Praise for *E-Myth Mastery*

"This fast-moving, practical book gives you the essential keys to think and act entrepreneurially for the rest of your career."

—Brian Tracy, author, *Getting Rich Your Own Way*

"Regardless of the business, we all struggle with the same challenges. The E-Myth concept is universal. I have recommended Michael's books to every franchisee in my organization."

—Roger McCoy, field vice president, American Express Financial Advisors

"There are few people that I consider to be masters of business —Ray Kroc was one of them, and Michael Gerber is another. This book is a masterpiece. It tells you exactly what you need to know to build a world class company. But it will also tell you something even more important: how to live fully and creatively while you're doing it. No one—entrepreneur, business executive, small business owner, or manager—should go one more day without reading it!"

—Kevin Dunn, retired president, Great Lakes Division, McDonald's Corporation

"Michael Gerber's *E-Myth Mastery*—the latest in his E-Myth series—is another absolutely must-read for anyone who cares about building a successful business. It has certainly caused me to rethink some of my "myths" which has, without doubt, made me a better businessman."

—Sid Feltenstein, chairman, International Franchise Association

"As a lifelong entrepreneur and CEO of many successful (and not so successful) enterprises, I have been delighted, inspired and deeply moved by Michael Gerber's E-Myth message. Michael is not only a master at what he does, he is a true genius at finding a way to help all of us do it. If you don't know the E-Myth, this is your chance to discover a remarkably powerful way of thinking. If you do know the E-Myth, sit back, set aside the time for some serious reading, and enjoy!"

—Sig Anderman, CEO, Ellie Mae, Inc.

"There is no greater marketing thinker than Michael Gerber. His innovative approaches to building sales and profits at the store level have served the small business community for over 30 years. No man or book promises such record profits in record time. Read it and weep."

—Tom Feltenstein, bestselling author, speaker, and strategic marketing consultant to the world's largest companies

"Of the more than two thousand franchisees we have brought into our companies almost all of them are technicians. Michael Gerber is the leading expert on teaching people to transition from technicians to entrepreneurs. We give the E-Myth to every new franchisee! *E-Myth Mastery* is a must-read for those who are ready to go to the next level."

—John T. Hewitt, CEO and founder, Liberty Tax Service,
former CEO and founder, Jackson Hewitt Tax Service

"Michael Gerber teaches us how we can profoundly increase the performance and productivity of our companies. Each one of us can gain something from the E-Myth that is immediately practical that we can take back to our companies and utilize. You will want to reflect on what you have learned so that it becomes a part of your business. It has been said that knowledge is power, but the truth is that real power comes from the utilization of that knowledge."

—Richard Liddeke, past president,
Painting and Decorating Contractors Association, owner, Capitol Painting

"With *The E-Myth Revisited,* Michael Gerber established himself as the world's small business guru. In the years since, multitudes of entrepreneurs have been inspired by his powerful *vision* of small business at its best—the coexistence of a rich and joyful personal life and a state-of-the-art, highly profitable business. With *E-Myth Mastery,* Mr. Gerber shows us the *path.* Small business, and the lives of their owners, will never be the same."

—David M. Traversi, managing director, 2020 Growth Partners, LLC

"If you started your business because of your ability to "DO," E-Myth Mastery should be as important to you as making payroll. Mastery not only exposed my partner and me to the missing pieces of our business, but more important, Mastery gave us a methodology to create those pieces. Since starting Mastery, our revenue has grown 48% but our bottom line has grown 317%! Our employees make more money, our clients are happier, my partner and I have better lives because of it. It was the single best expenditure my partner and I have made to intelligently grow the business."

—Tracy Butler, president, Acropolis Technology Group

"E-Myth is making a profound difference in my life and in my business and it's starting to show. My thinking is changing and the vision of what I'm creating brings excitement to the here and now. I've never had this kind of energy before."

—Adena Franz, the Adena Franz Group

"The E-Myth Mastery Program helped me to transform my passions, dreams, and values into a dynamic and thriving business. It is where passion meets purpose. It energizes and inspires. I am well on my way to creating a legacy that I could never have achieved on my own."

—David Gunning, president, CEO, Alternative Finance Corporation

"Michael Gerber's philosophy of E-Myth embodies everything a small business needs to be more successful. I have strongly encouraged all of our business partners in Aquatech to study and participate in the E-Myth."

—Jeffrey Fausett, president and CEO, Aquatech Corporation

"I saw Michael Gerber speak a few years ago and his idea of working on your business instead of in your business had a big impact on me. Two months ago I began the E-Myth Coaching Mastery series. I've been in business 26 years and I have that same feeling of excitement I had when I first started my company. I realize now that with the right systems, anything is possible! I look forward to more improvement over time as I go through the series."

—Leon Shaw, Audio Advice

"I listened to some of Michael Gerber's early E-Myth tapes and was very impressed. I used a lot of the ideas from those tapes in my business but wasn't able to put everything together. The E-Myth Mastery Program gave me the whole framework where everything fit together and my Certified E-Myth Coach worked with me to accelerate the process of building the business, one system at a time. I found Mastery so valuable that I encouraged my wife to enroll for her company, and she did. We each spent more than a year in Mastery (with our separate companies), and are so much better off for it. When a partner and I started a new business recently, I insisted that he also enroll in Mastery, and he's currently working in Module 3, and is equally impressed."

—Keith Lowe, Chief Financial Officer, Conditioned Air Solutions

"Over the last 2 years of being involved in the E-Myth Group Mastery Program, I have watched my business transform from mess to Masterpiece. I was lucky enough to have a coach who frequently went above and beyond the call of duty by helping me to develop and implement systems other than those we were currently working on in group format. Her caring and well-educated persona worked great with me! She truly held my hand when necessary and held my feet to the fire when necessary, truly the sign of a great coach. I appreciate the program and what it has done and will continue to do for me and my business(es)!"

—Jason Silverman, EEMA Fitness and Martial Arts

"The E-Myth Mastery Program has opened doors I previously did not know existed in business. It has changed the way I think and the way I act and the way I engage my life."

—Bill Lougheed, Entrepreneur Expansion, master licensee

"Michael Gerber's E-Myth principles changed my life and my business. I learned how to work on my business, not in my business. I used to have to get in early and stay late, always worried about the many balls I was juggling. Today, my business works for me and provides me with a great deal of flexibility and a large income."

—Scott Hanson, cofounder, Hanson McClain, Inc.

"E-Myth has been the single most life-changing factor in my career. As a professional speaker to small business owners, I always recommend reading Michael Gerber's work as the first step to business success. I honestly believe that *The E-Myth Revisited* should be mandatory reading for all business majors. I'm so thrilled that Michael has chosen to follow up with *E-Myth Mastery*."

—Laura Harris, entrepreneur, speaker, and author

"We took a risk having this caliber of presentation at our trade association's annual convention. Michael Gerber exceeded our expectations in every way. Our members continue to marvel at the insight he seems to have into their formerly perceived unique situations. He clearly has the handle on what drives the entrepreneurial spirit, and more important what it takes to make it a success."

—Mark McSweeney, executive director, National Chimney Sweep Guild

"The teachings of Michael Gerber and E-Myth have had a strong impact on the National Network of Estate Planning Attorneys and its members. After two years of engagement with E-Myth, we have now created a "Franchise Prototype" for an individual law firm called LifeSpan™, and we have implemented E-Myth strategies in our own corporation; E-Myth "systems-thinking" has permeated our culture. We believe that Michael Gerber and *E-Myth Mastery* are simply among the very best and most effective methodologies for enhancing the lives and businesses of today's professionals and small business owners."

—Richard L. Randall, chairman, Network of Estate Planning Attorneys

"The innovative E-Myth concepts and principles presented by Michael Gerber have served to dramatically reenergize hundreds of Pak Mail franchisees around the world. Mr. Gerber's book *The E-Myth Revisited* is required reading for every new franchisee, and its principles are integrated into their initial training. With these tools, our Pak Mail owners are armed and empowered to overcome obstacles that have plagued small business owners throughout history."

—P. Evan Lasky, president and CEO, Pak Mail Centers of America, Inc.

"I discovered *E-Myth Mastery* at the perfect moment in the life of my business. After reading Michael's book, I suddenly realized that my years of hard work working IN my business instead of ON my business were actually keeping me from getting where I wanted to go. After just 4 months into the Mastery Program, it now seems like a new business with less stress and more opportunity. The systems we have put in place have allowed my business to operate with less of my involvement. These processes are applicable to all businesses. Already, I have gained increased wealth, salary, and time with my family to pursue our dreams. Thank you, Michael!"

—Patrick Crowley, Patrick M. Crowley, Inc.

"The E-Myth Mastery process is truly transformational. Michael Gerber's focused, no-nonsense approach has allowed our software and consulting business to grow 150% since we began E-Myth Mastery. Our business is all about metrics. And E-Myth helps us see the right metrics and objectives to keep our business moving forward."

—Mark Palmer and Mike Haney, cofounders, ProfitMetrics Inc.

"I have been in the E-Myth Mastery program for over a year. I cannot imagine growing my business without it. I thought my business was pretty well organized and poised for growth, but after participating in the Mastery program I realized I had a lot to learn. All of my key employees have embraced the program and have learned how to solve their own frustrations by building systems to solve them."

—Tim Koehler, President, ReBath of the Triad

"My bible for continuing success is Michael Gerber's E-Myth. Adaptable to any business venue, there are no greater marketing tools than Gerber's principles. The E-Myth explains the pathway to entrepreneurial achievements. Since implementing his winning strategies on a daily basis, I celebrated the millennium as Rhode Island's Re/Max Realtor of the Year 2000."

—Dolores DiMeo Duffy, CRS, GRI, CBR, RE/MAX 1st Choice

"Michael Gerber ranks among the top ten most influential people in my life. He taught me that employees are to report solutions, not problems. He also taught me that I need not focus on my role as CEO but rather as the visionary."

—Gib Snow, Snow Orthodontics

"I began the E-Myth Program with the expectation of being able to streamline my daily operation and to give it a 'check-up', so to speak, by comparing how we operate with the model I had learned about while reading *E-Myth Revisited*. The business was so dependent on me that if I was not present it didn't work very well. I am now in the closing stages of *E-Myth Mastery* and find that the business now works very well without my being there every minute of every day. It sometimes works better without me. I firmly believe that Michael's model will enable any business to operate at maximum efficiency with minimum friction. The end result will be a working environment that brings both harmony and fulfillment to both those in management and those working on the front lines of the company."

—William R. Ammons, president, United Financial of NC, Inc.

"I am living the American dream thanks to *E-Myth Mastery*. I will never work IN my business again; any time I spend on my business is spent working ON the business! Thank you Michael Gerber for opening my eyes to the mistakes that most small business owners make!"

—Steve Distante, CEO & president, Vanderbilt Financial Group

"As a distributor to thousands of small businesses, we know firsthand how important it is that small business hears what Michael Gerber has to say. Most small business owners don't realize that they are really caught in a life-and-death struggle with themselves. Michael Gerber shows them this reality, then leads them to salvation."

—Matt Sheeleigh, president, Wallwork Group

"Michael Gerber and E-Myth Worldwide's Programs have the uncanny ability to provide a simple but powerful bottom line methodology to a complicated subject. By implementing E-Myth methods, I have not only significantly increased my business but simplified my life!"

—Gregg W. Whelan, certified financial planner

"I want to thank you for your help in convincing me to give E-Myth Mastery a chance. I have gone through a complete transformation. When we met, I was a hardworking, 12-hour-a-day, *self-employed,* panic-attack maniac! Now I'm retired at 39! . . . Not bad for a kid who grew up in the projects."

—Shawn Gardell, entrepreneur

"We have been paying attention to Mr. Gerber's ideas for more than a decade. It's no accident he has twice appeared as keynote speaker for our annual international convention—and so far he is the only person to be invited twice. If success is important to you, pay attention to his advice and work on your business, rather than in it."

—Mike Etchieson, chairman and CEO of Signs Now Corporation.

The principles illustrated by Michael Gerber in *E-Myth* and now in *E-Myth Mastery* are universal for all businesses, regardless of size, and regardless of industry sector. Michael Gerber provides business owners and senior managers a clear-cut road map to building a better organization through steps that are achievable and measurable. This is a must-read for any entrepreneur seeking to maximize their businesses' or organization's potential."

—Bennett Napier, CAE, executive director, National Association of Dental Laboratories

E-MYTH
MASTERY

ALSO BY MICHAEL E. GERBER

The E-Myth Revisited
The E-Myth Manager
The E-Myth Contractor
The E-Myth Physician

E-MYTH MASTERY

The Seven Essential Disciplines for
Building a World Class Company

MICHAEL E. GERBER

COLLINS BUSINESS
An Imprint of HarperCollins*Publishers*

Portions of this book were previously published in Michael E. Gerber's *Power Point, The E-Myth Revisited,* and in course materials made available through E-Myth Worldwide.

HarperCollins books may be purchased for educational, business, or sales promotional use. For information, please e-mail the Special Markets Department at SPsales@harpercollins.com.

FIRST COLLINS PAPERBACK EDITION PUBLISHED 2006

Designed by Ellen Cipriano

The Library of Congress has catalogued the hardcover edition as follows:.

Gerber, Michael E.
E-myth mastery : the seven essential disciplines for building a world class company / Michael Gerber.
p. cm.
ISBN: 0-06-072318-1
1. Entrepreneurship. 2. Success in business. 3. New business enterprise. I. Title
HB615.G47 2005
658.4'21–dc
2004060769

ISBN-10: 0-06-072323-8 (pbk.)
ISBN-13: 978-0-06-072323-1 (pbk.)

16 17 18 DIX/RRD 20 19 18 17 16 15

To Ilene, my partner, an irrepressible lover of the truth and the most heroic woman I have ever known. Thank you.

"If from now on you will treat everyone that you meet like a holy person, you will be happy."

From The Holy Man *by Susan Trott*

■

"Free yourself from all beliefs, all norms. See that you live completely with beliefs. Free yourself from second-hand information. See in you clearly what is beautiful. All that is beautiful in you is right. Look at the situation with an open mind, free from hearsay. The solution is in the situation. So, see the situation clearly with an open mind. Then the choiceless decision comes."

From Beyond Knowledge *by Jean Klein*

■

"Just when I discovered the meaning of life, it changed."

From Napalm & Sillyputty *by George Carlin*

CONTENTS

ACKNOWLEDGMENTS

I would like to express my deepest appreciation to all those who have contributed, each in his or her own unique way, to the realization of my vision to bring E-Myth Mastery to small business owners throughout the world. . . .

To Ilene Gerber, who edited this book in a way that brings out the best of who I am as only she can. . . .

To our Certified E-Myth Consultants throughout the world, thank you for your dedication to the principles and magic we all share. . . .

To every member of the E-Myth Worldwide staff who renews every day the inspiration it's taken to come as far as we have, and to go as far as we're determined to go, thank you for your persistence, your humor, your love, and your commitment to grow. . . .

To all of our E-Myth Mastery clients whose commitment to life has been a treasure to me personally, thank you for your deep expression of trust in us to help you get as much of it as you want. . . .

To Steve Hanselman at HarperCollins, you're a breath of fresh air, a true champion, and a true publishing partner. . . .

To my children, from the youngest to the oldest, Alex, Sam, Hillary, Kim, Shana, you each hold a unique and deeply loved space in my heart. . . .

To David Traversi, whose commitment, integrity, and wisdom have helped to make the next stage of my life at E-Myth come alive with unbounded opportunity. . . .

To Bill Schlegel, who is making it all happen, I appreciate so much how you have taken on the E-Myth vision as your own. . . .

Thank you all.

FOREWORD

"The higher goal of spiritual living is not to amass a
wealth of information, but to face sacred moments. . . .
We must not forget that it is not a thing that lends
significance to a moment; it is the moment that
lends significance to things."

From The Sabbath *by Abraham Joshua Heschel*

The most amazing things have occurred in my life.

Things I could not have imagined until they happened.

That I'm sitting here writing to you at this very moment, a book that
you're holding, is amazing to me.

The story I'm about to share with you in this book is also amazing to me.
It's the story of a woman named Sarah, a baker of pies, a small-business owner,
who became, after experiencing the kind of frustration and despair that comes
when one discovers her business cannot fulfill the promise of joy and freedom
she thought it would, *a reluctant entrepreneur.*

I call Sarah a reluctant entrepreneur because, even after all of our conversations, after all of the work we did together to transform her relationship with her business, Sarah still did not feel like an entrepreneur. She hadn't
yet developed an intimate relationship with the entrepreneur in her, or the
natural response that is expressed when that relationship is nurtured and
alive and integrated. So at times, the entrepreneur in Sarah would flourish, and
at times it would languish. What pulled her through every day was Sarah's
intense desire to break free of the malaise that was confounding her in the
operation of her business. She was determined to discover what she didn't
know.

It is that intense desire, coupled with her childlike willingness to suspend
disbelief, that makes Sarah's story amazing. I watched her grow, day by day, giving up her beliefs, one by one, attempting to do something new as soon as it
was suggested to her, one step at a time, letting go, moving forward, and then
backward, and then forward again, relentlessly pushing the envelope of her

understanding, skill, and ability to see clearly. The progress she made was, and continues to be, amazing to me.

As I'm sure your story is amazing.

As are the stories I've heard of the thousands of small business owners who, despite their lack of knowledge and experience, despite how little they might have known about business, despite how much they thought they knew and then discovered they didn't, despite all of their dysfunctional habits and beliefs, despite all of that, have overcome monstrous obstacles that appeared insurmountable when they first showed up. "Oh my God, now what?" they would say, and then knuckle down, brace themselves, and let go of the huge "No" in their first response to discover the little "Yes" just behind it, which came from their heart, their determination, and their longing to overcome those obstacles. Each one of these stories is amazing.

Perhaps you haven't thought about it that way, but as you read this book, I'm certain you will come to find your story to be amazing. Just like Sarah's.

If you have read *The E-Myth Revisited*, you know Sarah. I shared our earlier meetings in that book, our process of discovery of what a business is and what a business isn't, and why her misconceptions so riddled her days with pain and constriction, only occasionally giving her the satisfaction she craved.

Everything I've had the good fortune to give to Sarah has come from my experience, all of the stunning failures and successes that have made up my life. My story has, in some real way, shaped Sarah's story, just like specific people, at specific moments, have shaped mine. I'd like to tell you about some of the ones who entered my life when I was a young man, searching for my calling.

All of my life, I've been blessed by miraculous events that produce the kind of insights or epiphanies that change everything, forever. Randomly happenstance, seemingly disconnected, electrical zapping experiences that unalterably affect everything that follows . . . Zap Crackle Spark . . . and I'm on a new path.

Like the time I was selling encyclopedias, and had been for a seemingly interminable length of time, and I had gone downtown to talk with an insurance executive who had been doggedly pursuing me to switch vocations, from the "disreputable dead-end" I was headed for, to the "limitless respectable opportunity" to become an insurance executive just like him.

"Anyone who can sell encyclopedias as well as you can would be out of his mind not to sell insurance," he told me.

He was an elegant-looking man. Tall, Waspy, with perfectly coiffed white hair, a true executive type. Unlike the type of guys I had been working with in the "book business."

Those guys could have been gangsters for all anyone knew. Black shirts, one-button sport jackets in bold checks, flashy, hip, quick to make a buck closers, or they wouldn't be around for very long.

And most weren't around. Except me.

So, of course, the insurance executive was right.

I actually can't think of another guy who sold encyclopedias for as long as I did. There was a good reason for that, but I couldn't tell you what it was then. At 32 years old, I realize now, I had created my life so that nobody could or would tell me what to do. For all practical purposes, I became the Invisible Man. It was the '60s, in San Francisco, and I was an anomaly. With all the social insanity going on around me, with all the drugs and the music and the flowers, nobody gave a second thought to an encyclopedia salesman! Nobody *cared* what I did, not my boss or even my wife, until I sent in a contract. That's when they remembered I was alive, and cheered me on, halfheartedly, to go out and get another one. It was enough to drive any reasonable man crazy. But, for all practical purposes—and, of course, that's what I told myself I was doing it for, all practical purposes—I was good at it, and I could always depend on closing enough deals to keep my life, and the lives of my loved ones, on an even, and sometimes respectably successful, financial keel. In short, knowing I could sell, that I could always come up with enough deals to satisfy the pragmatic reality of my life, gave me tremendous freedom. It meant that I could sit in my car and write poetry for all anyone cared. I could take a break for a night or two at a time to sit in at a jazz club just north of Fisherman's Wharf at Pier 23, playing the saxophone with a jazz band that didn't care either if I showed up or not. But, given my passion and my sometimes raw and brilliant addition to their music, they tolerated me when I did. And, despite their lack of conviction, I played madly, hotly, full of love, the music busting free from my lonely heart like the wail of a lost man.

What I didn't realize at the time, with two kids and a wife who had her own way of "sitting in," her own unexpressed passions, her own longing for something more true, was that the psychic exhaustion of our cacophonous life together had become unbearable, and that the prospect of making yet another cold call, on yet another unwary stranger, in the cold of the night, to engage them in my story about the fertile field of education awaiting them—and the serious gap between where they were in their hopelessly uninformed life and where they could be with the 30 dense volumes of my magnificent *Encyclopedia Americana* at hand, not to mention all the other richly bound volumes that were to be theirs if they could only come to a decision, the 20 *Books of Knowledge* for the children they would certainly have one day, and the 10 *Books of Art;* but that wasn't all, for if they said yes tonight and signed the piece of paper, not would they receive everything just mentioned, but in addition, on top of all the rest, they would be awarded, at absolutely no additional cost, the amazing, incomparable, 52-volume set of the red, faux-leather-bound *Harvard Classics!*—all of this had become dreadful to me.

It may be hard to believe but I wasn't aware at the time how dreadful it actually was, that this 32-year-old unremarkable guy, secretly yearning to be remarkable, was about to come crashing down solidly on the floor of his life. That's what happened, literally.

Some time after I said yes to the elegant, white-haired elder of insurance, and no to the gentleman in the black shirt and checked jacket, I found myself sitting alone at a counter in a coffee shop somewhere on Webster Street in San Francisco, early on a sun-drenched, crystal clear morning, trying to boost myself up to make a warm insurance call at Presbyterian Hospital next door on a doctor who had been referred to me, having a third cup of coffee to get my nerve up, to bolster my complete lack of self-confidence, finding myself in the strange early-morning world of insurance sales rather than the early night of encyclopedia sales that I had grown so perversely accustomed to. Still on straight commission, more visible at this time of day, unable to hide in poetry or my saxophone, and suddenly, just like that, it happened. One moment I was sitting on the stool at the counter and the very next I woke up with my face pressed to the cold hard concrete floor of the coffee shop looking at something that seemed like a guy's shoes planted directly in front of my face.

I had passed out!

Cold.

And I came face-to-face with that place that I have found myself in too many times in my life where I've discovered, to my surprise, that a choice I thought I had already made was really a step toward a collision with the fact that I had not made a choice at all. I had simply done what was apparently next. The choice was still there to be made. And if I made it, the right decision, my life was never going to be the same again.

And that's when the blessed moment occurred.

Right there on the floor, I came to the realization that I was marking time, that I was living in a closet of my own making, a small, tight, breathless closet called My Life, and I had closed the door behind me, thinking at the time that I was living in the real world.

I was living in a closet and I had just run out of air!

And suddenly, God opened the door!

That's what it felt like to me. God opened the door and I was called.

Right there on the cold floor in a coffee shop in San Francisco, I was blessed. First I wasn't, and then I was. Blam. Just like that.

And that's what set me on fire.
In one moment there was no fire, and in the next moment there was.
In one moment I was burned out, and in the next I was burning up.
They told me at the hospital next door that I had had a panic attack.
Get some rest, they told me.
I didn't go home to rest. I didn't need to.
I sold the doctor some insurance instead.

It's been *36 years* since I found myself with my face ignominiously pasted to the floor of a coffee shop next to Presbyterian Hospital in San Francisco.
The year was 1968.
Nine years after that, in 1977, I would start the company known today as E-Myth Worldwide.
In another nine years, 1986, I would publish my first E-Myth book.
And it is now 2004, 36 years later, and I'm writing my seventh E-Myth book, the one you're holding in your hands.
On some level, it is *inconceivable* to me that the 32-year-old man I was in 1968 could be the man I am today, writing this book.
If I could have told him what was going to happen to his life over the next 36 years, he would have laughed hysterically. He would have thought I was insane.
So what difference does all of this make to you?
I hope a lot. Bear with me.
But let me caution you in advance, that the insight this experience and others like it in my life produced is not science. It's not earthshaking. It's not conventional business wisdom or even good religion.
As best I can tell, the essence of the inconceivable turns my life has taken over the past 36 years is this: *I've been blessed, then on fire, then I acted.*

I had the good fortune not too long ago to talk with a rabbi who had read one of my books and was inspired by it. We talked about Judaism and miracles. He offered many, many examples of how the miracles spoken of in the Bible are not just biblical in nature, but happening around us every single day. Our problem, he said, is that we just don't see them for what they are. He went on to add, "If the Messiah were to appear on 42nd Street in New York City tomorrow in the plain light of day, it's probable that only a handful of people would even see him! And everyone else would think he was mad!" The rabbi said to me, "I have come to think that the Red Sea has parted for each and every one of us in our own singularly unique and miraculously unpredictable way, over and over and over again. The tragedy is we don't see it.

"If we saw it, our lives would be transformed."

Miracles happen, the blessing comes, the Red Sea parts, but then it's up to us. Are we ready to see it, are we moved by what just happened, are we open to the possibility, are we ready to catch on fire?

If not—and my life has shown me in countless, tragic ways how often I'm not open, not available, not willing to let go and jump—nothing will happen except more of the same. We'll continue to sell our metaphorical encyclopedias. We'll just drag our weary butts up off the coffeehouse floor and go back to doing it, doing it, doing it some more. The insufferably walking dead, shuffle, shuffle, shuffle, in a small, airless closet we call Life.

Being available. That changes everything.

For whatever reason, and I find it hard to explain, I have seen in my life that there's some part of me that's also been *sufficiently* available. Even when I felt like the walking dead. When the fire had all but died out, almost to the point of being completely extinguished, and my body and spirit were dry, dry, dry. When the absence of my own spark, my own sizzle, brought a lassitude, a dread, and the sallow, soul-sucking clamp of hopelessness.

Somehow, when I'm available to the miracles, to catch the fire when it inevitably returns, everything changes. None of this, not the miracles or the fire, are of my own doing.

I can't take credit for any of it. I don't have the ability to light my own fire. No matter how many times I've tried, no matter how much I have attempted to manipulate my feelings, nothing, no motivation or inspiration, no cosmological or earthly razzmatazz has had any impact on my being.

For me, success, forward movement, improvement has been about being open to enough or available to receive a *sufficient* number of the blessings or miracles that have naturally come my way.

That's when the fire returns.

And then it's my job. I need to act.

After the blessing, after the fire, I need to act.

And the action, I've also discovered, is more than the physical doing of something. Much more. It's first and foremost the *mental* doing of something. Magic, that's what it feels like to me, starts in my mind before it ever moves my body. Thought begins, sometimes out of the blue, sometimes as a result of something I see or hear. And then the words begin to go together, and a poem comes out, or a song, or a title for a book, or a new idea for the business, it could be anything. If I start moving before I start dreaming, which is what I call thinking without a clear, identifiable purpose, I lose it, more often than not.

The blessing produces the fire which produces the impetus for the action, first in my mind, as an amorphous idea, then as an idea that takes shape as I express it, share about it, write about it, and ultimately make it happen.

And when the thing that I'm doing meets the world as it is, and that meeting makes sense to both me and the world, there is an organic, sympathetic connection made that moves everything around me forward. That's when what I'm doing takes on an even bigger, more purposeful form that no one could have anticipated at the outset.

That's Magic.

I just *love* when that happens!

When I'm available to blessings and the fire they ignite, Life is Magic.

Come back with me to the coffee shop, and then move forward seven years. The year is 1975. A close friend of mine who owned a boutique advertising agency in Silicon Valley asked me to visit a small, high-tech, start-up business client of his. My friend thought I might be able to help his client. I had no idea how. "I don't know anything about business," I said. "Don't worry," my friend Ace said, "you know more than you think you do." I went. The client, I'll call him Bob, asked me what I knew about his business. I said, "Nothing, Bob." And I meant it. He said, "Well, what do you know about our products." I said, "Same, Bob, nothing." He said, "So, Michael, if you don't know anything about my business, and you don't know anything about my products, how can you possibly help me?" I said, "I don't know, Bob. But Ace thinks I can, and since he's left us here with an hour to kill, why don't we find out?"

So that's what we did. I started the meeting with two assumptions. The first was that I didn't know anything about business. The second was that since Bob owned one, he did. The conversation proved me wrong on both counts.

What I discovered in that meeting was that I knew that selling is a system.

What I discovered that Bob didn't know was just about everything except his product. He was a high-tech wizard. Unfortunately for Bob, it wasn't enough.

Every question I asked him produced an approximation or an anecdotal response.

I was astonished. And excited.

Here I was in a completely foreign world, a world Bob created, and he didn't have a clue what he was doing!

Fortunately for me, I found myself in a new profession and, though I didn't know it at the time, face-to-face with my calling.

I began working with Bob, building his selling system, watching it produce results, working with another of Ace's clients, and then another. While I was experiencing success, I was also trying to make sense of something that was deeply puzzling to me. Everyplace I went, the business was in chaos. Nothing seemed to work like it was supposed to.

And there I was, with absolutely no experience running a business, no knowledge about business, no *interest* in business, and yet I was producing results that astonished my clients. How could this be? What was really going on?

What blessing was about to unfold, what secret was about to reveal itself as I rummaged around in this increasingly strange world looking for a holy grail that had only in the last minute and a half of my discordant life become of interest to me?

And then I walked into McDonald's.

I've got to be kidding, right?

McDonald's? The Golden Arches? Is this what this philosophical rambling is coming down to: *finding salvation at the altar of a hamburger stand!*

Well, I hate to admit it, but yes.

That's how ordinary a guy I really am.

I am impressed by the seemingly ordinary things that surround us. I can't help myself.

McDonald's that day, for me, was exactly the parting of the Red Sea.

I was about to see the world, for the very first time, in a way I had not seen it before.

One moment I was doing it, doing it, doing it. The next moment I was enlightened!

Now here's the thing.

If you take what I'm about to tell you with a grain of salt, you will fail the blessing test miserably. And your life will be a living tragedy. The metaphorical encyclopedias you are selling today will drive you to drink. The bones of your spiritual body will one day be used to conduct experiments to discover what it was about you that led you to close the closet door of your life, *from the inside,* and then drive 16 penny nails through the door into the door frame to keep your spirit locked away forever.

I was a witness to the miracle of McDonald's.

What came to me at that moment was that McDonald's was far more than just a hamburger stand and far more than just a business. What came to me was that McDonald's was a metaphor for the world. That the world—any world—could be organized into any damn thing I could imagine wanting it to be. When that happened, by what appeared to be simply an accident of need, I was ready. The Spirit called and it connected with the spirit in me.

There is a logic to the Universe, the Spirit said.

And all *you've* got to do is see it.

. . .

Ray Kroc, the founder of McDonald's, has had a profound impact on my life and I never met him.

But, frankly, I didn't need to. It was enough that I knew we were kindred spirits.

The blessing came to Ray Kroc. The fire. He turned it into action.

The mental model of McDonald's went beyond the passion, but if it weren't for the passion, it wouldn't have mattered.

Ray Kroc's genius was his ability to see the simple in the complex. To turn the ordinary into the extraordinary, to produce incredible results with the blessing he was given when, at the age of 52, as a malted milk machine sales-man, he walked into McDonald's to sell the McDonald brothers a multi-mixer malted milk machine.

The genius of Ray Kroc is that he lived his life like a little boy.

Little boys play.

Ray Kroc played.

Little boys are moved by the most ordinary things.

Ray Kroc was moved by ordinary things.

Little boys get lost in dreaming all the time, only to find themselves in strange places.

Ray Kroc got lost in his dreams and found himself in strange places. Can't we stop the French fries from falling on the floor? Can't the hamburger bun be more perfect? Can't we deliver the food as soon as the customer asks for it?

There's got to be a way, Ray Kroc said.

There's got to be something miraculous hiding in here, said Ray Kroc, looking at any ordinary problem. There's just got to, he would say.

And that's what this book is about.

The miracle of magic, the magic of miracles, the inspiration that brings the fire roaring down the spiritual hill, to arrive blazing at one's feet, to lift us up to the top again, full of passion, enflamed with purpose, electrified by the wonder of it all.

Let's go there together.

Michael Gerber
Petaluma, California
July 15, 2004

INTRODUCTION

"Recognized geniuses may be rare, but genius resides within all of us. There's no such things as 'luck' or 'accident' in this cosmos; and not only is everything connected to everything else, no one is excluded from the universe—we're all members. Consciousness, like physicality, is a universal quality; because genius is a characteristic of consciousness, genius is also universal. It follows that that which is universal is available to each and every person."

From Power Vs. Force *by*
David R. Hawkins, M.D., Ph.D.

We're about to go on an adventure, you and I.

An entrepreneurial adventure.

Whether you're an independent business owner or a franchisee, whether you are self-employed and work out of your home, whether you manage a department, a division, any size organization at all, or whether you're thinking of starting a business of your own, this book will provide you with the insight and understanding, the rules, disciplines, mind-set, and perspective necessary to build a World Class Company.

Whether that company is a Company of One or a Company of 3,000 is unimportant. That you are determined to do what you intend to do in a world class way is all that matters.

Over the past 27 years, having consulted more than 30,000 E-Myth Mastery business clients, both large and small, throughout the world, the people at my company and I have come to recognize that all successful businesses operate in accordance with the principles, practices, and disciplines you will find in this book. No matter what the industry, no matter the size of the company, no matter what the personal preferences of the owner might be. As Gertrude Stein, the poet, might have said if she were talking about a business instead of a rose: "A business is a business is a business."

When our clients have honored the universal rules of the game, their businesses have soared and prospered.

When they haven't, or when they fought it tooth and nail, their businesses have struggled and sputtered aimlessly, never providing the owner with the lush gifts that could have been conferred upon him.

And those lush gifts are a spectacle to behold!

Nothing in my life has been more rewarding than experiencing firsthand what can happen when a small business owner, supported by her E-Myth Mastery Coach, the E-Myth point of view, and the E-Myth Mastery Program material, devotes herself with unremitting advocacy, evangelism, and dedication to the entrepreneurial perspective, passion, purpose and practice described in this book.

Their experience, time after time, flies in the face of the conventional wisdom about entrepreneurs:

- That entrepreneurs are born, not made
- That very few people have that unique entrepreneurial quality
- That entrepreneurship is an art, not a science

To be blunt, the clients I'm talking about didn't have a clue, when we met them, how to grow their company into a flourishing enterprise, but were able, over time, to break through the barriers of their own resistance to become true entrepreneurs.

A World Class Company has been the inevitable result of those break throughs.

As a result of these experiences, I've come to the conclusion that each of us is born with the inherent impulse, a creative center, which, when cultivated through disciplined learning and practice, can produce works in the world that defy the imagination. Entrepreneurial works. Works of the entrepreneurial kind.

And it all starts with a passionate commitment to that which is entrepreneurial.

This book is intended as a guide to take you into this stunningly imaginative, albeit highly demanding, world. To provide you with the tools, the ideas, the energy, the insight, the methods, the systems, and the inspiration you will need to integrate everything I am about to share with you in everything you do in order to make entrepreneurship a way of life for you and the people in your company.

In fact, entrepreneurship, once discovered, is a way of life.

That once entrepreneurship is alive and well in you, in form and in substance, the power of it, the unending power and passion of it will never let you rest.

Once you open the doors to the creative entrepreneurial energy within you, it just keeps rolling out, in continuous joy, misery, joy, joy, misery, joy, joy, joy.

For almost three decades at E-Myth Worldwide, we have been helping our clients open those doors. Inspiring, teaching, coaching, supporting, and training thousands of owners and managers throughout the world to utilize the system of business development processes we call the E-Myth Mastery Program. The E-Myth Mastery Program was designed to cultivate our clients' inherent, God-given entrepreneurial gifts through a rigorous process of entrepreneurial skill development. The skills that are essential to the creation of a World Class Company, an entrepreneurial company.

What is an entrepreneurial company? It is a company where the entrepreneurial consciousness is alive in all of its people.

And when I say all of its people, I mean it.

I mean the busboys, the waiters, the salespeople, the clerks. The person at the front desk. The accounts receivable person. The person entering data, and the person analyzing the data she entered. The person consulting with a client, as well as the janitor cleaning up the office at night. I mean the guy blowing the leaves off the lawn and the window washer. The chimney sweep and the roofer. The framer and the plumber and the electrician and the mechanic. The pool guy, and the truck driver who delivered his supplies. I mean the cook in a fast-food restaurant, and the person who manages him, as well as the person who manages the manager.

Everybody in a company must be entrepreneurial for a company to come alive as only an entrepreneurial company can.

Because each and every single one of your people conspires to make your company great or not. And greatness is achieved only when the entrepreneurial leadership in your company is passionately committed to inspiring every one of your people to plumb their entrepreneurial depths. In such a company, each person is expected to hold herself personally responsible for discovering, exploring, and expressing her own unique entrepreneurial nature in everything she does. In such a company, it is a steadfast mind-set that each of us possesses the gift to create. Not just for the company, mind you. But for our own personal growth and fulfillment as "owners" of our job here on earth: to be fully human, to participate in a team of people, each of whom inside their most private heart is seeking more than a life of simply getting by. People thrive by bringing alive their own personal brand of creativity in everything they do. Creativity, our God-given gift, is the calling of the entrepreneurial soul within each of us.

So it is a fundamental premise of this book *that every single, solitary person on this earth, no matter what his job might be, or what his experience has been, can discover within himself the brilliance, the genius, the captivating and captivated soul of an entrepreneur, once he knows where to look.*

Not just to create a great company, but to create a great life.

It is my deepest wish in this book to help you to look for that genius within you, and to teach you how to bring it out in all the people you touch.

To discover that stunningly alive, passionate, entrepreneurial soul just dying to come out, to be of purpose, to ply her miraculous trade, to explore the endless opportunities that abide in the world, to color the world lavishly from a palette of her own choosing. Or, if you have already come out only to be met with devastating resistance, and shrunk back to where it is safe, I want to help you leave that experience behind, to learn how to suffer failure with good grace, and to trust that there is a better way to fulfill your creative genius through the work you do and the results you create. I want to help you to see that, despite what might be your experiences to the contrary, the very world you live in is a world where creativity is honored, respected, nourished, yes, even loved, and that you already have everything it takes to live in that world.

Providing you're willing to learn how.

This book will reveal to you, in nourishing detail, the entrepreneurial method that anyone can learn in order to become a true entrepreneur. This method is a system of practices we have invented over the 27 years since I founded E-Myth Worldwide in 1977. This method was created, and continues to be re-created, through intense investigation, application and continuous improvement in the tens of thousands of small businesses we have been invited into. These practices touch upon all of the many things you will be called upon to do in the creation of your World Class Company. Though your business may be very small, the job of an entrepreneur is very, very big. There are so many facets to it.

This book is organized into two parts, **The E-Myth Entrepreneur** and **The Seven Essential Disciplines.** While every sentence, every page, of this book is about you and your skill development, Part One covers the life skills that are necessary for an entrepreneur's creative expression, and Part Two covers the business skills that are necessary to become the entrepreneurial leader of your company. Let's take a brief look at each part.

Part One of this book is about overcoming the real obstacles to building a World Class Company. Not the obstacles on the *outside,* mind you. Not the people you need to inspire who frustrate your every attempt to win their hearts and minds. Not the sources of capital that seem so difficult to convince to lend you the money you need to grow. Not the competition that is intent on eating you alive, or the fickle marketplace that relentlessly tests your marketing mettle to the max. Not the government that regulates you on every front and at every turn. As important as all of these obstacles are, Part One is not about any of that. It is about the obstacles *inside, the only ones that have the power to prevent you from seeing your entrepreneurial commitment through to the end.*

I'm talking about the emotional obstacles, the fluctuation of your energy, the loss of will, of vision, of conviction. The obstacles that are caused by your disconnection from your own life force, upon which the life of your company ultimately depends. The life force called Passion. Part One is first about passion, what it is, how you experience it, how it can consume you or, when seen for what it is, liberate you to pursue the path of the impossible as every entrepreneur is called to do.

What happens when you're overwhelmed by the necessity of doing more than you are humanly able or willing to do, when your very life and the life of your business depend upon your rising to the occasion one more time?

What happens inside of you when there's simply no more juice to fuel your day, when the doubts about your own ability to do what needs to be done are all you can see?

My objective in Part One is to speak to your entrepreneurial soul, to pursue these questions, to call your soul out in blazing, living color, to create the fuel you will need to build your World Class Company by enabling you to see clearly the mechanism by which you can inspire yourself when you're least emotionally available to be inspired.

Part Two of the book, on the other hand, is organized around Seven Essential Disciplines of business: Leadership, Marketing, Finance, Management, Client Fulfillment, Lead Generation, and Lead Conversion. Each chapter is devoted to one of the seven essential disciplines, and is designed to provide you not only with an understanding of the *passion* and sense of *purpose* essential to integrating that discipline into your life, your people, and your company, but also with a blueprint for the *practice* of each discipline, including a selection of the processes from the E-Myth Mastery Program. For you to become transformed into the entrepreneur you were meant to be, you must become a leader with passion and purpose, one who is committed to practicing the seven essential disciplines.

Part Two, then, is about entrepreneurial leadership. It is through leadership that an entrepreneur converts his vision into reality. It is through leadership that an entrepreneur moves people around him toward their own higher vision. It is through leadership that an entrepreneur inspires sources of capital to provide him with the money he needs to realize his vision. It is through leadership that an entrepreneur differentiates his company, distinguishes it as world class, and attracts the market to it. It is through leadership that an entrepreneur truly experiences the height of his creative power.

In Part Two, I will teach you how to lead by sharing with you some of the key processes inherent in the seven essential disciplines. Through the practice of these processes, you will come to understand what it truly means to lead, to move people and resources toward the development of a World Class Company.

As a reader of *E-Myth Mastery,* you are invited to register on our E-Myth Mastery website, www.emythmastery.com. There we will provide you with countless special opportunities for education, training, and coaching in the seven essential disciplines should you feel the need for it, as Sarah in this book did, and still does, and as our many thousands of small business clients have and continue to do.

As an *E-Myth Mastery* reader you will also find on www.emythmastery .com the worksheets you will need to help you complete the E-Myth Mastery processes that are included here in each of the seven essential disciplines in Part Two of this book. Registration on our website will additionally provide you with access to special offers for selected products and services from E-Myth Worldwide, all designed to assist you and your people to develop the skills, disciplines and practices necessary for building your World Class Company.

You will also find at www.emythmastery.com a sample of *Letters from an E-Myth Coach,* stunning examples of actual implementation of E-Myth processes in real client companies. These letters were written by a Senior E-Myth Coach, Tom Bardeen, an extraordinary man and mentor for the hundreds of small business E-Myth clients he has worked with over the past 10 years. Every week, at 6 A.M. on Saturday morning, Tom sits down to write his clients a letter covering one or more of the seven essential disciplines comprising E-Myth Mastery. These letters provide detailed illustrations of work done by Tom's wonderfully committed E-Myth Mastery clients to develop systems customized to their needs, using some of the very same tools you will be provided in this book. It is our hope that these examples make this book come alive for you in a very tangible way, with the result that your business becomes one that serves your life rather than consumes your life, as so many small businesses unfortunately do.

It's a good idea to register on www.emythmastery.com now, while it's fresh in your mind.

A NOTE OF APPRECIATION TO SARAH

As Sarah and I reengaged in dialogues about herself and her business, after a 10-year hiatus, she came to the realization that just wanting to bring the entrepreneurial spirit alive in her small business was not enough. She had to face the question that every small business owner must face: "Am I up to it?" Up to what, of course, is the serious question that's unanswerable at the outset of any journey. That's why it is such a complex dilemma. How to commit to something without a true understanding of what it will demand of you or whether you'll be up to the task? Sarah and I came face-to-face with that question, over and over again. How can I know, Sarah would ask, if I have never done it before? You can't, I would say to Sarah, over and over again. But that shouldn't stop you.

Trust is so important and Sarah gave me hers. Dear, courageous, thoughtful, determined Sarah. The woman she is came through every single time. She wished to know the truth and dedicated herself to it and her transformation as much as anyone I have ever had the pleasure to experience. Sarah was, and is, a wonder.

She would find herself completely overwhelmed by her ignorance, and suddenly break through to crystalline clarity. She would find herself completely determined to overcome some obstacle, only to discover, with a charming laugh that would burst forth from her at those moments, that she was the only obstacle. Time and time again she was reminded that if she could just let go of the obstacle of need, the obstacle of want, the obstacle of lust for a solution to feed her lust for control, love, always there underneath, was waiting to transform her, waiting to accept and to receive her. Sarah is a lesson for us all. If the entrepreneur is waiting within you, then Sarah will teach you in the following pages how she discovered the entrepreneur in her, and how stunningly alive that process can be for you as well. Sarah has been a gift to me. I feel so grateful to be able to share her with you.

Every World Class Company, every company marching to the tune of entrepreneurial wisdom and magic, must continually learn to reinvent itself. And with it, its people. And with its people, the place that it holds in the heart and mind of the world.

As Ray Kroc did at McDonald's, over and over again.

As Fred Smith did at Federal Express, again and again.

As Larry Page and Sergey Brin are doing at Google as we speak.

With every epiphany, with every new possibility they never saw before that moment, with every change they made, with every result that was successfully executed on behalf of the customer, life became infused with more passion and a deeper sense of purpose.

More than you can possibly imagine!

Welcome to E-Myth Mastery. And to the world of the entrepreneur.

PART ONE

THE E-MYTH ENTREPRENEUR

■

Epigram

■

**"Given the right circumstances,
from no more than dreams, determination,
and the liberty to try, quite ordinary people
consistently do extraordinary things."**

From Birth of the Chaordic Age, *by Dee Hock*

World class" is defined by Webster's dictionary as "being of the highest caliber in the world."

When you see a world class car, you know it instantly.

When you hear a world class musician, you know her instantly.

When you see a world class athlete, you know him instantly.

So it is with a World Class Company. There is absolutely no doubt.

The World Class Company looks, feels, and performs better than any other.

This book is about how to build one.

This book is not about survival.

It is not about getting through the day.

It is not about maintenance or eliminating frustrations or solving the day-to-day problems that make up the ordinary day-to-day experience of an ordinary person in an ordinary kind of company.

This book is about the extraordinary.

If you're committed to the extraordinary, read on.

The first and most important commitment to the extraordinary is personal. A true E-Myth entrepreneur on her way to building a World Class Company is committed to seeing herself as she really is, as opposed to how she wishes she were. To seeing the fears that inhibit her, the passions that consume her, the passivity that rules her, the things she avoids doing as much as the things she insists upon doing, the barriers to growth that keep her from growing and, as certainly, keep her company from growing. An E-Myth entrepreneur is also committed to understanding her gifts, all of the wonderful characteristics that live inside of her, whatever they may be, beyond the optimism, focused passion, willingness to take risks, perseverance, and discipline that are common to all. In short, to achieve Mastery one must achieve Clarity. And to achieve clarity, most often requires an outside influence, someone who can pull you out of yourself so that you can more readily see yourself, someone who can challenge your assumptions, your beliefs, the habits that determine what you do in reaction to what happens to you, the opinions you hold, the walls you set up to keep your life comfortable, unthreatened, unchallenged. It is hard to see ourselves without the eyes of another. A coach, a confidant, a mentor, a teacher. No world class entrepreneur has ever done anything on her own. She always surrounds herself with people who know more than she does, with people who are as good at what they do as she is at what she does, people who are committed to her growth and her vision, people who are inspired and inspiring, people who are so committed to engaging with life in a world class way that they never let the people who depend upon them play anything less than a world class game, people who are trustworthy and demand the same from the people they serve, people who accept nothing less than optimal results.

Building a World Class Company calls for a world class commitment to your own personal growth.

CHAPTER ONE

The E-Myth Point of View

■

**"Begin as creation, become a creator.
Never wait at a barrier.
In this kitchen stocked with fresh food,
Why sit content with a cup of warm water?"**

From Unseen Rain, Quatrains of RUMI
by John Moyne and Coleman Barks

And now we begin our journey together to find the entrepreneur, who he is, how he thinks, what he does, how he does it, how he moves mountains to make his dreams come true. Mountains on the inside of him, and mountains on the outside of him. Mountains of his imagination, and mountains with a stark overwhelming reality to them. What do mountains ask of the one who is determined to climb them? What preparation is in order? What role does your guide play in all this? How strong of mind and spirit does the one who would climb mountains truly need to be? You and I are going to ask all of these questions, over and over again. We will answer them, and then throw away those answers. We will discuss the harsh reality of them, and you will begin to understand them to be metaphors for something even bigger than the mountains we have set out to climb. Much bigger.

Tragically, few of the people who start their own business think like entrepreneurs, act like entrepreneurs, dream like entrepreneurs, or succeed and fail like entrepreneurs. Even more tragically, this is a crime against their very own nature. Most small business owners spend their entire small business journey in the foothills without ever starting to climb. And what's worse, they never realize what they've done.

By the time we're done with our journey, you will have learned, through your own experience, not only what entrepreneurship is, but what it is to *you*, what it is for you to take on the mantle of a true entrepreneur by doing work only true entrepreneurs do.

You will learn how to build a World Class Company.

You will learn how to create the extraordinary.

You will learn how to find magic inside of yourself, the kind entrepreneurs are famous for, and how to tempt it out. And then, how to be gentle with it, love it, nurture it, play with it, coerce it, cajole it, massage it, console it, cry with it, and be firm with it.

All of this, dear reader, you have inside of you. No matter who you think you are, no matter how you think you ought to think, this book can provide you with a completely new perspective on your life, and the business or businesses you create as you live it.

You will discover that entrepreneurship is not a trait, quality, or characteristic possessed by a rare and special few. It belongs to each and every one of us. It lives inside us all. It is a legacy, a birthright, which we are free to nourish or ignore, to claim or reject, to pursue or avoid, to develop or not, so help us God.

Entrepreneurship is, first of all, the power to create.

But creation is not something that you do.

Creation is something that is done *through* you.

Creation is like music. My saxophone teacher, Merle Johnston, used to say to me, "Michael, you don't make music. Music finds you. Your job is to practice to get yourself ready."

Likewise, your job is not to become an entrepreneur. It is not to create.

Your job is to commit to the process of becoming an entrepreneur and then to practice what entrepreneurs do so that entrepreneurship can find you when you've practiced enough to be ready.

Commitment and practice. Commitment and practice.

Because, just as I found the power to create music through the practice of music, you can find the power to create a World Class Company through the practice of entrepreneurship.

Understand, the power to create a World Class Company doesn't come from the practice. It comes from deep down within you. It's a calling, a potentiality; it's ineffable, unexplainable, and enormously exciting. It comes from your connection to your passion. Practice, I believe, is your signal to the power—to the passion—that you have taken it seriously. That you are committed. That you are earnest about the gift the passion will bestow on you. How do you know it will? Commit and you'll discover the trust over time. And even when you're completely unsure, as I'm certain many of you reading this are, even as I'm speaking to you, there's a knowingness in you, isn't there? That somehow you just know that entrepreneurship is your calling.

Unfortunately, the calling is insufficient on its own. Unless you commit to the practice of entrepreneurship, unless you get down to the study and the form and the skill-set of entrepreneurship, it is most likely that your entrepreneurial calling will turn into a nightmare of unbelievable proportions. You will be completely unprepared for what you are called to do.

I know. Because I've lived through that nightmare. I know because the coaches in my company have lived through countless nightmares with their clients. Nightmares about running out of money. Nightmares about losing an absolutely essential account. Nightmares about losing their marriage, or a significant relationship, or their kids, about not knowing what to do next as a catastrophe sits there on their doorstep just waiting to happen. I know about nightmares. And I know the toll they take on people who have been taken by the impulse to start a small business only to find out too late that they were completely unprepared for what it demanded of them. Nightmares are sweaty, painful, fearful, monstrous. They take your breath away. They put a bleak, flat, and hopeless face on reality that destroys any urge we might have had to create, to build a successful business.

That's why this book is so important to me. The terrible truth is that small businesses are killing most of the people who create and operate them. We all know the statistics. Most small businesses fail. And the vast majority of the rest are just dying a slow death. And it doesn't have to be that way. First, you need a different perspective.

What we call the E-Myth point of view.

If you've already read one of my E-Myth books, you probably have already verified in your experience what I'm about to share with you.

If this book is your first E-Myth experience, then it's important for you to know that the E-Myth point of view is the foundation for everything else in this book.

The E-Myth point of view is the essence of E-Myth Mastery.

It is the foundation for building a World Class Company.

The E-Myth point of view explains why most small businesses fail, and what the most successful ones do.

The E-Myth is the entrepreneurial myth.

The E-Myth says that most businesses fail because they are not founded by entrepreneurs, but by technicians, suffering from "an entrepreneurial seizure."

- A carpenter finds herself possessed by the urge to start her own business, becomes a contractor, and then goes to work, doing it, doing it, doing it.
- A hair stylist finds herself compelled to start her own business, opens a hair salon, and then goes to work, doing it, doing it, doing it.
- An attorney finds himself possessed by the need to start his own business, forms his own law practice, and then goes to work, doing it, doing it, doing it.
- A cook is taken by the impulse to start his own business, opens his own restaurant, and then goes to work, doing it, doing it, doing it.

The E-Myth says that all of these technicians, anyone who does technical work of whatever kind, make the same, fatal assumption: that because they understand how to *do the technical work* of their business—building a house, cutting hair, practicing law, cooking food—they understand how to *build a business* that does that work.

Untrue, says the E-Myth.

Untrue, untrue, untrue.

The truth is that knowing how to do the *work* of a business has nothing to do with building a business that works.

Failing to understand and appreciate, deeply, the difference between an entrepreneurial perspective and the perspective of a technician suffering from an entrepreneurial seizure is almost sure to be catastrophic for anyone starting her own business.

The result of that failure is predictable and verifiable by anyone interested in looking into it.

Let's look at the difference between the two. Between the technician's point of view and the entrepreneur's.

The technician builds a business that depends upon him, around his skills, his talent, his interests, and his predispositions. He devotes his time, his energy, and his life working for a living, albeit self-employed. In the end, there is little equity to show for the investment of his time. At the beginning, he bought a job. In the end, if he's lucky, he sells the job to a person who acquires it for little more than break-even, but most often at a net loss. The most a technician can show for the time he spent in his business is the income he earned, the feeling he had of being "independent," and whatever few assets he may have acquired with the income he earned over the time he was in business.

The entrepreneur, on the other hand, builds an enterprise that liberates her, creates endless amounts of energy, and increases her financial, emotional, and mental capital exponentially. In the end, there is significant equity to show for her investment. The enterprise runs itself in the hands of professional management. It has real value in the world. The entrepreneur is now free to invest what she's learned in another enterprise, depending upon what she wishes to do with the rest of her life. In any event, she has learned how to grow an organization, how to utilize her creativity in the real world, how to expand her reach, and how to add value to many people, all while creating income that she no longer has to "work" for, not to mention an estate for herself and the people she loves.

Same amount of time invested, significantly different return on investment.

The technician goes to work *in* his business.

The entrepreneur goes to work *on* his business.

The entrepreneur creates an enterprise, like Starbucks or Wal-Mart or Google.com.

The technician creates a job in a business of his own, like Jerry's Cleaners or Peggy's Diner or Dr. Kaplan's Chiropractic Clinic.

The result, in both cases, is predictable.

In the beginning, Sam Walton of Wal-Mart took on what would seem to be, on the surface of it, an enormous risk. In the end, he left a multibillion-dollar legacy. You know it today as one of the largest companies in the world.

On the very first day of Peggy's Diner, Peggy was doing pretty much the same thing she would be doing years later: waiting on tables, cooking meals, making ends meet. The only difference was she was older at the end and had a hell of a lot less time and energy left. In the end, she had debts to pay off. You've never heard of Peggy's Diner.

Sam Walton started his company the same year Peggy started hers.

Think about it.

The very same year that Sam Walton started Wal-Mart, Peggy started Peggy's Diner.

What a difference though!

Sam Walton was a true entrepreneur, one of the best ever. Peggy was a technician suffering from an entrepreneurial seizure. One of so many.

Same amount of time invested, significantly different return on their investment.

Knowing what you know right now, who took the bigger risk, Sam Walton or Peggy?

But wait, you say, where is it written that everybody has to want to build a big business?

It isn't, and they don't.

And that's not the point.

It's not *big* that's important here, it's *better.*

There's nothing wrong with building a small business. There's nothing wrong with Jerry or Peggy or Dr. Kaplan.

It's just that what they did could have been so much better!

They could only see what they could see.

And it's what they couldn't see, and what Sam Walton could, that moved them to invest so much for so little.

It's that they missed a huge, palpable something that could have altered their entire life's experience. They could have had a completely different life, a life that was richer, more zestful, less stressful, more productive, more contributing to everyone around them they knew, and so many people they didn't know, if they had only known where and how to look.

Not by creating a big company. Not by thinking bigger, or by being more ambitious, smarter, feeling more deserving.

But by understanding this simple distinction: that there's a profound difference between working *in* a business of your own, like a technician does, and working *on* a business of your own, like an entrepreneur does. And the distinction is of such life-changing proportions, that I'll say it again.

Most people who start a small business are technicians, moved by an all too short-lived entrepreneurial seizure. Because of the way they think about their relationship to their business, through no fault of their own, owning a business is nothing more than trading one job—working for someone else—for another job—working for themselves.

The technician goes to work *in* his business, doing everything he can possibly do to survive. He invests everything he has, and everything he doesn't yet have—his future, his home, his time, his relationships, his life, his options, everything—to get something he never clearly identifies or defines. He has an approximate vision, a vision of being on his own, a vision of being his own boss, a vision of financial independence, a vision of an idealized lifestyle that he's heard about in a seminar, or tasted in an infomercial, or read about in a self-help book, or heard about from his uncle, of miracles that happen without risk, without work, not truly knowing what that is, other than a dream of being a hero to his family, to himself, a dream of making it, like all the stories he has read or imagined.

These dreams are almost never realized.

Instead, he ends up putting in enormous amounts of time, of grueling, brain-numbing energy, of money he never earns, because he's got to take care of all the expenses he never anticipated: the rent, the overhead, the inventory, the people, the government. So that the dinners he hoped to serve, the products he hoped to sell, the services he hoped to deliver, never materialize to the extent he had imagined they would. Owning a small business like this is a hard road to hoe. The magic that shines at the beginning loses its luster long before the end.

It's like this. When you were working for someone else, it was their payroll that had to be met. Whatever their problem was, you got your check. When it's your business, you're the one who's got to meet payroll. When you can, you're often left feeling like your people haven't earned it, that they aren't quite producing the way you hoped. And when you can't meet your payroll, it's just plain excruciating, no, humiliating. Whether you have people working for you or not, most of what's produced in your business is produced by you. And if you're not producing it, you simply go without. Despite what you thought when you started your own business, you don't have a lot of options. You can work or not. You can produce or go without. You're like a straight commission salesperson. Either you get the sale or you don't. Who pays the price for that? You do, of course. In stress, in anxiety, in depression, in impatience, in overweight, in illness. Your loved ones also suffer. You just don't have the time or energy to give your family what you know, in your heart, they not only want from you but deserve.

And what about vacations? The truth for most small business owners is that they don't take them very often, if at all. That's fine in the first few years because you're, understandably, just getting started. And, in the years to follow, there are the obvious questions that can't be answered: Who's going to watch the store while you're gone? Who's going to take care of the cash? Who's going to take care of your most important customers when, all the time you've been doing it, doing it, doing it, busy, busy, busy, you're the one who's taken care of your most important customers. You're the one they've grown to count on. You're the one who's been making the promises and keeping them. Isn't that how you planned it when you built your business around yourself and your own ability to perform? It seemed like a good idea at the time. Did you really have any choice? You know there is no one you can really trust. So taking off from the business is out of the question. It's like turning over your bank account to a complete stranger, for goodness' sake! Can I do it? What if I make a mistake? What if I trust someone to take care of my business, and discover, after spending all that money, he screws it up! "Then what?" has dashed more thoughts of time off than you would possibly imagine. Because "Then what?," most small business owners will tell you, is worse than you can possibly imagine.

So is it any surprise, with a situation this tenuous, that the bank doesn't want to give you any money? Is it any surprise that your suppliers want cash on delivery? Is it any wonder that you can find yourself with no dial tone if you don't pay your telephone bill on time? Is it any wonder that the IRS and the state taxing authority will come down on you like a ton of bricks if you don't pay your payroll taxes? Do they know something you don't? Well, actually not. They're just ramming it home. Who *knows* when a small business is going to have its last gasp? It could be at any moment. And, unfortunately, it often is. Tens of thousands of small businesses close their doors around the world every single day. Sound dismal? Well, it is. More dismal than most will admit. They don't call it sweat equity for nothing. And when it's all said and done, a small business owner has little left to show for it other than the sweat.

As a result, most small business owners get to the point in their business, as the world changes around them, as new businesses move into the neighborhood, as new business owners, with the optimism you once had, join the game, where they just give up. You might tell yourself that you're maturing and developing wisdom, but it's really a deeply held cynicism, hard-earned through deeply felt experiences that convince you that you can't trust your people, you can't trust your bank, you can't trust your customers to stay with you or to care about anything other than their own, small needs, you can't trust your partner, you can't even trust yourself to remain enthusiastic, after all the hand-to-hand combat you've engaged in out there in the jungle you know small business to be. At its best, owning your own business frees you from having to work for a lunatic. At its worst, it enslaves you to the lunatic you've become. At its best, you can do whatever you want. At its worst, whatever you want invariably ends up being the worst choice imaginable. You can tell everyone you know that business is great, the money's fantastic, you love what you do, and that the downsides are just the price you have to pay for freedom. But part of you knows, though you might not admit it to anyone, that the clock is ticking and you're not going any place you haven't already been. In fact, you're dying inside, convinced no one else could possibly understand.

Thank heaven there's a better way.

The E-Myth says that Jerry and Peggy and Dr. Kaplan—and you—deserve much, much more than you're accustomed to getting in your lives.

You deserve More Life.

The more life that can only be found through the discovery of the entrepreneur that already lives inside of you.

A part of yourself you don't know very well.

What an incredibly exciting notion!

That all is not lost.

That seemingly ordinary people like Jerry and Peggy and Dr. Kaplan can transform their small business into a truly stunning company.

That anyone can.

That anyone can discover what Sam Walton so obviously knew.

Which brings us to the other side of the E-Myth. The E-Myth is both the entrepreneurial myth and wonder of the entrepreneur.

The E-Myth unabashedly proclaims the extraordinary magic of the entrepreneur, how absolutely essential entrepreneurship has been to the ascent of man, to the creation of the world in which we live, to the astonishing inventions in technology, in medicine, in entertainment, in education, in manufacturing, in distribution, in services of every conceivable kind. Entrepreneurship has been so important to great art and great music. To great architecture and great engineering of great buildings and great ships. To great works of every imaginable kind which people, throughout the world, strive for, whether it's better food, shelter, healthcare, education, wealth-building, whatever. It is entrepreneurship, and the remarkable imagination and creativity of man, the endless torrent of innovative commercial and noncommercial enterprises, the bewildering and miraculous array of things we see and use to make our life work, the continual discovery of what we never imagined because we never cease looking, that is our passion. To travel to the stars, to the bottom of the seas, to every niche and cranny of the earth, to live more richly, more fully, more wonderfully, more deeply than we had ever thought we could. All this we owe to the entrepreneurial instinct, the entrepreneurial desire, the entrepreneurial urge and dedication, the entrepreneurial perseverance, the entrepreneurial gift that lives deeply, I believe, like a throbbing underground current in every single man and woman, and always has, whether you know it or not.

Which brings us full circle. Back to the beginning.

Going to work *on* your business, rather than *in* your business, is the key to building a World Class Company.

And going to work *on* your business needs to be learned. It is not something you automatically know how to do. It is not simply doing it, doing it, doing it, like Peggy did. It has nothing to do with the work of your business. It has to do with the practice of becoming an entrepreneur. It has to do with the question: What is it that Sam Walton knew that I need to know? What is it I need to practice? The key to becoming an entrepreneur is to be willing to start your business all over again.

CHAPTER TWO

Passion, Purpose, and Practice

∎

**"You need to have passion to end sorrow,
and passion is not bought through escape.
It is there when you stop escaping."**

From Krishnamurti's Notebook *by J. Krishnamurti*

"I want to start my own business."

How many times have I heard that in the last almost three decades? More times than I could ever count. And from all types of people. Middle managers in large corporations who've come to the end of their corporate road. Executives in large corporations who've achieved most everything one could expect in terms of income, power, perks, and prestige. To them, it wasn't enough. Something was missing that only a business of their own could provide. The same could be said of the carpenters, electricians, obstetricians, contractors, attorneys, accountants, hairdressers, dentists, veterinarians, and therapists I've met, all of them at a certain stage in their lives where they needed, craved, something more, something that seemed to be promised by a business of their own.

At the same time, if there's anything I've learned about small business people, the ones who want to start their own business as well as the ones who've already done it, it is that they have no idea what they are going to be called upon to do. And if they did, if they really knew what they were going to be called upon to do, they still wouldn't believe that they couldn't do it! Most people who start a business believe that all it takes is good common sense. That any dummy can run a business. That given the will and the wish, they absolutely already possess what they need to pull it off.

Unfortunately, they don't. Few people do. It takes much, much more than good common sense. It takes *uncommon skill*. And to develop uncommon skill requires, first of all, that you know what skills are required, and second, that you are committed to the practice of developing those skills in order to become a master of them. And to pull *that* off takes uncommon passion. The skill and the passion. A dance between the two is essential, a dance that requires practice.

The unfortunate truth is that few people want to practice. Most people, in my experience in fact, *refuse* to practice. "Practice what?" they argue. "Building a business isn't practice, building a business is work. Work and creativity. You go to work, you don't go to practice. And even if you did," they continue, "even if there was something that people who go into business are supposed to practice, I don't need to. That's what *other* people need to do. All *I* need to do is . . ." They usually don't say this part, but they imply it, "All *I* need to do is be creative. To follow my heart." Well, there is something to be said for that, but it's never enough.

So let me say what absolutely needs to be said for what will prove to be the first of many times throughout the following pages:

To build a World Class Company you have to become a World Class Entrepreneur.

Becoming a world class entrepreneur takes an enormous amount of uncommon skill.

Developing that uncommon skill takes uncommon practice.

And without the uncommon commitment to the practice of entrepreneurship, without the intense and purposeful willingness to give yourself up to the down-and-dirty, nitty-gritty process of step one, step two, step three, over and over and over again—in the same way a musician practices the scales—without the thorough, experiential understanding of the logic of the craft of entrepreneurship, neither your creativity, even if it's brilliant, nor your determination, even if it's rock-hard, will ever take you where you want it to. Neither creativity nor determination are ever enough.

I learned this lesson for the very first time, the value of practice, as a young boy of 12, from my saxophone teacher who demanded that I practice, like a madman, very specific exercises he gave me. That's how he put it, "Like a madman." To say I resisted is an understatement. I didn't want to practice. I didn't want to do the grueling, unsatisfying work that practice called for without an obvious and immediate outcome to it. But when it became obvious that I had no choice, that my teacher would send me home without a lesson if I didn't practice, and cut me off entirely if I persisted, I got with his program. The impact was not immediately self-evident. My fingers didn't get remarkably faster. My sound didn't get remarkably sweeter. The honks and squeals didn't immediately transform into music. But, then, imperceptibly at first, when I finally began to give up looking for what I hoped to get, when I gave myself up to doing what was asked of me simply because I trusted that my teacher knew what was important for me to do, and I didn't, something new came into my practice. Something fresh. I like to say that the something new was "It." "It" began to practice. And "It" wanted to do nothing *other* than practice. And "It," the part of me that was born to practice, not to play, not to make great music, but simply, intensely, passionately, to practice, that "It" and I came together to work every day, three hours a day, to do the work that my saxophone teacher expected us to do, and to do it with passion. Not for any reason in the world other than I knew, deep in my heart, that this was the work great saxophone players do.

Likewise, the true entrepreneur is not only passionate about the enterprise he is there to create, but about the craft he is responsible for practicing.

Because after all is said and done, entrepreneurship *is* a craft. And learning it is no different from learning music or any other demanding craft.

Professional ballplayers, for example, would never dream of questioning the dedication to practice, the hitting the ball in between at bats that's required, to prepare the players for every possible opportunity that might present itself.

We've all seen the miracles that can happen in the ninth inning, with bases loaded, where the game is won in the last seconds by a successful hit or a successful play in the field. Well, those miracles happened long before those players met those balls. They happened one swing at a time, one catch at a time, one practice at a time, one day at a time. Why should entrepreneurship be any different? Why is it we expect so little of the aspiring entrepreneur?

The difference between our expectations about entrepreneurship and baseball or any other craft has everything to do with the conventional wisdom that we've come to accept. We've bought into the notion that entrepreneurs are born with a certain charisma and know-how that is unique, that can't be learned. That all great entrepreneurs need to do is to surround themselves with great people, people who know what entrepreneurs don't need to know. It's the great people they surround themselves with that make it possible for the entrepreneur to achieve great results.

This is a myth, a story based on our cultural wish to turn entrepreneurs into rock stars. A false belief that great entrepreneurs get to do what rock stars do: perform, perform, perform what comes naturally to them while everyone else in the company, the ordinary guys, the operators as they're called in the business world, do the gritty, down-and-dirty, amazingly boring stuff, the stuff that needs to be done every day in every single business to make the entrepreneur successful.

Every great entrepreneur knows that building a World Class Company is not show time, that this is hard work, and that nothing, absolutely nothing, is more important than understanding, accepting, and surrendering to the mechanics of the music, the mechanics of the processes, the mechanics of the skills, and practices, and systems of this thing we call entrepreneurship. To ignore this means death.

Death to your dream. Death to your enterprise. Death to the time you've invested, doing it, doing it, doing it, without any concept of the context of your entrepreneurial odyssey or what it demanded of you. Entrepreneurship demands rigorous practice. But with an open heart. The openheartedness that can only be expressed through the release of one's passion in service of a higher purpose.

Building a World Class Company is a commitment to the integration of passion, purpose, and practice.

Passion is at the heart of entrepreneurial energy.

Without passion, nothing of entrepreneurial significance will happen.

So much is said about passion, but so little is really understood. Perhaps because it is so experiential, so emotional, so not of the mind, that it's so difficult to put into words. But I'm going to try.

Passion is a powerful, organic arising. It is a surge of energy that has nothing to do with commitment, determination, resolve, or a hardy hunger for getting what you don't have. I don't know of anything more potent than the passion that rises up in my body for no obvious reason whatsoever.

Passion is a strange thing. It hurts, even while it's thrilling. It radiates around your body like a shocking blue halo of electricity; it puts hot flashes behind your eyes, rings in your ears, brings up giggles without the slightest warning, causes you to leap and jump and want to run without anyplace to go for any reason. It wakes you up too early in the morning, keeps you up too late at night, makes you pick up food without the slightest interest in eating, creates strange words that bump out of the ceiling when you're lying on the couch, and even stranger words that bump out of the wall when you're trying to read a book you're not really interested in, or watching the *Tonight Show* without seeing anything, without hearing anyone, without understanding what Jay Leno is saying, or why you're even watching the *Tonight Show,* looking for something else to do, anything, wanting to write, wanting to talk, wanting to . . . no, *I don't think I'll go there!*

Passion is the heart of the matter.

It's what keeps you moving.

Passion is the juice in the battery that can be plugged into at any time, for any reason. It is the force behind the words and the music of the song you must sing.

People ask me all the time where I get my passion.

The most honest thing I can say is that it just pops up. It's always been there. When I was a little kid running around in circles, laughing like a lunatic. When I was a bigger kid bumping into walls, reading endlessly, startled by strangers who would come up to me on the street and ask me for directions. Passion has always been a part of my life. It kept me sliding in my seat at school, unable to pay attention, yawning off in the middle of a lecture, fading out as the afternoon wore on, until three o'clock finally showed up. You know what I mean, you've been a kid waiting for something good to happen, waiting for the deadly stupor to wear off, feeling the itch in your body, the craving for action, the breathing that keeps breathing, even when you can't catch your breath, it's so hot in here, so intimate out there, so empty, so full, so energized. Passion is what makes the ideas pop up. The ideas that are disconnected from the past and the future, and disconcerting in the present, making absolutely no sense, at least not in the moment, at least as far as you can tell. You know what I mean. The thoughts just keep moving, moving, moving, and then, suddenly, something unpredictable clicks into place, and you're at a crossroads, a fork in the road, and you know exactly where you're going, if not why, at least where, and you follow it. Because it's taking you and you're letting it. That's passion. At times, you've got to let it take you. It's the soul of your being, the core of your appetites. It's what creates colors rather than black and white, makes apples sweet and tangerines a pleasure. It's the wrinkle in your suit that you don't notice simply because you don't care, simply because you're on to something else, something that has sizzle in it, something that has rhythm in it, something that taps and stretches and runs around the block. What else can I say about it? Okay. Sometimes you've just got to let it rip, to feel it in your loins, to feel it rising up in your heart, the sheer joy of being alive, the sheer, unrestrained, itching wonder of it all.

Yes, passion is the heart of the entrepreneur.

Passion is what moves her. Because she allows it.

Passion is the force that brought you into this world. And makes it possible for you to keep going, wherever it takes you. Passion keeps you company on that journey into the unknown, singing in your ear, whispering in its strange language, in words that your mind doesn't understand, though your heart is touched in the sweetest, most intimate way, to move you forward.

"You're getting closer," the words say in the silkiest way. "You're getting closer," they say until you break out laughing or into a sweat, or simply collapse from the overextension of your energy, the longing, the aching, the deep satisfaction of connection with yourself.

Passion keeps me awake at night.

Passion puts color in my words, and words in my head, and heart in my music, and music in my voice. It is what connects me to every living thing, even those I have never seen or heard of.

Where do you get your passion, everyone asks me?

What turns *you* on? I ask them in response, without even a grin.

Where's the magic in your life?

What takes you away, out of your mental notions of appropriateness, to mindless soaring, creative bursts of energy and fresh discovery?

Passion is what passion is. You can feel its current coursing through your body. You can feel the water breaking against your inner emotional rocks. You can feel the waves of wanting rise inside of you without the slightest warning. You know how it feels, you know what passion is even when you don't. There's not a soul on the face of the earth who hasn't been taken by that energy that is so innately, so organically, so uniquely Me. Passion is who we are and why we're here. Passion is so understandable and so unmistakable that it's a wonder any of us get anything done with such a racket going on inside.

"Okay, Michael, I know that feeling. But what does that have to do with my business?" you might be saying to yourself.

It's this.

The passion I've been speaking about is the life force that *drives* everything you do, but it isn't the life force that *chooses* everything you do.

To build a World Class Company, you need to engage both of these life forces, what I'll call the passion of the soul and the passion of the mind.

It's the passion of the *soul* that keeps jumping off rocks, that yearns to fly like a bird; it's the passion of the *mind* that pursues visions.

It's the purposeful integration of the two that puts the juice to work in the invention of a great business. And it is the living heart of every entrepreneur.

Without the passion of the mind, the passion of the soul spins out of control, chasing first this thing, and then that, pursuing this appetite, and then that, being consumed by this obsession, and then that. Our passions can consume us until our life force is spent, leaving a shell, a burned-out corpus. Some become depressed, others, like so many in retirement, simply die. Still others just get old, simply glad to be left to rest, doing nothing of any importance, content to be living, no matter how little living they're actually doing.

Without the passion of the soul, however, the passion of the mind creates an endless stream of empty suits, dreams without heart, abstractions that fill the dead vacuum of soulless ideas, academic pursuits, dreams without feet, idealism disconnected from life. Like communism, fascism, terrorism, ideas borne of the mind's passion, ostensibly pursued on behalf of mankind, that end up killing people in an effort to save them. This is what the mind's passion, without soul, does. It creates forms without substance, huge promises without any connection to the real people who are impacted by them.

The integration of the two passions, in pursuit of an entrepreneurial vision, makes the E-Myth entrepreneur come to life.

CHAPTER THREE

The Reluctant Entrepreneur

■

"I will not learn about fire by thinking about fire but by burning."

From The Work of Craft *by Carla Needleman*

We often let our passion down. Our connection to our passion is so tenuous.

We start a million projects, only to forget two days later, or three months, or a year, why we were passionate about them. Half-completed projects become a way of life, unfulfilled dreams, crowded closets, files that stack up, the sign on the store, once new, now faded, the bike parked in the garage, idle, that we were going to ride, every day without fail. Sum it all up and it comes down to this: we lose interest. Somebody wakes up in us, and sometime later, somebody else goes back to sleep.

It's the same for all of us, to one degree or another. And yet, how do we explain that we all stay the course successfully at times. Does it mean that entrepreneurs are born, not made? That our passion is highly specific? That the absence of passion is evidence that we're missing something innate, or that we don't have the right stuff? I don't think so. I think there exists in each of us the aptitude for striving, and that the passion is there to fuel it. Understanding your passion is the key. Understanding how it works, the unsubtle and subtle shades of it, is critical to your finding your entrepreneurial gifts.

Sarah, the owner of All About Pies, will help you get there.

·   ·   ·

In *The E-Myth Revisited,* I first told the story of Sarah, and how I worked with her to transform her relationship to her business.

Taught her a different way of thinking about her pie shop.

Taught her what she needed to do instead of what she elected to do.

Taught her to work *on* her business, not just *in* it.

Taught her about the three personalities in every business owner, the Entrepreneur, the Manager, and the Technician.

I taught her that, like most small business owners, her dominant personality was the technician, and that all the technician in her really wanted to do was to go to work, to give herself a job: to make pies, sell pies, clean the shop, talk to customers.

And as long as she nourished the technician in her at the expense of her other parts, she would, ultimately, only feel enslaved by a business of her own, not enlivened by it.

It took the entrepreneur, I told her, to free her from the tyranny of routine that the technician willingly submits to.

It took the manager to manifest the entrepreneur's vision as a system that operates the business.

In short, it took all three personalities playing out their designated role, working in harmony, for the business to fulfill its promise.

Sarah was a great and willing student, and she took what I gave her to heart.

Almost 10 years ago, at the end of *The E-Myth Revisited,* Sarah and I parted company. Sarah went back to work *on* her business, not just *in* it.

She went to work to apply the entrepreneurial principles she had learned during our time together.

But all was not well at All About Pies.

Almost 10 years from the day I watched Sarah leave my office for the last time, filled with the energy, desire, and perspective to create a new life, she reentered mine.

I was the keynote speaker at her Association's annual convention, where I shared the E-Myth point of view with a large, enthusiastic audience of retailers, owners, managers, and employees.

Afterward, Sarah appeared in front of me. I couldn't believe it.

"Michael," Sarah said, extending her hand to me. "Remember me?"

How could I forget?

"Hello, Sarah," I said. "Wow, what a surprise! It's good to see you. How are you?"

"Okay," Sarah responded, "but not as well as I could be." Her hand lingered in mine and then she placed her other hand over both of ours, and said, "It's good seeing you again, Michael. I've missed you."

Sarah looked exactly as I remembered her, a little older maybe but so were we all. She was an imposing woman, by anyone's standards. Tall, elegant, with an air of authority about her. Her hair was brushed tightly back from her face, revealing bright, sharp, steady eyes, which look right at you, with interest, without imposing themselves on you.

But there was sadness in Sarah's eyes I hadn't remembered seeing there before. Frustration, yes, overwhelm, yes, but not sadness.

I shook her hands warmly. "What's up, Sarah?" I asked, almost, at the same time, regretting the question. For whatever reason, standing as we were outside of the conference hall, surrounded by a crowd of milling people, yet feeling very much alone with her, I wasn't sure I wanted to hear her answer.

"Your talk . . . ," Sarah began haltingly, "it brought back so many memories of things you and I talked about."

I hesitated, and then asked the obvious question: "And . . . ?" anticipating the response.

"Yes, somehow, it's been more difficult than I thought it would be. Than I guess I hoped it would be." She sighed and dropped her hands to her sides. "I need help, Michael. I need help. Do you have a few minutes to talk?"

"I really don't, Sarah," I said apologetically and sincerely. "I'm on my way to the airport to head home."

"I promise, it will only take a few minutes," Sarah said.

The resistance I was feeling must have showed. She said, "Michael, honest, I just need five minutes. Hearing you talk about E-Myth again brought up so many things, so much frustration and disappointment in me. . . ." She stopped talking and looked at me and smiled, knowing she had me.

What could I say?

"Why don't we sit down over there for a few minutes?" I pointed to a set of couches in the lobby, took her elbow, and started walking.

As we sat down, Sarah began talking. Her intensity built up with each word, her feelings welling out, her passion for what she was saying to me all-consuming.

"The last time we talked, I left feeling completely in control of myself and my business. I knew that what you had shared with me was going to make all the difference in my business and in my life. I knew that the confusion I had felt from the day I started my business was a thing of the past. I could see clearly, for the first time, that I was called to work on my business, not in it as I had been doing. I made the commitment to myself that I would do exactly what you said. I saw the wisdom of it and felt the excitement that the clarity created for me, like nothing else I had ever experienced.

"I went back to my business, knowing deep in my heart what I was going to do, even though, admittedly, I had no idea of how I was going to do it. I even printed up a little sign that I put over the cash register, and over my desk, that said, "Work ON it, not IN it!" as a constant reminder to myself that my role was not to go to work in the business every day, but to go to work on the business every day, to build a business I could replicate, as you said again today"—she smiled—to be run by ordinary people, doing business in an extraordinary way.

"For some time, that's exactly what I did, Michael. I built manuals, I built special trainings for my small staff. I measured everything I could. I became an E-Myth Maniac. My girls laughed at me, every chance they could: 'Did you ask Michael Gerber about that? Do you think Michael Gerber would do it that way?' You would have been embarrassed by how often your name came up at All About Pies, Michael. The driving question was always, What would Michael Gerber say about that?

"And, I loved it!" Sarah continued.

"It felt like a huge adventure. My business stopped being all about work, and all about pies. It became all about development, growth, getting our little business ready to become a big business, doing what great businesses do.

"And then, something began to change. Slowly at first, so slowly that I didn't even notice it. So subtly that none of us really noticed it. But it changed. And I didn't realize until much, much later what actually happened.

"What happened was that I went from doing it, doing it, doing it as a technician, to doing it, doing it, doing it as an entrepreneur. I changed one kind of work for another kind of work. Even though I was building systems like crazy, and even though I was documenting everything we did, even though we were doing what I thought you had taught me, I was slowly but surely becoming as overwhelmed by working on it as I had when I was working in it. I had shifted my intention, as well as my attention, but the intensity, the overwhelm, was exactly the same as before. Somehow I had lost my sense of purpose in my passionate pursuit of getting everything exactly right.

"And I didn't know what to do about it.

"To tell you the truth, Michael, when I found out that the Association was inviting you to speak, I made up my mind that day to come here, and to talk to you, because I need you to help me break free of this place I'm in. I need help in moving to the next step. I came here determined to ask you for help, once more, but this time, to see it through to its conclusion."

Sarah paused for a moment, took a deep breath, and said, "Michael, you can't say no, you've just got to say yes, no matter what it's going to cost me. I can't keep struggling like this!"

Sarah smiled, painfully, but, cleanly.

"Don't say no," she said.

I shuddered to myself thinking about everything Sarah and I would need to confront, to work through, to overcome, in order to even engage in the process she was contemplating.

"Sarah," I began, "I can see things have gotten pretty painful. And I so appreciate your sincerity. Honestly. And I'm honored that you would think so much of me to ask me for help. But knowing what I know about what you are asking for, and how much time and care it would take, and the projects I'm already committed to . . . and that I don't have all the time in the world left. Knowing all that, I just don't think. . . ."

She stopped me in mid-sentence and laid her hand on mine again. "Michael, I have no illusions about what I'm asking for, and I also know I have no reason to expect that you should give it to me. But, somehow, I know that it is exactly what we should do, and I'm simply asking you to trust enough to take the first step with me. If it doesn't feel right to you then, so be it. I will drop it in a second. But, somehow, I believe in my heart that this is going to be well worth your time. I don't know how exactly, but I feel it. Could we just take the next step?" She moved her hand away from mine, but the touch of it was still there, warm and insistent.

I sighed, smiled, and said, "Okay, call me when you get back and we'll set up a time to talk. But no promises," I said, still very much ambivalent.

I got up, as did she, we hugged, and I said, "I've got a bear of a schedule over the next several weeks but call my assistant and she'll fit you in." I gave her my assistant's name and her direct line.

"But no promises," I said again as if to convince myself that there still was a possibility that I wasn't in this for the long haul.

Sarah smiled brightly. "I can't wait," she said.

CHAPTER FOUR

The Little Girl Who Wanted to Write a Book

"Being, not doing, is my first joy."

From The Abyss, The Collected Poems of Theodore Roethke

When I arrived home from the meeting, an email was waiting for me from Sarah. It said, "I loved seeing you. I've been thinking about nothing else. If we can find a way to make this work for both of us, I can finally get this right. I was moved to write this story on the plane and send it to you. A good place to start, I think. Warm regards, Sarah."

As soon as I read Sarah's story, I immediately knew what she meant. It was a perfect metaphor for the delicate balance between the part of us that dreams, creates and plays—the entrepreneur—and the part of us that works—the technician. Think of it as a parable. Think of it as a message from Sarah about how easily we give up what is most genuine in us and most important.

· · ·

Once upon a time, there was a little girl named Sarah.

Sarah was 9 years old.

She was a quiet, little girl. She didn't make too much of a fuss about anything. She pretty much did what her mother expected of her. She cleaned her room, did her homework, helped around the house, was courteous to her mother's friends and well behaved in school. Sarah was the kind of little girl every busy parent dreams of. Not any trouble at all.

All of this changed when Sarah closed the door to her room behind her for the night.

Sarah's mother would never have imagined that Sarah had another life when she was supposed to be sleeping.

Sarah had an amazing internal life at night, alone with her thoughts and her journal.

The pictures, the stories, the visions, the music, all came alive in Sarah in full color, taking the form of internal talk, whispering, laughing, crying, raging, hot, hearty, boisterous voices, of girls, of boys, of men, of women, none of whom Sarah knew, except there at night, in her imagination.

And gradually, as Sarah became 10, and then 11, the stories began to take the form of chapters. And the chapters began to take the form of a book. And the book began to take the form of pages, numbered sequentially, with chapter headings and copious notes scrawling tight little words, up and down each side of every page, and above the Middle Words, as Sarah liked to call the words in the center of the page, and below the Middle Words, and in the middle of the Middle Words, to the point where Sarah gradually began to discover the something that had formed all on its own, the something Sarah called My Book, her wonderful book, a book that had come out of her heart and head almost as a surprise, like it appeared one day and said, "Hi. How are you? Here I am. Aren't I wonderful?"

And that's how Sarah came to the decision to write a book. She had already been doing it without even realizing it, and suddenly, there it was. And suddenly, too, there appeared in Sarah the person she called The Little Girl Who Wanted to Write a Book.

The Little Girl Who Wanted to Write a Book lived in Sarah now all the time. Sarah loved her.

The Little Girl Who Wanted to Write a Book would plead with Sarah to get home so they could go to work. "I've got to get busy on the book," the little girl would say to Sarah.

And for the first time in Sarah's life, Sarah began to worry. She began to worry that there wouldn't be enough time to write her book.

She wouldn't be able to think up enough ideas for her book.

But these thoughts were not Sarah's. It was The Little Girl Who Wanted to Write a Book who put them in Sarah's head.

To Sarah, writing was a calling.

To The Little Girl Who Wanted to Write a Book, writing was a necessity. The Little Girl's needs eventually took a toll on Sarah.

Sarah's face started to look worried. Her room began to be a mess. She was always late to everything. She snapped back at her mother, she was rude to her mother's friends. And most of all, she dreaded going to her room at night. She dreaded closing the door at night. Because now, when she did, The Little Girl Who Wanted to Write a Book was waiting, the little girl who was fast becoming for Sarah, The Girl I Really Hate.

Of course, Sarah's mother's friends told her mother not to worry. They said Sarah was, after all, turning 12, a time when all little girls begin to act very strangely. Who knows what little girls becoming big girls are thinking about, if it isn't boys, if it isn't their bodies, if it isn't romance, if it isn't, well, you know. Aren't all little girls impossible to understand?

But, of course, Sarah wished all the time that her mother *could* understand her. Just like her mother wished she could reach Sarah. Neither of them knew how. If they could have just talked to each other about the mystery of the battle going on in Sarah's life, Sarah could have unraveled, at this tender age, a major source of internal conflict that would remain unresolved for most of her life.

. . .

Little did anyone understand what was actually going on inside Sarah.

It was a war. Between the Creator in Sarah and the Need in Sarah.

It was a war that started out harmlessly enough, and naturally enough, as the Creator in Sarah came face-to-face with the Producer in Sarah. The war gradually grew in size and temperament and energy and weapons and strategy. Unfortunately, as is usually the case, the producer in Sarah gave way to the need in Sarah. And The Little Girl Who Wanted to Write a Book turned into the part of Sarah who really, really, *really* wanted, really *needed* to win, at all cost.

All the creator, the emerging entrepreneur, in Sarah wanted to do was to dream and let the feelings and the words that captured those feelings come out.

Not even 12, the entrepreneur in Sarah was in a battle for her life.

CHAPTER FIVE

The Reluctant Coach

*"I was so determined to break all routines . . .
(that) I developed a routine for avoiding routine
and eventually had to change that, striving to make
of the whole process a spontaneous adventure
rather than another routine path."*

From The Vision *by Tom Brown, Jr.*

The session I promised Sarah didn't take place for more than a month. My time was consumed by previous commitments, a book I hadn't yet completed and needed to, four more speaking events, two on the East Coast, the beginning of a search for a CEO for E-Myth Worldwide, so much to do, so little time.

When I finally did have the time to talk with Sarah by phone, we spent some time catching up. Then I revisited the subject of my misgivings about taking on a consulting assignment like hers.

"I've asked myself a dozen times why I'm even considering doing this, Sarah. I swear, the only answer that comes up is that this is a way for me to complete the process we started, that we obviously never finished, 10 years ago. The process called how to successfully make the transition from technician to entrepreneur. What you're asking of me is a major commitment, bigger than I think you imagine."

Sarah barely waited for me to finish my sentence.

"Come on, Michael, I think I get it. I have the same concern about how much all of this will add to my already impossible schedule. But I know in my heart it's right. The real question, as I see it, is with everything you've already got on your plate, how are you going to give me what I need?"

I laughed. "That's my question, Sarah! And you're right. With everything else I've got to do, this is impossible. There's no way I can do this. What am I thinking? I've got to be out of my mind!"

She laughed with me, and then grew playfully serious again.

"So why don't we just start and see what happens?" she said. "We've got an hour to kill. What do you say we just use it?"

What do you say we just use it? Isn't that exactly what I asked Bob, the high-tech wizard who didn't know anything about business, in 1975? And look at how perfectly that turned out? What was I doing here with Sarah for an hour?

What was my purpose? What was my entrepreneurial purpose?

Why was I even contemplating working with her? There wasn't a day that went by since *The E-Myth* became popular that someone didn't ask me for help. Help with their business plan, help in finding money, help in marketing their product, help in developing their business model, help, help, help.

And every time I succumbed to giving the little bit of help I could give, the inevitable happened, I could never give enough!

The need for help was endless.

And, ironically, that's why I created E-Myth Worldwide in the first place. My company was my entrepreneurial answer to the infinite need I saw, everywhere I looked, for help, for affordable help that, most of all, didn't depend upon me. I wanted to help, but I didn't want to *be* the help.

Just like Ray Kroc never wanted to make hamburgers, I never wanted to be a business consultant.

I wanted to invent a consulting system that would make it possible to deliver world class help to small business owners through people who were not consultants either, but were passionate about helping others and could learn to use the consulting system we invented for just that purpose: to make business consulting affordable to anyone, like Sarah, who needed exactly what she was asking from me right now.

So, why didn't I just turn her over to one of our E-Myth Coaches and be done with it? Why, why, why?

All this was going through my head as I listened to Sarah, on the other end of the line, implore me to do something I wasn't really feeling compelled to do. And then it hit me. What if I were to start all over again? What if I were to imagine that Sarah was my very first client? And that I could create the consulting system from scratch. What would I do differently given everything I've learned since 1977? What an intriguing idea! The chance to revisit the entire business development process with someone like Sarah who is deeply committed to the process. That's why we're here, I thought. That's what my purpose is. Suddenly, I was jazzed and thoroughly engaged.

I said, "Yes, Sarah, let's just use the hour we've got. I have a sense it'll be interesting."

I imagined I left her smiling.

I told Sarah what I was thinking. That this could be a really interesting way for me to rethink everything we had done from the beginning of our business, and to engage Sarah as though she were my very first client, as though we were beginning from the very beginning.

"How would we do that?" she asked, truly interested.

I thought about Sarah's question and, suddenly, there it was, the space to explore the right questions for the right reasons, which I had wished every new client could have done when we'd started our relationship. The space that is inevitably there before they start their business but is lost as soon as problems start appearing, inevitably, almost immediately. How many times had I wished that I wasn't being asked to solve problems, problems of money, problems of competition, problems of too little of this, too much of that? I saw, in that moment, in the space that I had created around Sarah and me, how the entire essence of our business rested on the one thing that was missing in almost every small business we worked with: the entrepreneur, the entrepreneurial ethos, the entrepreneurial mind-set. Our clients were the living, breathing expressions of the E-Myth, the Entrepreneurial Myth, the missing entrepreneur, the person who wasn't there at all, who needed to be.

What a place to start!

"Let's start at the beginning," I said.

"You're an entrepreneur. You're not interested in pies, you're not interested in customers, you're not interested in anything specific, other than this pressing need you've got to invent something, a business you can grow. How would you go about this in a way that would produce something significant, something exciting, something remarkably different from all the other ordinary businesses struggling to make ends meet out there?"

I felt the need to find something I had not found before. A way of expressing this that I had not yet expressed before, using the same words I had said time and again to small business owners. I was looking for something that had eluded me in the past, a new path, a new discovery, a new way of transforming the mind of a client who had not yet engaged with me, to discover what was missing in her life that she needed in order to create what she wanted. Where was it? How to find it?

"Sarah, this is truly difficult for me. Difficult, because I haven't done it before. Difficult, also, because I *have* done this before, and I'm struggling to break free of all of the words and thoughts and ideas that have already been expressed, to find something new, something fresh, something deeply entrepreneurial. I'd like you to give me the room to do that, even if I stumble in the process. I have no idea where this is going to take us. But I'm willing to experience the discomfort of not knowing if you are. Okay?"

"Yes," Sarah said simply. She seemed genuinely happy to be able to give me something. "Whatever you need."

"Okay, then let's start with nothing. There's nothing here in front of us, just the wish to discover what it is that entrepreneurs do. How do entrepreneurs think? How do entrepreneurs invent? How does invention happen? How does something emerge out of nothing? How does one take the first step? Does the business emerge out of an insight, or does the insight emerge out of the business? This sounds hopelessly abstract, I know, because I feel it, and yet, somehow I know that this is moving, this question, this interest, this excitement, is moving us someplace where something significant can reveal itself."

"Sarah," I said, "the entrepreneur in me feels such a wish to break free. And yet this other part, my technician, just wants to get it done. I can feel the conflict as I'm talking to you. This wish to break free is a wish to discover who I really could be in this moment, with you, in pursuit of your wish to break free of who you've been in your business. It's pretty juicy stuff if you think about it. But I'm still looking for it. I'm still looking for something I haven't heard before. For both of us. So, let's push the window open a bit more. Let's see what shows up."

Sarah didn't say anything. She simply waited. It was up to me. I sat quietly for a moment, feeling somewhat embarrassed, but also knowing that something would come up, and whatever it was, would be worth waiting for. I waited. We both waited. The only sounds were the clock ticking in my office and Sarah's breathing.

Nothing.

Nothing.

The silence was deafening.

I felt the need to speak.

I waited some more. I could feel my body settle in the chair, I could feel the soles of my feet in my shoes resting heavily, it seemed, on the floor. I breathed deeply. And then Sarah spoke.

"I think I understand something I didn't before," Sarah said softly.

"I suddenly realize that in all the time we were together before, in all the time and energy I invested after that to apply what I learned to my business, I never really struggled with freeing myself from how I was. It was simply a new way of thinking about my business. I didn't want to do anything more than *use* how I was to get better at doing business."

Sarah paused but I didn't say a word. It was obvious to me that she had more to say that I wanted to hear.

"It struck me, as you were struggling to find something new, that I rarely, if ever, do that. I have no idea how to do that. I'm aware that when I tracked you down at the hotel, all I wanted to do was to solve a problem. That's all I really wanted from you. To help me out of my pain. The direction you're pointing me in is very different than that. And I feel the pain of my resistance to it. To being as interested in the pursuit of the question as you are. And, on the other hand, I can feel a part of me that wants to be. I just don't know how."

"I understand, Sarah, I get it." I said. That's exactly the question you have to face: Do you want to change how you are so that you can change your business? Do you really even buy into the notion that in order for your business to change, you have to change first? It's an honest question. It's the right question for you to think about.

"Miraculously, we've come to exactly the place we needed to today. If you can find interest, deep, genuine interest, in looking at yourself, struggling with yourself, changing your habits that don't work, discovering your unexpressed passion—pursuing the question of the nature of the entrepreneurial mind-set—I would feel honored to pursue it with you. If you simply want to solve a problem or two in your business so you can feel some temporary relief from your pain, I'm just not interested."

I looked at my watch and said, "We're just about out of time. Think about it."

CHAPTER SIX

Creating the Room to Create

■

"Creativity is, foremost, being in the world soulfully, for the only thing we truly make, whether in the arts, in culture, or at home, is soul."

From Care of the Soul *by Thomas Moore*

Sarah emailed me two days after our first phone meeting to ask me if I would have a short session with her to help resolve her resistance to my proposition. She told me she knew that most of her resistance was fear, fear of really looking deeply at herself, fear of discovering that she wasn't world class enough for World Class, fear of giving up and then feeling like she failed, fear of disappointing me, among others. She said that she was also having moments of feeling her entrepreneurial energy intimately and a deep wish to give it to the creation of her business. Sarah and I arranged to talk on the following Saturday morning.

I was now thinking about the whole question of entrepreneurship all the time. It became clear to me that we probably had made a huge mistake with clients by moving too quickly to what they were concerned about, getting their business to work. That some clients had paid a price for our willingness to respond so readily to their perceived need. We should have been more resolute in defining what was missing in the client, the entrepreneur, rather than what was missing in the client's business: the money, the manuals, the systems, better people. Because we so often responded to the condition the client was reacting to, we too often ended up working *in* the client's business under the guise of working *on* it.

"I've been in such conflict, Michael, for the past few days," Sarah burst at me. "Part of me wants to flee, and has been screaming, 'Get me out of here!' and another part of me wants to know what's really missing in my business. I want to understand this entrepreneurial thing you talk about so passionately, and I can't stand that I can't just give in to it. All I ever seem to want to do is to get busy, and make things work. Remember the little girl who wanted to write a book?" Sarah inserted with a smile. "There's an impatience in me that just drives me to get busy. I can't stand still for a minute without doing something. So I do whatever comes up. And that fills my day. Because there's always something that needs doing. And there I am, willing to do it, no matter what it is."

"And that's why it's so important for you to find a way to stop, breathe, and feel into who you are, and who you want to be, in relationship to All About Pies," I said to Sarah. This very old habit of doing whatever comes up won't cut it, not if you want to create a World Class Company. If we don't spend time right now discovering who you are, you will find yourself back at this very same point before too long. Something will be missing again, Sarah. And you'll think that it has something to do with not knowing how to create better manuals, or build better systems, or train your people better, or sell better, or buy better, but that won't be it. Because 'better' in your business depends on the depth of your relationship to the fundamental emotional center of entrepreneurial energy. Otherwise, the mechanics, the practice, will consume your energy rather than feed it. The result, and I see it all the time, is a brittle, dry, deadly business. Because an owner who hasn't found her entrepreneurial passion will never find it trying to create systems and manuals and training programs. Eventually, all that will deplete her energy.

"And you have to be willing to engage with yourself and this process whole hog plus the postage. To create with me something that didn't exist before we came together. If we do that, if we pursue this with a vengeance while you're in it up to your eyebrows, we'll create magic. But I have to know that you're committed to hanging up the phone each time we spend time together with something completely different, more life producing, than you've ever had before. The magic of being an entrepreneur is manifested in the process of inventing. It transforms, but you have to be open to it."

The entrepreneur is nothing if not passionate.

The entrepreneur is passionate about creation. Creation is everything.

The creator is created through the act of creation. The act of doing what entrepreneurs do creates who entrepreneurs are. But it's not just the doing of it, it's the passionate commitment to it, like honing the edge of a sword, patiently, with dedication, persistently, lovingly, without a thought as to when you might use the sword.

The entrepreneur takes shape through the act of invention.

If there is no invention there is no entrepreneur.

If there is no entrepreneur there is no invention.

The two are inextricably bound.

The substance of the entrepreneur, his worth as an entrepreneur, is determined by the substance of his invention.

If you were to look at McDonald's when it was invented, early on, in the years when it morphed from one store to 100 stores, it not only increased in size, it established its meaning and fulfilled its purpose. All you have to do is think about McDonald's, as a business, for a few minutes and you begin to comprehend the substance of it. It became, by doing what it did and accomplishing what it accomplished, a standard for all business. It exemplifies the best model for growing a small business, any business, there is. You can see the substance of the man who created McDonald's, Ray Kroc, in his invention.

If you can see the invention as only an entrepreneur can.

Most would look at McDonald's and just see hamburgers, French fries, milk shakes, lines of people, fast food, cheap food, fats, carbohydrates, the cause of obesity, money, kids working for minimum wage, beef being unnecessarily slaughtered, capitalism, gross inequities and injustices, anything and everything but the unadulterated brilliance of the business model, the ultimate ingenuity of the entrepreneurial mind.

The entrepreneur is the creator, and the entrepreneur is defined by his creation. And his creation, at first, is of interest only to him. It does not exist except for him. It is the product of his solitude. It is private, personal, and deeply internal. It lives where the fire is, inside not outside. It bakes in the internal oven of his burning passion, over the hot coals of his imagination and his heart. It will collapse, like a soufflé that is removed from the heat prematurely, unless all of the heat is kept inside.

The entrepreneur, however, is never passionate about work. Creation is discovering something new. Work is not for the purpose of discovering something new. Work, the work we all do, is for the purpose of getting something done. The minute creation becomes about getting something done, it turns into work. Work is not unimportant. Things must get done. But getting things done is not creation. It has a result in mind. Entrepreneurs do not set out with a result in mind, though they always discover a result. They set out to create. Creation is discovery. Discovery is magical. Discovery is the juice that an entrepreneur lives for. The juice of discovery comes from the passion that creates it. The passion that creates it is everything to the entrepreneur. It is what makes entrepreneurs, the entrepreneur inside of us all, so absolutely, wonderfully, miraculously alive.

"That's why," I continued with Sarah, "you came back. You're still a reluctant entrepreneur. You still want to use E-Myth Mastery as a way out. As a way of improving the circumstances you find yourself in, making your business run better. And, of course, it will do that. But it won't last. There is so much more of lasting value here for you. There is the potential for establishing a deep connection to the passion at the heart of an enterprise. The foundation for inventing All About Pies isn't simply something to bring back to your business like a newfound skill, like a tool acquired at a two-day training. The foundation for inventing your business is *you,* Sarah. And you've been missing. The creator in you. The connection between the you who started your journal as a little girl, passionately, with abandon, and the you who will go back to your business to do something different. These two parts of yourself need to come together into a totally new person, someone who is both a stranger to you and someone you trust to take over. This is a tall order, I realize, but the only real way out.

"Because you never really changed, Sarah. You simply took the ideas you learned while we were together and implemented them, and for a time, you looked different. But, eventually, the facade wore off. Can you see that?"

"Something you're getting at here, Michael, is starting to hit home," Sarah responded, haltingly, as if a part of her were wishing I would keep talking so she didn't have to. "I realize that I'm feeling some sense of loss of that little girl who so passionately went about writing in her journal only to have her joy thwarted by my need to produce a result. By my need to turn what was a labor of love into a love of labor. My need to turn what had no practical purpose at all into something that served some use, something that I could justify to the rest of the world. No wonder I never shared my secret. There was simply no room for that much passion in my life."

"That's it, Sarah!" I said. "You need to *find* the room! And when you do, I promise you, there will be no going back again."

CHAPTER SEVEN

The Heart of the Matter

■

"To me the desire to create and to have control over
your own life, irrespective of the politics and the time
or the social structures, was very much part of the
human spirit. What I did not fully realize was that
work could open the doors to my heart."

From Body and Soul *by Anita Roddick*

The next phone session with Sarah, almost two weeks later, was a challenge for
both of us. I was trying to do something with Sarah that I had never done before, something that would truly help Sarah make the transition from technician and reluctant entrepreneur to a true entrepreneur.

I could feel myself drawn to old solutions that I knew in my heart worked
some of the time and for some of the people who worked them. Somehow it
wasn't enough to say it was up to them anymore. If the vision I've had for almost 30 years, transforming small businesses worldwide, was going to become
a reality for the vast majority of people who were in need of it, something significantly different had to happen.

The fact is that there is rarely enough passion to feed many of our clients
over the long haul, to sustain, enrich, and inspire them until the work we do together becomes a way of life. Sarah's experience is no different from that of so
many other small business owners I've known. Over time, the reluctant entrepreneur rears her weary head and everything that we've built together can start
to erode. If this were to happen to Sarah again, we would both end up despair-
ing, each for our own reasons.

My resistance to starting over, from the very beginning, is no different than

Sarah's resistance to turning her focus inward. Where to begin? How to begin? How to even know when, or if, I've begun? What if I can't? A part of me doesn't even want to ask these questions. It's so much easier to fall back on what I know.

Adding to the challenge were Sarah's pressing pragmatic needs, which weren't necessarily going to be satisfied by my agenda, at least at the beginning. And, even though she agreed to engage with herself and to trust that it would all work out in the end, I could also feel the part of her that just wanted to get on with it, the part of her that had come to depend upon her own ability to find the shortest distance between two points. And this little adventure of ours was anything but the shortest journey between two points. Sarah and I found ourselves engaged in a process in which the teacher was awkwardly attempting to learn a new teaching methodology while the student was anxiously trying to get through the class so she could graduate, get a job, and start earning a living!

How to do this so both of our needs were satisfied was the question.

But isn't this the kind of opportunity we are all faced with every day of our lives?

Haven't you worked hard to get where you are? To become who you are?

Hasn't your life, like mine, had its share of difficulties?

When I think about the story I shared with you in the Foreword of this book about the time I fainted in the coffee shop, 36 years ago, I'm struck by a wave of the pain of my life, an accumulation of the traumatic experiences I've had over close to 70 years. It reminds me of a book I read, a long time ago, by P. D. Ouspensky, *The Strange Life of Ivan Osokin,* during a time when the teachings of Gurdjieff, a brilliant Russian mystic in the first half of the 20th century and Ouspensky's teacher, played a significant role in my life. In *The Strange Life of Ivan Osokin,* Ouspensky says that reincarnation is not what we've been led to think it is, that we're not reborn as someone else, but rather that *we're reborn to relive exactly the same life we've lived, over and over again,* until we make a significant choice in a moment to do something differently than we've done it, life after life. In that moment we are instantly transformed. Ouspensky was saying that hell on earth is life as we have always lived it, and heaven on earth is breaking free of our long-standing patterns. I don't have to tell you that it takes an enormous amount of energy, passion, determination, and will to even *see* the patterns, let alone *break free* of them.

I can feel how unbearable it would be if I had to relive all of those traumatic moments, over and over again. I can feel them in my body, just as I felt them then. I can feel the hopelessness, the overwhelm, how bleak life looked. And yet, my life isn't bleak at all when I recognize that it was only my habituated way of engaging with life that made it look so dark. I can begin to think back and see how many different options I actually had, all of which would have produced less traumatic outcomes, none of which I saw at the time. But what about the choices I have right now? What could I be choosing right now, at this very moment, that I can't see, that I'm blind to, that all of my habituated patterns won't let me see? That's what I'm doing here with Sarah, both aware of the endless options I've already explored over the past 27 years at E-Myth, and open to discovering something fresh and new, to transform my understanding of how to help Sarah, and in so doing, my understanding of how to help others in the same position as Sarah. And, in the very same instant, I'm feeling the terror of giving up everything I know how to do! Because if I do that, if I give up everything I know, what, and who, would be left? Who would I be without what I've become, the person I've created?

Who would you be if not You?

Who would Sarah be if not Sarah?

Do you really want to find out?

That's the question, isn't it?

I can feel the tension in me as I pursue this path, a need to end it, a wish to continue it, the confusion I'm feeling, which turns into fear that I've reached a dead end, and I'll fall, like a house of cards, tumbling down, and then what? If I can let go of my anxiety for a moment and just let this be, I suspect something will come that will move the energy again. That's usually what happens but I don't always trust it.

"I think I've got it," Sarah said, as if in response to the monologue that was going on in my head. "Let me try this out on you, Michael."

"Sure, Sarah," I answered. Her voice held the promise of something fresh and comforting, like a warm pie just out of the oven.

"Okay then. Here is what I've gotten so far from what we've been talking about. Passion is the love of creation. Creation is its own gift. When I was a little girl and would go to bed at night and close the door to my room, I would close out everything that happened in my life: the day I just had, the things that happened, the schoolwork, the homework, things my teacher did, things I was expected to do around the house, my mother, my aunt, my friends, tomorrow, everything. I just settled down in my bed, took out my journal, opened to a blank page, and just waited. Something always came. A word, a thought, a picture, the entire world would explode anew there in my room. All I had to do was lie down in my bed, pull the covers up around me, pick up my journal, and the miracle would happen. There has never been anything quite like it for me, ever. Other than the pies. . . ." Sarah just stopped. It was obvious that something important had crossed her mind.

"That's it!" she said.

"The journal and the pies I used to make with my aunt. They are both creation. But there is something very different about my experience in relationship to each of them. Until the little girl who wanted to write a book showed up, writing in my journal had no purpose whatsoever. It was pure love. The love of discovery. Discovering thoughts and words and ideas that I had never thought or said before. It was as if they were living in me, hiding, waiting, bubbling, laughing, crying, talking to each other, telling secrets that were going to be revealed to me, as soon as I let them come out in my journal. The pies, though, were creation of a completely different sort. The love of creating the pies was connected to our picture of who would eat them, of the pure delight on their faces. In some way, as my aunt baked, she was connected to the pleasure she would be giving through her pies, and she radiated in that pleasure, which in turn, permeated the pies she created. Writing in my journal had no purpose. It was pure creation. It was the pure love of creation.

"To me," Sarah continued, "there has never been anything quite like those private moments between me and my journal. Never. If there is such a thing as pure joy, that was it. And as I say this to you, Michael, I can honestly say that I have never experienced anything even close to that kind of pure joy in my business. And I realize I don't know how to. I'm not even sure it's possible.

"I also realize that this is the first time I have ever understood the difference between pure, solitary creation, and creation that has a purpose connected to my relationship with others. It really helps me understand the nature of passion at a subtler level. My journal writing was pure, expressed passion. It had no purpose, it filled no external need. The minute the little girl who wanted to write a book showed up, that purity was destroyed. I lost it completely after that. I tried to turn the ideal into the practical. I tried to use it to become something it was never meant to be. The journal was the discovery of myself. I turned it into a tool to define myself. An exercise designed to define who I am has nothing to do with creation, with passion, with love. I can see now that I have a choice. I can choose to create simply for the love of it. Or I can turn creation into mechanics and sentence my creativity and passion to death. I can build a business out of some need, or I can create a business free of any need to do it at all. Then, I can go to my room at night, take out my journal, and discover things that are waiting there for me, as an expression of me, as an expression of the love that I am. That's how I want to fall asleep at night from now on.

"It's important to me, Michael, that you know that I'm beginning to get the entrepreneurial passion you talk about with so much love. I'm starting to feel your passion in my body, if that makes sense to you. Your passion for passion. Your passion for invention. Your passion for creation. Your passion for the entrepreneur inside of you, and the one inside of me. This is your sweetest gift. Thank you for sharing it with me."

Sarah stopped for a moment, and then said, more quietly, as though she were speaking to herself, "You know, I came to get answers. Answers about systems development and people development. Answers about how to stimulate my people to think on their feet, how to find the time to work on my business rather than becoming consumed with all the stuff that has to happen every day. But my questions and the answers seem insignificant right now. I've wrestled with you and I've wrestled with myself, and just like Jacob did with the stranger, all night, in the Old Testament, I've come away with a wound, touched and burned, a part of me forever marked and changed. And it took all I had. And that's what's been missing in my business. My willingness to give it all I've got. That's why you call me a reluctant entrepreneur. My body and my mind give into the passivity, and there's nobody home to wrestle."

Sarah stopped abruptly. The silence fell between us. The energy was intense. "What's worse, Sarah," I said, "is that there's been no one to wrestle with. There's been no stranger."

CHAPTER EIGHT

Wrestling with a Stranger

■

**"Jacob was left alone. And a man wrestled with him
until the break of dawn."**

From Genesis 32:23–32

Sarah had just given me a gift, one of many. Wrestling with a stranger. We are
all called to wrestle with a stranger, to engage with that part of us that refuses to
give up and the part that wants to flee, both at the same time, the parts that are
known to us as well as the parts that are unknown. Sarah and I were getting
someplace. She was changing. I could hear passion's voice again, "You're getting closer, you're getting closer."

To wrestle with a stranger, to engage in mortal combat, to risk yourself, particularly your beliefs about yourself, and to care more deeply about your relationship with the process than how it all turns out, is what passion is all about.

The reluctant entrepreneur does not want to wrestle with the stranger. The
reluctant entrepreneur wants to stay busy, busy, busy, doing what she knows
how to do until it bores her to tears or frustrates her to death.

The reluctant entrepreneur is completely attached to how things are and is
dedicated to keeping things exactly as they've been. As a result, the reluctant
entrepreneur tacitly commits to the entrepreneurial opportunity at hand, but
never wholeheartedly commits to it. The reluctant entrepreneur says, yes, I like
the idea of going to work *on* my business, as opposed to *in* it, but do I really
have to take it seriously?

There is no room in a World Class Company for a reluctant entrepreneur. A true entrepreneur is serious. He is interested in wrestling. A true entrepreneur wrestles completely, no holds barred.

And if you can't wrestle with yourself right away, go track someone down, like Sarah did, to wrestle with you, to take you to the mat.

You've got to wrestle with the stranger. God bless the stranger.

Sarah and I talked a few weeks later, late on a Monday afternoon. The rain had come and gone, the sun was out, the day was shining.

"I've had quite an experience with all of this since our last meeting," Sarah said. "I need to tell you about it, Michael."

I listened with great interest.

"I realize, for the first time, how much energy this thing takes," Sarah said evenly. "I realize how much interest, curiosity, and attention is required if I'm going to do this work, the work of the entrepreneur, earnestly. I've watched over the past few weeks how that interest rises in me and then falls. How my curiosity awakens and then evaporates, as though it never existed. How my attention wanders, so much so that I don't even notice it's gone until much, much later, and I suddenly become aware that I've been lost in activity, distraction. And I can't remember when it happened, what triggered it, what took me away. I feel my emotions go up and down, from excitement and extreme focus, to feelings of deep depression. And even through all of that, I realize that it doesn't matter which emotion it is, excitement or depression. In a fundamental way, they're both the same thing. I get attached to my feelings and then lose myself. I've begun to discover that there is something calling to me that is much deeper than the feeling, a transitory ebb and flow, a flux of thoughts randomly running through me like water running through a pipe without any true intention of its own. The water runs according to the angle of the pipe. If the pipe turns down, the water flows; if the pipe turns up, the water builds up until the pipe angles down again and the water follows its natural course. My thoughts and feelings are just like that. I recognize that they have nothing to do with me. I'm beginning to sense there is much more to me than that. I can't say what exactly, but I'm interested in finding out.

"I also know now what was missing for me after you and I worked together the last time, when I went back to my business to apply what I thought I had learned from you. I wasn't up to it. You can't do this work alone. Wrestling with a stranger is a perfect metaphor for this, Michael. I need someone in my life who understands the territory of entrepreneurship, and how to navigate it. A person who is not afraid to tell me the truth about myself, whether I like it in the moment or not. A person who's interested in working with me, first, be-

cause it serves his interests, his passion, his purpose. A person who is not willing to compromise the rules of the game to be liked or approved of. When you
told me that you weren't interested in working with me unless I was interested
in looking at myself, it made me so uncomfortable, but not just for the obvious
reasons. I finally realized that I couldn't simply do this any old way, that my
rules of the game were about to be revealed, tested, put into serious question. I
realized that the only way you would give me the time of day is if I really did it.
If I really met you halfway. If I generated my own energy in support of the
growth I was looking for. I realized that if you felt you were pulling me along in
any way, you would lose interest, and this would be over. I've never found myself in this situation before. It's embarrassing to say this, but I'm aware that, at
some level, I came to you hoping that you would have enough passion and energy for both of us. That I would get carried along in your wake. When it became obvious to me that you weren't going to play that game, it really forced
me to ask myself whether I should just take my marbles and go home. I almost
did a couple of times. But I have to tell you, Michael, I've been so inspired by
your passion, your uncompromising conviction, your determination to do
something that you didn't need to do, in a way you've never done it before, so
willing to be vulnerable and exposed at times, that all of my considerations col-
lapsed into a puddle of tears. Last night, in bed, I burst into tears and cried
deeply, for the little girl who just wanted to be free to be Me, for the little girl
who couldn't let her, and for all the years I've wasted being busy at the expense
of discovering my deepest passion, my most vital self. I have no doubt that I
want to do my life differently, that I want to create a very different relationship
to All About Pies. I'm in this game, Michael, because I feel the wish to discover
my entrepreneurial vitality. I'm committed to learning how to do this E-Myth
Mastery thing, as you always say, 'whole hog plus the postage.' I have absolutely
no idea whether I'm big enough, whether I have enough passion. Mostly, I'm
scared to death that I won't be good enough to make it through to the end."

Sarah stopped, breathed deeply, and then went on. "My difficulty right
now is that I don't know what I really want. How can I commit myself completely to what you're asking of me when I'm not sure what I'm asking of myself. I know now that I'm not certain what my purpose is in doing this. I need
to get grounded in what my passion is pursuing. Because if I am good enough
to see this through, I need to know what the end is."

"Sarah," I said, "what a beautiful place you've come to. I knew you would
get there. And your question is the most natural question in the world to ask.
Let's try to answer it."

CHAPTER NINE

The Purpose of Purpose

∎

"Now we have found that this is of paramount importance in order to progress. We absolutely must leave room for doubt or there is no progress and there is no learning. There is no learning without having to pose a question. And a question requires doubt. People search for certainty. But there is no certainty. People are terrified—how can you live and not know? It is not odd at all. You only think you know, as a matter of fact. And most of your actions are based on incomplete knowledge and you really don't know what it is all about, or what the purpose of the world is, or know a great deal of other things. It is possible to live and not know."

From The Pleasure of Finding Things Out *by Richard P. Feynman*

Most people seem obsessed with the notion of purpose. The world seems to be divided into those who believe they know their purpose and those who are searching for their purpose. I don't think I know anyone who is blasé on the subject—doesn't know, isn't searching, doesn't care. People who say they've found their purpose are judged to be mature, grounded, inspiring, on track. The ones who are searching, the majority it seems, are seen as anxious about it, frenetic, insecure, lost. Have you ever noticed how people don't want to admit that they don't know what they're doing here? It seems to be a good thing to know what your purpose in life is.

Unless, of course, your purpose is evil. We seem just as obsessed with ridding the world of bad purpose. The War on Terrorism has certainly consumed a lot of airtime since 9/11. We don't mess around when it comes to purpose.

Whether we know what ours is or not, whether we're on the receiving end of good ones or bad ones, purpose is a subject we take very, very seriously.

With such seriousness about the subject, why do you think it is that so many are at a complete loss when it comes to the question: What's the purpose of my life?

Let's look into it.

Sarah and I next met on the telephone one morning not long after our last meeting, to address the question she posed to me about purpose.

My mood that morning was a bit ironic, if not skeptical, a reflection of the ambivalence I was feeling about speaking with Sarah about the subject of purpose.

On the one hand, I knew how important this subject was to Sarah at this stage in her process and I wanted to serve her need. On the other, I knew that she probably wasn't going to like what I had to say.

When the subject is a prickly one, where I know I'm about to burst someone's bubble, I often rely on a little sarcasm to get me through.

That is, when I no longer can avoid the subject.

The subject of passion is something that most people can only take for so long. For most people, the conversation about passion inevitably turns to purpose, which is about results, which is about what do I want and what do I *get in return* for the time and energy and money I'm investing?

So I knew in my last meeting with Sarah that the jig was up.

Sarah needed to engage in an inquiry about purpose, what she would get at the end of all this, presuming she was committed enough, presuming she had what it took, presuming that I would deliver on my part of the bargain, what would the end game be? What was her purpose in doing all of this? And how would she know that she'd achieved it? And what difference would it make when she did, to her life, to her experience of being alive?

Dear reader, I'm about to rain on your parade. And here it is in a proverbial nutshell: *There is no purpose to purpose!*

There, I've said it. I'm glad. And it's exactly what I said to Sarah.

"What?" Sarah said.

She sounded deflated like I imagined she would. I told her that "purpose," the word, is deceptive. That there's a narrowness, a strictness, a rigidity to the word that is very different from the energy or essence of purpose. The meaning people give to the word "purpose" has a reality to it that is exactly the opposite of what Sarah needs to see and engage with right now. The common interpretation of the word "purpose" has to do with wanting and getting results. My purpose is to do or to get this or that. That's the business of the little girl who wanted to write a book, *but it is not the business of the Sarah I've been calling out over all these months.*

"Then, why is the E-Myth and the work you do so important to you, Michael? Why are you doing it?" Sarah asked incredulously.

"Candidly, Sarah, I have no idea. It just is."

"I don't understand," she said, without completing the sentence.

"What were you hoping I would say, Sarah? That business has always fascinated me? It hasn't. That the plight of people who own their own business is of deep concern to me. It isn't. That my father's failure in his small business, which literally killed him, made me vow to help others like him avoid his fate? It didn't. That my Primary Aim in life is to transform small business worldwide? It isn't and never has been. These are the reasons people most want to hear and are inspired by. But they're just stories, Sarah. Empty stories. They're stories that start out, 'Once upon a time . . . ' and end with the frog turning into a prince, or the poor tailor marrying the princess, or The Little Engine That Could puffing up the hill. They're stories speakers tell to their audiences because audiences eat them up.

"The only answer I can give you to your question about why the work I do with small business is so important to me is, I don't know. I do know it's important, though. More than anyone could imagine. And it's important because I have made the commitment to do it. Why I made the commitment to do it is beyond me. It was just there; it showed up. And it was more than just interesting. It was compelling. It was elegant. It took my breath away. And I didn't make the commitment all at once. It took time. All the rest is a fairy tale."

"But what about purpose?" Sarah asked. "How does what you've said fit with what you've said or at least implied about purpose for months? I thought it was important to you. You sure made it sound that way."

"I didn't mean to be disingenuous," I responded. "We have a purpose, Sarah, to create. And creation does not need anything other than itself to justify it. Creation, the act of producing something out of nothing, the love that one finds in the pure act of it, is enough to last a human being a lifetime.

"The question for me is not why this work is important to me, but do I behave like it's important to me? Do I give my creative focus the time and attention and passion it deserves? Do I take my life seriously, or not?

"I have asked myself the question you are asking me—Why is this important to me?—for years. And I have never been able to find a true answer, a completely satisfying one, other than the one I just gave you. All the rest is false. Empty. Lies, if I were to tell them.

"If I have any purpose in this life that feels real, it is to not lie to myself. That's how I want to live my life, not lying to myself."

"But what about telling the truth, Michael? Why do you say it in the negative? Aren't you really saying that the purpose of your life is to always tell the truth?" Sarah said.

"No, Sarah, it's different. To not lie to myself means that I will always be vigilant to smell the lie. To be that vigilant, to be that honest, to be that aware and interested, not to tell a lie to myself, is even bigger than telling the truth. I can believe I'm telling the truth, but if I do not know a lie when it presents itself to me, I'll never know whether I'm telling the truth or not.

"And that is what the true essence of purpose is. It's a vision, no matter how that vision comes to you. And vision comes to people in the strangest, most unpredictable ways. You can be standing on the corner about to walk across the street. You can be turning in your sleep, dreaming. You can be in the shower, or packing a suitcase, or cleaning out your closet, and a vision will all but knock you off your feet. Purpose, in the sense of a vision, is what passion serves. It provides passion with something to do, which is greater than itself, which is more productively focused than what passion finds when it wakes us up every morning. Vision is a reason to live. You can call it purpose, but the minute you turn it into a purpose, it calls forth the part of you that is more focused on results than process, like the little girl who wanted to write a book. Purpose doesn't free you. Vision can."

"So help me understand, Michael, what the difference is between purpose and vision. I don't get it yet."

"Okay, Sarah. A purpose has a clear, palpable construction to it. A vision is what you see through feeling. The passion of the mind and the passion of the soul creates vision. A vision makes you laugh out loud for no reason. A purpose makes you dig down deep to persevere. Managers have purpose. Entrepreneurs have visions. Vision is where the passion lives. Purpose is a doing that fills the space that passion cannot occupy. Vision leads. Purpose follows. Vision is the aura of enlightenment. Purpose is the work of the monk. Bottom line, vision is about magic, Sarah, the ecstatic experience of the magic of being human."

I stopped, and took a breath, and then said, "Vision is where the heart resides. It is the love of living."

Sarah was silent for a moment, but I could hear her breathing on the other end of the line. She said, "Michael, part of me is swept away by your passion and your vision, in the purest way. And part of me, maybe the manager in me, is still not getting something about this. I feel like there's something you're not saying that is keeping me confused. Does that make any sense to you?"

I laughed, feeling a little exposed, but grateful that Sarah invited me to reveal my motive. "To be honest with you, Sarah, I made a somewhat overly dramatic point of telling you that I didn't believe in purpose to move you to see something important. And that is that purpose is a lesser thing in the scheme of things for an entrepreneur. A true entrepreneur finds her truest joy envisioning the reinvented world of a poem or a work of art rather than an essay or a work of engineering. It's the same difference you experienced between writing in your journal and trying to turn it into a book. There is a role in our lives for each. But we invariably give up the vision, which may have little, apparent practical value to it, for the purpose, which has so much. And in so doing we give up our lives. The vision is what calls us. The purpose is what manifests the vision. The passion is what fuels us to achieve what we can't clearly describe in a way that we are made able to describe it."

"Oooooh, now I can follow you. Thanks for letting the charade go," Sarah offered lovingly with a grin that I could only imagine in my mind.

"And that's why your letting your passion express itself is so important, Sarah. Unless we do what we're doing right now, unless you form a deeper understanding and relationship with your passion, you will never be able to sustain an entrepreneurial pilgrimage because you will not have sufficient energy for it. The entrepreneur pursues the impossible. Not because it is impossible, but because it will remain impossible until he pursues it with the belief that it isn't impossible, that somehow, some way, he will manifest it into being. The four-minute mile and the Golden Gate Bridge and the summit of Mount Everest and so on and so on. All of them have been impossible. And all of them have been the product of a vision first and a purpose second. The pursuit of the impossible calls for enormous amounts of energy, fueled by passion, the juice of vision."

"So I guess what you're saying," Sarah said with some disappointment in her voice, "is that I'm not going to find my purpose today, that the part of me that wants to, *needs to,* is attached to producing results, getting things done. Okay, okay, okay. You're asking me to trust that my passion will bring me to vision. More of the impossible."

"Yes, Sarah," I said, "yes."

CHAPTER TEN

The First Exercise

■

**"If it is the quality of your consciousness at this moment
that determines your future, then what is it that
determines the quality of your consciousness?
Your degree of presence. So, the only place where
true change can occur and where the past
can be dissolved is the Now."**

From The Power of Now *by Eckhart Tolle*

Sarah and I had been working together now for more than four months. And we had still not focused on her business. It would be some time before we did.

Hopefully, you see why.

For Sarah to break free of the overwhelm, the busy, busy, busy, the tyranny of routine she was experiencing in her business, Sarah needed to change. Regardless of what her vision turned out to be, regardless of how big she wanted All About Pies to become, Sarah needed to commit her attention to learning about Sarah. Only then would she prove herself ready to practice the disciplines necessary for building a World Class Company.

Sarah has certainly come a long way in the last several months. She came to me hoping I'd help her fix her business and she's changed her perspective dramatically about what that will really take. Her perspective has shifted from her business to herself, but she hasn't yet learned how to *practice* changing herself so she can then change her business.

Our next few meetings will give her what she needs to do just that.

Do you remember the movie *The Karate Kid?*

In the movie, the hero, a boy who is beaten up by bullies and starts studying karate with a wise, old karate master to learn how to defend himself, is asked by the master, before any karate instruction, to wax his car.

As the boy resentfully does what he's asked—what does *this* have to do with karate?—the old man patiently instructs him: "Wax on, wax off. Wax on, wax off. Wax on, wax off."

The karate master knows that "Wax on, wax off" has everything to do with mastering martial arts. But the boy, impatient to get on with business, doesn't know that.

Of course, he doesn't. That's why he's studying with the karate master. To learn what the karate master knows. Because the boy doesn't know what it takes to become a master. He's never mastered anything. He doesn't know that mastery has everything to do with the relationship between the *outset* of the process and the *outcome* of the process.

The impatience of the apprentice, borne of inexperience, is legion in every story like this, causing most to lose interest in the process before they even get a taste of mastery.

Like the Karate Kid, Sarah is an apprentice. In the E-Myth context, she's never really engaged in working *on* her life. Like so many people, she only knows how to work *in* her life.

Everything Sarah and I have done during the last more than four months has been in preparation for Sarah *to take herself on*. It's taken her this long to genuinely accept that her commitment to a deepening relationship with herself must precede mastery over her business. And that her commitment to her own growth must forever operate on a parallel track with her commitment to building a World Class Company.

So far, what Sarah has proven herself ready for is the "Wax on, wax off" part of the process of mastery, exercises designed to demonstrate her ability to work *on* her life. All of these exercises will prepare her for the practice of the disciplines for building a World Class Company. Only if she achieves a level of mastery of the entrepreneurship version of "Wax on, wax off" will she prove herself ready to engage in E-Myth Mastery.

Through these simple, but challenging, exercises, she will begin to understand, in her body, how passion moves through her, how it affects her behavior, how it plays itself out from day to day in her life, how she uses it, or misuses it, how it serves her or sabotages her, how her passion uses *her*. And believe me, it does. Passion can be merciless. It can distract you, confuse you, lie to you, and take you. Everyplace but where you want to go, again and again. Sarah's task at this stage is simply to see it clearly. Until she does, she will never know the price she pays for allowing herself to be subject to its whims. Until she sees her passion clearly, Sarah will never discover what a gift it is!

• • •

Sarah came to this meeting with an aliveness I hadn't yet seen in her, in all the time I've known her. As soon as she felt how she had abandoned her passion as a little girl, her passion began to flow again. As soon as she gave herself permission to let her passion move her, her energy dramatically shifted. Some new connection or, better yet, reconnection, with herself made all the difference.

"What would it be like for you to feel your passion and purpose coming together through your electrified vision whether we're together or not? How about starting there, Sarah?" I asked.

"Can you see the smile on my face?" she said through the receiver. "Well, that's a no-brainer."

"Remember, Sarah, a while ago, I told you about a time in my life when my heart and mind were captivated by the teachings of G. I. Gurdjieff?" I asked.

"Yes," she offered.

"One of his students told me a story about an exercise he asked his students to practice, called the Stop Exercise," I continued.

"His students worked on the property Gurdjieff created for the purpose of doing his spiritual practice, what he called 'The Work.' Gurdjieff would occasionally walk by a student and say, 'Stop!' The student was expected to stop instantly whatever he was doing, no matter what it was, and freeze, exactly as he was in that moment. So if his hand was scratching his face, if he was bending over to pick up a rock, if he was walking or talking or cutting a carrot in the kitchen, he was expected to freeze in that position until Gurdjieff released him to go about what he was doing, sometimes minutes later, sometimes hours, depending on the student, for whatever reason Gurdjieff had for challenging the particular student he was working with.

"And it was challenging. The impact of stopping in one's tracks, when the student least expected it, was profound. Suddenly he would see himself in a way we rarely, if ever, do. The student would, in remarkable moments of clarity, 'remember' himself, as Gurdjieff called it, which would give him a moment of stunning realization, that 'I am alive!' And in the same moment he would see, usually with surprise, and sometimes, with outright shock, that he had been alive all the time, but completely asleep to it! Completely lost in his imagination. Completely caught up, or 'identified,' as Gurdjieff called it, with whatever he was doing. All of us, Gurdjieff said, live most of our lives lost, lost in doing, asleep to the moment, and never realize our life is going by.

" 'Remember yourself!' Gurdjieff would exhort his students. Your life depends on it!"

The very frustration that Sarah was feeling about her business and her inability to change it could only be addressed once she was able to see how completely identified she was with her pain. And as long as she *was* her pain, and could not create enough distance from her pain to see herself being in pain, she would never get free of it. Which brought us to an interesting place to begin this phase of our work together.

"So what I would like to suggest, Sarah, is an exercise for you to do. The purpose of the exercise is to discover the passion in you even when you don't feel there is any. Even when you feel completely disconnected from yourself, or exhausted, or depressed, or frustrated or lost. I'm suggesting that, even in those times when you feel completely depleted, your passion is alive and well. You just need to see it. Yes?"

Sarah was quiet on the other end of the phone. "How do I do that, Michael?" she asked, finally. "What's the exercise?"

I laughed, and said, "Sarah, I'll give you the exercise, but first, would you mind telling me where you went just a moment ago? What happened to you when I asked you the question about whether or not you got what I was saying? You went away. Where?"

"I did?" Sarah said with true surprise. "I didn't even notice that I was gone. I was simply thinking about what you said."

"What were you thinking?" I asked her.

"I don't know!" she said, surprised to discover that she really didn't.

"Well, think about it," I continued. "What did my question trigger in you?"

Sarah was quiet again but quickly came back. "I know," she said, suddenly interested in the question. "After hearing your story about Gurdjieff, I was thinking that you were going to ask me to do something I didn't want to do. And I was feeling afraid about how I was going to respond to you."

She continued, "I guess I was feeling pretty resistant. The funny thing is, I never would have told you that if you hadn't noticed it and asked me where I went. It's the kind of thing I probably do all the time. And yet, I have never really noticed how my perceptions of other people's expectations of me make me feel resistant. And then I get really suspicious of them. What are motivations? What's really going on with them? Which probably has a big impact on them. And even as I tell you that, Michael, I realize that no matter how energetic I appear, how open to learning I seem to be, there's a part of me that's really stubborn and resistant to having to do what other people want me to do. And I just noticed it."

"Yes, a very good thing to notice, Sarah. Not just that you got lost, but that as soon as you sunk into the truth about what was really going on, your aliveness reappeared. As soon as you wrapped your head around my question about where you went, you came alive. Can you see that?"

"You're right, Michael. Underneath my tra-la-la, superficial take on my experience was real interest in what was going on. I came out of feeling shutdown by what I thought you were asking of me into passionate interest in what just happened."

"Exactly," I responded. "And that passion lives in you every single moment of every single day.

"I don't think I'm going to give you an exercise to practice today. This *was* the exercise. Think about this some more before our next meeting. I think you're going to discover that, no matter how you're feeling at any particular time, whatever you're doing, or whatever you're afraid of doing, your passion is alive and well underneath, whatever is standing in the way. All you need to learn how to do is to observe the form it takes at any particular point in time.

"Your fear reaction to something you felt threatened by took you away from the moment we were sharing, yes?"

Sarah agreed with me so I asked her another question. "What part of you was threatened, Sarah?"

Sarah laughed nervously. But only for a moment.

"It's the me who doesn't want to be seen because she feels so small," Sarah said.

"It's the me who doesn't believe she is up to it," she continued.

"It's the me who is terrified of all the passion I have that could blow me away in a flash," Sarah said, now softly.

"I never saw that before," Sarah added, almost to herself.

"I would say she needs you to take care of her, Sarah," I answered. "I think she deserves more than she's accustomed to getting."

CHAPTER ELEVEN

The Second Exercise

■

**"If the greatest mania of all is passion: and if I am
a natural slave to passion: and if the balance
between my brain and soul and my body is as wild
and delicate as the skin of a Ming vase—Well, that
explains a lot of things, doesn't it?"**

From Kingdom of Fear *by Hunter S. Thompson*

Passion is the fuel that drives an enterprise forward. The passion to invent. The passion to create value. The passion to build something that has a life of its own. The passion to lead, to inspire, to put the pieces of your world together in such a way as to blow people's minds, not the least of all your own. And most of all, the passion to do something remarkable with your life. It is the connection with this passion that enables a small business owner to move through all of the inevitable external obstacles that get in the way, that, of course, each come with their own set of internal obstacles to be overcome. It is the relationship with this passion that can transform a reluctant entrepreneur into an electrified entrepreneur. Sarah was struggling once again with her relationship with her passion.

The weather was cool, the sky overcast. Sarah and I had been working together, by telephone, for not quite six months as I sat in my office preparing for our first meeting in person since we reconnected at the hotel. The themes had been clarified for both of us. She was afraid that neither she nor her business would ever grow. She felt inadequate to deal with the powerful energy that moved through her, the passion that she felt. So, she shrank from it at the very moment it called her to do something much bigger than she felt capable of doing. She felt obliterated by the dead spaces that showed up after extreme bouts of work. She felt fooled, betrayed, tricked, rapped about the head and shoulders as she went from Go for It to Get Me out of Here, all in the course of one week. She needed to understand why this was happening, and what she could do about it. She needed help.

As we worked together we had found that it wasn't that Sarah was without passion. It was that her passion was huge but without a clear, unifying vision, so the energy she expended always turned out to be unproductive. It was like an ominous storm that, in a moment, would well up in her and threaten to consume her. She was helpless in the face of it. Her first attempts were always to control it, or to use it to work, and when she did that she would work herself into a frenzy, and work everyone around her into a frenzy. And, for a time, that worked. For a time, it felt like she could do anything. And so she would. Anything and everything, except the right things. She would *become* her passion, identify with it, become the storm. Inexhaustible, combustible, frenzied, until the storm worked itself out, that is. Until it simply blew itself to smithereens. And then, even then, even after the storm of her passion would burn itself out, the residue of it, the memory of it, in her body, and in her mind, would drive her even further and she'd crash.

At times like that, Sarah felt hopeless. The pall in the void that the storm of her passion left was disastrous. It was like the ground torn flat by a tornado as it ripped through and devastated the countryside, pulling the trees up, crashing the buildings down, tossing the cars and trucks and glass and timber and signs and streetlights and electrical wires all into a catastrophic mess, unlike anything that existed before the storm went recklessly charging through with little or no warning. Without care for the havoc it would create. Because it was obvious that storms don't care. And when Sarah was possessed by the storm in her, she didn't care either. Afterward, though, was something else again. Afterward was the other side of the storm, the other side of the passion, the dark side of the moon that Sarah always forgot when she was taken by her passion. Sarah felt like that often, following the rampage her passion would create, like a wreck looking for a place to hide. Her passion was a continuous threat to her sense of order, for it could come at any time, and would, without notice, without warning, without care for the catastrophic impact it would have on her sense of well-being, or anyone else's.

But, even with all that, she loved her passion dearly. Despite all the chaos her passion created, it also gave her a sense of life. With all the unreasonable mayhem it produced in her and in everyone around her, it was also her strength. Her passion could make molehills out of mountains. Her passion was her will. Her wish in the moments of consuming passion could be fulfilled, despite the fact of her inability to control it once it got moving.

And, though it moved her, it had no interest in her, it bludgeoned her balance, it kept her smaller, self-concealed so she didn't have to feel its pain. And that was the terrible truth to Sarah about passion. It could be used to avoid coming face-to-face with the other truths that could hide so cunningly amidst the wreckage. Her little self, the little Sarah, the one who was not big enough to go where she had never gone before, could hide while her passion ran amuck doing the things she could easily do: technician's work, washing floors, cleaning the oven until it shined, opening the doors, closing the doors, locking up, going to the bank, and eventually, manager's work: building systems, training, delegating, and so forth. What was really going on, we found, was that the little girl who wanted to write a book in Sarah would preempt Sarah's vision with Sarah's purpose. Sarah's vision was the rich, textured technicolor context for continuous creation. Sarah's purpose was to put that vision to work in black and white. Do something useful, Sarah's purpose said. Be something remarkable, Sarah's vision said. Sarah's passion didn't care which master it was serving. Sarah's intent was key to making that decision for her. My job with Sarah was to help her clarify her intent, by helping her to see how destructive her passion would always prove to be if it were used in service of her need to be useful, her need to be productive, her need to be practical, her need to be of use. Our job together was to work the field in which Sarah was going to plant the seeds for her own transformation, for her new growth. From being a little person with a big purpose, to being a big person with an electrified and electrifying vision. The vision first, the purpose second, the passion in service of her aim.

Today's session had been rescheduled twice over five weeks as a result of both of our particularly hectic schedules. In frustration, Sarah finally decided she wanted to spend time with me face-to-face. During the intervening weeks, we talked on the phone about her experience with the second exercise I had given her to do. An exercise called Seeing Through It. It's something I've done when I've felt in conflict, when I didn't want to look inside, when I was deeply stressed, when I was called upon to do things that felt beyond me because they were so threatening. I shared some of those experiences with Sarah. And I shared the exercise with Sarah, and suggested she work with it. This was the instruction:

"When you feel overwhelmed, Sarah, or exhausted, or simply wrung out, say to yourself, 'See Through It.' That's all, nothing else. Just, See Through It. And then, tell me what happens."

Sarah said, "So what am I supposed to see?"

"Whatever you see, Sarah, nothing other than that. And then let's talk about it. Just remember that our passion never leaves us. It's always there on call. But until you see it as a willing and trusted servant, it will be undependable, and at times, it can be even dangerous. At the very least, our passion can be spent unproductively. No rules other than just see what happens, okay? Are you willing to try it?"

Sarah agreed but quickly discovered how difficult it was.

"I don't know what to look for," she said to me one afternoon in a call we had planned the previous day. "And if I don't know what to look for, how in the world will I know when I find it?"

"But that's the point, Sarah," I responded. "It's simply a different way of looking. So you can see something that you wouldn't normally see. If you could see everything there is to see, your business would be growing through the roof and you'd be in heaven. You know there's something you can't see. That's why we're talking, right?

"Here's something that might help. I'm sure you've seen one of those books where each page is a picture that has another picture underneath it that you can't readily see? You're supposed to hold the book at a certain distance from your face, and then pull it slowly away without focusing on the picture, sort of looking through the picture, and suddenly another picture shows up?"

"Yes," Sarah said. "In fact, I think I have that book somewhere around here. I couldn't do that either. It drove me crazy for a while. And then, for no reason whatsoever that I can remember, I picked the book up, opened it to one of the pictures, and without trying at all, there it was! The other picture behind it just appeared. Even after I did that, I couldn't do it again for quite a while. I thought the trick was sneaking up on the book as though I wasn't interested. And that wasn't it. Then I thought that it was putting my eyes out of focus, and for whatever reason, that wasn't it either. Sometimes it comes to me, and sometimes it doesn't."

"Did you ever practice it?" I asked Sarah.

"Practice it? No. It was never that important to me."

"Ah," I said. "*It was never that important to you.* And that's the key. The key to discovering your passion, and how dependable it can be. If you want to use your passion to your advantage, if you want to tap into an enormous resource for anything you want to do, if you want fuel to power any intention you have, then make it really important to you. So important that you will do anything to see it for what it is. It's being interested in it, deeply interested in it, that will give you the power to see. So, let me suggest a way to do this that might make it easier for you, okay?"

"Yes," Sarah said with genuine interest.

"Okay. Then try this. Three times a day, any time at all, but most specifically when you're feeling consumed by something you're doing, or you're dreading the prospect of something you need to do, try the Stop Exercise. Only I want you to be your own master, as though you were walking by yourself and ordered whomever you are in the moment, doing whatever you're doing, to stop! I want you to remember to stop. That's all there is to it. Just stop. Look. Listen. See. And something remarkable will make itself immediately apparent."

"So what you want me to do is to practice stopping myself whenever I'm feeling particularly distressed, anxious, harried, overwhelmed, busy, and freezing exactly where I am and just looking at myself?" Sarah asked.

"Yes, that's it. That's the practice, or at least one of them, for Seeing Through It. A way of seeing without being what you see. A way of beginning to separate yourself from yourself so that you can see yourself being yourself, which will allow you to see yourself in a completely new way."

"So that's what you mean when you talk about not being identified. It means just watching myself doing whatever I'm doing, and seeing what comes up in me," Sarah said.

"Yes, Sarah, that's it," I responded. And it's the most important thing you can be doing right now if you want to build a World Class Company. Isn't that interesting?"

Sarah and I finally met face-to-face. She looked radiant. Her face glowed and her eyes shined. I swear, if coaching by telephone weren't so damned efficient and effective, our coaches would be meeting all of our clients like this. Sarah smiled brightly, we hugged, lingered for a moment, and then, without words, sat down in the two chairs I had placed face-to-face in front of the fireplace. The fire was burning, the dark leather of the chairs gleamed orange and red, the clouds moved across the sky through the skylight above, cutting off the sun, and then letting it through, creating patterns of light on the white walls of the room, my home office, the place where I love to work, write, make calls, visit with people from the world outside, or just to think and read.

Sarah spoke first.

"Michael, these past several weeks have been amazing. I didn't really need to meet in person, but I wanted to see you and, even more to the point, I wanted *you* to see *me*." She smiled an electric smile, and almost as an afterthought, she spread her arms dramatically as if to say, Voila!

I burst into a smile as big as hers. "What's the secret?" I asked. "What happened to you?"

"I saw my passion," Sarah said. "I did what you suggested I do. I did 'See

Through It.' I did the 'Stop Exercise.' I did whatever I could do to see myself as I really am, to break free of my identification with my moods. My mood called 'I Can't Do Anymore,' or 'I'm Exhausted,' or 'Oh No, I Forgot to . . .' or whatever it is in any moment. I saw how absolutely consumed I am with My Moods. They eat up my passion by filling the space with something else to do. I found out"—Sarah leaned forward in the chair, her elbows on her knees, pushing her face forward so there was no chance I wouldn't get this—"I found out there's more passion than I have ever imagined underneath my moods. An enormous reservoir of juice—to use your word—just waiting there to fuel whatever it is I want to do. It was the stopping that made it possible for me to see it. Because I saw that I am not my feelings, not my moods. I am something apart from them that is so alive. This has been illuminating for me!

"You said something, Michael. And I don't know whether or not you said it purposely. But it turned everything around for me and made it possible for me to do the exercise and to see what was there waiting for me. You told me to become my own master, to be like Gurdjieff instructing a student, as well as the student. When I tried that, I saw myself. I literally *saw* myself, and I saw myself seeing myself. It created a dimension that I have only accidentally bumped into in rare times in my life. A sudden moment of clarity, where I see myself as separate from myself. But in the last few days, I've even been able to see myself seeing myself! Do you get what I mean, Michael?" Sarah asked passionately.

"I do, Sarah. I do," I said. "And it's thrilling what you've discovered about yourself. You're so willing to be interested in finding out. That's all it takes. This new dimension to your experience is the foundation for a completely new relationship to life. It's a fourth dimension, a parallel universe to the one we live in. And it was there all the time! A dimension beyond the dimension we're accustomed to living in. And, I would imagine, one beyond that, and one beyond that, like the galaxies in the universe which we thought not that long ago were only stars but now understand are other worlds of planets. The universe is more immense than we can possibly imagine. But so is yours.

"And your experience is a gift to me. It supports *my* wish to see myself. It inspires me to see how meaningful the simple act of a practice can be."

Sarah was thrilled that I was sharing her excitement.

"There's one more part of this, Michael." Sarah leaned forward again, but this time not so energetically. There was a quiet, a calm, to her that was palpable. She went on.

"My passion was there when I least expected it to be. When I was exhausted and felt completely overwhelmed, when a part of me felt certain that I didn't have any energy left, when I stopped, and observed myself, in this disidentified way, I felt an endless amount of passion and energy just waiting there in me. It's like there's a part of me that *makes* me exhausted, *makes* me overwhelmed, *makes* me tapped out, because that's what it does. I don't fully understand this myself, Michael, but I had an insight into something that I feel so moved to understand better because I can feel how it could alter my life. It's that big."

"Can you tell me any more about this part that *makes* you?" I asked Sarah.

"Let me see." Sarah paused. "The exhaustion is a strategy, not a result. I have this sense that I choose to be overwhelmed, or exhausted, whatever the negative state is, because I have found it to work for me. Again, I'm not sure how this works or why. I just saw clearly that, no matter how at the end of my rope I thought I was, I had an abundance of energy to do anything I wanted to do. These two realities were there as plain as day. And if that's true, Michael, then what *else* is true about how I'm feeling at any particular moment?

"And that's why I just had to see you, so you could see me, the way I'm feeling right now. I wanted you to see what you've had a big hand in creating. Because I know that if you hadn't insisted, Michael, that we first discover the nature of my passion, we would have spent our time immersed in doing all the stuff I feel compelled to do, all the stuff that makes me feel competent, all the stuff that keeps me from seeing what I don't want to see!"

"And do you know what that is, Sarah?" I asked with particular care.

"Yes, Michael. I'm really terrified to be, as they say in the Army commercials, All I Can Be."

CHAPTER TWELVE

The Third Exercise

◼

"Everything that is really precious is right here,
in our hearts. Everything is already right here."

From The Heart of Learning *by Steven Glazer*

In the months that followed, Sarah went up and down like a yo-yo. It was actually more like two steps forward and one step back. She would lose herself in
her emotions and forget to Stop, and then, almost miraculously, would find
herself again. But when she found herself, she would have the most amazing
epiphanies and insights, which provided her with a clarity her obsessions never
did. Her obsessions called, "So much to do, so little time to do it." Of course,
that's how we all put it. But, remarkably, the more she looked at herself, the
more Sarah discovered that it simply wasn't true. The deeper she investigated
her passion and how it played itself out in her day-to-day activity, the more
Sarah saw that not only *wasn't* there too much to do, there was more than
enough time to do what she needed to do. And that what she had to do in her
very small business was significantly less than she thought. The question of
what she should do with her time suddenly became a real one, a painful one to
Sarah. Given the huge reservoir of passion she possessed, and an equally huge
reservoir of time available to her to put that passion to use, what was she going
to do with it?

This question led to other questions, like: If everything seems limited, and
time and energy are a lot less limited than I thought, then what about money?
What about love? What about life? What's really true?

In one of our next conversations, Sarah seemed particularly subdued. I asked her what was going on. She said, almost timidly, "I don't know, Michael. But *something* is. I'm spending a lot less time working in the shop. In fact, I'm going home early more and more often and simply watching television. I think I'm addicted to *Oprah*. This is so embarrassing to tell you. Sometimes I don't go in at all! I call one of the women who works for me and she opens up. I've given two of them keys, something I never would have done before. But it's not as if I finally trust them to run my business without me. Somehow I don't seem to care. This feels like resignation more than breaking free of my lifelong intense need to control everything. It feels dark, and heavy. I've never quite felt like this before."

"Tell me a little more about your resignation, Sarah, if you can," I said, hoping I could better understand what she was dealing with. "I understand that this is new territory for you in your life."

"It is," she replied. "I'm tired all the time. Bored and tired. All of a sudden, I have so little interest in All About Pies. The more I have been doing the exercises you gave me, the more I stop, the more I try to See Through It, the more I see how frenetic I am as I work. It disgusts me and makes me want to flee. To be honest, I'm not liking myself very much lately. And I don't know what to do about it. I also feel afraid. I have no idea what's going on, but somehow I've lost my way, and I don't know where I'm going anymore. The thing that really scares me is that I don't seem to care."

"Oh, Sarah," I responded. "While I can completely understand why it feels to you like you no longer care, this is not about *not* caring. This is about caring too much. I know you're in pain but this pain is the answer to your prayers. You're beginning to really see yourself, how your passion plays through you, how you are taken by it, the unproductive impact the way you've learned to express your passion has on you, first physically, on your face, the way you hold your mouth, your head, your eyes, your body, and on your feelings and the way you express them. I once heard someone say, I can't remember who it was, 'Work seduces us all. It takes all of our attention. It drugs us to sleep.' As you have been stopping yourself so successfully, as you have been Seeing Through It, as you have courageously attempted to become the master of yourself— rather than doing whatever comes up like a willing servant, or even worse, a slave to your passion—you can't help but come face-to-face with stuff that's incredibly uncomfortable to see. Sarah, you're waking up! And it's inevitable that you wouldn't like the person you've avoided seeing for so long. I've been waiting for this to happen."

Sarah looked puzzled, so I asked, "Do you know why I would say that?"

"Not really," she responded. "But I'm interested in what you meant."

"Because now," I said, "you can begin to change in earnest. You're seeing some of your habitual patterns that don't serve you or your business, and you're feeling the kind of pain about them that is necessary to move you to want to change. I'm so sorry about the pain and the malaise you're feeling but I can assure you that it's temporary.

"Over and over we've talked about the fact that your business will never change until you do. If you can't see the relationship between your behavior and the results you're not achieving in your business, there's nothing to change. And if you didn't *care deeply* about achieving different results in your business, you wouldn't have taken the steps that have brought you to this moment of seeing the condition of your life so much more clearly.

"Think about it like this, Sarah. You have become identified with your re-action to what you're seeing about yourself, in the same way you became iden-tified with your passion. Your reaction, the depression, the heaviness, the need to remove yourself from the path of the tornado, where all this is going on, your desire to stay home and watch television, is simply your way of saying 'I don't want to play this game anymore.' Not the game called All About Pies, but the game called All About Sarah. 'I don't want to play this game anymore, *be-cause I don't know how to play it!*' What I want you to consider, Sarah, is that no one knows how to play it. Not really. I've never met anyone who truly knows how to play the game called My Life. But I *have* met people who play it with all their heart anyway. And they're living life with remarkable aliveness.

"The pain you're experiencing will become a gift to you when you can cre-ate some distance from what you're experiencing. Your ability to see yourself—get lost in unproductive passion, feel afraid that you're too small to act, whatever it is—is one level of dis-identification. The next level is the ability to see it without becoming completely emotionally involved with it. To see your-self, dispassionately, with some objectivity, so you're able to spend your energy on changing it, rather than emotionally obliterated by it, is the next step for you, a step I trust you'll take as courageously as you've taken all of the others. And when that happens your relationship to life will be forever transformed. Building a World Class Company will become a joy rather than a burden.

"Try this mantra I created for myself, 'Just stop, see it, don't be it.' It's like holding yourself out in front of yourself, as if you were standing in the palm of your hand, watching yourself. Observe all of your feelings in the moment, all of your fears and dreads and angers and hurt, right now, out there, as you watch the you who's standing there in the palm of your hand.

"With practice, you'll be able to see the passion that runs through it all, in its different colors. You'll learn how to discriminate, how to choose, how to be a master of your passion, what the mechanics are, how it all works, what happens when you do this, when you do that. The whole picture of your life will change, Sarah, just like it already has. What's on *Oprah* will become boring in relation to the excitement of your own life."

When I stopped talking, Sarah remained quiet in a way that told me that she was touched, and processing the implications of what she was experiencing. I could feel in the silence that she understood, at a deeper level, what it could mean for her to make a true commitment to play the game called All About Sarah in her pursuit of the game called All About Pies. And that All About Pain was, unfortunately, a necessary step in the process.

After several seconds, I felt free to continue. "This is all quite amazing, Sarah. As a result of doing these little exercises, Stop, and See Through It, relatively consistently, you started staying home instead of going to work. *And you have never, ever done that before.* And I'll bet you, even though you're not there to solve all the problems, check up on all of your people, say hello to your favorite customers, even though you're home in bed watching television, for God's sake!, your business is just fine. Is that true?"

Sarah laughed, a mixture of sadness breaking free and sudden relief. She said, "Michael, you know it is. In fact, it's even better. That's funny," Sarah said, almost to herself. "How come I didn't see that until you said it?"

"Because passion can distort our ability to see, Sarah. Until we understand how to work with our passion, we only see the emotions we're consumed by, everything else is hidden. If we're angry, we only see red. If we're depressed, we only see blue. You might consider that you couldn't see that your business doesn't really need you anymore, Sarah, *because you need to feel needed.* Every technician needs to feel needed, which is why every technician builds a business around his own ability to produce results.

"But the thing is that while you're feeling needed by your business, you're ignoring what you really need: More life. More life than the business you've got can give you. More true vitality. More true spirit. More variety of vitality and spirit. You need to *take care* of yourself, Sarah, not *care for* yourself. You need to take care of yourself by feeding yourself the kind of food you need. And by 'food' I mean impressions, experiences, ideas, dimensions beyond the current tiny dimension of the business you own. You are and always have been much bigger than your business, Sarah. You couldn't see that as long as you were consumed by your passion, doing it, doing it, doing it. But as this new experience takes root in you, as you begin to realize what a gift your wish to flee from the business has been, as all this begins to make sense to you, there will be new room for you to appreciate yourself, your richness, your unseen dimensions, your unrealized capacity. Your passion will fuel that if you ask it to. If you direct it to."

"I guess I've been so consumed *that I never really felt anything*," Sarah responded. It's exactly the same as when I was a little girl, writing in my journal at night, I became consumed by my need to produce something other than what my passion was producing. It's very tricky trying to explain this, Michael, but I need to try. Can we take just a few minutes more so that I can make sure I'm clear?"

"Of course, Sarah. I would love that," I said.

Sarah went on, "There's such a squirrelly thing about passion, the energy that moves in me and around me and through me. I'm always getting sucked into it, getting lost. Even when I'm feeling powerful, even when I'm feeling absolutely charged in a positive way, even then, I realize I'm not in charge like I thought I was. I'm simply charged. On a tear. And this Stopping thing, when I remember to actually do it, has the true power to enable me to actually see what's going on, to actually stop, to come back to myself, to a place from which something quieter, something more balanced, something with greater authenticity can begin. I realize that the practice of Stopping, the practice of Seeing Through It, the practice of engaging with myself as an observer can, when I remember to do it, provides me with a place from which to be. And that place has little or no identification in it. I'm not reacting. I'm contained within my experience, and I contain it within me. There is something more genuine in it than any of the passions, the inflammations, the exaggerations, the helplessness and hopelessness, and whatever other feelings that take me over will ever be. I see so simply right now, Michael, what you mean when you talk so passionately about practice. It's one day at a time, and then the next, and then the next. There is never an ending to seeing clearly. It feels good to say this to you."

"I'm glad, Sarah. What you've just said tells me that we've completed our journey to the foothills. I think now is the perfect time to start climbing the mountain."

Sarah's voice revealed her surprise. "What? What do you mean 'time to climb the mountain'?"

I couldn't help the delighted laugh that came out of me. Her voice expressed so much of the little girl that I had grown to love in Sarah, the part of her that was so willing to show how she was really feeling in the moment. "You're a treasure, Sarah. You've so alive, you're so ready to take on the challenges in front of you, and so immediately available. That's what's so disarming about you. You're obviously a mature woman, and yet you're like a child. It's the balance of the two in you that makes this possible. So let me tell you what I mean by 'it's time to start climbing.'

"Everything we've been doing together has been, in one respect, a test of your emotional mettle. And to put it succinctly, you've passed the test with flying colors! You now have enough appreciation, through your own experience, of what's going to come up, continuously, on the emotional front, to challenge your achieving your long-term objectives, your discovering your vision, your nailing down in concrete terms what your purpose is, your sustaining the passion you have for building a World Class Company.

"I know you understand now, Sarah, that your ability to meet those challenges rests in your emotional strength, your ability to see yourself clearly in the middle of the storm, when everything seems to be going horribly, when you find yourself completely lacking in resources, when you're suddenly confronted with the need to move higher on the face of the mountain and the weather turns ugly, with absolutely no advance warning, and the choices you make are life-and-death. How you respond to your feelings and how you manage them in those moments is everything.

"When the storm is brewing, and the winds are picking up all around you, moving to a different place in yourself is much more important than moving to a different place on the mountain.

"You've demonstrated to me that you see that, Sarah. I know in my heart that you're a trustworthy climber. And as your guide, I'm honored to take you anywhere you want to go."

Sarah didn't speak for a moment, and then said, "I don't know what to say, Michael. Only that I'm more ready for this than I have ever been in my life. I'm just surprised, and moved, by what you just said. I'm honored to be doing this with you. I know it's going to take everything I've got. And yet I also know I'm not sure what I've got. And that's the most exciting part about all this. Finally, in my life I don't have to know and I'm going to learn what I've got as we move forward. I'm ready. So all I can say is, what's next?"

PART TWO

THE SEVEN ESSENTIAL DISCIPLINES

■

Epigram*

■

"A warrior accepts that we can never know what will happen to us next. We can try to control the uncontrollable by looking for security and predictability, always hoping to be comfortable and safe. But the truth is that we can never avoid uncertainty. This not-knowing is part of the adventure. It's also what makes us afraid."

From Comfortable with Uncertainty *by Pema Chodron*

Sarah and I have climbed together. We have tested each other and our readiness to move up the mountain. Sarah has discovered how to stop and observe herself, to liberate the passion within her to flow, to move unrestricted, to find its own level, its own pace, as water does. And this has made all the difference to Sarah. The liberation of her passion means that, finally, Sarah's passion can

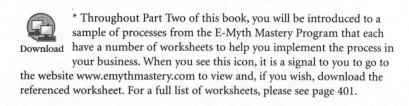

* Throughout Part Two of this book, you will be introduced to a sample of processes from the E-Myth Mastery Program that each **Download** have a number of worksheets to help you implement the process in your business. When you see this icon, it is a signal to you to go to the website www.emythmastery.com to view and, if you wish, download the referenced worksheet. For a full list of worksheets, please see page 401.

serve her rather than consume her. Sarah now understands how to allow her passion to lead her to her vision, how to translate her vision into purpose, and how to clarify her purpose without it interfering with her creativity or her access to the aliveness that's brewing inside of her all the time.

This preparation, this "Wax on, wax off," is critical to the development of the depth and vitality of the entrepreneurial mind-set.

This has been a rich and rewarding experience for Sarah, awe-inspiring at times, uncomfortable, if not painful, at others. All of it has brought Sarah great insight. Over the many months Sarah and I have worked together, she has come to realize that when your heart is broken, as all of ours are, as hers was as a little girl by the people who didn't "get" her or make her feel safe, it can only begin to mend once you *recognize* that it was broken, probably many times over. That awareness has allowed Sarah to see that her broken heart has been making decisions throughout her life that she would never have made had her heart been whole. Her broken heart has caused her to believe she was someone she wasn't. And her inability to see herself, as she really was, made seeing her business, as it really was, impossible. Sarah has discovered in herself a genuine interest in seeing herself. But this seeing, if it is to possess the clarity we all crave, the wisdom we all wish we had, is not the looking that most of us have grown accustomed to. It is a separate way of looking, separate from the aspect of yourself you are looking at. So that the you who is doing the looking, and the you that you see, are separate, distinct parts of yourself. It is looking as though from above, while at the same time from within, completely engaged with the aspect of yourself you are looking at but able to see it with some objectivity.

As Sarah and I found our way to the foothills of the mountain, I tested *my* readiness to climb as well, to let go, to give to the process what it demanded of me as Sarah's guide and as a reluctant coach to Sarah's reluctant entrepreneur. We were both preparing ourselves for what was about to come, the practice of serious climbing, the Seven Essential Disciplines for building a World Class Company.

Before we start, a few words about how to best think about the climb.

The seven essential disciplines to follow are first and foremost about leadership. They are the practices, processes, and perspectives that establish that inextricable connection between entrepreneurship and leadership. Entrepreneurship is the strength to lead. And the disciplines are about the leadership every entrepreneur needs to possess through understanding if his vision is to become a world class reality.

Because, above all, for an entrepreneur to evoke in the world a concrete world class representation of his imagination—visual, emotional, functional, and financial—he must possess a kind of *leadership resonance.* Leadership resonance describes the connection between an entrepreneur and the leadership he is called to bring to everyone around him. It means that the thing that follows an entrepreneur's imagination is a creation that all but rhymes with it. The leader moves the imagination's energy forward. The leader makes the rhyme of the entrepreneur's vision and the purpose of the enterprise sound like one thing. He makes them look like a replica of each other, but not exactly one thing. He makes sure that they resonate with each other. The vision is excitingly vague but moving, a representation of the picture the entrepreneur sees in his head and his heart. The actual expression is something that the entrepreneur has never seen in real life. "So *that's* what it looks like, my vision!" the entrepreneur is likely to say. And the entrepreneur who is also the leader must understand the leadership disciplines, the seven essential disciplines you and I are going to investigate together, if he is ever going to succeed at manifesting his vision through other people, the only way he can. Otherwise, his vision will always remain unformed. It will never become concrete. It will never find in reality what the entrepreneur experiences in his imagination. It will never become what it needs to become, what it deserves to become, a faithful expression of his imagination in real life: a real enterprise, coupled with a real vision, each with its own purpose, but each with one purpose, to make the body of the enterprise sing. But as the entrepreneurial leader grows with understanding, and begins to create, the resonance is felt like a deeply dozing drum, the skin tight, the drumstick radiating from the skin, the sounds welling out and far away, the music that makes the body begin to dance in sync, in step, in the hugging loving motion of the passion's lover embracing this, embracing that, forever, for everything.

That is what leadership resonance is. It connects the world with the entrepreneurial passion. It connects the passion of the entrepreneur with the world. It is above all what the disciplines are there to do. They are the practice through which the resonance comes alive, finds itself, humming with everything it's got. They are what the entrepreneur must learn to do. Not once, not for a certain length of time, not first this, then that. But forever. They are the disciplines that never end.

Finally, though the seven essential disciplines are brought to you one at a time, each of them is only complete as part of One Thing, a thorough comprehension and internalization of the seven disciplines. As you perform the assignments and the exercises, as you begin to develop skills and produce results, remember that the accomplishment of it all is less important than an understanding of the process of it all, and your total immersion in the "wax on, wax off" part of the process of becoming an entrepreneur. One step at a time, yes, but every step is everything.

Let's begin at the beginning, with the discipline of the enterprise leader.

CHAPTER ONE

The Discipline of the Enterprise Leader

■

" 'How come you never told us any of this?'
the bosses inquired. 'How come you never asked?'
the workers replied."

From Gonzo Marketing *by Christopher Locke*

Sarah and I agreed that it would be good, for this phase of our journey, to meet in person instead of on the telephone. It hadn't been that long since we met at my home, but, strangely, I was looking forward to seeing her again. Despite the fact that we had met many times in person, most of our contact this time around was by telephone, so when I thought of Sarah, rather than seeing her, I could only hear her voice. To me, Sarah *was* her voice. We accomplished so much, we shared so much truth and vulnerability, so much life and vitality, all over the telephone. So, even though a part of me, of course, knew what Sarah looked like, I couldn't wait to see her, to see how the work we had done together since the last time we met had changed the way she looked.

It was a delight to see her!

Her face was bright, flush with life, her eyes clear and excited, her smile beaming. We hugged each other like old, old friends do, and spoke each other's names—"Hi Michael," "Hi Sarah"—and then moved apart to look at each other again.

"I'm so glad we decided to meet in person, Sarah," I said, feeling the truth of it as I looked into her laughing, warm eyes. "It's perfect. I can't wait to get started."

"Me too, Michael," Sarah responded, sweetly, truly meaning it. "I've got so many questions, and so much to say. But I know you've got an agenda, Michael, you always do!" She laughed, wholeheartedly, and then said, "So my questions can wait. Just as long as I've got some time to pursue them."

"Sarah, you'll have all the time you need. So rather than standing here in the doorway, why don't we go to my office where we can sit down and get started." I took her by the hand and led her where we needed to go.

Just as there are universal principles that determine what works and what doesn't in a business, the same can be said about leadership. The social role of the leader may be perceived differently in different parts of the world and in different types of institutions, but *the discipline of enterprise leadership, and the rules, standards, and practices that define it, are the same no matter where they are practiced, regardless of the type and size of business.* When it comes to building a World Class Company, what is first and foremost is the entrepreneur's readiness to wear the mantle of leader.

"Easier said than done," I said to Sarah as we made ourselves comfortable at the table we set up between us in my office.

"I think I know what you mean but what do *you* mean?" Sarah asked.

"Because of the discomfort it creates in most people," I answered. "While we may be comfortable leading in circumstances where we feel we know best, because we've proven to ourselves and to others that we do know best, in circumstances where we're unsure, as in the creation of a company we're not certain we can create, most of us would rather sit it out to figure out the rules of the game and to become competent at them, rather than risk making a fool of ourselves.

"Leaders are always risking making fools of themselves," I continued.

"The willingness to risk how they look is one of the things that makes them leaders.

"And in the process of creating All About Pies and establishing yourself as the leader, you're going to risk yourself again and again, Sarah. If you didn't, and if you don't, nothing other than what you've already created would be created. It's your commitment to create something significantly different than what you've already created that's going to challenge your leadership capability, because the more unknown the outcome is, the more stress will be created as you not only attempt to lead your people, but challenge yourself to rise to the occasion. And the more stress that's created by your fear of the unknown and by your unknown and yet untested ability to push beyond it, the more challenged you will be as a leader. Challenged to find the right words to say. Challenged to make the right decisions. Challenged to hold yourself and your people on target, when the target itself is unclear, and constantly shifting. Challenged by your constant feeling of being hopelessly alone. That after you have said what you have said, done what you have done, concluded what you have concluded, argued, deliberated, debated what you have believed in and fought for, after all of that, still there will be that deathly uncertainty in your own mind, your own heart, about whether you were right, or whether you will be successful, or whether the decision you finally made is going to come crashing down in the future. And that feeling of being alone, late at night, or early in the morning, or even in the middle of the action when you are being forced to make a decision, that feeling is more isolating than anyone can ever know until they've experienced it. What happens then is what will determine your ability to lead.

"Because ultimately, Sarah, when everything is said and done, when the leader has made her best decision, the only one left at the end of the day is her. The leader is always alone. With the decisions she's made and the ones that she didn't make but were made on her watch. A leader must be able to stand in them alone.

"And that's why the reluctant entrepreneur is almost always a reluctant leader.

"Because she is always alone, even when she isn't, even when she is surrounded by people, clamoring for her attention.

"And being alone can be no fun."

The first practice of an enterprise leader is learning how to live with being alone. How to come to grips with it. Learning how to accept the hollow reality of it, the tiny sound of your own voice in your self-induced vacuum, the sound of your voice when you know you have no idea what you're saying, when you have absolutely no idea whether or not the decision you're making or, even worse, about to make is correct. Is this the right decision? Is it? Am I about to do something stupid? Did I *just do* something stupid? The leader is always thinking to herself. She never thinks to ask those around her whether the decision she has just made, or the decision she is about to make, is stupid. Are you kidding me? I'm supposed to be the leader. Of course, feeling alone is made worse because some part of her knows that there are a lot, oh, a lot of people, who are thinking how very stupid she can be. They would never tell her. But they think it. And the worst part is, if she's at all honest with herself, she knows they're right! But only off the record, in the privacy of her own thoughts. In her own monkish mind, and in her own solitary heart, the lonely leader is always alone, and always stuck with the plain, unvarnished truth: When it comes to the really hard decisions, she can be as dumb as a stump.

So why do it, you ask? Because in the thick of the action, leading is *god-awful* fun. If it weren't, who could bear the rest of it? You'd have to be a moron to bear up under the sheer, incredibly insufferable, chilling, no-escaping-it lucidity of seeing one's own massive dullness, one's own stultifying lack of clarity, unremarkable vapidity, downright stupidity, if it weren't for the fun.

You might add to that the belief that it's either lead or be led, and leading is the only way to create the company you want to create. In my experience, these are the only three reasons for taking on the challenge of leadership. And taking it on is obviously something you're determined to do, so you might as well do it wholeheartedly.

THE FIRST ASSIGNMENT

"Learning to live alone, the first practice of leadership, means learning to take full accountability for everything on your watch. Which means, the buck stops here. Which means, the fish stinks from the head down. Which means, there is nowhere else to turn, but to yourself. What does that feel like to you, Sarah?"

"To be honest, I never feel like I know enough. I constantly feel inadequate to the task. I feel that there are decisions I need to make that I don't know how to make, that I've never taken the time to learn. It brings up a lot of stuff about not really being a leader. The word itself doesn't fit me. Being 'the boss' fits. I feel big enough to be 'the boss' but being 'the leader' feels like my sense of my own importance is all out of whack. Leadership is what big people do, not people like me, running a pie shop, doing the insignificant things I do. And when I think about some of the dumb decisions I've made just to get through the day, believe me, I'm not a leader."

"Exactly," I said. "And that's why this conversation about leadership is so important. The word 'leader' is used academically, but not personally or functionally. Nobody I have ever met has been comfortable referring to himself as a leader, even when they are. People will discuss the *subject* of leadership all day long, but because leadership is not a function or a job or even a role in any company, only an arrogant son of a gun would refer to himself as the leader in reference to a position he holds. But everyone will agree that leadership is critical to the success of anything that calls for organization.

"To become a leader, you first have to learn to live with the word, accept its importance, and its responsibility. You have to learn to feel at home with 'I am a leader. I am called upon to do the work of leadership.' The first assignment is to say that to yourself, over and over again, until it begins to find a comfortable place to rest in you.

"No matter how silly this seems to a part of you, Sarah, your first responsibility to yourself as a leader is to become comfortable with the fact that you *are* a leader. And that it doesn't matter how large or small an organization you are leading. Leadership is leadership. And learning to lead in a small organization will prepare you for the large organization you're determined to create.

"So, that's your first assignment, in our new and evolving relationship, Sarah, which also, and not coincidentally, calls upon the **first essential skill of leadership, Concentration,** to pull off. And that is this, to remember to say to yourself, whenever you find yourself alone, with a decision you need to make, with your mind running a mile a minute about this problem or that problem, when you're simply sitting watching television, say to yourself, 'I am a leader. I am called upon to do the work of leadership.' And say it over and over again. Say it every chance you get. Say it when you're confronted with the choice to either do the work or get someone else to do it. Say it when you're feeling exasperated beyond all belief. Say it, say it, say it: 'I am a leader. I am called upon to do the work of leadership.'

"To do that will call for concentration, which is really focusing your attention, remembering your commitment to this exercise, not just the words, but the emotional experience of living into the meaning of the words. You have to mean them. And to mean them you need to concentrate on the feeling those words evoke in you. You have to take them in as deeply as you can. You have to own them. 'I am a leader. I am called upon to do the work of leadership.' The words have a weight to them that 'being the boss' doesn't. The word 'leadership' imparts to every activity a significance the activity would not necessarily have in itself. The word 'leadership' has a gravity to it that no other word in this context possesses. That's why people feel so uncomfortable using it to describe themselves. And that's exactly why you need to do it, Sarah. To take in the size of the word and to grow to meet its size, not reduce the word to the size you feel you can fill. The discipline here is to remember to do it.

"Any questions, or thoughts about it?"

Sarah answered immediately. "I'll do it, but I can't help but feel silly even thinking about it." She put a fake frown on her face, raised her head squarely, threw back her shoulders, and with mock sincerity, said, "I am a leader. I am called upon to do the work of leadership. Oh, really."

"Yes," I said, "you *are* a leader, and you *are* called upon to do the work of leadership. But not by me, and not by anyone else. But by the entrepreneurial commitment you have made to build a World Class Company. That's a serious commitment. If you truly want to build a World Class Company, no matter how big that company may be in the end, then everything we commit to do with each other is serious. And nothing is more serious than this first assignment. Because it pushes the window of your willingness, your determination, to take yourself seriously. *You won't take your commitment seriously if you can't take yourself seriously.* If you take yourself seriously, even if you don't feel like a leader, even if this feels silly, you'll find how much this exercise will move you in the right direction."

"Even though this is sooo embarrassing, I really do get it, Michael," Sarah said. "A part of me is just afraid. That part of me feels like I'm jumping off a cliff. But, in some strange way, I also trust that I'll fall into something soft and safe."

The second practice of the enterprise leader is choosing *where* to focus your attention. It's not a question of what's important and what isn't—in a World Class Company everything is important—it's a question of what is most important and what is least important from a leadership perspective. This calls for the skill of **Discrimination, the second essential skill of leadership,** learning how to choose between one alternative and another. If concentration is the skill of *how* to focus one's attention, discrimination is the skill of *where* to focus one's attention. Concentration makes discrimination possible. If you can't focus your attention, you will never learn how to use it to select the most important things to do. A leader who can't concentrate, cannot discriminate. A leader who can't discriminate will spend as much energy on the least important things as the most important things.

So, what are the most important things to the leader of an enterprise? They are the strategic drivers of the enterprise: **the vision,** its substance and how it is communicated, with intention, with conviction, with sincerity, and, most of all, with clarity; **the business model,** the unique way the enterprise works that differentiates it from the rest of the market; **the consciousness of the enterprise,** how people are regarded, how they are compensated, the core ideas that are important to them and to the enterprise that provide meaning to what they are expected to do every day, and how that is reflected in the look, feel, and function of the enterprise; and, finally, **the end game,** what it is, when it is expected to happen, what has to happen between now and then to make sure it does, how much capital is needed to assure its success. In short, the focus of the leader is to assure that the enterprise will function in a world class way.

THE SECOND ASSIGNMENT

"To be clear about where you are going, and why, is the leader's responsibility, Sarah. Lack of clarity about outcomes, about the end game, about what your company needs to achieve when it's finally done, when you've completed your mission, feeds uncertainty in your people. Clarity provides people with the certainty they need. Your number one job is to provide that clarity."

"But, how do I provide my people with clarity when I don't have it, Michael?" Sarah said. "One moment I'm clear, then something happens I didn't expect and I lose it. Everything seems to change, based upon circumstances, upon what's important in the moment. First, we're focused on this, and then on that. That's what doing business has been about for me, being able to respond to what comes up. That's my version of clarity. The clarity you're talking about sounds so unrealistic."

"And that's why there are so few leaders in business, Sarah. Especially in small business," I said. "Because there are so few who start out with a clear, long-term vision, most are just reacting to what comes up, confusing their ability to react with their ability to lead. The two are very different. A leader is someone who can remember what he wants. And what he wants has little to do with what comes up. What comes up is called **tactical** work from a leadership perspective. What he wants is a **strategic** question through which a leader evaluates everything that comes up. Which brings us to the next assignment I'd like to give you, Sarah.

"Your second assignment is to begin to develop the brand of clarity I'm talking about through the practice of discrimination. Every day, I want you to write down what you do. *Everything* you do. Make a list of what you do, no matter how insignificant it is. And at the end of every day, I want you to assign a work designation to the items on your list: **E** for entrepreneur, **M** for manager, or **T** for technician. Work you assign an **E** to is leadership work. Work you assign an **M** to could be leadership work, but for our purposes here, it's management work. Work you assign a **T** to is absolutely not leadership work, it's the work of a technician."

"So, how do I know which letter to assign to which task?" Sarah asked.

"Let's look at that," I answered. "Let's start at the bottom. If the work you do is related to something that needs to be done to fulfill an objective *in* your company, that falls within the operation of your company—you make a sale, you bake a pie, you hire a new person—it is either the work of a technician or the work of a manager. Think about your store, and think about the operation of that store as though it were separate from your corporate offices. None of what's done in that store called 'doing business' is the work of the entrepreneur. The entrepreneur may *visit* the store, but the entrepreneur doesn't *work* in the store. Does that begin to clarify it for you, Sarah?"

"Yes, it does," Sarah answered, "but all I do is work in the store."

"Exactly!" I said. "And that's the point of this exercise. To see clearly how much leadership work you are truly doing.

"That's why," I continued, "this assignment is really important. Take it to heart, Sarah, and you will discover more about what you do and the implications for growth than just about anything I can imagine you doing. Not only will it help you to develop your ability to concentrate and discriminate, it will give you clarity about how you spend your time.

"Every day you go to work, you discriminate. The problem is that you don't do it consciously. Discriminating consciously is a learned skill, one that will cause you to see yourself more clearly than you ever have before.

"Conscious discrimination is one of the leading indicators of whether you are a practicing leader. Your people will grow to depend on it."

As a leader learns how to concentrate and to discriminate, he is able to develop **the third essential leadership skill, Organization.** Organization defines the functional component parts of the whole and relationship between the parts.

Organization is the skill through which chaos is turned into order.

Organization is the skill through which sense is made out of nonsense.

Organization is the skill through which the things of your business that have a place are discovered and put into the place they are supposed to be in, and the things that do not have a place are discarded or put aside. Just like when puzzle pieces are put together, the sense of order is a sense of completion. A leader drives organization in his company, the desire for it, the need for it, the perfection of it, the will to achieve it. Organization is essential to the growth of a company, and no company can achieve world class status to the degree it has not developed a world class ability to continually organize itself and reorganize itself into an ever-increasing sense of order and predictability.

THE THIRD ASSIGNMENT

"The completion of the second assignment will bring you naturally to this one, the third assignment. I know you already get how uncomfortable, but necessary, it is to make the transition from thinking of yourself as the boss to thinking of yourself as a leader. Once you start writing down everything you do every day, and identifying whether it is the entrepreneur's, the manager's, or the technician's responsibility, you'll notice how little you've been discriminating between the strategic work a leader does and the tactical work that a technician does. This discrimination alone will have a profound impact on your day and the choices you make, Sarah. The third assignment will take this to the next level by giving you an opportunity to organize your day into strategic and tactical segments, and an experience of spending your time accordingly. I'd like you to set aside certain times every day dedicated to entrepreneurial work, management work, and technician work. It doesn't matter which times are devoted to which work, but for the purpose of organization, discrimination, and concentration, it is critical to you that you do this faithfully every day, and that you confine yourself to doing the work you have committed to doing in each of those daily segments you have selected for each."

"I haven't a clue," Sarah said, "how I could possibly determine in advance what I'm going to be doing in any particular day? That isn't how my business works, Michael. I do what I'm called upon to do."

"I know that, Sarah. But that's what we're doing this work for. To show you that there is a completely different way to do what you do, the way it's done in a World Class Company by leaders who are living a life that is completely different than yours.

"Until you can make the distinction between strategic and tactical work, and make choices accordingly, stuff will continue to happen to you, and the stuff you want to happen to your business will never happen. You *can* determine what you do every day, once you make up your mind that this is what your relationship to your business will be. And once you make up your mind to do this, it will become a reality if you practice it. So this is your third assignment, to practice organizing your day into work segments, during which you only do the work you have committed to do during that segment. Your job is to do that, and then to tell me what happens. Okay?"

"So it doesn't matter when or how much time I commit to each type of work?" Sarah asked.

"Well, yes and no," I said. "The only thing that matters right now is that you do it. What will matter *once* you do it will become obvious to you. Right now it's only important *that* you do it."

As you begin to consciously focus your attention, discriminate where the maximum leverage is, and begin to organize your day in such a way as to reap maximum benefit from this new awareness, you will recognize the need for continual improvement in everything you do and everything your business does. This call for continual improvement creates a demand for **the fourth essential skill of leadership, Innovation,** in you and your people, and, ultimately, as a core capability resident in your company. Innovation depends on discrimination. If improvement is the objective of innovation, the standards by which current performance is evaluated are defined by the vision of the end product, a World Class Company, and nothing else. At E-Myth Worldwide, for example, our vision is to become the preeminent provider of small business development services worldwide, with the objective of transforming small business worldwide. Everything we do and how we do it can only be measured by how well it contributes to achieving our objective. And since the methods, systems, and processes we utilize to fulfill our objective are always subject to improvement, it is critical to us that we possess the ability to improve them.

The process of improvement is very straightforward. **Step One:** Select the aspect of your business that you wish to improve. **Step Two:** Determine what the process is for doing what you have selected. For example, if you wish to improve the way you acquire new leads, determine what the current process is for acquiring new leads. If there is no process in place for acquiring new leads, create one. If there is, go to **Step Three:** Quantify how effective your lead-generation process is. **Step Four:** Rely on your quantification to tell you where you can and need to improve your lead generation process. If your ad isn't pulling, change it or test other lead generation methods. If your call center results are insufficient, rework the call center script. If your lead conversion rates are low, change the system for following up on leads. Only change one thing at a time so you can perform **Step Five:** Test it. Then go to **Step Six:** Quantify the results of your test. **Step Seven:** If the results of your test are positive, orchestrate the use of your new process or system. If the results of your test are not positive, go back to Step Four again. And do this, over and over again, continuously, in every part of your company.

THE FOURTH ASSIGNMENT

"So now we come to your fourth assignment, Sarah, to begin practicing the discipline of improvement in your company, through the development of the skill of innovation. What you choose to improve at this point doesn't matter, Sarah. As you begin to do the first three assignments, it will become obvious to you what is in need of improvement. Those things usually stick out like a sore thumb. Just begin the seven-step process. Pick something to improve. You simply need to focus your attention right now on practicing the skill of innovation, through an effort to improve one result your company produces through people other than yourself, using a systems approach for improving it. I want you to improve your *ability* to improve your company **by leading the process of improvement,** *not* by improving a process in your company by yourself. The improvement of your company will be a function of your enhanced *ability* to improve your company, which is the skill of innovation.

"What you're going to discover as you begin to do this, Sarah, will be the need for strong, effective communication with your people, the essence of the fifth assignment. So let's go right there and then I'll answer the questions I know you have."

THE FIFTH ASSIGNMENT

"The fifth essential skill of leadership is Communication, Sarah, how you communicate to your people what you expect of them, how you listen to their understanding of what you communicated, and how you improve your communication to diminish the gap between what you communicate to them and their understanding of it over time.

"So here's the assignment. Once you have completed the fourth assignment, and measured the effectiveness of your process improvement, I'd like you to do a review of each and every benchmark of the process. I want you to look at the scripts you used to communicate what your expectations were of your people, the words you used in those scripts, where you used scripts and where you didn't, and the implications of your decisions for the effectiveness of the process. In short, your fifth assignment is to complete a critical assessment of the effectiveness of your communication during the fourth assignment, including what you would do differently next time. The essential question you want to answer is: Did you organize the communication of your expectations to your people in a clear, compelling, and inspirational way?

"In my experience, Sarah, business owners spend far too little time, energy, and attention on increasing the effectiveness of their communication skills. People simply do what they do. And they have no idea the price they're paying for it. Communication is the skill through which a leader moves people, and is moved by his people, to build a World Class Company.

"And there are five essential functions for increasing the effectiveness of your communication: Inspiration, Education, Application, Implementation, and Continual Improvement.

"Let's take a brief look at each step in the communication process, Sarah.

"Inspiration is the result of seeing clearly. It is the result of suddenly, in a moment, understanding the world differently than you did, discovering that your relationship to the world possesses possibilities you never realized before. Inspiration, borne of organic, impossible to contrive, epiphany moments, provides you with the motivation to act. Inspiration is food for the spirit. Inspiration touches the deepest part of all of us. It awakens our passion.

"Education moves inspiration to a deeper level of understanding of the discipline we're discussing. This is where the usually formless idea—of leadership, of marketing, of finance, etc.—is given form, where the magic of the epiphany is filled with content, where the pieces of the puzzle, and the picture they make, come together in a logical, pragmatic, sensible, justifiable way. 'Oh, so that's what it looks like!' is the response to education I'd be looking for. Education doesn't require the student to do anything other than to study the content, and to develop an intimate understanding of the relationship between the components of the finished puzzle. Education is food for the mind.

"**Application** is the logical result of education. It is the process through which one validates what she's learned by testing it out in the real world. The inevitable result of the application of education is skill improvement. Whether someone is engaged in learning how to plan or manage money or generate leads, application turns training into competence. Until ideas work in your life by improving your ability to navigate through life, it's all academic. Application, therefore, is doing. Application is food for the mind and the body.

"Once you can demonstrate to yourself that education can be applied to produce real results in your day-to-day work, you are then ready to expand your reach through **Implementation** company-wide. By introducing the inspiration, education, and application steps to your employees so they can be in alignment with this process of transformation. Having successfully learned how to plan, or manage money, or generate leads, personally, and demonstrated the pragmatic results of it to yourself, you are now ready to communicate what you've learned and experienced as a strong advocate to others. The intent here is to drive the E-Myth perspective and process down into the operating level of the organization, to produce a planning system or a money management system or a lead generation system or a whatever system. Implementation is food for the mind, body, and emotions.

"**Continual Improvement** is the watchword of the entrepreneur. To the entrepreneur, nothing remains static. Everything always improves and changes. When people seem to resist change like the plague, how is it possible to create an environment in which people are engaged with the change that continual improvement drives? In which people are willing to give up their attachment to something they just learned how to do well and start down a new path without the same sense of competency? The answer lies in the integration of **Innovation, Quantification, and Orchestration** into the culture. These processes are the learned systems and practiced skills that every entrepreneurial company needs to build into its operations and its people so that continual improvement becomes a lifestyle, a way of being, rather than simply a way of doing.

"So, Sarah, you've been so patient. What are you thinking?"

"I know I told you weeks ago, Michael, that the change in my thinking was changing my sense of time, that I had much more time to do the important things than I thought, but I'm feeling pretty overwhelmed by all of this right now. I'm not sure how I'm going to fit these assignments into my already busy day," Sarah said.

"These assignments are designed to organize your attention differently.

That can only occur even if a sizeable chunk of the tactical work you do as a technician is sacrificed for some period of time. You have to begin to study your *attention* for the time being, not your work. If we can alter the way you think about your day, how you approach your day, how you engage your mind in your day, how you relate to your role as leader, everything you do will change, Sarah. So will the results your business produces. *After one month of doing these assignments faithfully, you will be on your way to being a different person, the leader of a World Class Company in the making.* When that happens, you will answer the question you're asking me better than I ever could. In fact, at that point, you will be asking a very different question. Right now, your technician is worried about time. As you move through these assignments, and your perspective changes, the emerging leader in you will be speaking for you."

Sarah smiled in acknowledgment of what I just said. "I know you're right, Michael. Old habits die hard. I understand that what you're saying to me is that I need to focus my attention on fulfilling my obligation as a leader if my company is to grow in a world class way. And that the five essential skills of leadership are critical to that discipline. What happens while I'm developing those skills? What happens in the meantime? Does the company have to wait until they are fully developed in me?"

"Oh Sarah, I so understand your concern about how all of this will work. But of course not. Both you and the business will transform in a parallel way as you make the commitment to do these assignments. The commitment to doing them is everything. As soon as you begin, you will be well on your way. And as you proceed, the new leader in you will awaken a new, more mature and more aware leader who will lead you to what's next. Our work will be done, Sarah. The rest of the process will be miraculously guided by you. You will become not only the leader of All About Pies, but the leader of your own journey toward the creation of a World Class Company. It is the only way. And it starts with your commitment, the commitment you've demonstrated so beautifully in the months we've worked together.

"You're already in the throes of leadership work, Sarah. Your interest in the truth, about yourself and your business, in both freeing and harnessing your passion, about why you lose interest only to regain interest again, about what it really takes to build a World Class Company, and whether you're the person to do it, whether it's something you really want to do. All this, Sarah, has been the work of a leader, going through your process, digging down deep with an earnest wish to know.

"You're ready to take on the E-Myth Mastery processes on enterprise leadership. I'm going to give them to you today and ask you to complete them on your own. As you go through them, Sarah, questions will come up. Most of them will be answered through your work with the other six disciplines but, of course, I'm available to answer any questions you might have. By the time we're done working through the seven essential disciplines, we will have answered a lot of questions, and raised a lot more. Many will remain unanswered for some time. But, of course, that's what building a World Class Company is all about, raising questions that create answers and more questions. The process never stops. It's like the movie my kids watched when they were little, *The Never Ending Story.* Building a World Class Company is a never ending story."

SELECTED E-MYTH MASTERY PROGRAM PROCESSES IN ENTERPRISE LEADERSHIP

The Business Plan That Always Works: Making Your Vision a Reality

■

A business without a vision is directionless. It lacks purpose. It lacks the essential idea from which commitment, growth, and the sense of personal achievement arise and flourish.

But a vision without a plan is only a hope. A vision needs a plan to make it come alive, to make it a reality.

The vision of your business reflects thinking and feeling on a grand scale. It then requires smaller scale strategies and even smaller scale tactics to make it happen. Like the tiles of a mosaic that first form individual pictures and then a grand mural, your business tactics will accomplish your primary strategies, building to the overall impact and results you want your business to have.

So your vision needs the form, direction, and clarity of a business plan to give it relevance to the day-to-day operation of your business. Your business plan is the link between the work of your business and the vision that work is intended to produce.

THE "TRADITIONAL" BUSINESS PLAN VERSUS THE BUSINESS PLAN THAT ALWAYS WORKS

A plan is a plan, right? It's a document that's intended to help you start a new business or make a success of the business you're already operating. It's a document you can hold in your hand, read, and show to other people.

The Business Plan That Always Works

MAKING YOUR VISION A REALITY

Business Planning "Productive Points of View"

Start with what's important to you.

Approach planning as more of an art than a science.

Create a planning framework that accommodates change.

Recognize those things that are "hard" for you and how you avoid them.

Treat the plan as a living, growing document.

Tips for Getting Started and Making Your Business Plan Work

- Be clear about what you want to achieve.
- Choose an appropriate time horizon.
- Get organized.
- Get others involved.
- Make the process easy.
- Make your plan robust and flexible.
- Build in "frames of reference."
- Use common sense.

Overview

The "business plan" is a common tool used by many companies. But why? Too often, preparing a business plan is done because "that's what businesses do" and, as such, it becomes a rote exercise that inevitably yields little or no productive results. Otherwise known as "the business plan that doesn't work."

What you're about to discover is a completely new version of the business plan—the business plan that always works. It always works because it's a plan that starts with your passion, your vision. And rather than denying the impact of change on the planning process, it recognizes that change will be your constant companion.

The business plan that always works begins with a different set of operating assumptions than does the "traditional" business plan. Your attitude and your own relationship to the plan will be the key factors that will make it a success.

Benchmarks for Producing Your Business Plan

Create a Mental Picture of Your Business Plan's Impact

Outline Your Business Plan

Prepare Your Business Plan Binder

Gather Materials You Already Have

Identify What You Need to Produce

Conduct Planning Meeting

Prepare, Review, and Revise Materials

Produce "Final" Business Plan

Create Change Mechanism

But why is it that business plans almost never come to life? Why do almost all of them, once written, sit on a shelf and gather dust, while the futures they describe never see the light of day, and the businesses they describe wobble their way into their uncertain futures?

A traditional business plan is head-centered; it's an exercise in what business owners think they should do. Writing a traditional business plan is usually precipitated by one of two thoughts: either (1) we'd better write a business plan because "that's what successful businesses do," or (2) we need to write a business plan if we want to go out and borrow some money.

A traditional business plan is also static. The expectation behind its development is that the plan will be "decided" and then implemented. Case closed. There's usually no room for change in the plan. A company sets its "best" people to work on developing the business plan, and it's their job to account for all possible contingencies in the plan. Otherwise, why bother creating the plan in the first place?

These first two characteristics of traditional business plans are quite intentional. That's the way business plans are done. Thoughtful, analytical, complete, decisive. All the hallmarks of a supposedly "smart" business. And, ironically enough, they're precisely the reasons that result in the third characteristic of the traditional business plan, that is, a traditional business plan doesn't work. It's the one that ends up in the drawer, collecting dust, only to emerge sometime in the future with the "whatever happened to . . ." or "do you remember when we planned . . ." remarks.

Traditional, head-centered, static business plans don't work. Can you see why they don't? A plan that starts in the head, with logic and reason and thoughts, lacks passion and excitement and purpose. And a plan that starts with the assumption that it's been able to capture and account for all the relevant changes that will happen in the future is obsolete before the "ink is dry on the page." Any employee in your company could tell you that! Traditional business plans are not alive and they're not realistic. Why would anyone feel a sense of commitment or pride or accountability around a business plan like that!

The bottom line is that a traditional business plan simply won't give you the results you want or need—it won't work if nobody's committed to working it.

The business plan that always works *looks* a lot like the traditional business plan. You could put them side by side and not notice any difference. But their appearance is where the similarity ends.

The business plan that always works *does* work, and can *only* work, because it starts from a completely different place, with a different set of operating assumptions. It starts from a heart-centered planning approach, which means it starts with the experiencing of the feelings you'll have, and your people will have, and your customers will have, when your plan has been accomplished. When you start by defining the true end result, how you'll feel, then all the logic and analysis and numbers will really mean something.

The business plan that always works also assumes, and rightly so, that at the time you're creating the plan you can't possibly predict all the changes that will occur. So this plan not only tolerates change, but relies on your building in change as a key factor that will keep you on the best course. With a clear vision, and a business plan that adjusts its strategies to account for the world as it really is, the work of your business can be best positioned to achieve great results.

The real difference between the business plan that always works and the traditional business plan is in how you think and feel about the plan—it's your attitude and your relationship to the plan that will make all the difference.

THE MYTH—AND THE TRUTH—ABOUT PLANNING

When business gurus and management experts talk about building and growing a business, one central topic that usually comes up is planning; that is, the need for a plan to achieve the growth.

The idea of planning is very comforting. It makes people feel safe and secure to know that there is a plan guiding business activities in the "right" way. But the kind of planning you'll need to do in the 21st century is probably not the same planning that you're used to.

The pace of change in today's world, which will be even faster tomorrow, makes traditional planning virtually meaningless. The forces of technology and social change, among others, and their reach into our lives, call into question everything we do in business and everything we believe to be true about the way business operates. What we accept as reality today, changes in the blink of an eye.

So it's time to dispel the most common and dangerous myth about planning:

Plans do not insure that what is planned will actually come to pass; plans do not predict the future.

This requires us to reexamine what it takes to grow a business. How does one lead when the future is so uncertain? How does one plan when the outcomes of what we envision today and begin implementing tomorrow are so unpredictable?

In this mass of uncertainty, one thing is—or should be—certain: your vision. So that's where you start. Your business plan will be a statement of your vision and a current description of the main strategies and tactics you'll use to make your vision come true. From the strategies and tactics discussed in your plan, each department and position will be able to develop the additional strategies, tactics, and systems to achieve their results and, ultimately, the Strategic Objective and Strategic Purpose of the company. Not only do your Strategic Objective and Strategic Purpose create pictures of what you want your company to become, they provide the head-centered and heart-centered foundations for the choices you'll make in your business plan.

Here are some "productive points of view" about planning that will make it a truly worthwhile endeavor:

- **Start with what's important to you.** A mediocre plan that you (and others) feel passionately about will serve you better than a technically superior plan that you don't feel strongly about.
- **Approach planning as more of an art than a science.** Documented business plans that are professionally formatted with charts and graphs and lots of quantification give a false impression of certainty and precision. Use your best thinking when you plan, but don't forget that even the best thinking involves guesswork. Educated guesswork, to be sure, but guesswork nonetheless. Remember that even the best-looking business plan contains guesses based on assumptions. If you're aware of this, you can use it to your advantage as you create and implement your plan. Be sure that you and anyone developing portions of the business plan document all planning *assumptions* that underlie the actual content of the plan.
- **Create a planning framework that accommodates change.** Don't think of your plan as a rigid "final product" with every detail pinned down. Think of it more as a series of guideposts of key topics to focus attention on and targets to aim for. Welcome opportunities to add to or revise any parts of your plan, or even eliminate parts of it, when the talent and judgment of those around you and your own inclination tell you it's the right thing to do. Don't follow through with something in your plan simply because it's "in the plan." And don't forgo opportunities that are staring you in the face, simply because they aren't in the plan. Develop a system for building change into your business plan (you'll see one way to do this later in this process).
- **Treat the plan as a living, growing document.** Make a conscious decision to review your plan periodically, evaluate it, and revise it. Keep questioning your assumptions. Stay flexible and open to change. Don't let your pride or inertia get in the way of reworking the plan and moving forward.

GETTING STARTED

Many people approach writing a business plan as a daunting, burdensome task. If you approach it that way, then it certainly will be! But it doesn't have to be that way. If you have a vision for what you want your business to become, and if you really want to make that vision a reality, here's where you get to draw the map that will get you there. Just jump right in. You'll probably see that you've already done a lot of the necessary thinking and documentation. Use the *Getting Started on Your Business Plan* worksheet to Download clarify the thinking you've already done.

Here's an easy way to begin:

Be clear about what you want to achieve. This is a thought process that actually has two steps. First, you need to be clear about your vision for the business—what you want your business to achieve as expressed in your Strategic Objective and your Strategic Purpose. Second, you need to be clear about how you'll use your business plan to achieve that vision.

Your business plan can be the "call to action" for your people because it lays down the overriding goals and fundamental strategies your company will use to achieve them. With this map in hand, every person in your business can determine how they will individually contribute to making it happen.

Another way to use your business plan is to communicate with the "outside world," usually potential lenders, shareholders, or the community at large. If this is the kind of plan you need, you have some choices in how to approach it. The easiest way, which happens to also be the most productive way, is to start by creating the more internally focused plan, as described in this process. Then you can adapt the contents and format, if necessary, for the particular external audience you want to address. When you get to this stage, you could even bring in an outside professional to fashion this plan, because you'll already have most, if not all, of the essential ingredients.

Choose a time horizon for your plan. Company visions come in all shapes and sizes; some are very long range and others are more immediate. Building your business plan so that it covers a specific time span will help you maintain its focus and direction. There is no right or wrong time frame to use; many business plans are written for three- to five-year periods, but you should do what feels like the most sense for you and your business. Remember that you'll be building your business plan to embrace changing conditions, so the time horizon you choose shouldn't feel like a constraint, but more like a temporary frame of reference that will help you see the elements of your plan more clearly.

Get organized. This is as much a state of mind as it is a physical phenomenon. Make a commitment to yourself to devote the time, attention, and resources to creating your plan. Make it your *intention* to produce a plan that *will* work based on this new way of thinking about a business plan. Then assemble all the physical elements that will allow it to happen.

Think about how you'll get others involved. As a general rule of thumb, the more involvement, the better. You'll not only get the benefit of more knowledge and more help, you'll also create a sense of shared commitment and participation. The emotional impact that people feel when given the opportunity to engage at this level of business planning is more than worth the extra time and coordination it may take. Group involvement leads to group learning and a more "intelligent" company.

BENCHMARKS FOR PRODUCING YOUR BUSINESS PLAN

The concrete steps reviewed in this section will lead you through the process of producing the physical document of your business plan. These are not, however, the steps of the business *planning* process. The distinction is that the business planning process is how you actually formulate the content of your plan—the reasoning and proposed activities that arise from it. This is discussed in the specific business development processes that relate to the various systems in your business: marketing systems, financial systems, sales systems, management systems, and so forth.

The following benchmarks will help you pull all the pieces together into a document that combines heart-centered and head-centered planning to become the living, breathing "game plan" for your organization.

Benchmarks for Producing Your Business Plan

- Create a Mental Picture of Your Business Plan's Impact
- Outline Your Business Plan
- Prepare Your Business Plan Binder
- Gather Materials You Already Have
- Identify What You Need to Produce
- Conduct Planning Meeting
- Prepare, Review, and Revise Materials
- Produce "Final" Business Plan
- Create Change Mechanism

1. **Create the mental picture of the impact you want your business plan to have.** How would you feel if your plan actually had that effect? The premise for this step lies in the concept of heart-centered planning, which describes the importance of feeling a sense of passion or excitement as a necessary prerequisite to any plan in order for that plan to work.

    Picture in your mind a coach handing out the season's new playbook to the team. Or a director passing around new scripts to each member of the cast. Everyone is silent as they wait to get their hands on a copy, or murmuring excitedly to one another. They open it up and leaf through the pages. You hear oohs and ahhs, some gasps and a few laughs. You see the intent and animated expressions on their faces. . . .

Now imagine you're that coach or that director. You're distributing your company's new business plan. Look at the faces of your people. What do you see? What kind of feeling is in the room? How are people responding as they read it? How is everyone using the plan as they go back to their individual accountabilities? How are departments working with each other differently as a result?

Picture it exactly the way you want it. And don't go on to benchmark 2 until you do.

2. **Outline your business plan.** This will become the table of contents for your business plan, and a "pre-plan" that will help you organize this effort and distribute development accountabilities to others. The next process will give you a sampling of the items you can include in your plan and the *Business Plan Contents* checklist Download will help you get your outline started.*

3. **Prepare your business plan binder.** The best way to begin assembling your business plan is in an everyday, three-ring binder. This way you can move sections or pages around, replace old versions with revised ones, and continue to build your plan over time. Start by creating your cover and/or title page and insert dividers for the major business plan sections as identified in your outline.

4. **Gather the materials you already have.** Depending on how long you've been engaged in business development, and how diligently you've been documenting as you go, you should have a good number of the items for your business plan partially or completely ready. Some examples of materials you may already have are your: Strategic Objective, Strategic Purpose, organization chart, descriptions of your target markets, positioning statement, marketing plan, financial strategy, financial statements, and product/service strategy. Put all the pieces you have in your business plan binder. Decide whether each piece is complete as is or, if it

* Throughout Part Two of this book, you will be introduced to a sample of processes from the E-Myth Mastery Program that each Download have a number of worksheets to help you implement the process in your business. When you see this icon, it is a signal to you to go to the website www.emythmastery.com to view and, if you wish, download the referenced worksheet. For a full list of worksheets, please see page 401.

needs to be revised, use the *Business Plan Development* worksheet to indicate who should be accountable for the next step,
and a due date. Download

5. **Identify what you need to produce.** What pieces of your plan don't you
   have? What will be needed to produce them? Who should do it? Start
   your thinking about these things, but don't come to any final conclusions (unless you're going to develop the entire business plan yourself).
   Now you're ready to leverage yourself, bring others in to participate,
   and complete your business plan sooner rather than later.

6. **Conduct a planning meeting.** Gather the group of employees you've
   identified to move the business plan through its remaining steps. "Enroll" them in this process; don't just dictate assignments. Paint the big
   picture. Get them excited. Ask for their suggestions, and really listen.
   The end result of this meeting (or it could be a series of meetings), in
   addition to getting people's commitment to the business plan, should
   be to have a clear understanding of who will do what by when.
   In other words, each piece of your business plan should have
   someone accountable for completing it and a specific due date Download
   for completion. Record what's been decided on the *Business Plan Development* worksheet.

7. **Prepare, review, and revise your business plan materials.** This is the
   "tactical work" step. This step will involve all the accountable people
   thinking, analyzing, developing, writing, meeting, reviewing, rewriting,
   until each section is done. You should review every piece before it's fi-
   nalized and make any additional changes. Also it's important that you
   make sure all the pieces are consistent and work together as an integrated whole (for example, that you have the production capacity to
   meet sales forecasts, etc.).

   Beware "analysis paralysis" at this stage—the endless revising and revising based on continuing thinking and analysis to the point where no
   plan seems acceptable. To combat "analysis paralysis," remember that
   your plan will change and adapt over time to reflect and meet changing
   circumstances. Of course, do the necessary analysis. Get your best
   thinking and planning on paper now, finalize it, and be ready to make
   changes down the road.

8. **Produce your "final" business plan.** Now you're ready to put your plan
   together and craft the "look" of your document. (Final is in quotes because it's not really final—you'll revise and update it for as long as
   you're in business.) Give your plan a polished, easy-to-read appearance.
   Do what you need to do in order for your business plan to have the im-

pact you want it to have, but don't go overboard. Keep the three-ring binder format for your working version so you can easily make changes. If you want to produce variations of your business plan for outside parties (lendors, investors, shareholders, etc.), you're now ready to do that, too. For these audiences, professional printing and bindery may be a good idea.

9. **Create the mechanism for building change into your business plan.** This last step is absolutely vital if your business plan is to really work. Do it now—don't put it off! Think about how you'll accommodate change into your business plan and create the system for doing it. Because you know that no sooner will you dot your last "i" and cross your final "t" than something will happen that you didn't expect. The best system is a two-pronged approach: First should be establishing a "formal" review period, either quarterly or semiannually, when you review the entire plan and update it, as needed. Second is to review part or all of your plan when something significant changes (for example, a major competitor enters or leaves your market, Download an unexpected regulatory change, natural disasters, etc.). One tool for helping you do this is the worksheet called *Building Change into Your Business Plan*.

WHAT'S IN IT? THE INGREDIENTS OF YOUR PLAN

This section presents one model for the contents for your business plan. It's based on the "seven centers of management attention" so that your plan will contain the goals and strategies you'll use in each of the main arenas of your business to accomplish your overall vision. Use this as the basis of the outline for your company's business plan (see benchmark 2), modify it, or create your own.

The items listed are self-explanatory or are described in detail in other business development processes within the E-Myth Mastery Program.

GO FOR IT!

You've read the lists, you've read the rules, you've read the logic. You understand it; it makes sense. But how do you feel about it all?

If you feel that writing your business plan is going to be a waste of time and energy, don't do it! It will be a waste of your time.

But if you feel passionate about what you want your business to become, do it! If you feel excited by the idea of your vision becoming a reality, do it! If you want a way to drive the sense of shared commitment throughout your company, do it!

SAMPLE BUSINESS PLAN CONTENTS LISTING

I. Introductory Elements

* Cover and Title Page
* Table of Contents
* Statement of Purpose of the Business Plan
* Company Strategic Objective and Strategic Purpose (may also include Core Organizational Values and Beliefs)
* Company Story

II. Overall Company Development/Growth Plan

* Goals, including Key Strategic Indicators and major business indicators
* Assumptions
* Schedule
* Budget and Sources of funds

III. Overall Corporate Plan

* Systems Development Plan
* Organizational Strategy
* Organizational, Leadership, Management, and Personnel Goals
* Management Strategy and Personnel (Staffing) Strategy
* Description of Key Management Systems
* Quantification Plan, Reporting Vehicles (how you'll measure and evaluate performance)

IV. Marketing Plan

* Marketing Goals
* Overall Description of General Market, Company Image and Positioning, External Market Forces (competition, laws and regulations, societal forces)
* Descriptions specific to different market segments:
    * Target Market Description (demographics, trading area, and psychographics)
    * Positioning, Sensory Package, External Forces, Marketing Strategy
* Quantification Plan, Reporting Vehicles

V. Financial Plan

* Financial Goals
* Overall Financial Strategy, Pricing Strategy
* Description of Key Financial Systems and Reports
* History of Recent Financial Performance
* Pro-forma Financial Statements
* Financial Summary

VI. Client Fulfillment Plan

* Client Fulfillment Goals
* Products/Services Descriptions
* Production Strategy
* Service Strategy
* Delivery Strategy
* Customer Service Strategy
* Quantification Plan, Reporting Vehicles

VII. Lead Conversion Plan

* Lead Conversion Goals
* Description of Lead Conversion/Sales Personnel
* Description of Lead Conversion/Sales Process and Key Systems
* Quantification Plan, Reporting Vehicles

VIII. Lead Generation Plan

* Lead Generation Goals
* Description of Lead Generation Channels
* Description of Lead Generation Messages
* Description of Lead Generation Process and Key Systems
* Quantification Plan, Reporting Vehicles

IX. Other Unique Strategies and Factors
(NOT PREVIOUSLY DISCUSSED)

What are the remaining ingredients that will make your business plan really work?

Make it easy. It doesn't have to be hard. Use what you've already got. Build on it. Include the elements that make the most sense for your business. Don't load it up unnecessarily for the sake of volume. Delegate what you can. And have fun with it.

Make it robust and flexible. What would a robust and flexible business plan look like? It would be easy to use and easy to read. It would be "attractive" to its audience. It would adapt easily to change. It would have a clear purpose and be appropriate for the result it's intended to produce. It would be balanced in terms of how it addresses the different areas of the business. It would have a clear monitoring and follow-up mechanism. And it would have "energy" and reflect the passion you feel for your business.

Build in "frames of reference." These are intermediate completion and celebration points that will help keep everyone motivated as you develop the parts of your plan. Make it a practice to create individual and group frames of reference.

Use common sense. Don't be swayed by any "logic" and don't include any "plan" that doesn't make sense to you.

Can you see that the business plan that always works is not just a planning and implementation document? It's a "catalytic converter" that takes the ingredients you put into it and intensifies them. If you put passion, excitement, and commitment into your plan, they'll come back out, and become magnified as they spread throughout your company and become fundamental to the way you and your people operate every day.

You, your people, and your business deserve to have a meaningful, honest business plan to give your efforts direction and to guide your path toward the results you all want.

Business Quantification: Looking at Your Business Objectively

▪

Quantification is one of those habits that can become so basic you do it without thinking. That's good and bad. It's good if the idea of quantification is so ingrained that you automatically use it to understand every part of your business. But it's not so good if you do it mindlessly, without carefully thinking through what you're quantifying and how it will tell you what you need to know.

Quantification isn't an afterthought—it's an indispensable part of the business development process of innovation, quantification, and orchestration. Without quantification you don't know

Business Quantification

Key Points

Key business indicators tell an integrated story. They reveal how the entire business as a whole, not just its various parts, is behaving.

Key business indicators are organized and presented in "management reports" in order to present the information in digestible form and to distribute it to those who need it.

Exception reporting—focusing your attention on the out-of-the-ordinary—is used to direct your attention to the indicators that point out problems and exceptional results. Your attention is where it needs to be for decision making and problem solving.

There is no universal set of key business indicators. You should establish the indicators that give you the information you need, that make sense to you, that fit the situation in your business. A table of common key business indicators is provided for your reference in this booklet, but be sure to think through what will be best for you.

Definitions

There are three levels of quantification:

Key strategic indicators, which show how the business is progressing toward its Strategic Objective and indicate the general health of the business;

Key business indicators, which enable you to monitor and manage the business and its major functions as an integrated whole; and

Key system indicators, which show exactly and in detail what is right and wrong with every system.

This process focuses on key business indicators.

There are financial and operational indicators. Financial indicators are generated in financial statements and reports and are not covered in this process.

Operational indicators give you an objective view of what is happening in your business and how well or poorly it is being done. They include indicators of activity, productivity, efficiency, quality, and even subjective evaluations of intangible elements of your business.

The Key Business Indicators Process

Identify Activities and Results to be Quantified

Establish Management Report Structure

Create Data Collection System

Design Management Reports

Create Systems for Producing Management Reports

Continually Refine Reports

if your innovation has worked, and you lack the controls to orchestrate it properly.

YOU DON'T KNOW YOUR BUSINESS
UNTIL YOU'VE QUANTIFIED IT

All business owners can walk through their businesses, listen to their employees, look at their business activities, and get a sense of whether things are going well or poorly. Some do it better than others, but all business owners do it.

It's a valuable skill, but it's not nearly enough.

If you haven't quantified your business, you're not objective about it. You're seeing it through a distorted lens no matter how objective you try to be. Without quantification, you make judgments based on what you personally see and hear, and that's both limiting and biased. Because your eyes and ears can't see everything, and they're *your* eyes and ears and are, therefore, attached to your personal biases and beliefs, your personal view will always be distorted. Despite your best efforts, your decisions will be based on misinformation.

But by creating an effective quantification process you can pinpoint exactly what's going on in your business, for better or for worse. You can anticipate problems before they materialize. You can know exactly which areas need your personal attention, and which do not. You can be completely objective and accurately informed. Your decisions will be sound because they'll be based on good information, not belief, not opinion, and not on an incomplete view of the business.

Quantification, if you do it right, gives you a "sixth sense" about your business. It's not at all mysterious. It's a logical, practical process. And it's a process you can comfortably manage because it's one based on your own needs, abilities, and preferences.

So when the question is "Do I quantify?" the automatic answer is "Yes!" And when the question is, "What do I quantify?" the answer is "Everything."

THREE LEVELS OF QUANTIFICATION:
STRATEGIC, SYSTEM, AND BUSINESS INDICATORS

At the highest level of information, there's strategic quantification. You strategically quantified your business when you established your key strategic indicators. You should be reviewing your strategic indicators at least quarterly.

Strategic indicators give you a sense of your progress toward your Strategic Objective, and they give you a feeling for the general health of your business.

They give you the "big picture." But they aren't meant to help you navigate the day-to-day management of your business, and they aren't precise enough to help you detect and diagnose problems within your business.

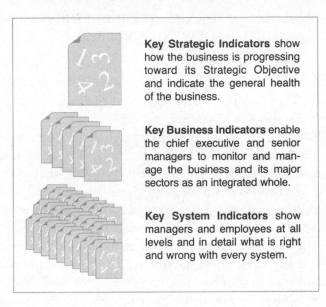

Key Strategic Indicators show how the business is progressing toward its Strategic Objective and indicate the general health of the business.

Key Business Indicators enable the chief executive and senior managers to monitor and manage the business and its major sectors as an integrated whole.

Key System Indicators show managers and employees at all levels and in detail what is right and wrong with every system.

At the most detailed level of quantification, there are key system indicators. Every time you develop or innovate a business system, you determine its key indicators and establish a baseline against which to measure performance and progress (see *Systems Innovation*, pp. 294–296). You, or your employees, should be watching your systems indicators continuously.

Key system indicators are detailed and precise. They're the best way to detect when something in your business is going awry and what's causing the problem. For day-to-day and minute-to-minute management nothing beats key system indicators for knowing *exactly* what's happening *within any one system*. But they don't tell you about the business as a whole or even significant portions of your business.

That's what Key Business Indicators are for.

KEY BUSINESS INDICATORS
TELL AN *INTEGRATED* STORY

It's an obvious point, but it bears repeating. Too many business owners lose sight of the fact that a business is an integrated organism. What happens in one corner of the business impacts what's happening in the other corners. If you're only managing the *parts* of your business, you're not managing the *business*.

When you look over the listing of suggested key business indicators later in this process notice how they form a complete picture, covering all areas of your business. They're multidimensional, multifunctional, and all-inclusive.

The concept of a business as an integrated organism goes over the heads of most business owners. And without that insight, it's impossible to manage a business in this integrated way. It's one of the things that makes an E-Myth manager stand out from the crowd of would-be managers who only think they understand their businesses, but actually only understand pieces, and even those not very well.

OPERATIONAL AND FINANCIAL QUANTIFICATION

When you look at quantification across thousands of companies, you notice that financial quantification is highly uniform and operational quantification is extremely diverse. Financial quantification takes the form of financial statements (balance sheet, income statement, cash flow statements), highly standardized accounting and bookkeeping conventions, and even a whole set of conventional approaches to financial analysis.

By contrast, operational quantification is infinitely varied with few standardized practices. In this process we focus on operational quantification. But always remember complete business quantification must include the financial quantification.

Thus, when you monitor your key business indicators, your budgets, cash flow, and financial statements are an integral part of it all.

YOU DON'T HAVE TO BE A ROCKET SCIENTIST

If you can add, subtract, multiply, and divide, and if you can use a pencil and a pad of paper, you have the essential tools of business quantification. If you can use a computer and draw graphs (or have employees who can), so much the better. You don't have to be a rocket scientist. In fact, it's better if you're not because scientists sometimes get caught up in their own numbers and lose sight of the fact that the numbers are a tool, not an end in themselves.

A FEW GUIDELINES FOR DEVELOPING
YOUR BUSINESS QUANTIFICATION

Start with your highest priorities. You've already quantified your highest priorities. Those are your key strategic indicators, the ones that directly reflect your progress toward your Strategic Objective. To quantify your key *business* indicators, start with those aspects of your business that are most critical to your success. You'll probably classify the critical parts of your business something like this:

- People
- Production and productivity
- Customer satisfaction
- Lead conversion and lead generation
- Market standing and competitive position
- Administration and support
- Profit margins and other financial indicators

You'll create your own quantification for your own situation, but the table that appears later in this process shows examples of the more useful and common key business indicators.

Start small and build. Don't overwhelm yourself or your people with measurement and tracking. Sounds like a contradiction, doesn't it? Quantify everything, but don't do too much.

It's a matter of finding the balance point. Learn as you go. But make quantification a priority, and continue to improve and add to your quantification systems. It's not just a numbers exercise. It pays dividends, and it can save your company by revealing problems when they are small and manageable. It can also help you identify opportunities before your competition finds them.

GIGO. Remember, "garbage in, garbage out." When you measure something, make sure the measurement means what you think it means.

For instance, take the case of a small metal products manufacturer (mailboxes and lawn furniture) who measures the days of raw materials inventory on hand by getting the information from the shipment notices his suppliers fax to him. He thought he had a 15-day supply, but he neglected to account for the fact that supplies arrived at his plant an average of 7 days after they were shipped out of his suppliers' warehouses. So he actually had only an 8-day supply of raw materials. No problem, until a big customer doubled the size of his order for lawn chairs. He ran out of raw materials, and his plant virtually shut down for three days while he panicked his way through the situation. It cost his company thousands to rectify the problem.

Minimize the work of measurement and tracking. Whenever possible, draw upon existing systems, procedures, and paperwork. But don't shy away from installing systems and creating work in order to get the information you need to understand and manage your business.

Focus on the meaningful. You can measure and quantify anything you want, but some things just aren't worth the effort and some things don't tell you what you think they do. Usually it'll be obvious, but not always.

There was a management consulting company that measured and tracked the number of clients served. That's an interesting number and useful for public relations and a general overview of the scope of the company. But the economics of the company were driven by the *hours of consulting labor* that were spent doing the consulting work, not by the simple number of clients. They paid too much attention to how many clients they had and too little to the economic realities of their kind of consulting.

CONVERTING DATA INTO INFORMATION— MANAGEMENT REPORTS

It's just as important to put your business quantification into usable form and distribute it where it can do the most good, as it is to gather the data in the first place. All your measurement is merely data—facts—until you make sense of it and convert it into information. You do that by organizing the data, possibly performing some calculations, and displaying it so that it makes sense and helps you understand what's really going on in your business.

The primary tool for making sense of data is the management report. A report is simply an orderly display of information. Its purpose is to present information so that it can be quickly understood and absorbed. The tools of management reporting are familiar to everyone—tables, graphs, and charts. They are easy to scan, efficient to produce, and convey large amounts of information in a compact format. They are also easily computerized.

EXCEPTION REPORTING— SEEING WHAT'S IMPORTANT

Anyone who works with management reports quickly learns the value of "exception reporting." As your quantification systems grow, you'll find that most of the numbers fall within normal ranges most of the time, and that your attention is drawn to abnormal measurements, those that fall outside your expectations either favorably or unfavorably.

In time you'll become adept at setting up your management reports to highlight these abnormalities. It's called "exception reporting," and it's the most efficient way to keep your attention focused on what is important.

Graphs and "variance analysis" are two useful ways to focus your attention on exceptions. Graphs are visual and quickly draw attention to spikes and dips, which are nothing more than "exceptions" to the norms for your business. Variance analysis accomplishes the same purpose with a little subtraction. For each measure that you are tracking, you simply subtract last year's (or last month's, or the average of the previous x months) readings from the current reading. This shows you how much the current activities "vary" from your business's norms, hence the term "variance analysis."

TIMING AND FREQUENCY OF MANAGEMENT REPORTS

How frequently should you collect and report information? That depends. A retailer will collect sales information at least daily, maybe even two or three times a day. He'll probably want to review customer complaints and compliments less frequently, say monthly. A manufacturer will probably want to look at inventory and production information daily, but only needs to review downtime information monthly. It depends on both your need for the information and your personal preferences.

Data collection and management reporting do not have to follow the same schedule. You may measure store traffic and collect the data continually as people enter and leave the store. But you may only report that information weekly or monthly.

As a rule of thumb, you should collect the data for efficiency and report it for utility. Collect the data in ways that require the least effort and annoyance to you and your employees. Report the information when it will be most useful. Looking at store traffic information as it is collected, at 15-minute intervals, is nearly useless—you can't detect any patterns. But looking at weekly or monthly patterns gives you information on which you can base staffing decisions and special promotions.

REPORT FORMAT . . . WHATEVER WORKS FOR YOU

The format of management reports—tables, charts, and graphs—is a matter of personal preference. Some owners prefer narrative descriptions. Most owners like to look at tables and charts where they can run their eyes down columns and across rows and immediately spot the items that stand out from the company's norms. Others like everything put in graphical format. Bar charts, pie charts, line graphs, scatter diagrams—they all draw the eye immediately to unusual activity, which is exactly what a manager needs to focus on. That's why the "exception reporting" approach is so useful.

EASE INTO IT

If you and your employees are not accustomed to this kind of information gathering and reporting, you can expect some resistance. (You may feel a little resistance yourself.) That's normal. After all, quantification to the inexperienced can seem like busy work and bureaucracy. But as you experience the benefits of quantification—early detection and prevention of problems, feelings of professionalism and greater control of your business, clarity, the ability to make more realistic (and more aggressive) plans, the competitive advantage of spotting opportunities first—the skepticism vanishes.

Plan to ease into quantification a step at a time. Select your most important management information needs and begin your quantification with them. Then, as quickly as you can, but keeping pace with your own growing familiarity with the quantification process and the ability of your people to implement quantification, introduce more data collection and reporting processes.

It's a never-ending process, just like systematization is a never-ending process.

DISTRIBUTION OF MANAGEMENT REPORTS

If your business is a five-person operation where you manage everything, then distribution is easy. All management reports go to you (you probably produced them all, and "them all" probably means only one or two reports of key information).

If your business has several dozen or a few hundred employees, and you have a number of subordinate managers, then you will probably produce numerous management reports of different kinds, and distribute them to several different levels in your organization. The key is to get the information to the people who can do something productive with it. We can't tell you what reports should go to what people, but we do provide worksheets and guidance on how you should structure your management reporting system.

And now it's time to do just that.

THE BUSINESS QUANTIFICATION PROCESS— CREATING YOUR MANAGEMENT REPORTS AND THE SYSTEMS THAT BRING THEM INTO BEING

The process of quantifying your key business indicators has the following steps:

The Key Business Indicators Process

- Identify Activities and Results to Be Quantified
- Establish Management Report Structure
- Create Data Collection System
- Design Management Reports
- Create Systems for Producing Management Reports
- Continually Refine Reports

1. **Identify the business activities and results to be quantified.** Determine appropriate measures and timing of measurement. You can select quantification measures from the list provided or devise measures of your own. The *Business Quantification* worksheet can be used to keep track of the measures you want to use. As you identify specific measures, also be thinking about the source of data, who in your organization should be accountable for reporting it, and what Download management report will be needed to present the information.

2. **Establish your management report structure.** Identify and give a general description of each management report that will be created in the future. The *Menu of Management Reports* worksheet will help you do Download this.

Most owners organize their management reports by functional area. That would result in a menu containing reports with titles such as "Monthly Staffing Analysis," "Production Tracking Report," "Sales and Marketing: Month of Xxx and Year-to-Date." You might prefer to structure your management reports along organizational lines, reporting marketing information to your sales and marketing people, production information to your production people, and so on. You might want "top line" information (key indicators of company performance) for yourself and detailed reports for your managers, or you might want all the details yourself. It's all up to you.

Every report, in addition to its title, should show the period of time for which the data were gathered, and should have the name of the person to contact for questions.

For *each* management report to be produced, use the following development procedure:

3. **Create a system for collecting the necessary data.** Your data collection systems should cover:
   - Source of measurement data ("piggyback" on existing information flows whenever possible)
   - Frequency and timing of data collection
   - Person (position) accountable for collecting data
   - Data collection procedure

4. **Design the management report.** The design should cover:
   - Format and layout of the report (graphs, charts, tables, narrative, and combinations of these)
   - Information content and any calculations (formulas) used
   - Time period covered by the report
   - Frequency and timing of report distribution
   - Distribution list
   - Contact person (person who can be contacted to answer questions about the report)
5. **Create systems for producing the management report.** Often the people who collect the data are not the same as those who produce the report. Your report production systems should cover:
   - Report specifications
   - Obtaining data from those collecting it
   - Organization and storage of data
   - Processing the data into report information
   - Reproducing and distributing the report
6. **Continually refine and upgrade the report.** Produce the first report; obtain feedback and experience using the report; modify the report and the process as appropriate.

A very small business will probably simplify this process. The owner might be the one who designs the format, collects the information, and produces the report, and is the only user of the report. A larger business may want to add other steps to the process. Either way, the same tasks must be accomplished.

THE QUANTIFICATION PLAN

Once you've identified the management reports you'll need and you have the basic development process in mind, it remains to convert this information into a plan. *The Quantification Planning* worksheet will help you. Simply list the management reports by name in priority order in the left-hand column. Then write in the time intervals (weeks, months, quarters) across the top, and estimate the timing of each report's development across the rows using the benchmarks indicated by steps A, B, C, and D at the top of Download the worksheet.

"LIES, DAMNED LIES, AND STATISTICS"

Mark Twain once said, "There are three kinds of lies: lies, damned lies, and statistics." Some feel the same way about business quantification. The truth is that in some businesses, quantification is misused, twisted to cynical purposes by dishonest or incompetent managers in pursuit of self-serving ends. Too bad, because they would be better served by honest, insightful quantification.

Quantification reveals problems and suggests solutions. Quantification eliminates personal biases, decisions based on anecdotes and personal observation, and confusion. Quantification gives you control, objectivity, and a deep understanding of your business.

Quantification is the magnifying glass, the X-ray machine, the telescope, and the microscope that allows you to see into every corner of your business and, at the same time, enables you to see the integrated whole of it.

Quantification isn't just numbers. It's insight. It's understanding. It's the path to a business that works.

EXAMPLES OF KEY BUSINESS INDICATORS

PEOPLE		
Total staffing	# FTE (full time equivalent employees)	Number of employees, including part timers based on their weekly hours as a proportion of full-time weekly hours. For instance, if A works 40 hours per week and B works 20 hours, then they total 1.5 FTE.
Full-time employees	# FT	Number of employees working full time.
Part-time employees	# PT	Number of employees working less than full time.
Turnover	# T/O	Number of employees hired to replace departing employees (do not include new positions or positions being eliminated).
	% T/O	Employees hired to replace departing employees as a percentage of total FTE.
Absenteeism	Days/Hours Absent	Number days or hours employees were absent from work for any reason.

PEOPLE (cont.)		
Absenteeism (cont.)	% Absent	Absent days/hours as a percentage of total available days/hours.
Overtime	Overtime hours (#)	The total number of overtime hours in the period.
	Overtime cost ($)	The total dollar cost of overtime hours in the period.
	Overtime hours (%)	Overtime hours as a percentage of total non-overtime hours.
	Overtime cost (%)	Overtime cost as a percentage of total non-overtime payroll.
Staff/labor costs	Payroll ($)	Total payroll amount in dollars for the period. Can be broken down by organizational unit or type of employee.
	Total personnel costs ($)	Total payroll plus benefits and incentive payments paid by the company for the period.
	Contract labor ($)	Cost of contract labor paid during the period.
	Contract labor (%)	Cost of contract labor as a percentage of payroll cost.
New hires	New hires (#)	Number of new hires during the period. Can be broken down by type of employee.
Terminations	Total terminations (#)	Total number of personnel leaving employment of the company for any reason during the period.
	Voluntary terminations (#)	Number of people who voluntarily left the company.
	Involuntary terminations (#)	Number of people who were fired, laid off, disabled, or left the company for reasons not of their own choosing.
PRODUCTION AND PRODUCTIVITY		
Production volume	Units produced (#)	Number of units of the product manufactured or assembled into finished goods during the period.
		Also, numbers of important components or work-in-progress items.

PRODUCTION AND PRODUCTIVITY (cont.)		
Production volume (cont.)	Production capacity (#)	Number of finished units you're capable of producing at full utilization in the period.
	Production utilization (%)	Percentage of capacity utilized in the period. Units produced divided by production capacity.
Downtime	Hours downtime (hrs)	The number of hours that production was interrupted and unable to operate for any reason. One can measure downtime for the entire company, for a single operation, or for any number of important components of the company's production capability (entire factory, assembly line, bakery, computer, printer, telephone system, etc.).
Production quality	Rejects (#) (%)	Number of units rejected due to poor quality, rejected items as a percentage of total units produced.
	Rework (#) (%)	Number of products that were rejected but were repaired or reworked to make them acceptable for sale; reworked items as a percentage of total units produced.
	Waste (#) (%)	Select important (costly, hard-to-get, etc.) materials in the production process and measure the amount of waste that has to be discarded or sold as scrap.
Inventories	Finished goods (#) ($)	The amount and dollar value (cost-based value, not sales price) of finished products on hand.
	Work in process (#) ($) (days)	The amount and dollar value (cost-based value) of partially finished products on hand. Also, the number of days, at current rates of production, that these items will last before inventories would run out if not resupplied (divide the number of units on hand by the number of units required for one day's production).
	Raw materials, components (#) ($) (days)	The amount and dollar value (cost-based value) of raw materials, components, and other supplies on hand. These are materials and items

PRODUCTION AND PRODUCTIVITY (cont.)		
Inventories (cont.)	Raw materials, components (#) ($) (days) (cont.)	purchased for the production process, but that have not yet been utilized or worked on. Also, the number of days, at current rates of production, that these items will last before inventories would run out if not resupplied (divide the number of units on hand by the number of units required for one day's production).
Backlog	Backlog (#)	The number of units on order to customers but not yet produced or available for shipment. Also, for non-manufacturing companies, the work that has been committed to clients, but not started due to lack of resources or some other reason.
Productivity	Labor productivity (units/worker/day) (units/man-hour)	The amount of production obtained by the labor force. One can measure productivity of individuals, teams, or the whole organization. Labor productivity is usually thought of as a measure of manufacturing efficiency, but it is appropriate for any labor-intensive activity.
	Machine productivity (units/machine-hour) (units/plant operating hour)	The amount of production obtained from machines and technology.
On-time performance	On-time delivery (%) Late delivery (%) Average time delivered late (avg min/hrs/days)	Occurrence of late delivery of promised products or services. Measure percentage of deliveries that are late and the average duration of time before delivery is made. Target should be zero occurrences of late delivery.
CUSTOMER SATISFACTION		
Customer ratings	Excellent (%) Satisfactory (%) Unsatisfactory (%)	Measure customer satisfaction with surveys or service evaluation cards. Use any scale that includes at least 3 ratings, one for exemplary service, one for satisfactory service, and one for poor service.
Customer surveys	Various	Periodically survey customers to determine not only their levels of satisfaction with your business, but

CUSTOMER SATISFACTION (cont.)

Customer surveys (cont.)	Various (cont.)	also their attitudes, their perceptions about your business and your competition, ideas for product improvements, etc.
"Onions" and "orchids"	Onions (#) (%) Orchids (#) (%)	An "onion" is a customer complaint, an "orchid" is a compliment. Count all onions and orchids, whether they come in person, by telephone, by mail, etc. Track the number as well as the percentage based on total customer transactions.
Merchandise returns and refunds	Returns (#) ($) (%)	A count of units and the dollar value of items returned by customers as well as the percentage of all units sold. If possible also track the reasons for the returns.
Disputes	Disputes (#)	Customer disputes, not including merchandise returns. Disputes are more serious than simple merchandise returns and customer complaints. Track the nature of the disputes and any dollar impact of resolving the dispute.
Extra service activity	Occurrences (#)	Track non-standard service and assistance provided to customers, as well as their reactions. Service in this sense means activities that are above and beyond the normal products or services that are sold to your customers.

LEAD CONVERSION AND LEAD GENERATION

Sales "funnel" TARGET MARKET REACH LEADS APPTS SALES	Market population (#) Reach (#) (%) Leads/contacts (#) (%) Appointments (#) (%) Sales (#) (%)	Measure and track lead conversion and generation effectiveness by measuring the response rates at each step of the process. 1: Estimate the target market size. 2: Measure the number of prospects your message reaches and the % of the target market. 3: Measure the number of leads/contacts made with prospects and the % of your reach. 4: Measure the number and % of appointments made from among the leads. 5: Measure the number and % of sales made from the appointments. Measure and track for individual

LEAD CONVERSION AND LEAD GENERATION (cont.)		
Sales "funnel" (cont.)		salespeople, teams, and organizational units. Set goals and strategies to increase "response rates" at each step.
Response rates	Attempts (#) Contacts (#) (%) Sales (#) (%)	For direct mail and telemarketing, total the number of attempts to contact prospects (# of pieces mailed, # of calls made), the number and % of actual contacts made, and the number and % of sales. Set goals and strategies to increase response rates.
Store traffic	Store visitors (#/time) Sales (#) ($) Product mix (#)	For each store, measure the number of visitors, the number and dollar amount of sales, and the types of products sold. Measure and track for appropriate time periods: for instance break the sales day into 15-min, 30-min, or 60-min time intervals. Take note of days of the week, holidays, paydays, unusual occurrences in the community, and special events.
Advertising tracking	Store visitors (#/date) Telephone inquiries (#/date) Sales (#/date) ($/date) Awareness source (#)	Measure advertising response by tracking activity (store traffic, inquiries, sales) and correlating it with advertising dates and media types. Ask people how they became aware of your store/company/products and track responses. Increase successful advertising techniques, and eliminate unsuccessful ones.
Telephone inquiries	Inquiries (#/time/source/type)	Track telephone inquiries received at your stores/company. If possible, capture time and date, source (advertising, yellow pages, word-of-mouth, etc.), and type of caller.
Promotional events	Attendance (#) Responses (#) (%) Sales (#) (%) ($)	For each event (a sale, seminar, trade show, etc.) track total attendance, responses (expression of interest), and sales.
Collateral materials	Distribution (#) Responses (#) (%) Sales (#) (%) ($)	Track effectiveness of brochures, flyers, handouts, giveaways, and other items given to prospective customers. Measure number distributed, responses (number and percentage of distribution), and sales.

LEAD CONVERSION AND LEAD GENERATION (cont.)		
Customer acquisition costs	Cost per customer ($) Cost per sale ($)	Gross acquisition costs = total marketing and sales costs divided by total number of sales or total number of customers acquired. Also track acquisition costs of different sales or marketing campaigns by totaling all related costs of the campaign and dividing by the number of sales or new customers resulting from that campaign.
MARKET STANDING AND COMPETITIVE POSITION		
Market size	Target market population (#)	Define the Central Demographic Model of your target market and estimate its population. This will be the total number of potential buyers of your product or service. Depending on your line of business the "units" of measurement could be consumers, households, companies, business units of companies, government entities, or combinations.
	Market potential (#) ($)	Calculate the maximum possible number of sales or sales dollars that could conceivably be achieved in the target market. Ignore competition or the feasibility of your company's achieving that level of sales. Later, combining your expectations of market share and the effectiveness of sales/marketing efforts, you can estimate and set goals for your "share" of the available market potential.
Market reach	Reach (#) (%)	The number of target buyers who are "reached" by your advertising, sales, and other marketing efforts. Consider the reach of each separate effort, and of your total marketing/sales capability. Reach translates into "awareness," meaning that the number and % of your target market you have reached has some awareness of your company and your products, however superficial that awareness may be.

MARKET STANDING AND COMPETITIVE POSITION (cont.)		
Market penetration	Customers (#) (%)	The number and the percentage of the target market who are customers of your company or your products.
Market share	Share of business generated by all competitors (#) ($) (%)	The number of sales, the dollar value of sales, or the percentage calculated by dividing the number or dollar amount of sales by the total sales generated by all competitors. Hence, your "share" of all the business generated in your market. Note that "penetration" and "share" are not the same. Penetration is based on market size and the amount of the available market your company has "captured." Share is based on the total amount of business generated in the market, and your portion of it. For instance, in the home computer business, the target market and the market potential cover all households in a market area. But the total penetration of all competitors amounts to only about 40% more or less. So a competitor having a 20% market share would have only an 8% market penetration. On the other hand, in the television market, since virtually 100% of households have televisions, market penetration and market share would be identical. Strategies for increasing market penetration can be very different from strategies for increasing market share.
Reputation, Image	Survey ratings	Your company's reputation and image can be hard to measure. The best way is market research. Appropriate measures are defined by the specific surveys. Customer satisfaction measures can be a good indication of reputation and image. Tracking of press clippings and other publicity can also provide good indicators of reputation/image.
ADMINISTRATION AND SUPPORT		
Admin headcount	Admin FTE (#) (%)	The number of people in admin and support (overhead) positions, and their percentage of total staffing.

ADMINISTRATION AND SUPPORT (cont.)		
Admin headcount (cont.)		Admin positions are those that do not directly produce and sell products and services, or service customers. Management is an admin function, so are Personnel and Accounting and other positions that are "support" or "staff" in nature.
Admin costs (overhead)	Admin payroll ($) (%) Admin office expenses ($) (%) Admin services ($) (%)	Costs of administrative and support functions are "indirect" costs in that they do not contribute directly to production or selling of products or to customer services. Track the dollar amount, percent of total costs, and percent of total revenue.
PROFIT MARGINS		
Product profit margins **PRICE PER PRODUCT** –Direct costs =Gross margin –Indirect costs =Net margin	Gross margin ($) (%) Net margin ($) (%)	It is important to estimate profitability on a per-product basis. Many companies have fallen into the trap of thinking that they can price their products low and "make it up on volume." That is only possible if the product's gross margin is positive and sufficient so that a realistic volume of sales can also cover indirect costs. This "margin analysis" provides insights into product pricing and cost control. Margin analysis should be conducted, and margins should be measured and tracked for all products and services.

CHAPTER TWO

The Discipline of the Marketing Leader

■

"The intensity with which you impress your
subconscious with a picture of your plan directly
affects the speed with which the subconscious will
go to work to attract the picture's physical counterpart
by inspiring you to take the right steps."

From Napoleon Hill's Keys to Success *by Napoleon Hill*

It's not hard to find lots of information on marketing. There are thousands of books on the subject. Marketing is taught virtually everywhere. You'll find over *73 million entries* on Google on the subject. There is an incomprehensible amount of money and time spent by businesses, universities, governments, foundations, organizations, and individuals of every kind on market research, market tests, marketing in advertising, marketing in product development, in graphic design, in copywriting, in media, on television, radio, on the Internet, all designed to figure out how to do the single thing that marketing is supposed to do, to bring in a customer, to crack the code. And yet, despite this investment of resources, and the overabundant supply of marketing genius that exists out there in the world, there is a screaming, unfulfilled, and seemingly impossible need in business to get more customers. Is it really that marketing is as inherently mysterious and difficult as everyone seems to be making it?

Let's look.

Marketing, the way to do it, the mechanics of it, is relatively easy. In this chapter, I'll provide you with the basics of what you need to know to market your product or service. What isn't easy about marketing, however, is the demand that comes with it. It calls for an intense, focused, single-minded, tunnel-visioned discipline and desire. Desire to get the result, regardless of the cost. Desire to build a world class brand. Desire to build a singularly unique position in the mind of your chosen customer. Desire to get the customer to come in the door, and to buy, not just once, but over and over again. Desire to move the customer to refer the people they know. To open the floodgates. Desire to figure it out. Desire to be more than just a contender. Desire to be more than just somebody. Desire to be the One.

And to do that calls for the discipline of a marketing leader.

In E-Myth terms, the marketing leader is the one in the organization who is most passionately committed to growth, to building a brand, a franchise, no matter how small the business may be. It could be one, single operating unit in the middle of a single community or a thousand throughout the world. It doesn't matter. What matters is the franchise and the differentiation it represents.

Without this differentiation, marketing is futile, a lot of work for no return, an empty suit, a ridiculous investment.

So that's the very first question the marketing leader must ask about his business: What's our franchise?

What do we own, what do we do, how do we look, how do we act and feel and perform that differentiates our company from everybody else's? What's the defining sensory impact our company makes?

That's the franchise question.

And the key job a marketing leader has is to pursue that question until everyone knows the answer. It's a concrete answer. Not an abstract one. It's an answer you can see, touch, feel, quantify. It's an answer that everyone who buys from your company or works for your company knows. If they lend you money, invest in your company, or sell products or services to your company, they better know the answer. Because if they don't, they will leave you for dead.

Marketing has always been, and will always be, about the concrete. The concrete customer, the concrete trading zone, the concrete deliverable, the concrete promise your company makes, the concrete behavior of your people, the concrete, undeniable, hard-as-a-rock reality of what you do and who you are, and why that's important to everyone who comes into contact with your company. The more concrete it is, the better the franchise. The more concrete it is, the better the marketing leader has done her job.

Sarah and I had worked hard together to get through the first discipline of Mastery, leadership. As Sarah wrestled with the work she was asked to do, what I had promised her began to come true: Her commitment to be the leader she was called to be led her to discover the leader within her. The commitment to leadership, her commitment to the enterprise, coupled with the practice of leadership, to fulfill her purpose, to build a World Class Company called All About Pies brought amazing insights to Sarah. Sarah was ready to move on to the discipline of the marketing leader.

"The first thing I want to suggest to you, Sarah, is that just because we're moving through Mastery in a kind of linear fashion, don't make the mistake of thinking about each component as a step in a process. Each component is more like a puzzle piece than a building block. The result, a World Class Company, is a function of how well you put all of the pieces of the puzzle together. Each piece makes the most sense as part of the whole. And you'll never have a completed puzzle if any of the pieces are missing.

"The seven disciplines and each of their component parts are the pieces of the puzzle and comprise the whole of a World Class Company. Everything you do to build your company through the Mastery process will affect everything else you do in this process. You're beginning to see how the work you've done so far is impacting the work we're doing now. And that awareness will only continue over time. Your thinking will mature to the degree you're able to maintain this holistic perspective and see your business as the integration of its various parts. You, of course, are the key ingredient in all this, Sarah. If this is not compelling enough to you, it won't get done.

"So the discipline of the marketing leader depends on the discipline of the enterprise leader, the five essential functions and the five essential skills, as well as the disciplines that are yet to come."

Sarah leaned forward in her chair, her chin in her hands, her elbows on each of her knees, her eyes fastened on mine. Her look was intense.

"I understand what you're saying, Michael, in the sense that the business I'm creating is an idea that finds its reality through the skills I'm developing. What I'm struggling with is how to think about this as anything other than a series of steps in a linear process. I'm not sure why it's important to see it as one thing, as a conclusion, as opposed to something to build from the ground up. I don't even know if I'm asking the right question. I think I'm confused."

"I understand your confusion, Sarah. It can be confusing. Let me find another way to say it. In the mind of the entrepreneur, the business is already done before he starts it. In the mind of the enterprise leader, the objective then is clear, even if the process isn't. The disciplines for building a World Class Company already exist, just like the business already exists in the mind of the entrepreneur. The disciplines are already resident in the outcome they are intended to produce. They are already connected to and integrated with each other. Your job is simply to appreciate and be supported by the reality of this, in the same way you are by the completed picture of the puzzle on the top of a jigsaw puzzle box.

"The connection of all the pieces of a jigsaw puzzle, before we begin to search for the right one to go here, and the right one to go there, are already understood and accepted as reality. Assembling a 1,000-piece puzzle is not simply 1,000 steps. It's many more steps than that; try this one, now that one, and so forth. As each piece fits into the puzzle, the path to completion becomes clearer, the pace changes, the sense of fulfillment heightens.

"So it is with the work we're doing together, Sarah. In the beginning, all you and I can see is a picture of the finished puzzle and, of course, that isn't really very clear to us. But as you move forward into each discipline, as each skill you develop through practice makes you more effective at each step to follow, the picture of your business when it's finally done becomes clearer. All of the steps of the process are connected. You don't know what the connection is, you don't know how one step affects another, but you can be certain that every step impacts every other step. And if that's so, then every step is connected *even before you take it.* You might say that the future of your company exists even before you start the process to build it. Only your commitment to making it one thing, as opposed to another thing, will determine what the future is, at least to some extent.

"And that's the elegance of a system. And the miracle of this process, Sarah. It's the mystery of how all this comes together that's so fascinating. If you're deeply interested in it. It's your interest in it, and your passion fueling that interest, that will move you to discover what's next. I'm here to help now. But if I've done my job right, you won't need me when we're done here. The passion, the interest, the commitment, will live in you.

"So let's get back to the puzzle piece called the discipline of the marketing leader."

"Sarah, the discipline of the marketing leader begins with the vision of the entrepreneur, the intent of the enterprise leader, and the commitment to turn the vision of a World Class Company into sensory components that are solid and real in the world.

"The first discipline of the marketing leader is the ability to draw a picture of the finished company. To translate the idea and the words that express that idea into a concrete product that looks, acts, and feels exactly as it must look, act, and feel to differentiate it from every other product competing for the heart and mind of the company's most likely customer.

"The discipline of perseverance is required to see the process of marketing development through to the very end. To see every single detail, to scrutinize every single aspect of the company, to ask every single question that can be asked about what we do here, how we do it, why that way and not this way, what the impact is on our customer, why it's important, how we replicate that impact every single time, and so forth. The marketing leader drives the pursuit of those questions in the company. Everyone—in operations, finance, sales, customer service, information technology, product development, human resources, training, field management, etc.—is engaged in the process. The marketing leader is accountable for making certain that the hard, objective, concrete, visual, emotional, functional, and financial pieces of the enterprise puzzle come together in an integrated, definable, manageable, measurable, emotionally compelling, and, most important, replicable way.

"The marketing leader, Sarah, must be driven by a retailer's sensibility.

"Just as a retailer orchestrates every component of the retail system to meet the customer's needs and preferences with great precision—what the displays in the window look like, how welcoming the entrance to the store is, how the path the customer takes to the back of the store works, the way the customer is greeted, the way the shelves are stocked, the way the employees are dressed, how clean the store is, what sounds the customer hears—the marketing leader must orchestrate every aspect of the company's sensory package. Regardless of the kind of business and industry, the type of product or service, what the demographics of the customer are, or the level of experience and skill that is required of employees. The marketing leader knows that the business is his one and only product. And until it can be seen as a picture on the top of a jigsaw puzzle box, literally, it does not exist."

THE FIRST ASSIGNMENT

"So, Sarah," I continued, "that brings us to your first assignment as the marketing leader of All About Pies. No, I'm not going to ask you to create that picture for your company. Not yet, anyway," I said, seeing the relief on her face. "What I am going to do is to ask you to take some time to identify the picture other marketing leaders have created in other companies that obviously understand what a marketing leader does.

"It's not going to be as easy as it may sound, Sarah," I said. "Marketing leaders are few and far between. In fact, as you begin to look for evidence of the presence of a marketing leader, you're going to find yourself hard-pressed to find one. And the reason is that, despite how obvious the need for a marketing leader appears to be, very few companies are led that way. More often than not, companies are led by product-centered rather than business-centered people. Software companies are most commonly led by software guys; hardware companies are led by hardware guys; auto repair companies are led by auto repair guys. This retail sensibility I'm talking about, this orientation to the words, shapes, colors, etc. that a company's most probable consumer responds to, is relatively absent in the world of business.

"Having said that, I want you to look for three companies that are led by marketing leaders. Here are a couple of examples of the kind of companies I'm talking about.

"Federal Express is led with a retailer's sensibility. See the truck, see the package, see the person who picks up your package. See the way he is dressed. There is no mistaking it, FedEx is FedEx. There is no other company like it, no matter how many companies are in exactly the same business. FedEx is a franchise. And because it is a franchise, it is a distinctly unique and valuable brand. It owns a place in the world. It has earned it. On-time-every-time-exactly-as-promised is the FedEx way. Everybody knows it. Everybody uses FedEx when they want guaranteed, on-time delivery because it has pulled off its entrepreneurial vision in an inordinately dramatic and effective way. The marketing leaders at FedEx have made certain all the pieces have been put together in a visually, emotionally, functionally, and financially compelling way. You can see and feel a marketing leader's hand at work there. There is no mistaking it.

"Starbucks is another company that is driven by a true marketing leader's retail sensibility. Look at the sign, look at the displays, look at the names of the products to order, Venti, Grande, frappuccino. Starbucks appropriated those names; they own them. A big cup of coffee is what everyone else gives you, but at Starbucks you get a Venti. And you can't get a Venti anywhere else. And look at the young, bright, responsive people at Starbucks who take your order and fill it. Listen to the sounds of your order being filled, smell the fragrance of the obviously special brands of coffee Starbucks delivers, feel the ambiance of that special environment that is exactly the same no matter which one you're in, in a way you'll only find at Starbucks. Starbucks *owns* the hearts and minds of its customers. Starbucks' marketing leader invented the place and the position Starbucks owns. 'If it isn't Starbucks, it isn't coffee.' Starbucks coffee is *beyond* ordinary coffee. It's the Starbucks experience Starbucks is selling, and the customer is returning to experience.

"So, Sarah, I'd like you to find three companies on your own, big companies, small companies, it makes absolutely no difference. Look for the signs of a marketing leader. It may be the truck, it may be an ad in the newspaper; it may be the sign on the front of the building, it could be anything that says, 'this is a marketing-leader-driven enterprise.' But whatever it is that calls your attention to it, follow it up. Look for the marketing leader's presence in other ways. See how deep his impact goes. Follow your intuition. You'll be amazed what you find and, even more important, what you don't find. Make notes in your marketing leader notebook. Organize your notebook by the four components of marketing leadership: visual, emotional, functional, and financial. How does it look, how does it feel, how does it work, how is it priced? And when you're done with all that, you'll be ready to do the second assignment.

"Questions, thoughts, Sarah?"

"Yes, and I know I must sound like a broken record," Sarah said. "But how in the world am I going to find the *time* to do this?"

"You know what I'm going to say, Sarah," I answered. "You just do. You make it important. Because it is important. You make it important just like you would make it important to breathe if you had to. Because leading the marketing development of your company is as essential to its life as breathing is to yours. And the best way to learn what that is, what it looks like, what it feels like, what it acts like is to see the retailer's sensibility in action."

"Okay, Michael, I'm in," Sarah sighed. "I'm ready for the second assignment."

THE SECOND ASSIGNMENT

"You'll be relieved to know that the second assignment is pretty simple."

Sarah laughed, and I laughed along with her.

"Your second assignment is to define the word 'franchise' the way a marketing leader would.

"What is a franchise? Not, *how* does one franchise? But, what exactly is a franchise the way I've been speaking about it here?

"You can look the word up in a dictionary," I said. "But, I don't think it will tell you what a franchise is in the marketing leader's mind.

"The first assignment I gave you will certainly provide you with all the clues as to how you need to define the word 'franchise.' It will provide you with what resides in, or makes up, a true franchise. To help you answer this question, it is probably a good idea to first consider what a franchise isn't.

"For example, you might look at a directory of franchise opportunities. You might investigate some of them. In the process, you might compare them to the three companies you've chosen for your first assignment. Ask yourself what's missing in these franchise opportunities? Where are the weaknesses in their sensory package?

"It's no secret, Sarah, that you're likely to find that very few franchise opportunities actually measure up to the term 'franchise' as a marketing leader would use it. I'd like you to think about why that is.

"Thoughts?" I asked.

"Yes, well, I'm beginning to see where all of this is going. Maybe what's more true is that I'm suddenly feeling my willingness to go where it's going. Thank goodness. At least for the moment," Sarah said.

"If I can just stay the course, to see my vision through to reality," Sarah said, "I can see how the process of building All About Pies in this way will give me more life, more vitality, a real sense of fulfillment, and greater clarity. I want that at this point in my life. I also want to touch many more people than I'm able to playing such a small game. This will expand my reach. It will be a much bigger game than the one I'm playing. And I don't know how to play it, which is all the more reason I'm moved to push through it. If I don't do it, I know what the rest of my life will look like, not unlike what it currently looks like, even if I'm someplace else, doing the same thing, only differently. If I spend the next, I don't know how many, years building a World Class Company, I have no idea what my life will look like. All I can tell is that it will be somehow bigger, more inclusive, less confined. That's why it's important to me, Michael. I want to grow, to be as big as I can be. No, that's not true. What *is* true is that I'm *determined* to grow. And this is the most spectacular way I can dream of doing it."

"Do you see how easy this is getting to be?" I asked. We both knew I was kidding. And we both knew it didn't matter. Sarah's expression told me that she was sinking into a depth of commitment from which there was no going back. I was excited for her. I took a moment to feel that her life would never be the same.

"How about if we go on to your third assignment."

THE THIRD ASSIGNMENT

"Once you're able to get a clear picture of what a real business looks, acts, and feels like under the direction of a true marketing leader, once you really get what a franchise is and why it's important, once you accept your challenge as the marketing leader to invent the most successful small business in the world, your next task, Sarah, is to begin to put the pieces of the puzzle together so you can communicate your vision or, more exactly, the entrepreneur's vision, in an absolutely moving way, to the enterprise leader, to the board of directors, to the people who work for you, to the people who will invest in your company, to anyone and everyone who you are determined to influence in a positively dramatic way.

"I'm going to ask you, Sarah, for the first time since we started working together, to make a financial investment."

Sarah look concerned, like she was thinking, "How much is this going to cost me?" In response to her unasked question, I said, "Don't worry, it's not going to cost you that much. And it will be more than worth it.

"So this is your third assignment, Sarah. To convert your idea of All About

Pies into a visual reality. Now I know it is already a visual reality. You already have a store, space, a dress code, a kitchen, a place for customers to sit, and so forth. But that's what you have gotten by doing what you know how to do, not doing what you don't know how to do. In fact, there's been a bit of the marketing leader involved in everything you've done to this point, but not by intention the way I'm going to ask you to do it. I'd like you to commission an illustration of All About Pies the way a marketing leader would. And to do that, I'm going to ask you to hire a professional illustrator. But first, you're going to have to prepare. You're going to have to take the store apart piece by piece, think through the process of everything the store does, how it looks, acts and feels to the customer, and how it functions best. You'll need to create rough drawings to reorganize the store as if you could do anything and everything you would ever want to do in the store. You'll need to see it clearly, through your experience and your imagination, as a finished product, designed to fulfill its absolutely most important objective, to stand out in the mind of your customer as a spectacular example of a World Class Company. See it, see it, see it. Write down your ideas, your thoughts, your conclusions, your questions. Dig down into it as deeply as you can."

"Sarah. Let me tell you a story about a dear friend of mine. I watched her do exactly what I'm asking you to do when she designed her home from scratch. Before she brought in the architect, she had thought through every single significant and seemingly inconsequential piece of the finished product: the layout, the variety of designs for the layout, the pitch of every single roof, the exterior shingles, what colors and kinds of wood, the window frames and the windows, exactly what width of the frame, exactly what size windowpane, on the front door, on the rear doors, on each and every single one of the bedroom windows, detail, detail, detail. And space. How much space for each space in each part of the house? Why this amount of space and not that? I watched her in amazement, and awe, as she went through this extraordinarily diligent, disciplined, creative process, completely absorbed, completely fascinated with every single part of the process, with every single question that suddenly showed up, with every single new problem that appeared, from the style of the cabinets in the kitchen, to the space required for the microwave, the stove, the refrigerators, the sinks, the counters, what the counters would be made of, what finish she should select for the doors of the refrigerator, the microwave, the oven tops, white, black, stainless steel, wood panels, what the cabinets should be made of, how she could use contrasting woods, which ones would work—oak, ash, cherry, walnut, maple, why this wood, and why this wood with that wood?

"As I watched this process unfold, Sarah, the extraordinary dedication and heart and passion my friend committed to it, to the outcome, to the purpose that she could not completely define, other than through the endless array of pictures she collected from every place imaginable, of houses she admired and respected and adored, of architectural details, of furniture, of small sections of a house, a window, a window seat, a fireplace, a built-in cabinet, a view from the garden, a fence, an entire parade of fences, roofs, countless different types, styles of roofs, all of this she collected and rummaged through and laid out on the floor of the house she had which she intended to gut completely to create the house she envisioned. All of this would seem to the casual observer as a woman obsessed. And, in fact, in one way she was. She was obsessed by her intention and, as she said many times, she uncovered creative energy that she had never been in touch with as richly or as completely as she was in that process, in the creation of her new home.

"That's the process I'm asking you to engage in, Sarah. That's your third assignment. To take on the design of your new store, the store that you can imagine, the store that will fulfill the entrepreneur's vision and the marketing leader's inspiration to make All About Pies a world class reality, a company that will move your consumer to your store above all others.

"Just like my friend did, you simply make up your mind to do it with as much attention to detail as you can muster. You make up your mind to take it on with everything you have, and everything you don't have, trusting that you'll find what you need in the process of committing to it. And just like my friend did, you'll discover creativity that you never knew you had. Your passion, your vision, your purpose, and your practice will guide you. The answers to the questions you don't now have are waiting for you. So is a much bigger you. Now is your chance to unveil her. To love her. To embrace her. To fold her into a new sense of yourself.

"I know that if you were to ask my friend what it meant to her to discover this huge part of herself, this previously invisible part, she would probably come to tears, it was that significant to her. And then you would probably hug each other. This is an extraordinarily successful woman, someone who has achieved things in her life that very few people will ever achieve. She went to the best schools, became a successful consultant, a respected professional. And with all that, she had never discovered how immensely creative she was until she took on her house and, in the process, allowed what was to be created to emerge in her, to take her. What would her life have been like, texturally, had she not done that, had she not experienced that, had she not allowed herself to fall in love with her creative essence?

"Well, I feel deeply, Sarah, that few people give themselves the room and the permission to transform in this way. It would be a tragedy for you, for anyone, to settle for less than what's possible. When what's possible is so exquisite, so nourishing.

"That's what this assignment is, Sarah. To embrace your creative essence. Through All About Pies. No holds barred."

"But what good will it do if, once I go to all that trouble, to all that work, I can't afford to make it real?" Sarah said.

"My friend couldn't afford it either," I answered. She had no idea how she was going to afford it. She just started with the assumption that she would. And as her house took shape on a piece of paper and was translated into an architectural rendering, and was organized, piece by piece by intimately small and elegant but specific, concrete, definable, buildable pieces, she discovered exactly what she wanted, and then figured out exactly how to get it. It started with trust. Trust in herself, in life, in the way things work when you can truly see them, and are committed to them, and are fully in love with them, and are willing to live in that place that so few of us understand, that place of not knowing. Not knowing exactly what the house or the business is going to look like when it's finally done. Not knowing where the resources will come from. Not knowing if you have what it takes and doing it anyway. Not ever knowing anything but your willingness to persist. The marketing leader, with all her dedication to manifesting the entrepreneur's vision, to orchestrating the impact the company has on the people who buy from it, the people who work in it, all the people who are touched by it, will never, ever truly, absolutely, know what the finished product will look like until it's finished. But she, you Sarah, have to be determined to know as much as you possibly can. And that's what this assignment is meant to do, to take you from the entrepreneur's vision down to the detail of the visual representation of it.

" 'Let me show you a picture of your company,' you will say.

" 'Let me show you how I see it,' you will continue.

" 'Isn't it stunning?' you will ask, already knowing the answer."

"So, let's get down to business, Sarah.

"It's time to do the work of the marketing leader, to clarify what the marketing strategy is for All About Pies.

"That's what the discipline of marketing comes down to, Sarah, strategy. And the strategy of your franchise calls for a very specific understanding of who your customer is and why she buys, and how your company, All About Pies, is going to influence those decisions to become the brand leader in your industry, in your market, in your trading zone. Which means you need to create brand awareness, brand acceptance, and brand preference, which is what a true franchise, or brand, achieves in the hearts and minds of its customers. How to do that is the homework I'm about the give you, Sarah."

"Okay, Michael. I'm ready!" Sarah said with a sense of promise that I had been waiting to hear.

SELECTED E-MYTH MASTERY PROGRAM PROCESSES ON MARKETING LEADERSHIP

Your Most Probable Customer: Identifying Your Target Markets

■

Marketing starts with the customer.

No, that's not quite right. *Everything* starts with the customer. Everything about your business has to be focused on providing products, services, and communications that draw customers to you, satisfy them, and bring them back to you again and again. It's no exaggeration—your business lives and dies on its ability to attract and satisfy customers.

The foundation of your marketing strategy is an insightful understanding of your customers. It's a "three-legged stool"—who they are, where they are, and how they think and behave; or, more formally, demographics, trading area, and psychographics. This business development process focuses on the first leg of the stool—who your customers are.

TARGET MARKETING AND THE NEED FOR FOCUS

"Market" is a generic word used to describe any grouping of people or organizations who are or might become customers for your products and services. But not everyone is a customer for your products. Your products are perfect for some kinds of people, completely inappropriate for other people, and so-so for others.

If you had the ability to "target" only those who are most likely to buy—your most probable customers—think how successful your business could be! You could direct all your marketing efforts specifically to people who are likely to buy, rather than to a wide spectrum of people, many of whom are not likely buyers.

The first step in developing your marketing strategy, then, is to identify your target market. And that's what this process is all about. You're going to look at your overall market and identify its various subgroups, or "market seg-

Your Most Probable Customer

Overview

Marketing starts with the customer.

Effective marketing depends on identifying the customers and prospective customers who will produce the best results for your business, then focusing your marketing activities on them. It's called "target" marketing.

Your most probable customer—your primary target market—is the focal point of your marketing strategy. By dedicating your business to the satisfaction of that customer, you set the stage for success in the market, financial well-being, and competitive advantage.

Key Points

Market "segmentation" is the process of grouping your customers and prospective customers according to their common characteristics, and targeting the segments that produce the best results for your business.

The product-market grid is a tool for market segmentation that takes into account your customers' view of the product, as well as the characteristics of customers in the market segment.

A target market segment is one that has a high probability of purchasing your products and for which you have selected for focused marketing activities.

Your most important target market is your "primary" target market. Other, less important target markets are called "flanker" markets.

A market segment is best described in terms of its demographic characteristics in the form of a Central Demographic Model, or CDM.

Central Demographic Model Characteristics

For people:
Age
Gender
Occupation
Household income
Employment status
Education
Marital status
Family status
Location
Race
Ethnicity
Physical characteristics

For organizations:
Industry
Product line(s)
Size of business
Type of business
Location(s)
Geographic coverage
Financial status

Process for Identifying Your Target Markets

Set Up Product-Market Grid for Your Business

List Products or Services on One Axis of the Grid

List Customer Types on the Other Axis

Fill In Sales, Units Sold, and Profit Margins for Each Segment

Designate Primary Target Market and Flanker Markets

Create Central Demographic Model for Primary and Flanker Markets

ments" as they are called. Then you're going to evaluate them and select the market segment which will produce the best results for your business (that's your "primary market segment") and any other market segments that will produce desirable results (those are your "flanker market segments").

Before we get into "market segmentation," think for a moment about how you describe a market segment. What enables you to differentiate one market segment from another, while enabling you to identify the specific prospective customers you want to attract to your business and your products? The language of market segmentation is demographics, and you are already familiar with it.

DEMOGRAPHICS—
THE MEASURABLE CHARACTERISTICS OF YOUR
CUSTOMERS AND PROSPECTIVE CUSTOMERS

You use demographics all the time. Every time you speak of someone's address, age, income, college degree, the size of a neighbor's family, or the recent divorce of a friend, you're speaking the language of demographics. Demographics are the objective, directly observable characteristics that describe people and organizations. From your viewpoint as a business owner, demographics are the tangible facts that identify and describe your customers and prospective customers. Demographics of people include:

Age
Employment status
Location
Gender
Education
Race
Occupation
Marital status
Ethnicity
Income
Family status
Physical characteristics

For business and commercial customers, you must keep in mind that a person (not a business) makes the buying decision. Still, the decision process is different for organizations and is influenced by additional factors depending on the nature of the organization. The demographics of organizations include:

Industry
Product line
Size of business (sales, number of employees, etc.)
Type of business (manufacturer, distributor, retailer, etc.)
Location (headquarters and branches/operating locations)
Geographic scope of the business (local, regional, national, international)
Financial status of the business (revenues, profitability, leverage, etc.)

Use the *Central Demographic Model* worksheet and the *Customer Demographic Questionnaire* to help you determine your central demographic model.

Download

DEFINING YOUR CENTRAL DEMOGRAPHIC MODEL

Every market segment has a Central Demographic Model (CDM). The CDM is nothing more than a description, in demographic terms, of the typical or average person in the segment. Each market segment has its own CDM, but you are interested mainly in the CDM for your primary target market and your important flanker markets. In fact, it's a common practice to refer to the CDM for your primary target market as the CDM, and to the others as flanker models.

Later in this chapter you will add a Central *Psychographic* Model to your description. The "CPM" will pinpoint the way the customer thinks, perceives, and makes purchasing decisions. But that's for later. Let's stick with CDM for now.

The box on page 130 shows an example of a Central Demographic Model for a hypothetical furniture store serving upscale customers (notice that not all demographic indicators may be relevant to every target market).

Where can you get the demographic information you need?

The best source is objective, professional market research. If that's too expensive, you'll have to do your own research based on customer surveys and observation. Here are some good sources of demographic information:

Formal approaches

- Use professional market research firms.
- Get free information from sources such as:

Department of Commerce	Chamber of Commerce
Small Business Bureau	State and local governments
Bureau of Labor Statistics	Local newspapers

AGE	**40 TO 55**
GENDER	Couples; female is primary decision maker
OCCUPATION	Managerial, professional, sales, business owners
INCOME	Over $80,000 annual household income
EMPLOYMENT STATUS	Employed; high proportion of two-earner households
EDUCATION	College degree; high proportion of graduate degrees
MARITAL STATUS	Married
FAMILY STATUS	Traditional families with children
LOCATION	Boston Metropolitan Area
RACE	Not relevant
ETHNICITY	Not relevant
PHYSICAL CHARACTERISTICS	Not relevant

Census Bureau   Library reference sections
The Internet

- Have customers complete a demographics questionnaire.
- Conduct a telephone survey.

Informal approaches

- Collect data in-house through observation of your customers. Ask a few well-placed questions to get the information that can't be observed. Document your findings.
- Use the *Customer Demographics Questionnaire* to document your findings.
- Gather data on a monthly basis during seasonally different months of the year.

Download

THE PROCESS FOR IDENTIFYING YOUR PRIMARY TARGET MARKET AND YOUR FLANKER MARKETS

The steps to identifying your target markets and defining them in terms of a Central Demographic Model are:

1. **Set up a product-market grid for your business.** The product-market grid is a market segmentation method that takes into account both the customer and the product.

2. **List on one axis the products or services you sell *as they are perceived by your customers*.** Describe them in terms that differentiate them in the eyes of your customers.

3. **List on the other axis the various types of customers you serve.** You don't have to worry about detailed demographics or the CDM yet, just use descriptive phrases to identify your markets, such as "upscale households with children," or "fast-food restaurants."

4. **Fill in information for each segment in the boxes of the grid.** Define your product-market segments in terms of their importance to your business, usually by entering the dollars of revenue, the unit volume of sales, and the profit margins generated by each segment.

5. **Designate your primary target market and your flanker markets.** Select your most important segment and designate it as your primary target market. If you have other important segments, designate them as flanker markets.

6. **Create the Central Demographic Model for your primary target market,** as well as for each flanker market by providing a complete demographic profile of each. You may have to do some research. You may also have to establish tentative CDMs until you learn more about your markets.

Process for Identifying Your Target Markets

Set Up Product-Market Grid for Your Business

List Products or Services on One Axis of the Grid

List Customer Types on the Other Axis

Fill In Sales, Units Sold, & Profit Margins for Each Segment

Designate Primary Target Market & Flanker Markets

Create Central Demographic Model for Primary & Flanker Markets

SEGMENT OF THE MARKET USING THE PRODUCT-MARKET GRID

Although the term is often used for convenience, there is really no such thing as "the market." Instead, the market is a collection of smaller groups, or "segments," each of which is different from the others in some important respect. It's not to your advantage to pursue every segment in the market, but only those which constitute your "bread-and-butter" customers. When you create your marketing strategy, you'll want to get the greatest possible yield from your efforts. You'll want to focus on the market segments with the highest probability of buying your products. That way you'll avoid the ineffective process of selling to large numbers of people who don't need or want them. Begin the process of segmenting your market by taking a closer look at your products, your markets, and the relationship between the two.

DEFINE YOUR PRODUCTS AS YOUR
CUSTOMERS VIEW THEM

As you work through the E-Myth Mastery Program, your business as a whole will become the "product" that attracts and retains customers. As the E-Myth point of view says, "Your business, not your commodity, is your product." Keep this perspective in mind as you build your business.

In the more generic sense, however, products are what your company offers for sale. Products can be things, services, or a combination. When you define your products, you describe what they are and what they do.

Let's take a man who sells doughnuts, for example. One product. Simple, right? Well, not really. Does he sell doughnuts over the counter for walk-in customers? Does he sell packaged doughnuts to grocery stores for them to sell to their customers? Does he sell bulk doughnuts to restaurants for resale to their customers? Does he sell coffee and doughnut setups for business meetings?

You get the point. It's not enough to say you sell doughnuts and let it go at that. You have to identify each product that is distinctly different from the others you offer, taking the customer's viewpoint into account.

Let's look at it from another angle.

DEFINE YOUR MARKETS
WITH YOUR PRODUCTS IN MIND

You know that our doughnut shop owner sells to walk-in customers, to local businesses, and to grocery stores, but unless you know which product he offers to which market segment, you really don't know enough about his markets. Single doughnuts are a different product from packaged doughnuts and bulk doughnuts are a different product from the other two. The basic item is the same—doughnuts—but the product depends on how it is offered to the customer. It's of no use to think about your markets unless, at the same time, you think about the products you provide to those markets.

THINK IN TERMS OF PRODUCT-MARKET SETS

The nature of a product depends on the needs and preferences of the customers (the market segments) to whom you sell the product. You don't sell doughnuts to an Overeaters Anonymous group. Similarly, the nature of the market to which you want to sell determines the kinds of products you will sell . . . or it should. If your shop is in a lower-income neighborhood, you probably wouldn't sell fancy, expensive pastries.

In the real world, you can't isolate the product from the market, so it makes sense to recognize reality and think in terms of your company's product-market sets.

CREATE YOUR PRODUCT-MARKET GRID

The product-market grid is a simple device. You set up a grid with product types on one axis and market segments (customer types) along the other. If you have a simple business like a doughnut shop that only serves walk-in customers, your grid has only one product-market set. If your doughnut shop has a little more scope, like the one in our example, it will have more product-market sets. It's not uncommon, even for a small business, to have numerous product-market sets and not be aware of all of them. For the best result, consider all possible combinations. To set up your product-market grid, see the *Product-Market Grid* worksheet. **Download**

What goes in the boxes? You have some options here. You can use any kind of information that will help you understand which product-market sets do the best job of moving you toward your Strategic Objective. Usually that will include estimates of your sales, the number of units sold, and the profit margin

MARKETS → / PRODUCTS ↓	Walk-in Customers	Grocery Stores	Local Businesses
Single Doughnuts			
Packaged Doughnuts			
Bulk Sale Doughnuts			
Doughnut & Coffee Setup			

for each segment. But you are not constrained to those three pieces of information if additional information will help you select the "best" market segments for your business. Also, you can use actual information based on business you have done in the past or are currently doing, or you can make projections based on your future plans. In the doughnut shop example continued below, the figures are actual numbers from the most recent full year.

Products	Markets		
	Walk-in Customers	Grocery Store	Local Business
Doughnut & Coffee Special 75¢ donut; 25¢ coffee (200% profit)	# Sold: 38,000 $38,000	No Market	# Sold: 65,000 $65,000
Single Doughnut 50¢ each (100% profit)	# Sold: 370,000 $185,000	No Market	No Market
Packaged Doughnuts $5 for 12 = 42¢ each (68% profit)	# Sold: 5,600 $28,000	# Sold: 56,000 $280,000	# Sold: 7,000 $35,000
Bulk Sale Doughnuts $8 for 24 = 34¢ each (36% profit)	# Sold: 1,250 $10,000	# Sold: 9,375 $75,000	# Sold: 5,625 $45,000

It's clear from the grid that this company's sales have been concentrated in two product-market sets—packaged doughnuts to grocery stores (probably their primary target market) and single doughnuts to walk-in customers (their most productive flanker market).

Don't hesitate to add your common sense to the numbers. For instance, what if you knew that single doughnuts to walk-in customers had double the profit margins of packaged doughnuts to grocery stores? Would that make a difference to you? What if coffee and doughnuts setups for local businesses had the highest margins of all, and a new business park was about to open nearby?

The product-market grid is a great tool to help you run some important numbers, and just as important, it helps you organize the way you think and make decisions about your business.

Now try it for yourself with your own product-market grid.

DEFINE THE CENTRAL DEMOGRAPHIC MODELS FOR YOUR PRIMARY AND FLANKER MARKETS

The last step in identifying your target markets—your primary and flanker market segments—is to create a profile of the demographic characteristics of each market segment, its CDM. You saw how to do that at the beginning of this process.

HAVING TROUBLE WITH TERMINOLOGY? HERE IT IS IN A NUTSHELL.

Market: A generic term for any grouping of people who are or might become customers for your products and services. It is often carelessly used in place of the more specific terms listed below. "The market" is often used as a term for the total population of customers and potential customers.

Demographics: The observable, measurable characteristics that identify and describe populations of people and organizations.

Market segment: A subgroup within the market whose members have common characteristics, such as similar demographics, attitudes, or behavior patterns. For instance, households with children are an important market segment of the American population. College-educated, female, high-income, long-distance runners over the age of 40 with 2 or more children are a narrow segment of the same market.

Market segmentation: Analysis of a market, or of a market segment, into smaller groupings, each having common demographic and psychographic characteristics. The purpose is so that marketing, sales, and product development can be focused and more productive.

Product-market grid: A refinement of market segmentation that takes the product, as perceived by the customer, into account. A matrix or grid, with products and major variants listed along one axis and market segments listed along the other axis. The cells of the grid contain information describing each "product-market set." The grid enables you to compare and evaluate product-market sets based on the information you use to fill the cells.

Target market (also target market segment): A market segment you have selected or "targeted" for active marketing and sales.

Primary market (also primary target market segment and primary market segment): Your most important target market segment; the one to which you dedicate the most resources and effort, and from which you expect the best results.

Flanker market (also flanker target market segment): Market segments of lesser importance than your primary market, but still important enough to justify targeting for marketing and sales.

Central Demographic Model (CDM): A description, in demographic terms, of any group, population, or market segment. It focuses on the mainstream or "central" characteristics common to the group which distinguish it from any other group. Every market segment has its own CDM, although it is common to use the term "the CDM" to mean the CDM for your primary market.

The CDM of each segment is the key to pinpointing and reaching your most probable customers. The CDM tells you where they are and who they are, and even gives you some preliminary insights into the ways they probably think and behave.

IT'S A WAY TO WORK SMARTER

Too often business owners don't realize the power behind identifying their most desirable customers and targeting sales and marketing efforts to draw those customers to them. As a business owner, your responsibility is to make your business work for you and your employees in a way that will provide the best possible return on your investment. Knowing who your best customers are gives you a head start in working smarter, not harder.

Customer Perceptions and Behavior: Understanding How Your Customers Think and Make Decisions

■

The human mind is anything but simple.

But the mind is where marketing happens for you and your customers. So in order to do an effective job marketing your products and your company, you have to get an insightful understanding of the minds of your customers. The good news is that it's fascinating, and you'll enjoy the discoveries and insights you develop about your customers and yourself.

Where do you start?

You start by understanding the basics about how your customers' minds work, and how you can influence them for their benefit and yours. First, you'll develop the Central Psychographic Model, the CPM, for your primary target market and important flanker markets. Then you'll look at purchase decision making and something we call the Purchase Decision Chain, which will lead you to an understanding of customer needs and behavior and how best to communicate with customers.

The work you do in this business development process requires a great deal of in-depth thinking about some ideas that may be unfamiliar, possibly challenging, probably fun, and certainly valuable. You'll develop insights about your customers and target markets that will shape everything your company does. You'll put those insights to use immediately in the next three business development processes. You'll create your company's "sensory package" (the total

Customer Perceptions and Behavior

UNDERSTANDING HOW YOUR CUSTOMERS THINK AND MAKE DECISIONS

Overview

Effective marketing requires a thorough understanding of the way your customers' minds work—how they perceive themselves and the world, how they think, how they make purchase decisions.

You gain this understanding by studying the psychographics of your target markets, creating a Central Psychographic Model (CPM), and applying that knowledge to the Purchase Decision Chain in order to influence the buying behavior of your target market(s).

Psychographics are people's mental characteristics; specifically, their perceptions, their expectations, and their conscious and unconscious decision making.

A CPM is a written description of the key mental and emotional characteristics typical of the people in a market segment.

The Purchase Decision Chain identifies the key points in the decision process where you can influence the customer's decision for your mutual benefit.

The Central Psychographic Model

Psychographic characteristics of a market segment:

- **Self-perceptions:** How people see themselves, their personal image and their values.

- **External perceptions:** How they see the world around them and what they expect from it.

- **Drives:** What motivates them – their functional and emotional needs.

- **Emotional associations:** The unconscious associations they make.

- **Gratification mode:** The dominant way they get gratification in their lives.

- **Purchase preference:** The dominant justification they use for their purchases.

Key Points

Perception is reality. What the customer perceives, correctly or not, is real for that person.

People have, in effect, two minds: the conscious and the unconscious. The conscious mind is rational and logical. It is concerned with features and benefits—the way products and services perform, what they cost, what they do for you.

The unconscious mind is emotional and irrational. It seeks gratification. It is concerned with the way products and services make you feel.

Purchasing decisions are actually made by the unconscious mind. The conscious mind later provides the rational armament that justifies the purchase.

The Purchase Decision Chain

Awareness

↓

Purchase Motivation

↓

Product Acceptance

↓

Brand Preference

↓

Purchase Transaction

↓

Customer Satisfaction

impact of sight, sound, smell, touch, and taste that your customers experience of your business and its products and services). You'll establish your "positioning" (the place you want your company to occupy in the minds of your customers). You'll select your "marketing mix" (the specific communications, sales, delivery, and customer service activities you will use to attract and retain customers). And finally, you'll combine these elements to develop your marketing strategy. The knowledge and insights you gain in this work will be essential later when you create your lead generation and lead conversion processes. Don't be in a hurry. Take the time you need to get to the core of your customers. It will pay off handsomely—for both you and them.

So let's get to it.

WATCH OUT FOR THE "FATAL ASSUMPTIONS"

There are two "fatal assumptions" that can get in your way as you try to understand the minds of your target market customers—marketing to yourself and being too product-oriented. Marketing to yourself means thinking your customers think and act as you think and act. If you have ever said, "The way *I* would do it is . . . ," or "What I would want is . . . ," or "The way they *should* think is . . . ," then you have been guilty of marketing to yourself.

Being too product-oriented means thinking more about your products and their specifications, and less about what your customers need and how to communicate with them. It's thinking backward. The idea that "I'll create a product and then go out and sell it" is the product-oriented approach, and it's a poor one. The idea that "I'll learn what the market needs, then I'll create the product to satisfy that need" is the customer-oriented approach, and it's the more effective approach. Product-oriented thinking also means focusing your marketing and sales activities on the features of your product or service, rather than on the emotional gratification it provides your customers.

PERCEPTION IS REALITY

In marketing, there is no such thing as reality; only *perceived* reality. What the customer, or anyone else for that matter, perceives is what is *real* for that person. What the customer's mind perceives, accurately or inaccurately, is the truth in the eye of that customer. What the customer's mind doesn't perceive, in effect, doesn't exist. And perception rules all decision making, including of course, purchasing decisions. So much so that you could define marketing as "the art of managing customer perceptions."

The key to successful marketing is to provide the gratification the customer seeks. If this happens, it is a "win-win" situation. There is a different approach to marketing that should be discouraged because it benefits neither the customer nor the business serving the customer. It's the view that one should manipulate customer perceptions in order to make a sale, using any method that works, without regard to the customer's welfare. Ethical questions aside, it's a counterproductive approach to business. Customers always come to realize what is happening and turn away from the selfishly manipulative marketer. In the end, ethical marketing is practical marketing. If customers' perceived needs and preferences are served, the business wins. If not, it loses.

A TALE OF TWO MINDS

Imagine for a moment that you have a pair of tiny twins living inside your head. Their names are "Impulse" and "Reason." They do all your thinking for you, all your feeling, all your perceiving. They are your mind, but there are two of them—and they couldn't be more different from each other.

Impulse speaks no language, understands no words, has no ability to reason. She has no sense of right or wrong. She wants gratification; she avoids pain. She feels desire and fear. She is the ultimate amoral pleasure seeker as well as the ultimate avoider of anything unpleasant. She can be embarrassed, she has a sense of pride and shame, and when she's done something wrong, she is remorseful. She is always completely honest, straightforward—there's no deception in her. She is pure passion, emotion, and impulsive instinct. And she wants everything *now.*

Reason reads, writes, and does arithmetic. She is logical and rational. She seeks facts, information, knowledge, understanding. She is not passionless, but her passions are rational and follow her reasoning. She makes unemotional judgments about good and bad, right and wrong, ethical and unethical, moral and immoral, should do and shouldn't do, can do and can't do, valuable and valueless. But she can't be embarrassed because she has no sense of shame, and she is never remorseful. She thinks, she reasons, she judges, but she doesn't feel.

They're an interesting pair, these little twins, but the most interesting thing is that Impulse is the decision maker of the two. Believe it or not, every decision you make is made by Impulse. That's right, the little crazy person is making all your decisions. Unsettling isn't it?

Well, it's not really all that unsettling because Reason has a lot to say about it. The two of them work together in a very productive way. They both perceive through the senses—sight, sound, touch, smell, and taste. Reason takes whatever meaning is inherent in what it perceives and logically processes it, adding no emotion, drawing conclusions. The result is passed along to Impulse who interprets the result in terms of expected gratification or pain, and reacts emotionally. Impulse provides the emotional response to Reason's rational conclusions and judgments. Meanwhile, Impulse is also using her sensory perceptions to make associations with past experience and bring forth the emotions they trigger. So Reason deals in information and judgment while Impulse deals in associations and emotions. The more information Reason can bring to her judgments, the stronger her influence on a decision. The more associations and impressions Impulse can make, the stronger her influence.

THE CONSCIOUS MIND AND
THE UNCONSCIOUS MIND

The little twins are real. Of course they're not creatures inhabiting your skull; they are the two aspects of your mind. Reason is your conscious mind and Impulse is your unconscious mind. They exist in all of us. They are the key to the way we think, perceive, and make decisions. And they are the key to understanding and communicating with your customers and prospective customers.

If your marketing is to be successful, you have to communicate with *both* of them. And that's where most businesses fall short. They communicate mostly with Reason, and she's not the decision maker.

UNCONSCIOUS ASSOCIATIONS

Associations are as important as they are mysterious and unpredictable. Your mind—anybody's mind—makes associations that rule your behavior and the way you perceive the world. Impulse is the twin responsible for associations. Associations can be triggered by the most trivial perceptions as well as by major events. For example, a middle-aged man doing yard work hears the rustle of fallen leaves. He perceives the sound and unconsciously associates it with the rustle of papers at an award ceremony at which he was the guest of honor. He doesn't consciously remember the award ceremony, but he smiles and momentarily feels good because the association triggered pleasant emotions. Here's another, more dramatic example. A young woman—an ice-cream lover—is walking home one evening eating an ice-cream cone. Suddenly she is attacked by a couple of dogs. To this day, more than 15 years later, she can't bring herself to eat ice cream. Her unconscious mind has created an indelible association between ice cream and brutality, pain, and fear. It's an extreme example to be sure, but it makes the point.

Marketers seek to create associations favorable to their products or take advantage of existing ones. Think, for instance, of the last time you saw a television commercial for perfume or beer or an automobile. Yes, the advertisement presented information, but the real thrust of the ad was to trigger an association in your unconscious mind linking the product with a pleasant experience or impression.

You never know exactly what associations your advertising, your product, or your sensory package are going to trigger with any specific individual—people's experiences and perceptions are much too varied. But you can tap into the common experiences and perceptions of *groups* of similar people and be confident that the associations will be pleasant or unpleasant for most of them. And that's what you do in your business communications and advertising. You understand your target markets in as much depth as you can, but at least to the extent that you know their major common experiences and the way they generally go about their lives. That tells you the kinds of things most likely to have positive associations. And that gives you insights into the kinds of messages and images your advertising should carry, the way you should interact with customers, and the kind of sensory experience your customers should have when they do business with your company.

The idea, of course, is that if you have an in-depth understanding of your customers and how they make their purchasing decisions, you can influence their decisions for your mutual benefit. So let's take all this background information and put it into a framework that will help you understand customer decision making and enable you to establish the psychological profile—the Central Psychographic Model (CPM)—for each of your target markets.

ATTRACTION AND AVOIDANCE—
THE ESSENCE OF PURCHASE DECISIONS

A purchase decision, or any decision for that matter, is simply the emotional response to all the rational and not-so-rational activities in the conscious and unconscious mind. Yes, decisions are made emotionally by the unconscious mind, but with full attention to both conscious and unconscious perceptions, associations, logic, and judgments.

It's all a matter of attraction and avoidance. The conscious mind is drawn to purchases that make sense, are rational, and have objectively desirable results. It is repelled by purchases that are irrational and have objectively undesirable results. The unconscious mind is drawn to purchases that result in emotional gratification. It is attracted by pleasant associations, pleasant sensory perceptions, and the promise of good results based on the conscious mind's conclusions and judgments. It avoids anything unpleasant.

CONSCIOUS MIND

Responds to facts, logic, price, capability, qualifications
Attracted to the rational; avoids the irrational

AVOIDANCE	NEUTRAL	ATTRACTION
Costs too much, poor value	No information	Good price, good value
Quality is poor		Quality is good
Judged to be "bad" (illegal, immoral, unethical)	Not relevant to me	Judged to be "good" (legal, moral, ethical)
Doesn't have the features I want		Has the features I want
Doesn't function as it should		Functions the way I want it to function
I don't have the ability to use it		I have the necessary expertise or aptitude
Purchase transaction is difficult		Purchase transaction is easy

UNCONSCIOUS MIND

Responds to sensory stimuli, impressions, associations
Attracted to gratification/pleasure; avoids pain/stress

AVOIDANCE	NEUTRAL	ATTRACTION
Any unpleasant emotion	Indifferent, who cares?	Anything that makes you feel good physically or emotionally without regard to right or wrong
Distress or fear of any kind		
Sense of insecurity, inadequacy	No past associations	
Ridicule, embarrassment	No sensory or emotional impact	Beauty, excitement, accomplishment, clarity, belonging, admiration, power, victory
Physical discomforts		
Association with past unpleasantness		
Ugliness, boredom, confusion, isolation		Relief from fear, stress, guilt, sense of obligation
		Association with past pleasures and positive experiences

The next diagram is a good way to understand the interplay of unconscious/conscious mind and the push-pull of attraction/avoidance in the decision-making process. It's pretty simple. First you draw a blank diagram with one axis for "conscious" and another axis for "unconscious." Label each axis "attraction" at one end and "avoidance" at the other.

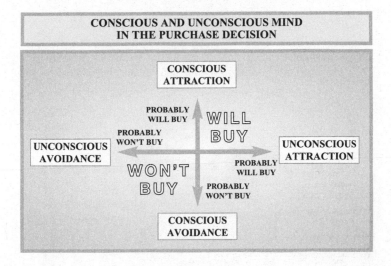

CONSCIOUS AND UNCONSCIOUS MIND
IN THE PURCHASE DECISION

If all reactions of the conscious mind and the unconscious mind make the purchase attractive, the decision will be to purchase. Similarly, if reactions of both minds are avoidance, the decision will be not to purchase. Most of the time, however, there is a complex interplay of reactions, with the purchase decision depending on the balance between attraction and avoidance.

It's best understood by following an example. Think of a man, call him Jack, deciding whether or not to buy a cashmere sweater that's more expensive than is usual for him. Jack's internal thought process won't be as neat and orderly as our diagram suggests, and much of it won't be conscious or in any particular sequence, but the perceptions that influence him are captured in a way that lets you see the interplay of conscious-unconscious and attraction-avoidance.

Starting at the neutral point in the center, follow the arrows and their "thought bubbles" to get a feeling for Jack's train of conscious and unconscious thoughts. Jack's first thought is "Hmm, pretty expensive." That's a conscious avoidance, but not a strong one, so you make a dot a little ways down the conscious axis in the direction of avoidance.

Next, Jack has a couple of negative feelings about the sweater. He doesn't consciously think about them, but unconsciously he registers an association of cashmere with snobbery; another with his extremely unpleasant uncle, George. The snobbery impression is a minor one, hence a short line in the direction of unconscious avoidance. Jack really dislikes Uncle George, so a longer line for that impression. He consciously notes the brand and workmanship of the sweater, and concludes that it is of very high quality and will probably last a long time. He also sees that he can buy it on his credit card, thus easing his fi-

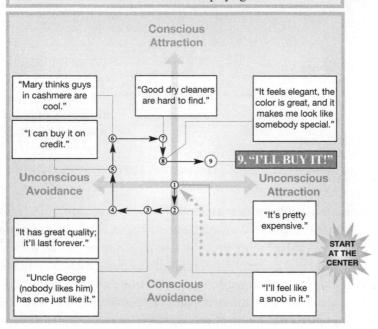

EXAMPLE: DECIDING TO BUY AN EXPENSIVE CASHMERE SWEATER

Start at the center and see how the attractions and avoidances of the conscious and unconscious mind play against each other.

nancial concerns—two more lines along the conscious axis in the direction of attraction.

Jack briefly pictures himself wearing the sweater in the company of his girlfriend, Mary, and the mental image sets off another association having to do with Mary's view of guys in cashmere. Jack smiles and is strongly influenced in favor of the sweater—a longish line in the direction of unconscious attraction. He has a passing thought about the need to find a good dry cleaner—a conscious avoidance. Jack tries on the sweater, and it makes him feel great and (in his own mind) look great—another long line for unconscious attraction. The end result, the balance of all those conscious and unconscious attractions and avoidances, is that Jack buys the sweater, with only minor misgivings.

So what does Jack's decision have to do with *your* marketing? More than you might think.

If, instead of Jack the individual, you think in terms of your primary target market, and if, instead of Jack's perceptions and associations, you think in terms of the collective perceptions and associations of your target market CDM, you now have a model for the purchase decisions of your customers.

PSYCHOGRAPHICS AND THE
CENTRAL PSYCHOGRAPHIC MODEL

Remember the three-legged stool that forms the foundation of your marketing strategy? You have looked at "who buys" (demographics) and "where they buy" (trading area) of your markets. Now it's time to build the third leg of the stool—"why they buy" (psychographics).

Psychographics refers to the psychological characteristics of populations, or in this case, of market segments. *Merriam-Webster's Collegiate Dictionary* says that psychology is the science of mental processes and behavior, or the emotional and behavioral characteristics of an individual or group. Let's take this definition a step further and define it in a way that is useful for marketing purposes.

Psychographics are the mental characteristics that typify the people in markets and market segments; specifically, their self-perceptions, their drives, their perceptions and expectations of the world around them, and their emotional associations.

Just as each market segment has a Central Demographic Model, or CDM, each segment also has a Central *Psychographic* Model, or CPM. The CPM of a market segment is a profile of the psychographic characteristics typical of people in the segment. There are six types of psychographic characteristics you should know to better understand your customers:

- Self-perceptions
- External perceptions
- Drives
- Emotional associations
- Gratification mode
- Purchase preference

The CPM characteristics are explained below, and there is a *Central Psychographic Model* worksheet to help you develop CPMs for your target market segments.

Download

Self-perceptions. People's self-perceptions have to do with their personal image and values. If they are satisfied with their self-perceptions, marketing messages that reinforce satisfaction are likely to hold the promise of emotional gratification and create attraction for your products and your business. If they are not content with their self-perceptions, messages that promise improvement are likely to generate a sense of emotional gratification and create attraction. There are two categories of people's self-perceptions:

- **Personal image** includes perceptions of your role in life, social status, economic class, special abilities (or inabilities), and distinguishing characteristics. People have either healthy personal images (nowadays they are said to have "high self-esteem") or unhealthy personal images (low self-esteem). Marketing messages should reinforce healthy personal images and promise improvement of unhealthy personal images. Personal image is the answer to the question "What kind of person are you?"
- **Personal values** are an important part of personal image, but they also include the element of interaction with others and preferences for the way the world interacts with you. Values include personal characteristics such as integrity, honesty, thrift, sense of responsibility, loyalty, generosity, and love. Values also include the importance you place on things such as family, friendships, career, material possessions, physical and emotional well-being, community, faith, and the environment. Marketing messages and any interactions with your business should be consistent with the dominant values of the market. Values are the answers to the question "What's important to you in life?"

External perceptions. People perceive the world around them in different ways. Some see it as a warm, friendly place while others see it as threatening, ready to do them harm at every turn. For instance, some customers view a salesperson as someone out to take advantage, someone who will sell them anything to earn a commission. Others see salespeople as helpful sources of information and guidance. Knowing customer perceptions, both good and bad, tells you a lot about their expectations. This helps you position your business in their minds and develop the most effective communications and ways of interacting with customers and prospects. Three categories of external perceptions are:

- **Environmental.** Is the world a safe place? Do they expect the best or the worst? Do good things or bad things tend to happen to them?
- **Behavioral.** Do they expect people to treat them well; with respect, in a friendly, helpful way? Do they view business people as helpful, friendly, and useful versus cold, unfriendly, and incompetent? Do they expect products and services to function as advertised, or do they expect shoddy products and shabby treatment?
- **Motivational.** Do they perceive others as "out to get them" or interested in their welfare? Do they expect salespeople to be after their money versus just being helpful? Are businesses caring and ethical or cold and greedy?

Drives. What is it that compels a person to take action? Physical and emotional needs? Desires? Obligations? Fears? Whatever it is, it's a drive. Drives can be positive (attraction) or negative (avoidance), but not neutral. Neutral has no emotional charge, leads nowhere, and prompts no action. And if a customer's drive has anything to do with purchasing, it's of enormous interest to you and your business.

Drives are either functional (the need or desire for something tangible) or emotional, and even functional drives are emotional at their most basic level. Take the functional drive of hunger, for example. Hunger is the need for food, of course, but at the more fundamental level, hunger is a desire for the pleasure of a good meal, or the need to relieve the unpleasant empty feeling in your belly, or in the extreme, the need to eliminate the fear of death—all emotional gratifications. So acknowledge functional needs and make sure your products and services satisfy them, but more important, understand the more fundamental emotional needs, and be doubly sure to satisfy them.

- **Functional needs** are what the conscious mind understands. They are satisfied by the tangible aspects of your products and services. What must your products *do* for your customers? What functions must they perform? What physical features must be present? How must they work?
- **Emotional/internal needs** drive the unconscious mind. They are the impulse for emotional gratification (and buying!). More powerful than functional needs, emotional needs underlie every functional need.

Emotional associations. What emotional associations are likely within this market segment, and what is likely to trigger them? You can't read minds and you can't know precisely what associations are true for your target markets, but you can learn about their typical histories and behaviors, inferring what communications and sensory impressions are *likely* to trigger emotional associations. And you can focus on what is likely to provide emotional gratification, avoiding what might trigger its opposite—emotional discomfort.

- **Positive associations** are those that trigger emotional gratification. Communications and sensory impressions that remind people of joyful events in their lives, or of wonderful sensory experiences (food, music, sex, athletics, luxurious comfort, etc.), or of achieving cherished fantasies.
- **Negative associations** are those that trigger emotional discomfort. If you are not attentive to communications and sensory impressions, you run the risk of inadvertently triggering negative emotional responses,

creating avoidance rather than attraction for your products and your business.

Be careful. Sometimes what is joyful for one market segment is unpleasant for another. Shopping for clothing is a happy, stimulating activity for some, an unpleasant labor for others. Running a marathon is a joy for some, unthinkable torture for others. Holding a newborn baby is deeply satisfying for some, uncomfortable for others. Attending an opera or symphony—entertaining for some, boring for others.

Gratification mode. There are three ways that people get gratification in their lives:

- **Interpersonal.** Their gratifications come primarily through interactions with other people.
- **Objective.** Their gratifications come primarily through interacting with inanimate objects or data.
- **Introverted.** Their gratifications come primarily from interacting with ideas in a solitary fashion.

Everyone gets gratification in all three ways, but usually one gratification mode dominates for any individual. For instance, even the most strongly interpersonal types occasionally take time to be alone with their thoughts or do something by themselves.

Individually, it's easy to observe which mode dominates a person by observing how they spend their time. But how can you determine the dominant mode for different market segments? The best way is through market research done by professional researchers. The next best way is to do your own research and observation. Another way, not quite as reliable as doing research but fairly quick, is to look at the mix of occupations in the market segment. People with different modes of gratification tend to settle into occupations that provide opportunities for their preferred type of gratification. You can use occupation as a fairly reliable indicator until you are able to complete the necessary market research. If you recall your earlier work on *"your most probable customer,"* occupation was one of the demographic characteristics in your CDM for each target market segment. With that information in hand, it's a simple matter to look at your demographic data, see which occupations are prevalent in your target markets, and determine from that which is the dominant gratification mode. Remember each mode highlights where these buyers get their emotional gratifications. Here's a listing of the occupations that tend to correlate with each of the gratification modes:

INTERPERSONAL	OBJECTIVE	INTROVERTED
Actors, performers	Accountants	Artists
Athletes in team sports	Bankers	Athletes in individual sports
Attorneys who litigate	Career military officers	Dedicated hobbyists
Consultants	Corporate attorneys	Designers (nonengineering)
Homemakers	Data processors	Elected politicians
Marketing executives	Engineers	Entrepreneurs
Physicians with people contact	Insurance executives	Inventors
Salespeople	Investment and stock brokerage personnel	Police officers
Secretaries		
Teachers	Manual laborers	
	Middle managers	
	Physicians with little or no people contact	
	Researchers	
	Senior managers in large companies	

Purchase preference. There are also three general reasons customers use to rationally justify the purchases they make. Remember that customers make purchase decisions based on unconscious-mind expectations of emotional gratification, but they explain those decisions, to themselves and others, in conscious-mind, rational terms. Here are the three general purchase preferences that indicate why customers buy:

- **Experimental.** These customers want products and services that are new, revolutionary, innovative. This purchase preference is most commonly associated with Interpersonal buyers.
- **Performance.** These customers want something reliable, dependable, of proven quality. This purchase preference is usually associated with Objective buyers.
- **Value.** These customers want something "worth the money." They either want the best price or the best sense of value in their purchases. This purchase preference is most often associated with Introverted buyers.

As with the gratification modes, everyone is concerned with all three preferences to some degree, but one preference dominates. And again, the best way to discover the prevailing purchase preference for any market segment is through market research. As it happens, occupation is also a fairly good indicator of purchase preference, and you can do the same kind of occupational analysis of your target market segments for purchase preference as you did for gratification mode. Here is the listing of occupations that tend to correlate with each of the purchase preferences:

EXPERIMENTAL	PERFORMANCE	VALUE
Actors, performers	Attorneys	Accountants
Artists	Bankers	Entrepreneurs
Athletes	Career military officers	Homemakers (low income)
Consultants	Data processors	Manual laborers
Dedicated hobbyists	Engineers	Police officers
Designers (nonengineering)	Insurance executives	
Elected politicians	Investment and stock brokerage personnel	
Homemakers (middle-and high-income)	Middle managers	
Inventors	Physicians	
Marketing executives	Researchers	
Salespeople	Senior managers in large companies	
Secretaries	Teachers	

It's important to keep in mind that the type of product or service can have a significant influence on the purchase preference. For example, Interpersonal buyers are usually Experimental buyers. But what if you're selling veterinary care? Pet owners are generally most interested in maintaining the health of their pet. They want assurance that the veterinarian is dependable, reliable, and well qualified. In other words, they are most interested in Performance. This holds true no matter how Experimental they might be with other products and services.

HOW DO YOU KNOW FOR SURE WHAT GOES ON IN THE MINDS OF YOUR CUSTOMERS?

You don't. You never know for certain what is going on in the minds of people and how their inner selves truly work. Most people don't even know that about themselves. The best you can do is observe what your customers do, listen to what they say, and use your own common sense and knowledge of human nature to develop the insights you need. You do this all the time with all the people you know. The challenge here is to extend your existing talent to consider larger groups of people—your target markets.

You can also do formal market research, but be careful. Normally, professional market research is the best way to get reliable information about markets. But when it comes to the subtleties of the mind, it's not clear that market researchers are any more insightful than businesspeople. The problem is that most research consists of asking conscious-level questions to learn about unconscious-level psychographics. It's a moot question for most small business owners anyway because this kind of research tends to be difficult and more expensive than they can, or wish to, conduct.

Don't be afraid to trust your own judgment. Be careful not to "project" your own way of thinking so that you believe your customers think the same way you do. Be objective. Base your conclusions on what you see, hear, and read. Use this process as a guide to focus what you already know about your customers and your product or service to identify what your customers most want from your business. Your experience with people, your growing knowledge, your logic, and your intuition will keep you close to the mark.

THE PURCHASE DECISION CHAIN— HOW IT ALL COMES TOGETHER

You've done a lot of in-depth thinking and research into the minds of the people in your target markets, and it may not yet be clear how it all comes together, let alone how this will be of practical use in your business. Part of that question will be answered in a moment as you look at the Purchase Decision Chain. The rest will become clear as you put what you have learned to use in the next three business development processes.

A purchase decision is actually a series of interim decisions leading, if all goes well, to the actual payment for your product or service. The links of the Purchase Decision Chain are diagrammed on the next page. Let's first review the links in the chain. As we do, we'll see what happens in the customer's conscious and unconscious minds, and your role in shaping the sequence of events.

Awareness. People want to be generally aware of what's available to them in the marketplace. They don't want much information—just a few facts such as the company's name, product names, some general impressions of what the product does, rough ideas about its quality and price, and some feeling of whether or not the product is appropriate for them. The name and a few general impressions are all they need.

Awareness is more important than it seems. While customers are consciously satisfied with minimal information to keep them "aware," their unconscious minds are at work balancing attraction and avoidance, creating powerful expectations of gratification or discomfort. Often the purchase decision is made at this early stage, but the conscious mind doesn't know it yet. When that happens, the rest of the decision chain is spent confirming and reinforcing the decision and coming up with the rational armament the conscious mind needs to justify it.

A quick word about first impressions and "selective perception." Selective perception refers to the fact that people, once they form a good or bad impression about something or someone, are more alert to information that supports the initial impression. If prospective customers form favorable early impressions, their selective perceptions will tend to reinforce and confirm their views. That means favorable awareness greatly improves the likelihood of a sale, and of course, unfavorable awareness makes the sale a longshot.

The Purchase Decision Chain

Awareness

↓

Purchase Motivation

↓

Product Acceptance

↓

Brand Preference

↓

Purchase Transaction

↓

Customer Satisfaction

That's why you *must* think carefully about your lead generation activities—your advertising, public relations, the external appearance of your facilities, business cards, Yellow Pages listings, signage—all the things you do to create awareness in your market. You're doing much more than creating awareness, in many cases you're actually making the sale at the unconscious-mind level, and you often have minutes or less to make a favorable first impression. That alone tells you how important it is to develop an insightful understanding of the psychographics of your target markets. The importance redoubles as you move through the remaining links of the Purchase Decision Chain.

Purchase motivation. At some point prospective customers are motivated to purchase, or at least consider purchasing a product or service. Something triggers their drives—their functional and emotional needs—and they experience "I need," "I want," "I should," "I have to." These drives can be triggered by events in their lives, they can evolve slowly, or they can be stimulated by your lead generation activities. You can't *create* motivation, but you can often stimulate it and intensify it with effective lead generation.

Here's an example. Our friend Jack, happy with his new cashmere sweater, is about to purchase a new home. He's excited about it, but a little worried too, because it's in a beautiful, upscale neighborhood that has become a hunting ground for burglars in recent months. He is developing a functional need for some kind of protection, and a cluster of emotional needs centered around fear and possibilities of loss. So his growing sense of need is beginning to generate the motivation to "do something."

Before he decides on his own to look into insurance, which he eventually would have done, he receives a mail solicitation from Rock Insurance Company offering property insurance. The mailer does two things: It increases his sense of need, thus intensifying his motivation to "do something," and it provides direction by focusing his attention on a product (property insurance) and a brand (Rock Insurance Company).

Jack is already aware of property insurance and has a perception that it provides the kind of protection that would be useful to him, and he unconsciously experiences some mild, but positive, emotions having to do with security and being taken care of. He knows about Rock Insurance Company, having seen its advertising (although he hasn't paid much attention to it), and having heard occasional favorable comments about it. In short, Jack has a general awareness of property insurance and Rock Insurance Company; he has a need he hasn't yet filled; and his motivation to buy has been triggered and directed by the lead generation activity (the mailer) from Rock Insurance Company.

The point is that nothing happens unless the customer's motivation is stimulated, but when it is, you want your name to be the first one in the customer's mind, and you want it to be favorably perceived.

Product acceptance. Before customers will buy your *brand,* they have to decide on the *product* they want. Keep in mind the difference between *product* and *brand.* Product is generic, brand is specific. An automobile is a product, a Ford Taurus is a brand. Potato chips are a product, Lay's potato chips are a brand. The product/brand idea includes businesses. A restaurant is a product, Chez Panisse is a brand. An airline is a product, United Airlines is a brand. Customers first decide on the product, then the brand.

Keep this idea of product acceptance in mind. It provides you with some important ways to shape your marketing strategy, and you'll see it again later in this module. For the moment, it's sufficient to understand the types of product attributes you can shape to best serve your customers, and to remember that at their core, purchase decisions are always driven by expectations of emotional gratification.

The diagram on page 154 outlines six general types of product attributes—incidentally, these attributes also apply to your business as a whole. Notice that these are attributes *in the mind of the customer,* not innate

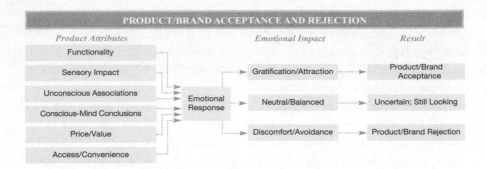

PRODUCT/BRAND ACCEPTANCE AND REJECTION

Product Attributes	Emotional Impact	Result
Functionality		
Sensory Impact	Gratification/Attraction	Product/Brand Acceptance
Unconscious Associations	Emotional Response	
Conscious-Mind Conclusions	Neutral/Balanced	Uncertain; Still Looking
Price/Value	Discomfort/Avoidance	Product/Brand Rejection
Access/Convenience		

properties of the product itself. Perception is reality. These perceived product attributes are the *only* product attributes that mean anything to the customer; therefore they are the only attributes that mean anything to your marketing strategy.

Our friend Jack was also approached by companies selling alternative products—a fireproofing service, a security patrolling service, and a security alarm service. The alternatives weren't exact substitutes for each other, but they all focused on some aspect of Jack's functional and emotional needs. In Jack's case, he quickly determined that property insurance was the product he needed.

Brand preference. Brand preference is determined by the customer's perceptions of which competing products are more appealing—which one promises the greatest emotional gratification.

Selecting from competing brands was tougher for Jack. All property insurance policies are pretty much alike, and they're hard to understand. He tried to compare six or seven of them, but he just got confused. He finally bought the Rock Insurance Company policy. When asked why, he said, "I just felt better about Rock. I don't know why."

From a marketing point of view, there is a difference between creating product acceptance and brand preference. Both can be illustrated with an example. Some years ago, Campbell's soup launched a major advertising campaign with the slogan "Soup is good food." They wanted people to think of soup as a main dish at mealtime, rather than something you occasionally have before a meal. The "Soup is good food" slogan plus advertisements that emphasized the hearty, mealtime nature of soup were an attempt to get customers to accept the *product,* soup, in a different way. Their advertising naturally focused on the Campbell's soup name as well, in order to maintain awareness and foster brand preference.

Purchase transaction. For some businesses, the purchase transaction itself is an important link in the chain. Insurance, especially medical and life insurance, is an extreme example. Forms, medical checkups, laboratory tests, long waiting times, more forms, and finally, a complicated policy document, all serve as a strong deterrent. Who wants to go through all that? It's only because the "attraction" aspects of medical coverage (functional and emotional needs) are so strong that the "avoidance" aspects do not overwhelm the decision.

Customer satisfaction. The customer's experience with the product or service takes place *after* the purchase, so why is it part of the Purchase Decision Chain? For two reasons. Satisfaction with one purchase leads to another. It's no secret that your best prospects are your existing customers. Unless you have no need for repeat business, you'd better make triple sure your customers are satisfied—*no, delighted!*—with your products and your customer service. Also, your customers' experience with your products and your business is part of the awareness of their friends and acquaintances. People talk, and they talk especially about the unusual—the unusually good and the unusually bad. Word of mouth from your customers to your prospective customers is the single most persuasive and credible kind of information available to most people about the things they buy and the companies they buy from.

Take time to study the Purchase Decision Chain Dynamics chart below. It

PURCHASE DECISION CHAIN DYNAMICS

The Purchase Decision Chain	The Customer's View		The Company's View
	Conscious Mind	Unconscious Mind	
1 Awareness	Knowledge of company, product names, and very few basic facts.	General impressions and feelings about company and products. "Do I like them or not?"	Advertising and Marketing Communications
2 Purchase Motivation	Functional needs recognized. Rational case for purchase beginning to take shape.	Emotional needs create sense of "I want," "I need," and "I should."	
3 Product Acceptance	Product meets functional needs. Rational case for purchase grows, but is slower than the emotional decision.	"Feels" right. Expectation of emotional gratification. Attraction outweighs avoidance. The "real" decision is made.	Sales
4 Brand Preference	Product is better for me than alternatives. Rational case for purchase is made.	I like this one better than the alternatives, and I feel good about the way things are being done.	
5 Purchase Transaction	Purchase conditions and activities are acceptable or are worth the effort.	Transaction is comfortable, not annoying. If it is annoying, it's worth it.	Customer Service
6 Customer Satisfaction	Product, service, company, employees live up to functional expectations.	Emotional gratifications live up to or exceed expectations.	

shows how you and your marketing activities interact with your customers' conscious and unconscious minds to move smoothly through the links of the Purchase Decision Chain.

YOUR BEST FRIEND—IMPULSE

Of all the things to remember about the psychographics of your target markets, first and foremost, don't forget the little twins in their heads. There's no problem with Reason—she's an old friend. You know her well, and you're comfortable with her. She thinks like you do. But get to know that rascal, Impulse. She's elusive, a bit crazy, and she doesn't communicate very well. But she's worth the trouble to know. And when it comes to understanding your markets, she's your best friend—she'll show you the secret of attracting customers in droves.

Positioning and Differentiating Your Business: Setting Your Business Apart from the Rest

▪

Positioning is the customer's general perception of your business and its products/services. Positioning takes place in the mind. If your positioning takes full advantage of customer perceptions and you communicate it effectively, it will set you apart from your competition and establish a solid first link in the Purchase Decision Chain—the awareness link. Remember, the awareness link shapes the whole relationship, and often the *real* purchase is made by the unconscious mind on the basis of awareness long before the actual sales transaction is completed. Good positioning makes for favorable awareness, and that sets you up for success right from the start.

Positioning can be tricky. It's under your control, yet it's not. To the extent that customers already have perceptions about your products, business, and industry, those perceptions already are your positioning. You need to learn about them because you can change your positioning—and thus change customer perceptions—with effective communications, an appropriate sensory package, and behavior that's consistent with the image you're trying to project.

Positioning has to be genuine. It has to be consistent with the reality of your business, and it has to be consistent with the perceptions of your target markets or it won't be believed. Positioning based on false claims or a misunderstanding of your target markets is a liability. It turns away prospective customers and weakens relationships with existing customers.

Positioning and Differentiating Your Business

SETTING YOUR BUSINESS APART FROM THE REST

Overview

"Position" is the place your products/services and your business occupy in the minds of your customers and prospective customers. It is the general perception held by their conscious and unconscious minds.

"Positioning" is what you do to intentionally establish the perceptions you want in the minds of your customers and prospective customers.

This section guides you through the process of developing an effective "Positioning Strategy."

Based on your Positioning Strategy, you will then create a "Unique Selling Proposition," or USP.

Finally, you'll restate the USP by writing a "Positioning Statement," using more literal terms and concrete language.

Process for Creating Your Positioning

- Determine General Classification of Your Product/Service
- Determine Your Relative Standing
- Determine Gratification Mode and Purchase Preference
- Identify Other Psychographic Characteristics
- Redefine Your Product
- Write Positioning Strategy
- Develop Unique Selling Proposition
- Develop Positioning Statement

Key Points

Your product's "general classification" as perceived by customers is either a "true" product, when it's one of a kind or has very little competition; a "commodity," when customers perceive it as just like all the rest; or a "brand," when there is substantial competition but your product is successfully differentiated from the rest.

Your "relative standing" indicates whether your Positioning Strategy should be:

Prestige identification: positions your products and business as "the best," "the most," "the only"

Preemptive persuasion: positions your products and business by identifying your product with the desired emotional gratification

Brand/product imagery: positions your products and business with images that stimulate favorable emotions

The "gratification mode" tells you what type of emotional gratification is best to emphasize in your positioning:

Interpersonal: emphasize personal interactions

Objective: emphasize things, information, systems

Introverted: show you've handled the details so buyers can be free to pursue their ideas

Your positioning should appeal to the "purchase preference" of your target market: If it is "experimental," emphasize the new, the innovative; if "performance," emphasize reliability and quality; if "value," emphasize price and value.

You will also revisit the psychographics of your target markets to identify their "key psychographics."

You will redefine your products by focusing on one or more of the six "key product attributes": functionality, sensory impact, unconscious associations, conscious-mind conclusions, price/value perceptions, and perceived access/convenience.

DIFFERENTIATION IS MORE THAN
SIMPLY BEING DIFFERENT

Mahatma Gandhi, Mother Theresa, and Martin Luther King Jr. differentiated themselves from the rest of the population. So did Al Capone and Attila the Hun. It's not enough to be differentiated; you need to be *preferentially* differentiated. And that's the purpose of positioning.

There is a systematic process for developing an effective positioning for your business. It's a step-by-step process, but it isn't automatic. It requires careful thinking and a lot of insight from you. It requires that you know your target markets thoroughly. And it takes time, but with a proper understanding of your target markets you have a foundation in place for building a Positioning Strategy that will draw your target customers to you.

THE POSITIONING DEVELOPMENT PROCESS

To begin the process, you will need all the worksheets you used in previous processes, including your *Central Demographic Model* worksheets, your *Central Psychographic Model* worksheets, and your trading area materials. You'll need them for your primary target market and for your flanker markets. You will be developing a Positioning Strategy for each primary and flanker market. Here's an outline of the positioning process. Download

1. **Determine the general classification of your products and services.** Any product or service can be classified in one of three ways: as a true product, a commodity, or a brand (there are special meanings for those words, which we'll define a little later). Think about what you sell, which category it falls into, and how that affects the way you're positioned in the minds of your prospects and customers.
2. **Determine your relative standing in the market.** Your relative standing is how the market sees you compared to your competitors. This will affect how you develop your marketing communications as you either reinforce your current relative standing or, perhaps, try to change it.
3. **Determine the dominant gratification mode and purchase preference of your target market.** You actually determined these psychographic characteristics in your previous work with *Customer Perceptions and Behavior,* pp. 136–157. The gratification modes are: Interpersonal, Objective, and Introverted; the purchase preferences are: Experimental, Performance, and Value. Now you'll apply them to the way you create your positioning.

4. **Develop other key psychographic characteristics of your target market.** Study your CPM worksheets, looking for clues to customer perceptions that will help shape your Positioning Strategy.

5. **Redefine your product.** Begin setting yourself apart and creating a unique place in your customers' minds by defining your product/service in terms of the features and emotional factors that are important to *them*.

6. **Write your Positioning Strategy.** This will be a brief paragraph for each target market segment that provides an overview of your positioning by "pulling together" all of the key positioning elements.

7. **Develop your Unique Selling Proposition (USP).** This is your *slogan*, your *tag line*, an expression that will become closely linked with your business. It should be catchy and easy to remember. It should also contain a basic message about your company that elicits in your prospective customers the emotional gratification they can expect from your business and its products and services.

Process for Creating Your Positioning

Determine General Classification of Your Product/Service

Determine Your Relative Standing

Determine Gratification Mode and Purchase Preference

Identify Other Psychographic Characteristics

Redefine Your Product

Write Positioning Strategy

Develop Unique Selling Proposition

Develop Positioning Statement

8. **Develop your Positioning Statement.** This is a more explicit, expanded version of your USP that explains and gives the rational justification for it by identifying what your business does, the result customers can expect, and how you're going to achieve that result.

YOUR GENERAL CLASSIFICATION: PRODUCT, COMMODITY, OR BRAND?

The Purchase Decision Chain shows us that before a sale can take place, customers must first accept the basic product, then accept your version of that product—your brand. First the product, then the brand. But there's a little more to it than that.

A product is what your business sells. It's a generic term that includes services for sale. But products fall into three categories that are important because your strategy should be different for each category. The categories are true product, commodity product, and branded product; or simply, product, commodity, and brand.

Product. When a new product is introduced into a market, or when there is a one-of-a-kind product with little or no competition, it is considered a "true product." The marketing issue is product acceptance, and the strategy is to focus marketing on the functional and emotional product attributes important to prospective customers. True products usually, but not always, appeal to buyers whose purchase preference is "Experimental." (See *Gratification Mode,* in *Customer Perception and Behavior,* pp. 148–150.) Most of the time, products don't stay true products for long. Competition moves in quickly, and competition changes the picture.

Commodity. As more and more competing products enter the market, and as customer acceptance of the basic product increases, customers begin to see the product as a commodity. "They're all the same" is the common comment. The product now begins to appeal to buyers whose purchase preference falls under "Performance." Now the marketing issue is differentiation—getting prospective customers to prefer your product over others in the market. If you are unable to differentiate the product, it continues to be perceived as a commodity, and the strategy is to compete on the basis of price or convenience.

Think of the banking industry. Banks want to differentiate themselves, and they pour huge amounts of money into advertising to do so, but they haven't been able to break out of the commodity category. Customers still perceive banks and banking services as essentially the same everywhere. Banks compete successfully on price (high interest rates for savings accounts, low interest rates for loans) and convenience (a branch on every corner, teller machines available 24 hours a day, and telephone information whenever you want it). Nevertheless, customer perceptions rule, and customer perceptions say "commodity."

Brand. As the market matures, it becomes more and more difficult for new competitors to enter the field. The growth potential for the product line as a whole begins to level off. The remaining players in the market must differentiate themselves, make their product stand out in the minds of their customers, in order to thrive.

When you're able to differentiate the product by altering its product attributes in the minds of consumers, it becomes a brand. This is also the point where you begin to attract "Value" buyers. The advantage of "branding" is that branded products enjoy higher profit margins and greater customer loyalty than commodity products of the same type. If your products have reached the commodity stage, the best strategy is brand preference. If you are unable to "brand" your products, then the commodity strategy is yours.

Take as another example the automobile industry: Objectively, based on their features and functions, you would expect automobiles to be perceived as commodities. They all operate the same, look very much the same, and for the same class of car, cost about the same. But the automobile industry has been extremely successful at branding their products. They have, in the minds of their customers, created huge perceived differences.

There are very few products that cannot be branded in some way. Even products that seem inherently commodity-like, such as fresh vegetables, gasoline, and hardware, can be branded with the right packaging and advertising that shifts branding to the business itself. Thus Safeway grocery stores, Chevron gasoline, and Ace hardware extend the benefits of store brand to the commodity types of products they sell.

In sum, you have three positioning strategies related to your product's general classification. The best strategy when your product is either unique or has little competition, is product acceptance. Once your product has reached the commodity stage in your customers' perceptions, the best strategy is brand preference. And if branding is not viable, then the remaining option is commodity selection—most likely via low price and/or convenience.

YOUR RELATIVE STANDING IN THE MARKET

Unless you are the only business of your type in your target markets, you have to be concerned with competition. The good news about your competitive standing is that while everyone would like to be "number one," you don't have to be number one to be successful. There are effective positioning strategies available for every level of competitor. Three general positioning strategies you can use to strengthen or shift your relative standing in the market are:

- Prestige identification
- Preemptive persuasion
- Brand or product imagery

Prestige identification—leadership position. If your products are the best, if you are the sales leader, if you are the most respected, if you are the only one with some distinctive product attribute, if you can promise some special status—if, in the customer's mind, you can make a legitimate claim to being number one in some important respect (or if no one else has)—you can make "prestige identification" part of your positioning.

Preemptive persuasion—instant association. If you can establish a link in the customer's mind between your product and the emotional gratification the customer is seeking, then when the need or desire surfaces, the customer automatically thinks of your product and you have "preempted" the competition. Remember the commercials for Rolaids, the upset stomach remedy? "How do you spell relief? R-O-L-A-I-D-S." Relief is the emotional gratification and Rolaids *is* relief.

How about "American Airlines, the Businessman's Airline?" Businessmen (nowadays businesspeople) are *the* experts on traveling, so American Airlines must be *the* airline to use. The consumer can read any emotional gratification they want into the message—speed, economy, comfort, status, safety—anything. In both cases there are no leadership claims, but there is a direct link with the emotional gratification sought by the customer.

When it works well, the brand name *becomes* the name for the product type in the minds of customers. Think of FedEx, Jell-O, Kleenex, and Xerox.

Certain words often signal the beginning of preemptive persuasion statements: "Because," "When," *"The"* (with emphasis), "If," "For," "To," and the like. They seem to suggest a certain exclusivity and imply that something special is about to happen, which the customer wouldn't want to miss.

Brand or product imagery—sensory stimulation and emotional associations. Images loaded with sensory stimulation and the potential for emotional associations are the key to brand/product imagery positioning. Little or nothing is ever said about the product and no explicit statement of uniqueness is made. The sensory package communicates practically nothing more than a stimulating sensation that is never explained. Examples include "The Pepsi Generation," "Coke Is It," "The Marlboro Man," and almost any soft drink, automobile, or beer commercial you've ever seen.

Brand/product imagery is always communicated through exciting graphics and sounds—sensory impact is the key.

Convention has it that, to be effective, any strategy for brand/product imagery must rely on high-end design, advertising, and other communications/images that require production and media costs small businesses usually can't afford. But if you've got some design and production expertise at your disposal, you might try a smaller-scale brand/product imagery approach. Remember that the key is to create some sensory image—usually sight and/or sound—that when seen or heard will be immediately associated with your business or product.

GRATIFICATION MODE AND PURCHASE PREFERENCE: HOW THEY AFFECT YOUR POSITIONING

Take a moment to look back at the *Customer Perceptions and Behavior* process (pp. 136–156) and refresh your memory about Gratification Mode and Purchase Preference.

In terms of positioning, it's important and pretty simple. The particular gratification mode and purchase preference you identified as being associated with your Central Demographic Model will guide the choice of language you'll use to position your product, service, and business in the minds of your potential customers. It works like this.

IF THE DOMINANT GRATIFICATION MODE IS:	USE LANGUAGE THAT EMPHASIZES:
Interpersonal	People and social situations
Objective	Information, systems, tangible items
Introverted	How you will handle the details and make it easy for them, so they can be free from unwanted involvement to pursue their ideas

IF THE DOMINANT PURCHASE PREFERENCE IS:	USE LANGUAGE THAT EMPHASIZES:
Experimental	Newness, innovation, cutting-edge quality, being first
Performance	Reliability, dependability, quality
Value	Best price, sense of value

Remember, you want your marketing and sales activities to connect with whatever is the dominant source of emotional gratification for your most probable customer.

It works similarly for the purchase preference component of your Central Psychographic Model.

KEY PSYCHOGRAPHICS OF YOUR MARKET

Here's where you get to be a detective. Every market segment has its own unique set of psychographic characteristics. The idea is to review the worksheets you've completed and look for the unique, high-impact characteristics that are most likely to be responsive to the attributes of your business and its products/services. You're looking for a "mental marriage." Anything that builds a bridge of positive perceptions from your business and its products into the minds of your prospective customers. It's hard to say what that might be. You already have the necessary tools: your own factual and instinctive knowledge of your business, plus your commonsense understanding of your market and human nature, and an openness to seeing the possibilities.

How might you go about the thought process? That depends completely on you. You might, for instance, notice that in target market "A" people tend to be suspicious of the motives of businesspeople. You might then couple that with an observation that they tend to be a low-self-esteem group and that their dominant gratification mode is Interpersonal. That paints a picture of a group of people who look for personal interactions with businesses, but who don't have much self-confidence and mistrust the people they will be dealing with. That presents you with the opportunity to position your business as friendly and filled with employees who enjoy helping customers. Or you might notice in target market "B" that honor and integrity are prized personal values and the dominant purchase preference is Performance (they focus on reliability, dependability, and quality). This could lead you to position your business as one that "goes the extra mile to make it work right for me." Once you learn to apply this approach, the possibilities are unlimited!

REDEFINING YOUR PRODUCTS

With so many similar and competing products and services out there, redefining *yours* so that it stands out from all the rest is an important part of your Positioning Strategy.

This component requires that you describe your product in terms of its key attributes *as perceived by the customer.* For purposes of positioning, you don't have to create a detailed product description—just a few words to identify the kind of product, plus a few phrases describing the one, two, or three attributes that make it stand out from all others.

Functionality. What the product does, especially what it does *for the customer.*

Sensory impact. The sensory experience of the product. What does it look like? Sound, feel, taste, and smell like?

Unconscious associations. What common unconscious associations is the product likely to trigger, and what emotional responses are likely to be stimulated by those associations?

Conscious-mind conclusions. What are the logical, rational judgments and conclusions the conscious mind is likely to reach regarding this product?

Price/value. Is the price of the product perceived as high, moderate, or low, and is the product worth its price?

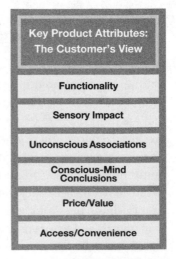

Key Product Attributes:
The Customer's View

Functionality

Sensory Impact

Unconscious Associations

Conscious-Mind
Conclusions

Price/Value

Access/Convenience

Access/convenience. Do customers have access to the product? How easily can they get it? Is it convenient—nearby, no hassles, minimal effort?

Consider these examples of products that have been "redefined." (We've noted the key product attributes used for the redefinition.) How do you respond to them?

- Not just a car, but *the ultimate driving machine.* (sensory impact, unconscious associations)
- Not just an investment service, but *your road to financial independence.* (unconscious associations, conscious-mind conclusions)
- Not only a restaurant, but *your best value in good taste.* (functionality, price/value)
- More than an insurance company, we're *round-the-clock security.* (access/convenience)

As you think about ways to redefine your product, keep in mind: (1) the product and company attributes that are most important to your customers; and (2) the attributes that make you stand out from your competition. You'll find it helpful to keep in mind the Central Psychographic Model—the type of buyer in your market segment—while also staying aware of what sets your business and its products/services apart from the competition.

All these product attributes need to be considered in the context of why people buy and how they get their emotional gratification. Building a Positioning Strategy founded on these essential elements will give you the best competitive advantage.

DEVELOPING YOUR POSITIONING STRATEGY

You should have a written Positioning Strategy for each of your target markets. A good Positioning Strategy contains all six components we've just covered in the first half of this process, in addition to an opening sentence. The six components are:

- General classification
- Relative standing
- Gratification mode
- Purchase preference
- Key psychographic characteristics
- Key product attributes

It's best to write your Positioning Strategy in two steps, which the *Positioning Strategy* worksheet will show you how to do. First, identify the *generic* components of your Positioning Strategy, then translate them into the specific language and wording that apply to your target Download markets.

You'll find it works best, especially the first time you do it, if you keep this book handy so you can refer to the process that discusses each component. When you're done, you'll have a list of the *generic* components and a lot of written comments about how each component applies to the positioning of your business. That's the raw material for your Positioning Strategy. Next, you'll compose a brief, tightly written paragraph that summarizes the essence of the raw material you just gathered. It will probably take more than one draft until you're satisfied you've captured the right positioning for your market.

When you write your Positioning Strategy, you should use, as much as possible, the exact words and style your customers will respond best to, given their preferences and perceptions. You will later use those same words in your marketing and sales processes. In fact, ***everything you do in your marketing and selling efforts springs from this Positioning Strategy.*** The written Positioning Strategy gives everyone in your company a feel for your positioning, and will make them more effective in the way they communicate with customers.

Writing your Positioning Strategy is not an easy task the first time. But like most new activities in the E-Myth Mastery Program, it becomes second nature with time and practice. There is a *Positioning Strategy* worksheet example for The Outer Edge Company to help you under- Download stand the process before you actually do it yourself.

YOUR UNIQUE SELLING PROPOSITION: THE ESSENCE OF EMOTIONAL GRATIFICATION

Your Unique Selling Proposition, or USP, is nothing more than a short phrase that conveys what it is about your business that brings emotional gratification to the customers in your target markets.

The most successful USPs are those that say nothing sensible to the conscious mind, but speak volumes to the unconscious mind. They are sufficiently vague to allow the unconscious mind to "read into them" any number of meanings and stimulate a wide variety of unconscious associations.

Remember Coca-Cola's "It's the real thing"? What *thing?* What does *real* mean? What does any of that have to do with soft drinks? Logically, "It's the real thing" makes no sense. But it gives the unconscious mind free rein to make lots of associations and imagine any kind of emotional gratification. The only logical part is its positive, upbeat tone and feeling. That's important because you want to stimulate *positive* emotions and associations.

Here's another one from Avis, the automobile rental company. "We try harder." Avis couldn't claim the number one position—Hertz had that locked up. But Avis turned its number two position into a plus: "We try harder" is vague, but it clearly says that Avis will do more for its customers. What would they do? That's for the unconscious minds of their customers to imagine.

A good USP may be so vague that it seems to have nothing at all to do with the kind of company it represents. "It's the real thing" and "We try harder" give no hint of the nature of the commodity but are highly effective. However, the USP cannot conflict with well-entrenched perceptions in the market. Some years ago, the National Cash Register Company, which had made a major commitment to computers, created the USP "NCR means computers," an attempt at preemptive persuasion. The problem was that in the minds of people everywhere, NCR meant *cash registers. IBM* meant computers! Of course, NCR's Unique Selling Proposition fell flat.

The real power of a Unique Selling Proposition comes from its connection to the unconscious mind.

You have already dedicated a great deal of careful thought to understanding the collective minds of your target markets, and you have concentrated that understanding into your Positioning Strategy. The way to craft a powerful USP, then, is to make sure it ties into the most emotionally stimulating elements of your Positioning Strategy (which you will capture in Part 1 of your *Positioning Strategy* worksheet). So how do you go about it? How do you capture the essence of your Positioning Strategy in a USP of a half-dozen words, making it vague, yet still keeping it focused on the promise of an emotional gratification that's important to your target market?

You do it by following these seven important rules:

1. Make it short—a phrase, not a sentence.
2. Keep it vague enough to leave room for the imagination.
3. Convey a positive feeling.
4. Give it impact, punch, and emotion.
5. Avoid defining product/service as a commodity.
6. Focus on the promise of emotional gratification, the result or benefit, not the technical work or feature(s) you offer.

7. Make it consistent with the relative standing, gratification mode, and purchase preference components of your Positioning (and differentiating) Strategy—they are most closely linked with market perceptions and expectations of emotional gratification.

There is a sample worksheet *(Guidelines for Developing Your Unique Selling Proposition)* with a set of USP guidelines that will be helpful. It gives you some examples you can use for your Unique Selling Proposition, based on various combinations of relative standing, gratification mode, and purchase preference.

Download

There's no foolproof process for creating your USP, but an example should be helpful. Let's consider the USP of L'eggs pantyhose: "Nothing beats a great pair of L'eggs." The key components of the Positioning Strategy are:

Relative standing:	Preemptive persuasion
Gratification mode:	Interpersonal
Purchase preference:	Performance

We'll look at the L'eggs USP in detail and see how it embodies the essence of the Positioning Strategy. The words "Nothing beats" address the purchase preference of Performance (nothing beats them, therefore, regardless of what "performance" means in the mind of the consumer, L'eggs does it best). Preemptive persuasion—identifying the product with the emotional gratification—is served (L'eggs pantyhose *are* great legs, and great legs *are* L'eggs). The gratification mode, Interpersonal, is served, not explicitly, but implicitly in that the USP implies the emotional gratification of being admired by other people for great legs. The customer has free rein to imagine whatever sensory images appeal to her, and the tone is distinctly positive because of the word "great."

If you're not satisfied that you have found exactly *the right* USP, it's probably because you have not yet reached a sufficiently in-depth level of understanding of your target markets. The more profound your understanding, the easier it is to write your USP. The main thing to remember is that your USP is built around your promise of emotional gratification. The acid test is to ask yourself, "What emotion am I selling?"

YOUR POSITIONING STATEMENT— MAKING THE USP MORE EXPLICIT

Just as a picture may have a caption to help the observer understand it, your Unique Selling Proposition should have a caption to make it more explicit. It's called your "Positioning Statement." The Positioning Statement restates and expands on the promised gratification of the USP, doing so in more literal terms with concrete language that should resonate with the people in your target market (your CDM). Yet your Positioning Statement should still be oriented more on emotional gratification than on the details of your product or service. It expands on the USP in a way that draws the customer's interest by redefining your product or service in an emotionally appealing way. The Positioning Statement is also a bridge from the USP to all the other marketing and sales communications you will be using.

The Positioning Statement may have as many as three elements: product, problem, and result.

Product. The Positioning Statement will almost always identify the product or service provided by your company, usually redefining it in a way that sets it apart from competing products and services. For instance, you could say "We manufacture widgets," or "We manufacture the nation's finest widgets." You could also redefine your product by saying "We're widget applications experts." The redefinition approach, in addition to helping differentiate your product, also prevents the customer from pigeonholing you as "just another widget company." It creates the impression that you have a lot more to offer than just widgets.

Problem. The Positioning Statement can be expanded and made more powerful by describing a problem that is solved by your product. Whenever possible, try to "package" your solution and make it memorable by giving your product or service a name that ties to a promise of emotional gratification. For example: "We're widget applications experts, and we've found that many widget buyers overbuy and waste money on unnecessary purchase and inventory costs. So we've developed the 'Perfect Purchase Program' to deliver *exactly* what you need, when you need it, at the lowest cost possible."

Result. This aspect of the Positioning Statement describes a result your product can achieve for the customer that he or she should find emotionally gratifying. Continuing the widget example: "We're widget applications experts, and we've developed a way for you to meet your production deadlines with lower costs and less effort than you're expending now."

GOOD POSITIONING—THE FOUNDATION OF ANY EFFECTIVE MARKETING STRATEGY

The objective of this process has been to help you develop a Positioning Strategy, a Unique Selling Proposition, and a Positioning Statement for each of your target markets. Just as important, you'll need to have a well-developed set of insights about your target markets. Your hard work will prove indispensable when you create your marketing strategy (and later as you create your lead generation, lead conversion, and client fulfillment systems).

Remember, positioning happens whether you do anything about it or not. If you do nothing, then you become positioned in whatever way strikes the fancy of a prospective customer. If you position carelessly, you can easily create the opposite perceptions from those you want.

When all is said and done, it's your positioning that first turns a customer's head in your direction. Positioning also creates the groundwork for successfully moving the customer through every link of the Purchase Decision Chain, and it's ultimately what sets you apart from your competition. Good positioning is the foundation of any effective marketing strategy.

CHAPTER THREE

The Discipline of the Financial Leader

■

*"Judge not, that ye be judged. For with what judgment
ye judge, ye shall be judged: and with what measure
ye mete, it shall be measured to you again."*

From Matthew 7:1-2.

Let's talk about money. Money is where the rubber meets the road. Where everyone on the face of the earth lives a good deal of the time.

If you're one of the very few who already has an easy, balanced, and mature relationship with money—or, more specifically, with yourself in relationship to money—you could skip this chapter. On the other hand, if you're one of those few, reading what follows will teach you an enormous amount about the 99 percent of us whose relationship with money is anything but mature. In either case, if you are determined to build a World Class Company, you've got to understand your people's relationship to money, in the business and in their personal lives. Their lack of understanding about and deep emotional resistance to how money works could cost you dearly.

I'm going to assume that, with some exceptions, if you are reading this book, you own a small business, want to own a small business, or you're a manager in a small business, and you know that something is missing in your understanding of how to create money and make it work for you. I'm also going to assume that money is a limited resource in your life, that you don't have a lot to burn, that you'd like more of it, and that you're hoping that I will say something here that will make it possible for you to begin making more money.

By all means, then, do take what I'm about to share with you seriously.

"That's condescending!" you might be thinking. "Why would I question your sincerity when we've come this far together?" Because the subject of money, if we pursue it with brutal honesty, will inevitably put you in touch with how out of control money makes you feel. Those of you who don't want to feel out of control—anything, please, but out of control—will want to run for the hills.

I hope you don't. There is a way out of this insanity. Unfortunately, as with anything in life or in the process of building a World Class Company, you have to face what's true first.

And what's true is that few people have a grip on their money. Even people who look like they have money handled, don't. They're just good at concealing it. We live in a world that expects us to "get" money but doesn't teach us anything of real value about it. People who don't have it long for it, dream about it, suffer from its absence, give the little they have to the lottery or the stock market in the unfulfilled hope of getting it. People who have it feel they never have enough, allocate it poorly, live in fear of losing it, mistrust other people's intentions around it. Because few people have a grip on their money, few companies do also.

How many times and in how many ways have I been called to face an issue related to money, with my clients, for my clients, with and for myself? After almost 30 years, passionately pursuing the quixotic subject of business, I have come to the steadfast conclusion that there is nothing in the creation and operation of a company that so seemingly conspires to confuse, intimidate, overwhelm, complicate, rationalize, and metastasize the plain ignorance of the average business guy, or woman, than money.

Well, perhaps I said that too strongly. Perhaps it's not ignorance, but an abiding resistance to dealing with money directly. Why, is a complicated question. It would seem on the face of it that everyone would want to know more about how money works in their company. Wouldn't you think? Well, you'd be wrong. They don't. What I've discovered is that most owners and managers ignore the money until it's too late to ignore it, and then become frantic to fix what needed to be fixed all along, but wasn't. And as soon as they fix it, if they're lucky enough to get a second chance, they go right back to sleep again. After all, if they were to pay attention to the money, to where it is and isn't, to where it's being produced or consumed, to the fluctuations of money and the causes of those fluctuations, well, then they would have to *do* something about it. Isn't that true? That to pay attention to money is to be *put* into question? Not the money, but you?

All the more reason, if you are going to build a World Class Company, why you need to learn how to get your arms around money. Not money, per se, but your relationship to money. There seems to be some gap in the synapses of the human brain when it comes to money. Some connection is missing. Some screw is loose. A man emailed me not long ago. He told me that he was a software engineer, a more than respectable position, working for a large software company for more than a respectable amount of money, had read *The E-Myth Revisited,* was inspired, was bored to death working for someone else, was just about ready to go out on his own, to start his own business, to pull the plug on his high-paying job. The only question he had was how to hire people if he couldn't afford to pay them? That was his question! Here's a grown man, earning top money working for somebody else, who wants to start his own business and he's asking me *how to hire people without any money?* You'd think he would know the answer to that question, wouldn't you? *Get the money! You can't start a business without money! Get the money!* Well, I didn't rave at him like that, but I should have.

Are you getting a sense of the problem? That the vast majority of small businesses are started without any money and continue to operate without any money. In the minority of cases that actually experience growth, the owner simply takes the "excess" money out of the business, first, so he can finally start making a living, and later, so he can improve his lifestyle. After all, wasn't that why he went into business for himself in the first place: to improve his lifestyle? The part of him that knows he's worked hard, *needs* something to show for it, and resents the fact that he's not earning enough will say, "I owe it to myself." Another part of him believes the exact opposite. That he's not working hard enough. Because, if he were, the business would be producing more money. All of this would have worked out much better. Wasn't it supposed to work out better? Wasn't owning your own business supposed to be significantly better than working for somebody else? Well, of course, it was. Being your own boss means that you don't have to put up with the boss's stupidity. On the other hand, though, when you were working for someone else, your paycheck just showed up; you didn't have to worry about it. Now the check doesn't get written unless you write it. And sometimes there's no money to write a check to yourself on a particular day. But, in a small business, you don't *have to* write the check to pay yourself right now. You can take the money out tomorrow, or the next day, or the day after that. Unfortunately, I've observed that, in some perverse way, this kind of control over money produces a false sense of well-being. This kind of control over money is like a drug. It numbs one to reality. The financial reality of the business. And the psychic toll of the financial reality of the business is enormous. The owner is always thinking about money. Or he's always avoiding thinking about money. And he never really knows what the future will bring. If the present is fuzzy, the future can't be anything but fuzzy.

There's got to be a better way.

The job of the financial leader in a business starts with the entrepreneur's vision. The entrepreneur's vision is the financial leader's marching orders. To the degree the enterprise leader is clear about her vision, the financial leader can build a financial model of that vision, she can determine the financial options that are available to achieve that vision, and she can create the financial systems that need to be in place in order for every aspect of that vision to be realized.

The financial leader's job, the financial leader's mission, the financial leader's accountability are directly proportional to the size of the entrepreneur's vision. When Steve Wynn built in Las Vegas the most expensive hotel ever at the time, The Mirage, it called for immense financial leadership to pull off. Of course, what Steve Wynn could have done was what most people do. He could have downsized his vision to what was possible and probable, to what had been done before. We downsize our lives, our visions, our goals, our missions, our purpose, our passion, all the time, without recognizing it, to what we perceive as acceptable, possible, guaranteed. We downsize our financial aims and our financial understanding according to our past achievements. Our past achievements are what we know we can do. Since it's reasonable to assume that you've yet to build a World Class Company, the enterprise leader in you will have to be willing to get behind a vision that is beyond your proven ability to realize. Likewise, the financial leader in you will have to take on the financial accountabilities associated with that vision and you may have no evidence of your ability to be successful at them. Therein lies the challenge, the thrill, and the opportunity for true aliveness.

Everything I'm sharing with you in this book, and in all of my books, has been validated in my own company, E-Myth Worldwide, and in tens of thousands of our client companies, over the past 27 years. Fortunately and not, in the course of 27 years, my company has experienced just about every success and every failure in the repertoire of small business experiences. We are our customer, particularly when it comes to our understanding of the price a small business will inevitably pay for the lack of financial leadership. I'd like to share our story with you because it so clearly demonstrates, perhaps more than you're quite prepared for, why the financial integrity required to build a World Class Company is so critical to your success.

The following is an excerpt from *The Power Point*, which I wrote in 1992. It is still the most compelling story I know to move you to honor, nurture, and commit to the development of the financial leader in your company.

Hold on to your hat.

Little did I know as I walked into my office at what was then called The Michael Thomas Corporation (MTC) on December 10, 1985, that neither my business nor my life would ever be the same again.

1985 was a significant year for many reasons.

It was the year our business more than doubled in size, from $2 million to more than $4 million in revenue.

1985 was also the year in which we inaugurated our franchise program in earnest, by selling, training, and starting up 57 franchises throughout California whose purpose it was to deliver the proprietary small business service we had been developing at MTC since 1977—a service we called The Michael Thomas Business Development Program.

In addition to the ongoing client base of 850 small businesses we served throughout California, we had a dedicated, enthusiastic, and well-trained staff of over 100 people in client support services, program development, marketing, and finance, not including our franchisees and their employees. In addition to everything else we accomplished in 1985, I also completed writing my first book, *The E-Myth*.

I had just married my wife, Ilene. We spent three, wonderful weeks traveling in Paris and the south of France and then came home and bought a large, elegant Spanish-style house in Hillsborough, California, just south of San Francisco.

In short, to me, my wife, and everyone else at MTC, 1985 was a year of unparalleled accomplishment, fulfillment, and promise.

Our company was an entrepreneurial dream come true.

My partner and I had started the company alone, with no money, a handful of clients, an office we couldn't afford, and the dream of creating a totally unique and affordable consulting service aimed at the millions of small mom-and-pop businesses in need of help the world over.

Ilene joined us in 1982. Her extraordinary ability to develop people and systems pushed the company far beyond the place she found us. We took on a new life, a new vitality, a new focus.

Eight years after starting the company, and three years after Ilene joined us, everything we had planned for, worked for, and struggled for was becoming a reality before our very eyes.

This year was the most exhilarating year of my life!

Until that day when the dark, worried frown on my partner's face revealed to me that something else was going on I wasn't going to like.

As I look back over the years that have transpired since I sat across from my partner and received the shock of my life, I have learned some things about money.

The most important thing I have learned is that we don't spend money as much as we consume it. Money is food.

We consume it and convert it into things—the feelings, associations, and symbols we believe in.

That's what a consumer society really is.

It takes the material idea of money, ingests it, digests it, and converts it into its idea of living.

To some, money is converted into power.

To others, money is converted into security.

To others, money is converted into getting by the best way they can, self-esteem, survival, scarcity, magic, sex, beauty, sin, and evil.

The fact is that money does not exist without people.

Money has no meaning without people.

Money is simply an idea we have agreed upon, an idea which represents to every one of us our net worth in the world.

I remember the exact words my partner said to me on the morning of December 10, 1985. I will never forget them.

He was sitting at his desk, his head hunched over his arms, his fingers pulling at his hair distractedly. He looked up at me briefly with a look that spelled disaster, and said in a voice I could hardly hear, "We blew it. We let it get away from us. I don't know what we were thinking about."

At first, I had difficulty understanding what he was telling me.

I thought that he was simply saying there was a problem we had to work out. Just another one of the many problems we had worked out together over the years. That would have been okay. That's what our partnership had been about, solving the problems as they got in our way.

But, that wasn't what he was saying.

What he was really saying, when I finally grasped it, was that this time we had really done it. We were broke! We had *really* blown it once and for all. As far as he was concerned, it was over.

I was stunned. It wasn't possible. How could it be? We had taken in more money this year than ever before. And, according to the financial information I had seen, we were operating at a healthy profit. Everything was working in the business according to plan. Franchise sales exceeded expectations, cash flow was better than expected, training of franchisees was completed and on schedule. Not one word had been mentioned to me about financial problems brewing. I stood there struck dumb with fear and self-loathing. I didn't know what to say, what to ask, other than, "How bad is it?"

He didn't even know that.

All he could say to me was that we were at least four months behind in our leases, five months behind with the telephone company, three months behind in our payroll taxes, add a couple of hundred thousand dollars or so in payables—almost all of which were seriously overdue—and you could get some sense of the size of the problem.

But that wasn't all.

Creditors were complaining, he said, some were threatening to cut us off, others to sue us, we didn't have any cash, and we couldn't get a line of credit. In short, other than our continuing client fees, we had no other source of revenue to which we could turn.

But that still wasn't all.

Our new franchisees, inexperienced and uncertain in the use of our systems, were beginning to lose clients faster than we could replace them.

Frustrated with their inability to retain clients, they were beginning to complain that our franchise didn't work.

There were rumblings out there that trouble was brewing.

Several were suggesting that there might be a legal problem in all this.

And they didn't even know the worst of it yet. None of them knew that we had run out of money.

What do you say to the woman you love when you have blown it?

What do you say when everything you believe to be true turns out to be false, and she has to help you pick up the pieces!

What's worse, what do you say to yourself?

Ilene and I were dumbfounded.

Nothing we had ever done had prepared us for this.

We had planned everything so carefully—or so we thought.

Certainly, the company had been on an aggressive path, but that wasn't the problem. We had hit every benchmark we intended to hit, and more.

The shock wouldn't leave us. It consumed us in everything we did and trailed us everywhere we went for weeks. (Indeed, the shock would trail after us for years.) It bewildered us; it suffocated us; it seized our very breath. We had no idea what to do since the problem at that point was too big to define, too sudden and overwhelming to fully comprehend.

I remember that time as a continuous stream of lunatic meetings with our accountant, with my partner, with our accounting staff, trying to make some sense out of the appalling ignorance and confusion Ilene and I encountered everywhere we went to talk about money.

They would look at each other. They would look at the floor. They would look at the ceiling, and then back at each other. I wanted to take them by the collar and scream, "What's going on with you? Don't you understand what you've done? Talk to me!"

I couldn't believe what was going on.

How could so many people who were so well-paid do so badly and be so ill-informed?

When I was alone, I would explode at no one in particular in an uncontrollable fit of rage at the absolute insanity of it all! I felt so absolutely helpless!

When I would talk to our accountant, he would explain things in a calm and reasonable voice, and yet, it was all so meaningless. He simply agreed with me that he and my partner and our accounting staff had screwed up, but nothing more. It was nobody's fault. We were growing so fast; we were all doing the best that anyone could given the circumstances. I can see his face even now, that dumb, bland, institutional look.

It was nobody's fault!

I could have killed him, and my partner, and our accounting manager, and all of the people who worked for them. And yet, they simply didn't seem to care!

I think that drove me crazier than anything else.

I felt like the only sane patient in an insane asylum.

Everyone looked at me as if *I* were the crazy one: they *indulged* me; they *understood* me; they *cared* for me; but no one would admit that they were to blame! There was no explanation that could justify our condition; there was no rationalizing it. It wasn't that we were growing too fast or that our systems were "outgrown" or that we were reaching too far. It was simply that everybody went to sleep and only woke up when we ran out of money!

My wife looked at me and said, "I think *we're* the crazy ones here. Let's stop for a minute and think."

January 1986 saw the beginning of what I think of now as my Education in Experts Phase.

Actually, my Education in Experts Phase is still going on today, but I'll get to that later.

In January 1986, thoroughly disgusted with my inability to achieve any clarity from the people in my company who were supposed to possess it, I brought in my first "expert" to help.

I've got to hand it to him. It didn't take long for him to come up with a solution.

He looked at me with the most pained expression, and then told me in no uncertain terms that we had to shut down the company immediately, give the business to the franchisees, and walk away, hoping that nobody found us out, hoping that I could still find a job after all I'd done. Perhaps I could perform seminars on behalf of the franchisees, or maybe I could manage a sales department somewhere where they hadn't heard of me yet!

There was no doubt in his mind that there was absolutely no hope. I can hear his voice to this day, *no hope, no hope, no hope, no hope, no hope.*

He was the first of my no hope experts.

The others would say, "There is hope, but there's no hope unless you can afford to pay for the only hope you have, Me!"

Meanwhile things were warming up on the franchise front.

One of our more successful franchisees—within ten months of opening his doors his franchise was producing annualized revenue of just under $500,000—was pressing hard for more results:

Why should he have to wait?

He expected to be on a million dollar course by this time!

He did love to talk on the phone.

He talked to my finance department at least once a day.

He also loved to talk to the other franchisees.

He soon became part of a chorus: More! More! More!

Everywhere I turned somebody was asking for more.

Money, money, money.

Ilene rented an apartment in southern California to run our recently opened operation there. Under her direction, sales were growing.

In March, my partner resigned. He couldn't afford to stay on any longer.

He wrote me a long letter after he left telling me how stupid I was. I agreed with him. But for different reasons.

To bring the cost of doing business down to a tolerable level, we closed our corporate offices, cut over 30 people from our payroll, and moved our remaining corporate staff into our northern California regional office across town.

Shortly after my partner resigned, I fired our accountant and our first expert and hired a new accounting firm to replace them, guys with the confidence I sorely needed at the time, that if the job could get done, well, by damn, they would do it!

By the end of 1986 I fired them too and ended up in court. The senior partner sued us for what he said we owed them, and I sued him for malpractice. I should have paid him the $30,000 he said I owed him after his firm worked our account for four months and left us in worse shape than they found us. They won, and with attorney's fees included, the final bill came to more than $195,000. What I saw in that senior partner's eyes in March 1986 was a resolute scrapper of a man—a real killer of a guy, somebody who would really go for the throat when he felt it was called for. That's why I hired him. I thought he would go for the throat of my problem. As it turned out, he went for my throat. When the final demand for payment came before he filed suit, Ilene wrote him a letter explaining that, given our devastated financial condition, the only beneficiaries of litigation would be our attorneys. He responded that he would be willing to accept anything as payment, "jewelry, furniture, rugs . . ." (a charming guy, a true, endearing expert, one of my favorites of all time!).

Money, money, money, the conflagration grew in intensity.

Ilene and I spent more time apart than together, she in southern California, I up north. We'd talk late at night on the telephone about what was going on. We felt sorry for ourselves; we were angry; we were afraid; we fought. We fought with each other about fights we had with other people. We loved each other on the telephone, and then we hung up in a fit of pique. She'd call me back, and then I'd call her back, and we'd apologize to each other, only to get angry again when something, anything, triggered our sense of helplessness and rage. We went on like that, day after day, week after week, month after month.

Every day brought a new threat, a new crisis, a new problem.

The franchisees weren't rumbling now; they were absolutely screaming threats.

Our people, too, had a problem.

To say I was losing credibility is the understatement of the decade. As each catastrophic day went by, I was quickly becoming the business pariah of the year to someone new.

"What really happened here?" they would ask me.

My answers satisfied some, but failed to satisfy others.

Unfortunately, the ones who weren't satisfied weren't always the ones who left.

Sometimes, as I discovered, the ones who thought the worst of me stayed on to watch what I'd do.

My new controller, a thin, young woman CPA my ex-accountant had recommended for the job, often came to me with complaints about our new accountants, about the people who worked for her, about the stress of working there, about life in general under the new conditions. Her face would get all pouty and drawn, her eyes moist; her lips would tremble. All I could say to her is that I was sorry; I understood what a problem everything was right now; but that she would have to take charge. I'm sure I didn't tell her to keep a stiff upper lip, but it must have sounded like that. I wasn't making good sense to just about anyone, least of all to myself. She would nod resolutely and shuffle back to her desk, as though in her slippers! I'm certain she thought that if she continued much longer in this degraded and deteriorating financial environment, her CPA badge (or whatever they call it) would be ripped from her breast forever at a meeting of her peers, that she would have to go back to the ignominy of being a lonely grunt bookkeeper in an auto parts store until she worked off the shame.

And still, no matter what we did to defend ourselves, to put things right, they kept getting worse.

If the franchisees had been angry before, they were now a mad raging horde.

Reasoning with them did no good. All they wanted was money.

In a moment of weakness, I felt so bad that I wrote one of them a personal check. He took it in a second, and then demanded more.

I felt as if I was locked in a room with a bunch of gangsters.

I don't know how I did it, I just kept working, trying to get things right again, trying to move out of the swamp we were in.

But the swamp was deeper than I was tall. I felt myself being sucked down, with nothing to hold on to. I was going to drown.

Money, money, money.

I fired my second accountants and our controller and hired a third expert with experience up and down his arm to replace them.

Dan was a godsend.

He took charge of our problem in a minute.

Everything settled down.

I couldn't believe it!

He was either one hell of a professional financial manager or a hypnotist! I couldn't be sure, but to be honest, I didn't really care.

The shells stopped going off in the middle of the office. The front lines were on the other side of the telephone, on the other side of the door, out there somewhere, and Dan and our people were in here, getting our house in order, making things nice.

He had such a calm and settled air about him!

"What about . . . ?" I would ask him.

"It's handled," he'd say.

Could things be finally shifting? He would reassure me.

I became a true believer. I took my newfound treasure, my financial maven, the proof of my sanity, to southern California with me to show him off to the franchisees.

Dan and I prepared ourselves.

We had a strategy.

He was going to show them how much we were prepared to do.

We had reports drawn up to show them the truth.

We were going to dispel the rumors once and for all. We were going to show them, finally, how everything was moving in the right direction, how Ilene's extraordinary efforts were really paying off, that sales were increasing to the point where all of us soon would be in tip-top shape.

Dan showed them, but they didn't like him either.

They got angrier and angrier.

They followed us down the hall as we left the meeting.

The worm had turned.

Only blood would do.

But, even then, Dan was unfrazzled.

Not me—I was a wreck.

Every place I went I felt like a criminal.

And, for the life of me, I had done nothing wrong!

I couldn't go to bed without hearing taunts.

The embarrassment was unbearable.

I gave seminars almost every day, trainings with my people, spoke to Ilene every night. On the outside I spoke about mastering business; on the inside I quaked in my boots.

To make matters even worse, my first book, *The E-Myth,* was beginning to take off. People were calling. They admired my work. They professed undying gratitude. My point of view about business was directly to the point; it touched them where they lived. They didn't know the half of it. I was dying a thousand deaths every day. I wished I could make the book go away until I was ready, until I got everything back under control.

. . .

Money, money, money.

My first expert sued me for $5,000. When the complaint was served, the person on our finance staff who received it gave it to Dan. He ignored it. Undisputed, my first expert got a default judgment, and as swift as a mouse, swooped the five grand from our bank account.

My first accountant must have gotten wind of how easy it was. He sued me for more than $20,000. The same employee gave the new complaint to Dan, which he ignored as well. Ditto, my first accountant grabbed twenty-two big ones from our now trembling account. Dan didn't flinch. At least not so I could notice. After all, *he* didn't create the problem, I did, the author, who was going to be famous, who was going to teach people how to avoid such problems. There was a lesson in all this. "Pay your bills!" he almost said.

How can a business work and not work at the same time?

I can prove to you that in a moment of inattention, it can all come down around your ears.

Have I been too hard on myself?

Or, perhaps, you think I have let myself off the hook, that I am focusing too much blame on all these people who let me down.

Perhaps you've already lost so much faith in my credibility that you're wondering, what in the world could I possibly teach you now about business? How could anyone make such a royal mess of things?

I can see my saxophone teacher, Merle, smiling in his grave. I can see my uncle Al, chuckling mirthlessly to himself, You dummy! You ignoramus! You let yourself get caught!

I can see my editor, my publisher, reading this manuscript for the very first time, asking themselves, how is he going to get out of this one? Have we tied ourselves to a nut?

Ilene grew our business in southern California from a dead start to an annualized rate of $2,000,000 in gross revenues in one year.

She then came back to northern California, fired Dan, and took over the finance department.

I never saw Dan again.

I forgot to tell you, before Ilene came home, a few other things happened. Not necessarily in the following order.

We received our first franchise rescission.

What that means is that a franchisee took *our* name off of his door, put his name on it, took our copyright off of *our* materials, put *his* copyright on them, notified the clients we gave to him to begin paying *him* directly rather than *us,* and in one fell swoop siphoned close to $60,000 a month out of our pocket!

That's right, you heard me, the guy who liked to make phone calls, who loved to talk to franchisees every day. The guy who got my personal check, *the guy whose business was growing through the damn roof,* that very same guy rescinded his franchise agreement!

Five more franchisees followed suit.

Hundreds of thousands of dollars stopped flowing into our company— just went away with a snap of the fingers.

Was God trying to tell me something?

Was Dan right?

What did Ilene and Michael do for goodness' sake?

What would you have done?

1987 saw the beginning of a new wave of threats. We now had a new accountant. Ilene was in charge of finance; we were truly getting our financial house in order; and then the lawsuits began. In earnest.

We were sued for fraud. We were sued for misrepresentation. We were sued for violations of the franchise laws. We were sued for enormous amounts of money.

We found ourselves a legal firm that came highly recommended.

Our first meeting included three attorneys, Ilene and I. We familiarized them with our problem. It took us about three hours. That first meeting cost us $1,600.

They told us we had a problem, but we were in the right.

I told them that I already knew both of those things.

They nodded and told us they knew how we must feel, but that was the way the world worked, how the cookie crumbled.

We simply didn't believe it could get any worse.

But, naturally, it did.

If our business had been a war zone before, we were now under atomic attack. All of the light weapons had been used up; major explosions were the normal course of every day. We'd arrive at the office—major explosion. We'd stop to eat lunch—major explosion. Ilene, our people, and I were suffering from shell shock, but somehow we went on.

The legal bills mounted. Yet the war persisted; it didn't care about cost. Cost was always the last thing to be considered; cost was always something that occurred *after* a shot was fired, *after* a bomb was dropped. Cost was never planned during those grim days; it was always the price of a shock.

Over the six years of unlikely, unimaginable, indecent events, our legal fees alone came to over $500,000! They simply added up: an hour here, a telephone call there, a marathon meeting here, a court appearance there. All we could do was defend ourselves. We didn't have the resources, emotional or financial, to go on the offensive. And we had the very best legal help money could buy. Our guys were known in the legal community as good. They said they knew what had to be done, but our financial condition wouldn't allow them, or us, to do most of it.

A prevailing sense of injustice dogged our every step.

What was illegal for the opposition to do, they did with impunity.

What was legal for us to do became, for the most arcane reasons under the sun, impossible to do.

There were reasons, of course.

The reasons sounded quite judicious, but only for a second.

It didn't strike us with a sudden trumpet blare, but somewhere along the way something shifted; and Ilene and I buckled down for the long haul.

We suddenly came to the realization that this simply wasn't going to go away; that it was going to take a long, long while, and a lot of money, to turn around.

We sold our home and put the money into the business.

We stopped paying ourselves and lived on my speaking engagements and royalties.

Ilene created payment schedules for the more than 100 creditors who were waiting in line, calling us every day for money we didn't have.

The schedules extended for years in some cases.

And yet, our creditors accepted our terms.

When Dan was there, he had hung up on them.

When our second accountants were there, they had made promises they didn't keep if they talked to them at all, which in most cases they didn't.

Ilene, God bless her, made promises, and then began to keep them, week after week, month after month, year after year.

She was committed to keeping her word, and did most of the time.

But still there was the need to produce the money to keep our promises, and the company's revenue was shrinking around our ears.

Our remaining franchisees were losing clients so fast that it was beginning to have a profoundly negative impact on our marketing people.

Who wants to sell something they don't trust?

Sales began to slide precipitously.

We rallied our people together; cut back on anything we could, again and again, and then cut back even more, to bring the company down to a financially manageable size; gained commitments from our people to help us to pull the company out of its tailspin; called in what chits we had; and found out that there were many chits we didn't even know about.

What we found out is that most of our people cared. They wanted to be included. They wanted to join the fight. They knew we somehow had blundered into a tornado but they also trusted that we could find a way out.

They thought our business was more than worthwhile.

Those who couldn't handle the chaos, the negative forces, left to do something else. There were some teary goodbyes.

Those leaving and those left behind felt an incomparable sense of loss.

Ilene and I developed a financial strategy to buy back as many of the remaining franchises as we could in order to save the remaining clients and work with them in-house as we had before we began to franchise.

We knew our coaches could keep the clients, and we knew that that would have a marked impact on our people. Clients produce cash flow, and cash flow was critical. But becoming a trusted business and producing results our people could be proud of was even more critical.

Ilene's negotiations with the franchisees were anything but easy. We didn't have any cash, so the only way we could buy their businesses was with a note and payments extending far into the future.

One by one most finally accepted our offers. Ilene bought their businesses back and even negotiated settlements with the landlords of the franchisees who had continuing lease obligations so they could be free to walk away.

The other part of our strategy was to work with our clients by telephone, fax, and mail, instead of in-person.

Everyone said that the strategy would fail.

I didn't think so.

My experience had shown me that the telephone could be an incredibly intimate instrument.

In any case it was a moot point.

If we were to stay alive we had to rescue our clients from our franchisees, and to rescue the clients we had to work with them long distance. We had no other choice.

And it worked!

Our client retention soared. Our productivity per client increased dramatically. Our profitability per client was substantially improved. And, best of all, our control over the entire client relationship increased exponentially.

Finally, we were turning things around.

We were pulling things out of the fire.

Our first real strategy since the tornado struck was beginning to pay off.

The only problem was that between the 100 creditors and the franchises we had agreed to buy back, Ilene and I had now incurred over $2 million we had to pay off!

Money, money, money.

The anger over money-gone-wrong knows no bounds.

If there is an ugly side to anyone—and there is, believe me, I've seen it at its virulent worst—there is nothing like money-gone-wrong to bring it out.

It is a demon from hell!

His little eyes flash red and yellow with fire; his little teeth grind unmercifully, gnashing, in the hope of red meat; his little fingers scratch and tear at anything within reach—for clumps of hair. They pull viciously at doors, at drawers; looking for the money, knowing it's hiding, knowing they're being deprived of their FOOD! Their flesh only appears to be flesh, it is in fact only wax with hair; their expressions and features constantly change in the heat of the moment from grimaces to grins to sneers to rage to lust. They are evil spirits brought up from the bowels of the earth, to annihilate, to scream bloody murder, to foul the air with their blasphemous bleatings and complaints, to tear and rend things apart until they can't be put back together again. To destroy until nothing is left.

At least that's what it seemed they were trying to do to us.

Every time I saw one of the six franchisees who were on the offensive, their faces grew darker, black, red, and purple; their eyes took on a yellow unhealthy cast; their mouths a perpetual snarl, filled with venom. They wanted everyone to know that prior to becoming franchisees everything was set for them, their lives had been stunning examples of fiscal, spiritual, and familial responsibility. Now, due to me—they were innocent victims of a diabolical scheme—their lives were destroyed. They were going to get even. They were going to have my soul for lunch!

Had they been as resourceful and as dedicated to the operation of their franchises, we would never have had a problem. But that was too much to ask.

It wasn't too long before the District Attorney called. "*Who?*" I asked my assistant.

"You heard me, the District Attorney!" she squealed. "*The god damned D.A.*" she screamed in a harsh whisper.

"The D.A.?" I thought to myself. I couldn't believe my ears! Was this going to become a television series? Was Judge Wapner going to call too?

I couldn't bear the thought of what would happen next.

Would he lean me up against my car? Would he tie chains to my arms and legs and walk me into court in front of all my clients, my children, my employees, the Chamber of Commerce, the Trucking Association?

Would I be forced to make a public apology to everyone I had ever delivered a seminar to?

Would the headlines in the *San Francisco Chronicle* scream out FRAUD! FRAUD! FRAUD! With my picture on the front page, my blue suit jacket pulled over my head?

I had my attorney talk to him. My attorney told me that the D.A. had received a complaint from one of our franchisees and they had been investigating the complaint for several months. He had talked to quite a few people who had a lot to say about us, about me, and about our little problem. He had to decide whether or not to indict us for criminal fraud. According to our franchisees there was absolutely no question about it, we were as guilty as sin. We had stolen huge amounts of money—the franchisees told him—millions had been stashed away in a Swiss bank; we had an extravagant lifestyle, taking from the little people what was rightfully theirs, and using it for our own insatiably greedy and multifarious ends.

As my attorney recounted his conversation with the D.A., I could see that the ugly little demons were having a field day.

The D.A. didn't sound as if he had to be pushed much further, my attorney said.

It sounded as if the cell doors were already being oiled to close.

It was about time guys like me got what we deserved.

As for me, I was about to pass out.

We reached an agreement with the D.A.

We told him that he could send his auditors into our company to look for any evidence of misdeed, of fraud, of misrepresentation, of evil.

We told him we had done nothing wrong; that our business did work; that the franchisees were simply being impatient; that no one had bilked them out of their hard-earned savings.

Come on in, we said. Take a close look. Look as long as you like; we've got nothing to hide.

So they did.

The D.A.'s auditors had themselves a field day.

What was supposed to take 45 to 60 days, at the most, took almost 9 months!

They dug into everything they could lay their hands on. We gave them everything we had.

And they found nothing, because there *was* nothing.

It cost us a bundle.

Money, money, money.

Our costs ran up; our money ran down. Every dime we made went to pay off our debt.

Ilene and I borrowed more money, from family, from personal lines of credit; all of it went into the business, to keep it running.

We created financial and operational controls so tight that the business couldn't squeak without us knowing it.

The business was insolvent, but it wasn't bankrupt. We were moving along.

Our new accountant, Dale, was a wonder.

Finally, a professional worthy of the name.

He worked with us, trusted us, developed our understanding, taught us, supported us in every way he could.

He was intimately familiar with everything that went on in our business, and he stood in awe of it.

There wasn't a day that went by when he didn't tell us how remarkable our business was, how extraordinary it had to be to have weathered such a continued and malevolent attack on all fronts. "Hang in there," he said, "it's going to work out." "Don't worry," he said, "the worst of it is behind you. We'll get it handled," he said, and damn if we didn't.

Day after day, an hour at a time, whittling it, molding it, nursing it, we faced the unfaceable and came through it so many times that we began to regain our former optimism.

Our people grew smarter, deeper, and more persistent. They learned to fight off the hounds. They learned to get what they needed. They learned that the world isn't always a safe place to be, but that you could make it safer if you had heart, discipline, a long lance, and good armor.

They learned that money was nothing to fool around with. It had a will all its own.

A word about money.

I have learned the hard way that money—the food of a business—must be tended to constantly.

Daily.

By the hour is best.

. I have learned that in a Free Market System, money is a monstrously complicated thing.

It is all some people have.

It is all some people are.

It is all some people want.

It is what lies down beside them in bed at night.

It is how they value their day.

If they think they have a right to it they will kill you for it.

If they believe it is sexy they will make love to it.

If they believe it is power they will make a club of it and beat you senseless until you give way.

If they believe it will keep them safe they will dress themselves in it.

In a Free Market System money is the only thing that stands between most people and the awful, bottomless, terrifying void.

Despite our *no-cash* position, despite our overwhelming debts, despite our legal battles and the negative energy we met on almost every front, Ilene and I paid off $1 million of our $2 million debt.

Our business continued to produce remarkable results for our clients.

We never missed a payroll during this entire madcap time, and we were proud of that.

We owned very little, owed a great deal, and continued to struggle with the imponderable.

Every day it felt like we won two and lost one. The continuing sense of forward movement only validated the decision we made in 1986 to find a way through.

Somehow, we never lost our drive to overcome all of this. In fact, we found in this experience the depths of our drive, something we never would have discovered had life been kinder.

There was a positive energy that continued to fuel our day, an extraordinary vitality which grew in us almost by the hour as we witnessed the minor miracles that occurred as a result of our persistence, our determination, our love of what we were doing, our appreciation of those who supported us, our unrelenting vision.

This was, to Ilene and me, an exceptional opportunity, a rite of passage, an odyssey of heroic proportions. I wouldn't have traded it for the world.

Sarah looked at me with both pain on her face and a question on the tip of her tongue.

"That was as excruciating to hear this time as it was when I first read *The Power Point* ten years ago. When we worked together last time, I remember it was still all too raw. How did you make it through? Why didn't you pull the plug? Was it worth it?"

"Let me just say," I responded, "that it was well worth it. The end of the story is an absolute miracle which I'm going to share with you before we complete our sessions together. Stay tuned. For now, I'll add that Ilene and I never seriously considered pulling the plug, despite how relentlessly desperate it was. We loved what we did, we couldn't imagine doing anything else, we knew our judgment about many things had been awful, that many people had suffered a great deal by our bad judgment, and we wanted to make things right. So we just didn't quit until the toxicity worked its way through the system. It took six years.

"But, what about you, Sarah? What impact did hearing that story again have on you? What thoughts or fears did it trigger?"

Sarah took my question in and let go into her most genuine response as I had seen her do many times. "The first thought I had, Michael, almost immediately, was that if this could happen to you, with everything you seem to know about business, what in the world could *I* hope to accomplish with the little *I* know about business? I could not have survived what you went through. I would have pulled the plug." Sarah continued, "I wanted to know, how did that happen? I mean, how did that really happen? Your experience of the advisors you paid to help you, who so obviously let you down, chilled me to the bone. How do I know I can depend on my attorney, my accountant, my financial advisor, on *you* for that matter?"

I smiled at Sarah, warming to her questions, feeling how she had opened herself up to the conversation we were having. "Sarah, thank you," I began. "These are perfect questions. Exactly the questions a leader needs to ask. How do you know who to trust? And how do you know if you can depend on the information they give you? What I've learned is that first you have to make sure you're delegating accountability, rather than *abdicating* accountability for your money."

I looked at Sarah firmly, determined that she get the point I was about to make. "You can never know whether anyone is providing you with the right information, unless you come to agreement, that is. Agreement about exactly what you need to know, how it should be provided to you, in what form, and in what frequency, and with the support evidence to back it up.

"The difficult truth is I was responsible for the near debacle in our company. I had handed over my accountability as CEO to my partner as chief financial officer, trusting him to be as good as his word, and then turning my attention completely to other things. Unfortunately, he wasn't as good as his word. In fact, his word didn't mean anything. But that wasn't his fault, Sarah, it was mine. I created a financial environment that was solely dependent upon the financial guy's word rather than on systems and information. In short, I abdicated my accountability as the financial leader of the company rather than delegated it. A big mistake, one that I've never made again.

"I can't say that I didn't know any better because I did. I did know what I should expect from my chief financial officer. But I gave in to the temptation to let the things I didn't want to focus on, in the areas where I didn't feel strong, be handled without my oversight. I also gave in to my fear that if I pressed my partner, something horrible would happen to our relationship, something that I couldn't clearly identify but was ever present. So I tolerated being without "the numbers." I tolerated the excuses, month after month, until the inevitable happened.

"Ironically, everything I was afraid might happen did happen. My partner's and my relationship completely fell apart and, as a result of the horrible financial mess we were in, he was forced to leave the company shortly thereafter. Had I faced my fear at the outset, perhaps none of that would have happened.

"At least not with the disastrous consequences that occurred. The horror was a function of my avoidance of reality, something I can talk about with some equanimity because I've had 20 years to digest this. Without giving any of the story's ending away, life has given me this wonderful second chance to acquire the discipline of a financial leader and to re-create my company with rigorous financial management. I've learned that you just can't pretend things don't exist when they do. And that's why I've written about this experience in my books and why I'm sharing it with you here. My hope is that you will listen to the voices that are beckoning you to address things you're avoiding before disaster strikes."

Sarah looked off into the distance as if she were thinking about some things she could no longer avoid. I just let her be with her thoughts for a few minutes. Then she looked back at me as if she wanted me to go on.

"Sarah, the only way you can know if your financial professionals are providing you with the information you need, if you're not an expert, is through a system of agreement between you.

"And it's the accountability of the financial leader to establish that agreement. It's the discipline of the financial leader that establishes that agreement, audits its integrity, monitors its reliability, improves its performance continually while, at the same time, increasing the value of the enterprise and driving everyone in the organization to better understand the role money plays in the health of the organization.

"Which brings us to your first assignment as the financial leader of your enterprise, Sarah. I want you to ask yourself the most serious question you can about the financial integrity of your company and your life."

THE FIRST ASSIGNMENT

"What is the meaning of money to you, Sarah? That's your first assignment. For one month, I'd like you to ponder that question and write about it. I mean, what associations does money bring up for you? What thoughts come up when you think of money? What feelings arise? Where do they go when you let them go where they go? How do your thoughts and feelings about money affect the rest of your day? Do those feelings make you weaker, less energetic, depressed? Or do they enliven you, move you to action, enhance your creativity? I want you to watch what feelings come up when you ask yourself this question, Sarah."

Sarah was already thinking about the question before I finished. Her face was flushed, tears were welling up in her eyes. Something had been triggered that was moving her deeply.

"Michael, this question and the story of your company have brought up a very painful reality for me. I have absolutely no skill when it comes to money. I've been so naive about it. I've spent it as I needed to spend it. I've worked too long without it, just making ends meet. I've avoided looking at the future financial needs of the company, living with the belief, no, that's not accurate, living with the hope, that things would miraculously change without having to deal with this question of money, and my complete ineptitude around it. To be honest, I'm feeling deep shame right now at how foolish and superficial I've been about money. And, I realize, how arrogant I've been to assume that just because I can imagine my company growing, I will somehow find the money to grow it without doing and being any different."

"Sarah, I certainly understand your shame. I'm sure you can imagine the shame I've experienced around all the people who were hurt by my foolishness and arrogance. I think you understand, though, without your willingness to feel your shame about this, which is so courageous, change is impossible. I wish it didn't have to be that way. Your integrity, right now, is what will carve a new path to a different result in your business and your life. This assignment is really going to help you flesh this whole issue out, to see the truth about your relationship to money. What needs to be done will naturally surface as you look into this question. By the time you're done with this assignment, Sarah, you will be well on your way to understanding and taking accountability for the role of the financial leader in All About Pies.

"Then you'll be ready for the second assignment."

THE SECOND ASSIGNMENT

"Create a list, Sarah, of the indicators of your company's financial health, the measures that tell you whether your business is on track or not and producing the results you expect of it or not. And rather than asking an expert or referring to a book on financial metrics, I'd like you to create this list from your own understanding of what you need to know. Simply ask the the question: What do I need to know about the financial performance of my company to know how well it's working?"

Sarah didn't think it was simple. "Maybe I'm just feeling particularly resistant this afternoon, but I don't get it," Sarah said. "I've already admitted I don't know anything about finance other than the little bit of bookkeeping I do to keep track of what's going on. Where are the answers going to come from in me?"

"From the same, natural place that your passion comes from, underneath your fear that you don't know anything, underneath your shame about your money history, underneath your wish to look good to me. Just as you have liberated your passion to work on your behalf, you can also liberate your knowing, about things that your mind will tell you you can't possibly know. Thinking about this list is simply a way of pursuing yourself, to see what happens as you delve deeper and deeper into yourself. You know more than you think you do, Sarah. Check it out.

"And let's talk about the third assignment, the organization of money."

THE THIRD ASSIGNMENT

"And here's the final step I want you to take before we begin the work of the financial leader, Sarah. Remember, for now, these assignments will give you perspective on the work. They are not the content of the work. The perspective provides the parameters for our approach to E-Myth Mastery, to a deeper appreciation and understanding of the disciplines that need to be developed to build a World Class Company. In E-Myth terms, the perspective is a system of thought that creates the platform upon which the work occurs. And each part of Mastery, whether it's a system or a discipline or a process or an assignment, touches every other part. Nothing stands alone. Everything touches everything in a World Class Company. As I've said, over and over again, Sarah, nothing you do stands on its own. When you get that, you really get that you will always look for the connections between things. You will always ask questions that reflect an interest in the implications for the whole. If I do this, then what? How will this change in Finance affect Marketing and Operations and Product Development? That's what leaders do, Sarah. They take in the whole and look for the connections between the parts. They know that you can't get anywhere without looking everywhere. Try to take this in, Sarah, as we move to the next assignment about the organization of money in your company.

"Here's what I'd like you to do. Once you have completed your list, after a month, I'd like you to organize the items on it into categories of information, which are essentially functions within your company. Functions like Operations and Marketing, you know what I mean. This is the organization of money. And it will help you to discover the organization of your company through the financial indicators that relate to it because: one, your financial system will reflect *your operating system* when it is finally done and at every stage of its development. The questions you will ask of your operating system will reflect the answers your financial system gives you about the health and well-being of your company; and two, your financial system will reflect *your management system* by providing each of your managers, and the people who report to them, with a framework for doing the work they do.

Structure, and the perspective it reflects, is critical to the success of your company. Without structure, without an architecture of understanding and a logic tree through which the rationalization of your enterprise is communicated to your people, you will not be able to realize your vision. The organization of money, and the organization of your enterprise, leads to the organization of your organization's mind around your vision. Despite what many believe, organization and the structure that supports it is the fountainhead for inspiration. Without it, people experience chaos and feel at risk. With it, people have a container within which to be their most creative.

"Any questions, Sarah?"

"Surprisingly, no," Sarah said. "All that's left is to do it, and I trust, as you've repeatedly said, Michael, that the process will reveal its meaning as I engage in it. Which is what's so exciting about all this. That you have no expectations whatsoever about what I need to discover. There is no test. It's liberating to feel that free to just pursue the assignments to discover their meaning to me, and to know that I will find whatever they have to reveal. As long as I don't think about all of the other things I have to do, I'm actually looking forward to getting started!"

"Great," I said. "Then let's go on to the work of the financial leader, the content of your homework around money."

SELECTED E-MYTH MASTERY PROGRAM PROCESSES ON FINANCIAL LEADERSHIP

Financial Strategies to Set You on the Right Path: Making Effective Financial Decisions to Get Your House in Order

■

There are strategic financial decisions you've been making (consciously or not) and will be making in the future (consciously, we hope) that determine how soon you'll achieve your Strategic Objective. It's time to take a look at your financial strategy and, if you haven't already begun to do so, make it a conscious part of the everyday management of your business. You'll soon see how your financial strategy, or more accurately, "strategies," fit into the overall scheme of things on the path to your Strategic Objective, and how a clear set of financial strategies helps make all your other decision making more effective and less clouded with uncertainty.

Also, there's one more critical component of your financial management system—pricing. Pricing is the key determinant of your revenue stream, and thus a critical driver of your profitability and cash flow. We'll provide you with a tool for effective pricing decisions later in this process, but first let's look at the big picture.

Let's stand back and look at some fundamental ideas about financial management; some key decisions you should make consciously, rather than by default; and ways for you to manage the financial side of your business, rather than letting it manage itself.

YOU HAVE TWO ROLES, SO YOU NEED TWO FINANCIAL STRATEGIES

Developing your financial strategy requires that you separate yourself from your business. It's not a literal separation. It's just the recognition that you have two different roles—you are the owner and you are also the chief executive officer (CEO). As the owner, your financial role is that of an investor. You want to invest your money in a business that is run responsibly and will provide you with handsome financial benefits. As the CEO, your role is that of running the business responsibly and making sure it is well managed financially.

Financial Strategies to Set You on the Right Path

MAKING EFFECTIVE FINANCIAL DECISIONS TO GET YOUR HOUSE IN ORDER

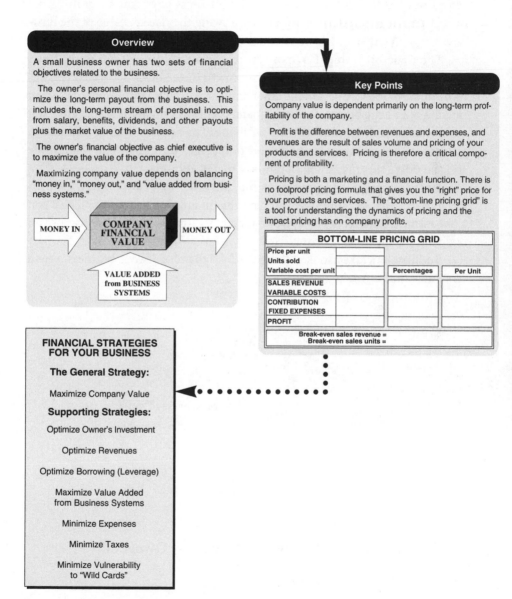

Overview

A small business owner has two sets of financial objectives related to the business.

The owner's personal financial objective is to optimize the long-term payout from the business. This includes the long-term stream of personal income from salary, benefits, dividends, and other payouts plus the market value of the business.

The owner's financial objective as chief executive is to maximize the value of the company.

Maximizing company value depends on balancing "money in," "money out," and "value added from business systems."

MONEY IN → **COMPANY FINANCIAL VALUE** → MONEY OUT

VALUE ADDED from BUSINESS SYSTEMS

Key Points

Company value is dependent primarily on the long-term profitability of the company.

Profit is the difference between revenues and expenses, and revenues are the result of sales volume and pricing of your products and services. Pricing is therefore a critical component of profitability.

Pricing is both a marketing and a financial function. There is no foolproof pricing formula that gives you the "right" price for your products and services. The "bottom-line pricing grid" is a tool for understanding the dynamics of pricing and the impact pricing has on company profits.

BOTTOM-LINE PRICING GRID			
Price per unit			
Units sold			
Variable cost per unit		Percentages	Per Unit
SALES REVENUE			
VARIABLE COSTS			
CONTRIBUTION			
FIXED EXPENSES			
PROFIT			
Break-even sales revenue = Break-even sales units =			

FINANCIAL STRATEGIES FOR YOUR BUSINESS

The General Strategy:

Maximize Company Value

Supporting Strategies:

Optimize Owner's Investment

Optimize Revenues

Optimize Borrowing (Leverage)

Maximize Value Added from Business Systems

Minimize Expenses

Minimize Taxes

Minimize Vulnerability to "Wild Cards"

The two roles can conflict.

As the owner, you want to maximize your financial benefit from your business. Your dilemma is the trade-off between current income and long-term wealth. You earn current income from the salary and benefits you make as an "employee" as well as any dividends the business pays you as an investor/owner. You earn long-term wealth from growing the market value of the business.

The trade-off is this: The more current income you pull out of the business, the less money there is to fuel the growth of the business, which reduces its ultimate market value. On the other hand, if you take a minimum of current income out of the business, you ultimately achieve a higher market value, but at the cost of your current standard of living. The art is in finding the balance point that gives you the current income to support the lifestyle you want, while still providing the business with funds to fuel healthy growth.

You're waiting for the answer to the dilemma, aren't you? Sorry, it's your job to figure that out. But now you have the financial tools (and we'll give you a few more in a moment) to arrive at a financial strategy that will work for you and your business.

But first, let's take a look at the financial dynamics of your business from a strategic point of view.

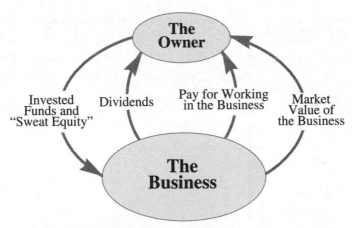

Financial Dynamics of Business Ownership

VALUE, LIKE BEAUTY,
IS IN THE EYE OF THE BEHOLDER

Think of your business as a device whose purpose is the creation of value. Value is a purposely vague term meaning "what is of importance to you." Value could mean a sense of accomplishment, prestige, belonging, contribution to society, power—anything of importance to you. It should be obvious that the overall objective for your business is to maximize its value, and value is what *you* say it is. Your Strategic Objective, if you think about it, is a way of describing your business when it embodies your idea of value.

Some part of the value of a business always includes the element of financial value. In other words, *the primary financial objective of your business is to maximize its financial value.*

You may have other objectives for your business that are more or less important to you than financial objectives, but the financial dimension is always there. And ultimately, that's the whole point of any financial management system—maximizing the financial value of your business. Use the *Financial Strategies* worksheet to help you define your strategies Download for maximizing the value of your business.

WHAT IS "FINANCIAL VALUE"?

For purposes of financial strategy, it is useful to view your company as a financial input-output device, a "black box" of sorts, that takes money in, adds value through its business systems, and puts money out. It's an oversimplification, of course, but it leads to some useful financial management ideas. The most important idea, from a financial point of view, is that of "company value" and the financial benefits to the owner of increasing company value. Large corporations make it a primary strategic objective and call it "shareholder value." It became something of a buzzword on Wall Street in the 1990s, but it's every bit as

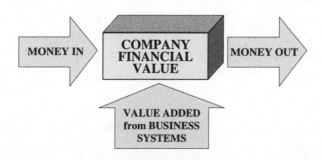

important to the small business owner.

The way you value your business depends on your perspective. There are four common views of company value: market value, book value, liquidation value, and the owner's perception of value.

Market value. This is simply the price you can get by selling your company as a going concern. No one knows for sure what a company's market value is until they actually sell it and the deal is done, but you can make a reasonable estimate (see the inset).

Book value. When you add up all your company's assets and subtract all its liabilities, what's left is the owners' equity, also called its net worth. That's book value, and

> **Estimating Your Business' Market Value**
>
> You can make an estimate of market value by calculating the "present value of the company's future net earnings." It's called the "capitalization of income" method for estimating the financial value of your company to a potential buyer. It's not very exact, but it serves as a rough indication of your company's market value . . . a very rough indication. Here's a simple formula you can use. Divide the normal amount of your company's annual net income by the total rate of return an investor would require for making a long-term investment. For example, say your company earns $250,000 in annual net profit, and the rate of return an investor would require is about 20%. Then a very rough estimate of your company's value would be: $250,000 ÷ .20 = $1.25 million. The idea is that, if your profits hold at the $250,000 level, then it would take an investment of $1.25 million to yield the 20% profit of $250,000 annually. The market value might be higher if your company's prospects seem bright, lower if it's a high-risk company or its future is highly uncertain.
>
> The tricky part is picking an appropriate rate of return. Small businesses are seen by potential buyers as highly risky and as having highly uncertain profits. You can't compare them with companies listed in the stock markets, which are much larger and much less risky (a perception one could debate with enthusiasm). As a "first pass," you might use "triple the bank prime rate" as a rule of thumb for the investor's required rate of return.

it's a measure of how much investment capital and profits have been retained in the company. Banks look at it as a key indicator of a company's financial strength.

Liquidation value. This is what you could get if you sold off your company's assets piecemeal. Usually liquidation occurs in distressed times, and the liquidation value is disappointingly small.

The owner's perception of value. Anyone who has ever been involved in the buying and selling of small businesses knows that owners tend to perceive the value of their businesses as much higher than does a potential buyer. The owner has a fuller sense of the value of the business, including all the nontangible aspects of value, and he tends to attribute a financial value to them that isn't shared by a potential buyer. These elements of value can be very real, but they don't always translate into financial value in the eyes of outsiders.

HOW DO YOU MAXIMIZE YOUR COMPANY'S VALUE?

If you refine the "black box" idea to focus attention on the key financial elements of your business, you can establish a strategy for each of them, and orchestrate them for the overall benefit of the business.

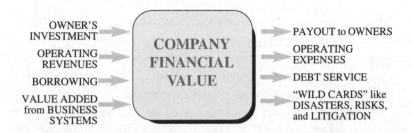

"Money In" breaks down into the owner's investment, operating revenues (normally the biggest, most important source of funds), money borrowed from banks and others, and value added from business systems. "Money Out" breaks down into payouts to the owner(s), operating expenses (normally the largest outlay of funds), debt service to repay loans, and outlays due to unforeseen "wild cards" that occasionally happen to a business.

OWNER'S INVESTMENT AND PAYOUTS TO THE OWNER

Owners benefit financially from their companies in two ways: from the long-term appreciation of company value, and from payouts in the form of salary, benefits, and dividends. There is an important trade-off to consider when owners think about their personal financial strategy, and whether to grow the company or use it to fund their current standard of living. The less money owners take out of their company, the better its prospects for growth, and the higher the price the owners ultimately will get when (and if) they decide to sell the company. The more money owners take out of their company, the lower the ultimate value of the company, and the lower the sales price when and if they sell.

The owner's personal financial strategy can be an important determinant of the company's financial performance. In general, whether on purpose or by default, owners follow one of three strategies:

- Maximize current personal income from the company.
- Maximize company value and minimize personal income from the company.

- Balance personal income and company value by limiting personal income from the company to a percentage (or $_____) of company net profits.

LEVERAGE: A DOUBLE-EDGED SWORD

The word "leverage" in company finance refers to the amount of debt in comparison to the amount of the owners' equity in the company. You measure leverage with the debt-to-equity ratio you learned about earlier in this module. The more debt (bank loans, loans from private investors, accounts payable, etc.), the higher the return on the owner's investment because the company can be bigger and grow faster when supported by large amounts of borrowed money. But debt, and the cash drain of paying off large amounts of debt, increase the company's vulnerability to downturns or events that reduce revenues and increase costs.

If you have high confidence in the sustained success of your company or a high tolerance for risk, you might want your company to be highly leveraged. It's usually not a good idea, but there are times when it can make sense. On the other hand, if you want your company to be able to withstand periods of difficulty and unforeseen events, you may want to take a conservative approach and minimize leverage. It's your choice, but we recommend the conservative approach.

Where does all that logic leave you in terms of financial strategy? It boils down to two overall strategies.

THE OWNER'S PERSONAL FINANCIAL STRATEGY FOR THE BUSINESS: OPTIMIZE LONG-TERM PAYOUTS TO THE OWNER

For most small businesses, especially those in their start-up phase and those struggling in hard times, optimizing long-term payouts to the owner means the owner may have to sacrifice current income in favor of building the company. The essence of the word "optimize" is balance, in this case balancing your personal needs against the needs of the business. Keeping the company's earnings inside the company gives the business the best chance for success. Then later, payouts to yourself, including the ultimate gain when (and if) you sell the business, should be much more rewarding.

You'll have to figure out the trade-off for yourself. There are no formulas or rules of thumb because the trade-off depends entirely on your personal situation, your need for current income, and the ability of your company to sustain payouts to you and still keep on track toward its Strategic Objective.

THE CEO'S FINANCIAL STRATEGY FOR THE BUSINESS: MAXIMIZE COMPANY VALUE

Whatever you decide personally to draw from the company in salary, benefits, and dividends, when you are wearing your CEO's hat, it should be your financial objective to build the company's financial value.

That's easy to say, but how do you do it? How do you maximize the value of your company? You break the main strategy down into more manageable substrategies, each of which you can identify and manage for best effect. Here are the main substrategies:

Optimize the owner's investment. As the owner, you probably want to invest the minimum amount of your own funds, but you also want to provide enough capital to assure the company's financial health and maintain control of your company. If there are other investors, your share has to be the largest, or theirs has to be in "nonvoting" shares in order for you to maintain control.

Optimize revenues. Normally you would think in terms of *maximizing* revenues. After all, the more revenues you earn, the more successful your business appears to be, and the greater is its value. But a more balanced strategy is called for.

Fast growth can be a serious problem—the kind of problem we might like to have, but a problem nevertheless. For many companies, fast growth can create significant cash deficits. It works like this: In order to grow, marketing and production have to take place before sales can happen. That means heavy cash outflows take place before the heavy cash inflows. The result is sizable cash deficits. This dynamic can create a situation in which a company can be highly profitable, yet be endangered because of a "cash crunch." Fortunately, you have the tools—cash flow statements and cash planning—to anticipate and prepare for fast growth.

Optimize borrowing. You may be tempted to leverage your investment with borrowed funds, but you need to be concerned about excessive leverage. Your company's market value will be diminished if potential buyers see it as too highly leveraged. From a buyer's point of view, leverage contributes to risk, and risk reduces the value of your company. Bankers take a similar view and will reduce the amount of loans they will be willing to make to your company if they think it is leveraged excessively.

But what is the "appropriate" level of debt? This becomes a balancing act because you want to avoid excessive leverage and minimize cash outflows for debt servicing, but you also want to fuel growth and increase the return on the owner's investment in the company.

Some say "appropriate" is whatever you can get lenders to give you. There's a superficial appeal to this approach—it requires the lenders to analyze your business and make up their minds how much debt they think you

> **FINANCIAL STRATEGIES FOR YOUR BUSINESS**
>
> **The General Strategy:**
>
> Maximize Company Value
>
> **Supporting Strategies:**
>
> Optimize Owner's Investment
>
> Optimize Revenues
>
> Optimize Borrowing (Leverage)
>
> Maximize Value Added from Business Systems
>
> Minimize Expenses
>
> Minimize Taxes
>
> Minimize Vulnerability to "Wild Cards"

can sustain. The appealing part is that you have an outsider's opinion of your debt capacity. That seems okay if you want to have outsiders tell you what's best for your business, but it's not *really* okay. *You* are the one who knows, or should know, what's best for your business.

And "what's best for your business" really is the only correct answer. But "what's best" is another way of saying "it depends." It depends on your Strategic Objective, your personal attitude toward risk, the kind of business you operate, the size of your business, your cash flow dynamics, the volatility of your sales, your competitive situation, the national and local economy, and on and on. So this is one time we're not going to give you a convenient rule of thumb. As you hone your financial management skills, the leverage question will resolve itself. You will develop a sharper, quantified view of how much debt your business can sustain, what your own tolerance for risk is, and what funding will be required to achieve the growth you want. The answer will come to you as a by-product of the process in which you are now engaged.

Maximize value added from business systems. Did you ever wonder where profits *really* come from? Yes, of course, profit is the difference between revenues and expenses, but that's just how it's calculated. What *makes* profits? What makes a customer willing to pay you more than the costs of materials and labor that go into your products or services? They're also paying you for the value your business has added to the resources used to create the product. It's your business systems that add that value. It's your business systems that create profit. You'll be covering your business systems extensively throughout the E-Myth Mastery Program.

Minimize expenses. No mystery here. Every dollar of expense savings goes directly to your bottom line. Every business, regardless of its size and no matter how successful, should have an aggressive, never-ending cost control program.

Minimize taxes. Minimizing taxes is not simply a matter of being clever about filing tax returns. It's also a matter of understanding the tax consequences of business decisions, and most of us don't have the knowledge to do this well. This is another of those areas where your accountant is indispensable.

Minimize vulnerability to "wild cards." The wild cards of small business are those unpredictable, sometimes disastrous, events that we cannot foresee. Even if we cannot foresee them, we can take steps to minimize their impact. Contingency planning, insurance coverage, computer backup files, and reserve funds are some of the tools to help limit your company's vulnerability.

THE KEY TO THE FINANCIAL VALUE OF YOUR COMPANY: PROFITS

When you look at the components that contribute to your company's financial value, it's clear that revenues and expenses—that is, profits—are the dominant components. To maximize financial value, you have to maximize long-term profitability. That means minimize your operating expenses and optimize your operating revenues.

We've put a lot of emphasis on revenues and expenses in this module. Now we're going to look closely at another key determinant of profitability— pricing.

PRICING IS WHERE MARKETING AND FINANCE MEET

If you price your products and services effectively, your prices will be acceptable to your customers and give them a sense that they have received value for their money, while at the same time producing revenue that covers your company's costs and generates the profits you want. Customer attraction and satisfaction is a marketing responsibility. Balancing the revenues and expenses of your business is a financial responsibility. Effective pricing requires both marketing and financial thinking.

The point is, don't think of pricing as just a financial function. And don't

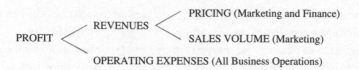

PROFIT — REVENUES — PRICING (Marketing and Finance) / SALES VOLUME (Marketing) / OPERATING EXPENSES (All Business Operations)

think of it as just a marketing function. It's neither because it's both. Like so many things your business does, pricing is an integrated activity requiring a whole-business thought process.

PRICING ISN'T A SCIENCE, IT'S A CRAFT

The "holy grail" of business is the foolproof pricing formula. Everyone wants the answer to the question: "What is *exactly* the right price for my product—the price at which my business will attract the most customers and produce the highest profits?" No one has found the holy grail and no one has yet found the foolproof pricing formula either.

Even the largest companies, with their extensive market research and financial analysis support, have difficulty with pricing. For them to obtain reliable pricing information, they have to accumulate extensive historical data and use sophisticated analysis to determine price/sales volume relationships, and even then, the relationships are constantly changing due to product advances, competition, and shifting customer perceptions.

We do know that pricing is linked with sales volume in an "inverse" way. If you raise your price, you can expect to sell fewer products. If you reduce your price, you can expect to sell fewer products. But the linkage isn't what the mathematicians call "linear." A 10 percent price cut doesn't necessarily create a 10 percent increase in sales. Furthermore, whatever the relationship between price and sales volume is, it's different in different markets and with different products. So a pricing formula that works for a company in one city won't necessarily work for an identical business somewhere else.

But the question is too important to leave to chance and guesswork. Fortunately, there are ways to make good pricing decisions—decisions that make maximum use of your market knowledge and your common sense.

BOTTOM-LINE PRICING— THE RIGHT TOOL FOR THE JOB

Knowing that pricing is a whole-business activity, doesn't it make sense to take a whole-business approach to pricing decisions? Of course it does.

We have a tool for it. We call it the "bottom-line pricing grid." The tool has more uses than pricing, but we're going to focus on pricing for the moment.

The bottom-line pricing grid isn't a formula that cranks out the "right" answer. But it is a structured way to think about the pricing question, to test any number of alternatives, and to know in advance the consequences of pricing changes so you can make informed decisions. It requires that you consider both the financial and the marketing implications of your pricing decisions. And it doesn't require you to be a mathematician.

Here's an example of a bottom-line pricing grid. Look at it for a moment. See what you can make of it. Then we'll discuss it in detail, show you how to use it for your own pricing analysis, and take you through a few examples. This example shows product profitability for a small company in the business of manufacturing men's shirts.

BOTTOM-LINE PRICING GRID				
Price per unit	$ 30.00			
Units sold	25,000			
Variable cost per unit	$ 18.00	Percentages	Per Unit	
SALES REVENUE	$ 750,000	100.0%	$ 30.00	
VARIABLE COSTS	450,000	60.0%	$ 18.00	
CONTRIBUTION	$ 300,000	40.0%	$ 12.00	
FIXED EXPENSES	225,000	30.0%	$ 9.00	
PROFIT	$ 75,000	10.0%	$ 3.00	
Break-even sales revenue = $ 562,500				
Break-even sales units = 18,750				

Per unit information { (brackets around "Price per unit", "Units sold", "Variable cost per unit")

Condensed income statement { (brackets around SALES REVENUE through PROFIT)

Income statement percentages (label right of title)

Dollars per unit information (label right of SALES REVENUE–PROFIT section)

Break-even figures (label right of break-even section)

Does it look intimidating? Wait until you see how easy it is to use! It only requires you to have four key numbers, and those come directly from your accounting information. The four key numbers are:

- Price per unit
- Number of units sold
- Variable cost per unit
- Total fixed expenses

The rest is simple calculation. The *Pricing Grid* worksheet walks you through the arithmetic.

To use the bottom-line pricing grid, the first thing you'll do is cre- **Download** ate a "baseline" for your existing business based on your recent history. That will tell you the critical relationship among pricing, sales, and costs.

Then you can use the same format to look into the future and evaluate any

BOTTOM-LINE PRICING GRID			
Price per unit			
Units sold			
Variable cost per unit		Percentages	Per Unit
SALES REVENUE			
VARIABLE COSTS			
CONTRIBUTION			
FIXED EXPENSES			
PROFIT			
Break-even sales revenue =			
Break-even sales units =			

number of "what-if" scenarios. What if you want to raise your prices by $X per unit? What if you want to launch an aggressive marketing campaign that will generate X percent additional sales? What if your fixed expenses are expected to increase? What if you can cut production costs by $2 per unit? What if your main competitor has just cut prices by 10 percent; can you match that price cut? What if . . . ?

Here are a few examples of how the pricing grid can be used (using the shirt manufacturing company's pricing grid illustrated previously as the baseline for all examples):

What if you raise your price from $30 to $33? That would probably reduce sales down to, let's say, 22,000 units.

BOTTOM-LINE PRICING GRID			
Price per unit	$ 33.00		
Units sold	22,000		
Variable cost per unit	$ 18.00	Percentages	Per Unit
SALES REVENUE	$ 726,000	100.0%	$ 33.00
VARIABLE COSTS	396,000	54.5%	$ 18.00
CONTRIBUTION	$ 330,000	45.5%	$ 15.00
FIXED EXPENSES	225,000	31.0%	$ 10.23
PROFIT	$ 105,000	14.5%	$ 4.77
Break-even sales revenue = $ 495,000			
Break-even sales units = 15,000			

The price increase does nice things for the bottom line, raising profits from $75,000 to $105,000, and boosting the profit margin up to 14.5 percent from the baseline 10 percent. How confident are you that the price increase will not depress sales more than you expect? You should be reassured by the fact that the price increase drops your break-even point down to 15,000 units from the baseline 18,750—a large margin for error.

What if you could increase sales by 50 percent? You estimate it would also increase your fixed expenses by $100,000. What would be the impact?

BOTTOM-LINE PRICING GRID			
Price per unit	$ 30.00		
Units sold	37,500		
Variable cost per unit $	18.00	Percentages	Per Unit
SALES REVENUE	$ 1,125,000	100.0%	$ 30.00
VARIABLE COSTS	675,000	60.0%	$ 18.00
CONTRIBUTION	$ 450,000	40.0%	$ 12.00
FIXED EXPENSES	325,000	28.9%	$ 8.67
PROFIT	$ 125,000	11.1%	$ 3.33
Break-even sales revenue = $ 812,500			
Break-even sales units = 27,083			

You can see that the increase in fixed expenses raises the break-even point from the baseline $562,500 to $812,500, but there's still a large margin of safety with sales revenue at $1,125,000. The sales increase more than offsets the cost increase. The key issue is, can you *really* increase sales? And will it only raise your fixed expenses $100,000?

What if you could trim your fixed expenses by $40,000 and still hold the same sales volume?

BOTTOM-LINE PRICING GRID			
Price per unit	$ 30.00		
Units sold	25,000		
Variable cost per unit $	18.00	Percentages	Per Unit
SALES REVENUE	$ 750,000	100.0%	$ 30.00
VARIABLE COSTS	450,000	60.0%	$ 18.00
CONTRIBUTION	$ 300,000	40.0%	$ 12.00
FIXED EXPENSES	185,000	24.7%	$ 7.40
PROFIT	$ 115,000	15.3%	$ 4.60
Break-even sales revenue = $ 462,500			
Break-even sales units = 15,417			

Again, the results look encouraging. Profits go up (from $75,000 to $115,000) and your break-even point goes down (from $562,500 to $462,500). The question is, can you really find ways to trim fixed expenses without harming product quality or cutting into your marketing activities? What if you could cut your production costs by $1.00 per unit? (Production costs are all variable costs for this company.)

BOTTOM-LINE PRICING GRID			
Price per unit	$ 30.00		
Units sold	25,000		
Variable cost per unit	$ 17.00	Percentages	Per Unit
SALES REVENUE	$ 750,000	100.0%	$ 30.00
VARIABLE COSTS	425,000	56.7%	$ 17.00
CONTRIBUTION	$ 325,000	43.3%	$ 13.00
FIXED EXPENSES	225,000	30.0%	$ 9.00
PROFIT	$ 100,000	13.3%	$ 4.00
Break-even sales revenue = $ 519,231			
Break-even sales units = 17,308			

Once again, the change, if you can accomplish it, will help your bottom line, and will lower your break-even point.

What if your competitors dropped their prices by 15 percent? Could you match their prices? Assume that you wouldn't be able to increase your unit sales because everyone's prices went down.

BOTTOM-LINE PRICING GRID			
Price per unit	$ 25.50		
Units sold	25,000		
Variable cost per unit	$ 18.00	Percentages	Per Unit
SALES REVENUE	$ 637,500	100.0%	$ 25.50
VARIABLE COSTS	450,000	70.6%	$ 18.00
CONTRIBUTION	$ 187,500	29.4%	$ 7.50
FIXED EXPENSES	225,000	35.3%	$ 9.00
PROFIT	$ (37,500)	-5.9%	$ (1.50)
Break-even sales revenue = $ 765,000			
Break-even sales units = 30,000			

Now you have some decisions to make. If you match the competitive price, you'll take a loss. If you maintain your price, how much business will you lose to your competitors? Can you counteract your competitor's pricing with aggressive marketing? What will the increased marketing and sales expenses do to your bottom line?

There are any number of questions, but the bottom-line pricing grid gives you a valuable way to assess the consequences of your decisions. It doesn't quite give you all the answers, but neither are you flying blind. You have a way to break the competitive problem down into alternatives that you can manage, and whose consequences you can estimate with the pricing grid.

You've noticed of course that each what-if case still depends on your own knowledge of your business, your markets, and your judgment. But now you know the financial consequences of your decisions, and the degree to which errors can hurt you. You can explore any number of decisions and potential consequences.

THE BOTTOM-LINE PRICING GRID
WORKS FOR MULTIPLE PRODUCTS, EVEN WHEN
YOUR COSTS ARE UNCERTAIN

What if you have more than one product? One approach is to average the prices of all your products or services and look at them in the aggregate as we did with the shirt company. But that doesn't help you evaluate the prices of individual products.

There's a better way. You set up a pricing grid for *each* of your products and see how each one impacts your bottom line. But you'll have to do two things a little differently.

When you have only one product, your income statement gives you all the information you need on variable and fixed costs. But your income statement doesn't break out your cost information for separate products; it just shows everything all lumped together. To look at separate products, you'll have to go into your accounting information, or have your accountant do it for you. If your accounting system (and your chart of accounts) doesn't capture product-by-product information, you'll have to do some estimating. (Incidentally, it's a good idea to set up your accounting system so that it *will* capture variable costs for separate products.)

Fixed expenses are a different matter. By their very nature, fixed costs aren't directly associated with your products and services. They support overhead, marketing, and other costs. But you can make some reasonable assumptions and *allocate* fixed expenses to products so you can see how profitable they are.

Think of it this way. What if your business has two products, say widgets and thingamabobs. And furthermore, about two-thirds of your manufacturing space, machinery, and people are devoted to producing widgets, and the other third are involved in producing thingamabobs. Wouldn't it make sense that, even though you can't point precisely to the amount of management attention, financial support, and other support activities that are dedicated to widgets, you could make the reasonable assumption that, since widgets are about two-thirds of your business, about two-thirds of your fixed expenses could be attributed to widgets?

The idea is to look at the way your business operates and allocate your fixed expenses to products based on some measurement that reflects the way your overall resources are used. It's not exact, but making reasonable assumptions is much better than making the false assumption that your fixed costs apply equally to all your products.

A MULTIPRODUCT EXAMPLE

Here's an example to illustrate: Imagine a company that sells baked goods. It makes all its own bread products, but it buys pastries from another bakery nearby. Almost all its people, facilities, and equipment are dedicated to baking bread products, and only a couple of people and some counter space are used for pastries, yet pastries make up 50 percent of sales. You could allocate the company's fixed expenses two ways. You could say, since pastries are half of sales, they should support half of your overhead. But that doesn't reflect the way you operate the business. It's more realistic to notice that most of the company's people, facilities, and equipment are dedicated to bread-baking with only a few people working on purchasing, receiving, and handling pastries. The bulk of the business operation is dedicated to bread products. So you could allocate fixed expenses on the basis of headcount, or any other measure that reasonably reflects the situation. For instance, if the company has 30 people in the business operation, 25 in bread-baking, and 5 in the pastry operation, it would be appropriate to use those proportions, 25 to 5, as the basis for allocating fixed expenses to products.

If you have no quantifiable way to allocate your fixed expenses, it's still better to make a judgment based on your perceptions, even if they're not exact, than it is not to recognize the differences at all.

Let's illustrate further by looking at another example, this time the shirt maker we talked about earlier. What if instead of one $30 shirt, the business sells three kinds of shirts: off-the-rack shirts for $22.50 each, upscale shirts for $50.00, and custom-made shirts for $100.00. On the next page are the bottom-line pricing grids for each of the three products plus the company totals shown in the "all products" grid.

The company didn't have detailed accounting information about the variable costs for each type of shirt, so they made some reasonable estimates based on their knowledge of the costs of fabric, buttons, thread, the labor required for each type of shirt, freight charges, and the like.

Fixed expenses were more straightforward. Off-the-rack shirts comprised the bulk of their business and the largest part of their sales revenues, amounting to 80 percent of the shirts they sold. It was clear that they could allocate their fixed expenses based on the number of each type of shirt they sold. So they allocated 80 percent of their fixed expenses to off-the-rack shirts (20,000

ALL PRODUCTS

		Percentages	Per Unit
Price per unit	$ 30.00		
Units sold	25,000		
Variable cost per unit	$ 18.00		
SALES REVENUE	$ 750,000	100.0%	$ 30.00
VARIABLE COSTS	450,000	60.0%	$ 18.00
CONTRIBUTION	$ 300,000	40.0%	$ 12.00
FIXED EXPENSES	225,000	30.0%	$ 9.00
PROFIT	$ 75,000	10.0%	$ 3.00

Break-even sales revenue = $ 562,500
Break-even sales units = 18,750

PRODUCT A: OFF-THE-RACK SHIRTS

		Percentages	Per Unit
Price per unit	$ 22.50		
Units sold	20,000		
Variable cost per unit	$ 15.75		
SALES REVENUE	$ 450,000	100.0%	$ 22.50
VARIABLE COSTS	315,000	70.0%	$ 15.75
CONTRIBUTION	$ 135,000	30.0%	$ 6.75
FIXED EXPENSES	180,000	40.0%	$ 9.00
PROFIT	$ (45,000)	-10.0%	$ (2.25)

Break-even sales revenue = $ 600,000
Break-even sales units = 26,667

PRODUCT B: UPSCALE SHIRTS

		Percentages	Per Unit
Price per unit	$ 50.00		
Units sold	4,000		
Variable cost per unit	$ 25.00		
SALES REVENUE	$ 200,000	100.0%	$ 50.00
VARIABLE COSTS	100,000	50.0%	$ 25.00
CONTRIBUTION	$ 100,000	50.0%	$ 25.00
FIXED EXPENSES	36,000	18.0%	$ 9.00
PROFIT	$ 64,000	32.0%	$ 16.00

Break-even sales revenue = $ 72,000
Break-even sales units = 1,440

PRODUCT C: CUSTOM-MADE SHIRTS

		Percentages	Per Unit
Price per unit	$ 100.00		
Units sold	1,000		
Variable cost per unit	$ 35.00		
SALES REVENUE	$ 100,000	100.0%	$ 100.00
VARIABLE COSTS	35,000	35.0%	$ 35.00
CONTRIBUTION	$ 65,000	65.0%	$ 65.00
FIXED EXPENSES	9,000	9.0%	$ 9.00
PROFIT	$ 56,000	56.0%	$ 56.00

Break-even sales revenue = $ 13,846
Break-even sales units = 138

of their total 25,000 units sold, or 80 percent), 16 percent to upscale shirts, and the remaining 4 percent to custom-made shirts.

With those estimates plus the product prices and unit sales figures, they completed bottom-line pricing grids as shown on the previous page, one for each product line, plus one for all products.

The first thing you should notice is that the company is making a comfortable 10 percent net profit on all its products in aggregate, and is operating well over its break-even point. In general, it's a pretty healthy picture, so there's no immediate worry. But there are some interesting strategy questions and some potential opportunities.

Take a look at the bread-and-butter product, off-the-rack shirts. It looks like a loser with a $45,000 monthly loss (−10 percent profitability), and a long way to go to reach break-even. But is it *really* a loser? On a contribution basis, off-the-rack shirts generate a monthly 60 percent ($135,000) of the company's total $225,000 fixed expenses. A lot of companies would like to have a product line that reliably covers its own costs plus 60 percent of company fixed expenses as this product does. Is it more important that each product be profitable, or that the entire company be profitable?

Normally, you want each and every product to be profitable in its own right, but what if that's not possible? What if you have a product like off-the-rack shirts that are the backbone of your business, but aren't profitable. You can't simply eliminate the "losing" product—it supports the rest of your business. If you eliminated off-the-rack shirts, you would be left with a two-product business generating a total of $300,000 in revenues and a very nice contribution margin of 55 percent. The problem is that this reduced-size business only throws off $165,000 in contribution to cover $225,000 in fixed expenses, resulting in a company net loss of $60,000.

Not good.

So, clearly, the business is better off with than without the off-the-rack product.

From a strategic point of view, however, there are a number of decisions brought to light by the bottom-line profit grids. In the short run, the business has to continue to depend on its mainstay, off-the-rack shirts. But it should be a high priority to increase the profitability of that product. Can prices be increased without losing sales volume? Are there opportunities to cut variable costs and make the product inherently more profitable? Can fixed expenses be reduced without hurting company operations or reducing the future potential of the more profitable products?

In the longer term, what are the opportunities to grow the upscale and custom-made shirt businesses? This is more of a marketing question than it is a financial question. The company has to take a close look at its markets—how large are the markets, what are the psychographic profiles, what will it take to grow sales volumes of these highly profitable products?

The truth is that these are neither marketing nor financial questions—they are *business* questions. And the bottom-line pricing grid doesn't give you answers, it gives you a better way to think about your business and come up with strategies that work best for you.

BUSINESS STRATEGIES, NOT FINANCIAL STRATEGIES

You may have noticed a theme developing as you work your way through the modules and business development process of the E-Myth Mastery Program—the theme of integration. Business schools teach functional specialties like marketing, finance, organizational behavior, and production. Businesses themselves organize into functional units. The instinct of both is to deintegrate the way businesses are managed. They have to. It's the only way to make the complex job of business manageable.

The essential fact, however, is that businesses are living, integrated entities. What is done in one part of a business has effects elsewhere in the business and in the company's markets. The owner of a small business and the CEO of a multinational corporation have one thing in common. While the people reporting to them can take a narrow, specialized view of the business, the person at the top has to take the *integrated* view in order to produce the desired result.

"Maximum Cash":
Unleashing the Cash Power in Your Business

▪

Do you remember the idea that cash is the lifeblood of your business? It's never more true than when your business is growing. The faster the growth, the more cash you need. And even if "growth" for you is getting better rather than getting bigger, it still takes cash.

If you're getting bigger, it takes cash to gear up your lead generation and lead conversion, and to build your inventories and set up your client fulfillment systems to serve the greater business volume that growth will bring. If you're getting better, it takes cash to fund your development work, establish quality control improvements, and create customer service systems.

Where will you get the cash you need to grow?

You'll either look internally to get the most out of your business's re-

"Maximum Cash"

UNLEASHING THE CASH POWER IN YOUR BUSINESS

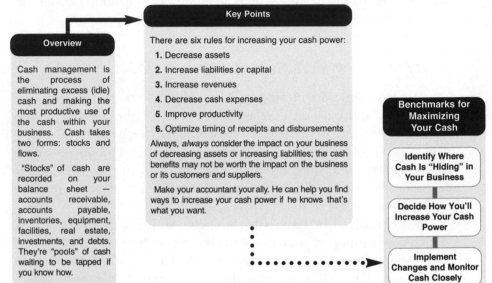

Overview

Cash management is the process of eliminating excess (idle) cash and making the most productive use of the cash within your business. Cash takes two forms: stocks and flows.

"Stocks" of cash are recorded on your balance sheet — accounts receivable, accounts payable, inventories, equipment, facilities, real estate, investments, and debts. They're "pools" of cash waiting to be tapped if you know how.

"Flows" of cash through your business are shown on your income statement — revenues and cash expenses (but not non-cash expenditures). They're the result of the productivity of your people, systems, and technology.

"Cash Power" is financial momentum. It's both the *amount* of cash flowing through your business and the *velocity* with which it flows. Anything that increases cash or speeds its flow adds to your cash power.

The arrow-shaped diagram shows how various parts of your business contribute to your cash power.

Key Points

There are six rules for increasing your cash power:

1. Decrease assets
2. Increase liabilities or capital
3. Increase revenues
4. Decrease cash expenses
5. Improve productivity
6. Optimize timing of receipts and disbursements

Always, *always* consider the impact on your business of decreasing assets or increasing liabilities; the cash benefits may not be worth the impact on the business or its customers and suppliers.

Make your accountant your ally. He can help you find ways to increase your cash power if he knows that's what you want.

Benchmarks for Maximizing Your Cash

Identify Where Cash Is "Hiding" in Your Business

Decide How You'll Increase Your Cash Power

Implement Changes and Monitor Cash Closely

Balance Sheet: "Stocks" of Cash

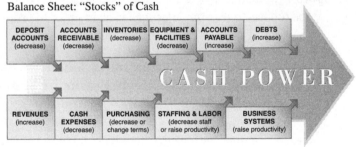

Business Operations: "Flows" of Cash

sources, or you'll look externally to find ways to bring in outside funding. Fact is, you'll probably do both.

This process looks internally. It shows you how to get "maximum cash" from your assets and business operations by increasing your "cash power." That way, even if you do have to use outside funding sources, you can minimize your external cash needs and minimize the costs of obtaining funding from outsiders. You start by understanding where cash is hidden in your business and knowing how to free it up to fuel your growth.

YOU HAVE MORE CASH THAN YOU THINK YOU DO . . .
PROBABLY A LOT MORE

There are two places cash hides in your business—in your assets and in your business operations. You have to understand a few basic ideas to find it. It's like those picture puzzles you played with when you were a kid.

Remember, for example, the picture of a jungle scene in which you were supposed to find the "hidden" animals? If you weren't looking for animals, all you saw was a simple jungle scene. But if you knew you were looking for hidden animals, you looked at the picture a different way . . . the two coconuts weren't coconuts at all but the eyes of an elephant. The hanging vine, not a vine, but a snake, or the tail of a hidden monkey. The fanlike fern, not a fern, but the spread tail of a peacock. If you knew how to look at the picture, the animals revealed themselves—some obvious, some obscure, but all visible if you knew how to look.

It's like that with hidden cash in your business. Accounts receivable, inventories, accounts payable, and other assets are pools of cash waiting to be tapped if you know how. Your revenues and your operating expenses are streams of cash running through your business, some draining it (you can reduce the drain) and others nourishing it (you can increase the "nourishing" flow).

THINK OF STOCKS AND FLOWS . . .
LAKES AND RIVERS OF CASH

How do lakes differ from rivers? Rivers move. Lakes just sit there. Rivers are "flows" of water. Lakes are "stocks" of water. They're both made of water; they just behave a bit differently from each other. Stocks and flows. If you want to make a lake larger, you either increase the flow from rivers that feed it or you decrease the outflow from rivers that drain it. More important, for those who depend on the lakes, you can increase the availability of water by either increasing the flow, which reduces the size of the lake, or increasing the speed with which water flows into and through it. If you have complete control over the rivers emptying into the lake *and* those draining the lake, you don't need the lake at all; you simply need to control the inflows and outflows so you have the water you need when you need it . . . "just in time" water.

You see where all this is headed, of course. The stocks and flows of water in nature are an exact analogy for cash in your business. Your business has stocks and flows of cash, and you can control them in ways that reduce your need for cash, that release hidden cash, and that increase the "velocity" of cash through your business, thus releasing the "cash power" available to you.

The "stocks" of cash in your business are recorded on your balance sheet—accounts receivable, accounts payable, inventories, equipment, facilities, real estate, investments, debts—each represents something real in your business. Each "account" on your balance sheet also represents a lake of cash that either soaks up cash, immobilizing it and making it unavailable for use in growing your business, or, if you know how it's done, can release cash to use elsewhere in your business.

The "flows" of cash through your business are quantified on your income statement—revenues and cash expenditures—and are speeded up or slowed by your business operations—the productivity and efficiency of your staff, technology, and business systems.

You'll see how to release the cash in your business in a moment, but first take a look at this idea of "cash power." Think of it as a form of momentum.

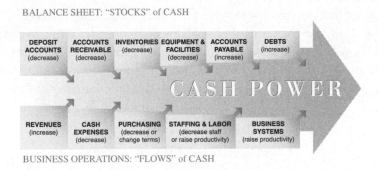

BALANCE SHEET: "STOCKS" of CASH

| DEPOSIT ACCOUNTS (decrease) | ACCOUNTS RECEIVABLE (decrease) | INVENTORIES (decrease) | EQUIPMENT & FACILITIES (decrease) | ACCOUNTS PAYABLE (increase) | DEBTS (increase) |

CASH POWER

| REVENUES (increase) | CASH EXPENSES (decrease) | PURCHASING (decrease or change terms) | STAFFING & LABOR (decrease staff or raise productivity) | BUSINESS SYSTEMS (raise productivity) |

BUSINESS OPERATIONS: "FLOWS" of CASH

"CASH POWER" IS THE FINANCIAL "MOMENTUM" OF YOUR BUSINESS

"Momentum" is the result of both speed and size. A bullet has tremendous power even though it weighs less than an ounce. The faster the bullet flies, the greater its impact. It gets power from its speed. But an avalanche also has tremendous power. It may move slowly, but it's huge, and it derives power from its mass. The idea of momentum is that the larger an object is *and* the faster it's moving, the greater its momentum, its *power*.

And that's the idea of the "cash power" of your business. The more cash you have at your disposal, and the faster it moves through your business, the greater your financial momentum, your cash power.

So cash power is what happens when you get *more* cash by releasing it from the stocks that appear on your balance sheet, and when you also move cash through your business *faster* by accelerating the flow of cash through your business operations.

SIX RULES FOR CREATING CASH POWER

So how does this work? How do you wring the maximum cash power out of your business? There are six rules:

1. Decrease assets
2. Increase liabilities or capital
3. Increase revenues
4. Decrease cash expenses
5. Improve productivity
6. Optimize timing

Most business owners think only in terms of increasing revenues and decreasing expenses, but, as you can see, there are many more ways to skin this particular cat.

There are pitfalls and risks associated with each rule, and differing ways to get maximum cash from differing businesses.

1. **Decrease assets.** Simply decreasing assets can be foolish. You employ your assets to conduct your business, and decreasing them indiscriminately, while that will free up cash, can also cripple your business. So the idea is to reduce assets, but do so in a way that doesn't hurt your business.

2. **Increase liabilities or capital.** Increasing liabilities or capital gives outsiders—lenders, vendors, or investors—a greater claim on your business. That can reduce your control, reduce the income you receive from the business, and can have other undesirable effects. Of course, if you, as the owner, pay in more equity capital or make loans to the business, there is no effect on your control, but it is money out of your

pocket, and that can be burdensome. The onetime inflow of cash may or may not be worth its side effects.

3. **Increase revenues.** Growing revenues is often the most desirable way to increase cash power, but it usually takes up-front cash to generate the revenues, which is the reason you need the cash in the first place. In this case, your strategy is usually to increase prices (be careful!), speed payment, or even arrange for payment in advance.

4. **Decrease cash expenses.** Reducing any expense has the effect of increasing profits, but cutting *cash* expenses—those expenses paid out in cash—has the added benefit of increasing your cash power. Often you don't even have to reduce the expense to get a benefit, for instance, when you can slow payment or pay over a longer period of time.

5. **Improve productivity.** The never-ending opportunity for any business owner or manager is to improve business systems and the efficiency of the people and other resources used in the business. Profit increases are an obvious result, but improved cash flow can be every bit as important in a growth period.

6. **Optimize timing.** When it comes to cash, you may not be able to do anything about the *amount* of cash you receive or pay out, but you can still benefit from the right *timing.* Think "stretching," "accelerating," or "just-in-time."

   - Stretching payments means delaying payouts or paying them over an extended period of time. It's a good way to conserve cash, but pay careful attention to your relationships with vendors and other third parties, and be sure that you're not losing the benefits of discounts or incurring unnecessary interest or other "penalties."
   - Accelerating receipts means receiving payments due to you sooner (maybe even in advance) or over a shorter period of time. Again, make sure you're not giving up more than you're getting.
   - Just-in-time means receiving supplies, services, and other goods just as you need them rather than "stockpiling" them in inventories. JIT (just-in-time) requires you to plan ahead, and to manage your business systems precisely so you always have the resources you need when you need them, *and no later.* With JIT you run the risk of interrupting your business if you run out of materials or services, but you also benefit from cash flow that more precisely matches your business processes.

Not all of these opportunities for improving cash power exist in every business, and they take differing forms in different businesses. You'll have to see what works for your situation in your business.

Those are the general rules. Let's look at how to apply them to the situations most often found in small businesses.

WRINGING CASH OUT OF YOUR BALANCE SHEET WITHOUT SHUTTING DOWN YOUR GROWTH

You need cash to fuel your growth, but if you're too aggressive about it, you can cut into productive assets and slow down the very growth you're trying to create. So don't be single-minded about it. As always, take the systemic view—your business is an integrated organism each of whose parts has an effect on the others. Think about the effect that reducing assets or increasing liabilities will have on your ability to produce and deliver your products and services. Be balanced about it.

Use the *Cash Power* checklist to help you determine where cash is hiding in your business.

Download

YOUR BANK ACCOUNTS— THE FIRST PLACE YOU LOOK FOR CASH

If you're one of the lucky ones whose business throws off cash like sparks off a grinding wheel, you have only to look to your bank deposit accounts for the cash you need. But for most of us, that's not reality . . . not in a growth situation. So careful cash management is a must. And the first step is to know the normal behavior of your business's bank accounts.

You need to know four things: the amount of your cash balances (that's easy, the bank will tell you anytime you ask), the amount of deposits needed to cover your normal operating cash requirements on a weekly or monthly basis (or daily if you're really in a tight situation), the amount of "cash reserves" needed to cover unexpected peaks in your cash outflows (these can be covered also by lines of credit with your bank), and the amount of "excess deposits" you maintain on average.

There are some things you should know about your deposits from your banker's point of view.

TOTAL BANK DEPOSITS

"Excess" deposits

Cash reserve

Operating cash requirements

Small businesses are a rich source of what bankers call "excess deposits." Bankers *love* excess deposits because they amount to free money that the bank uses to generate income from investments and loans. Bankers use other people's money to invest and lend, thus earning income on the "spread" between what they pay for the money they use and what they earn from their loans and investments.

Your bank deposits have a measurable value to your banker—it's called the "earnings credit rate" or some similar name. It's the value they place on your deposits, expressed as a percentage, and it changes continually in step with interest rates in the "money markets." Bankers won't usually tell small business depositors about their earnings credit rates because it's to the bank's financial advantage to have as much "free money" in excess balances as possible. And small business depositors rarely know about the earnings credit rates, so they don't ask.

You should ask.

Why? Because the earnings credit rate of your excess balances can pay for all or part of your banking services. And if your balances pay for your services, the money you're now paying for those services can be put to better use elsewhere in your business. It all adds to your cash power.

And while you're at it, you should also ask your bankers about their cash management services.

There's a long list of banking services you can take advantage of to get the most out of your cash and the balances you keep in your bank. Ask your banker to explain the ones that make sense for you. Some of the more useful ones are:

- **Accounts "on analysis."** This means that your account balances pay for your other banking services at the "earnings credit rate." It can pay for all or a portion of your banking service fees.
- **Zero balance accounts or interest-bearing accounts.** This eliminates "idle" cash in your accounts. The bank pays you interest for your account balances. Your banker will tell you several ways to do this.
- **Electronic banking.** Bank by computer, and you'll be able to monitor and control the flows of cash in and out of your accounts more closely, and you'll also eliminate paper and make your financial staff more productive.
- **Lockbox services.** This service is a way to speed collection of payments due to you. Your customers send their payments directly to a "lockbox" operated by your bank, thus speeding the movement of their payments into your accounts.

■ **Remote disbursement accounts.** There are ways to take advantage of "float" (float is the time it takes to get your money from your customers' accounts into your accounts after you deposit customers' checks).

There are other services as well, and there are almost as many variations of each service as there are banks, so you'll have to talk with your banker to see what's available to you. The point is to make the very best use of your bank accounts and your bankers to get more cash and to move your cash faster.

So, clearly, your bank balances have a value to you that you may not be taking advantage of. See the *Bank Account Valuation* worksheet to help you calculate the value of your bank balances to you and also Download their value to your banker.

You should actively manage your bank accounts. Manage your cash daily, not weekly or monthly. Put "excess" balances into interest-bearing bank accounts. Make sure you're minimizing the money sitting idly in bank accounts. Keep it working for you. Keep it moving quickly. Keep your "financial momentum" high.

And finally, there are risks. Make sure you *do* keep the deposit balances you need—to cover your operating requirements plus an appropriate cash reserve for unexpected outflows. Don't skinny down your deposit balances so far you can't cover your legitimate needs. But do *know* your legitimate needs, and keep your balances at that level.

ACCOUNTS RECEIVABLE—AN UNDERMANAGED ASSET WITH GREAT CASH POTENTIAL

If you're on a cash basis with your customers, receivables aren't a worry for you . . . you don't have any. But if you extend payment terms or credit to your customers, you have accounts receivable. You can look at your balance sheet to see how much money is tied up in your receivables. Whether it's a lot or a little, it's probably too much. So let's take a closer look.

Let's answer several questions: How much is too much in your accounts receivable? What's that worth to you? What can you do to release cash from your receivables?

How much is too much? If you have "past due" receivables, your receivables are too much. You should be producing a monthly Accounts Receivable Aging Report to show how much of your A/Rs are past due and how much past due they are.

Even if you have no past dues, your receivables may still be too large. If your payment terms are too generous, if you grant credit to customers too easily, if your collection efforts are too lenient, or if your record keeping isn't timely, you can bet your receivables are too large, and you have cash unnecessarily tied up in them.

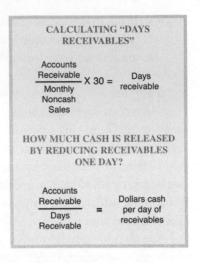

First you need to quantify your receivables in a way that tells you the value of changing the way you manage them. The inset box on this page shows you how to calculate "days receivables," a number that tells you the average number of days that customer receivables are outstanding. In other words, the average amount of time in days between the time you make a noncash sale and the time you receive payment for the sale. The inset box also shows you how to calculate how much cash you free up for each day you can reduce the average time from sale to receipt of payment.

With that information, you can make some decisions. For instance, if your sales terms are net 30 days, you can see the value of reducing your terms to net 20 days (make sure you know the impact of such a decision on your customer relationships before making a change). Or, if the time it takes you to collect on past due accounts is 45 days, you can see the benefit of making your collection system more aggressive, thus collecting more quickly and freeing up much-needed cash.

There's another way to get cash out of your receivables. Sell them.

Commercial finance companies and many banks will lend you money with your receivables as collateral for the loan. The amount you borrow is a percentage of your receivables (usually 40 to 80 percent), and you repay the loan as you collect the receivables. Factoring is another way to get cash for your receivables. In factoring, you don't borrow against your receivables, you sell them. Then the factor is responsible for collections and absorbs bad debt losses. There's a lot more to it than that, and it costs more than conventional borrowing, but in the right situation, it can be a valuable way to convert receivables to cash.

DECREASE YOUR "STUFF" AND INCREASE YOUR CASH

The only reason for having any inventory at all is so that your business won't run out of "stuff." If you're a manufacturer, the "stuff" of your inventories might include raw materials, components, work-in-process, and finished goods, not to mention materials and supplies used in your production process and all the supplies that are used in administration and management. If yours is a purely service business, your "stuff" might only include inventories of office supplies.

What if you didn't need any inventories at all? What if the "stuff" you need magically appeared just in time, when and where you needed it? Well, there's no magic, but there is a useful idea here—it's the idea of "just-in-time," or JIT. What if you could order minimal inventories of "stuff" that could reliably arrive just in time for your business to use it. Wouldn't that dramatically reduce the amount of inventories required? You bet it would. And it doesn't take magic. It takes planning and close attention. But it can be worth it to free the cash bound up in all those inventories of "stuff."

You have to plan carefully just how much and when you'll need the materials required for your production system. You'll have to make precise arrangements with your suppliers, and the suppliers will have to be utterly reliable. You'll have to monitor inventory levels carefully so you can quickly adjust to changes of sales volumes. It's more than merely a faster way of doing what you're doing now . . . it's a different way of doing business, with its own risks and rewards. But the rewards, if yours is one of those businesses with large inventories, can be a huge release of cash into your business, and an ongoing rapid flow of cash through your business. And that means . . . more cash power!

In some important ways, inventories resemble your bank deposits, in that, for each kind of inventory, you have a required amount you need to have on hand (like your deposit balances), a reserve in case of unforeseen situations (like your cash reserve), and anything beyond that is excess (like your "excess" balances).

The idea is to minimize the inventory required for production and reserve inventory (consistent with minimizing the risk of running out and interrupting production, of course) and eliminate excess inventory.

And just like accounts receivable, you can calculate "days of inventory" to help you manage your inventory levels. Days of inventory (or "days inventory") tells you how many days you can continue operations without running out of inventory. You divide the dollar amount of inventory (from your balance sheet or from your accounting records for each type of inventory)

TOTAL INVENTORY

"Excess" inventory

Reserve (safety margin)

Inventory required for operations

by the monthly cost of goods sold (or the monthly inventory costs from your accounting records), and you multiply that by the number of days in the month. That's your "days of inventory." You do that for each kind of inventory of significance in your business.

Days inventory gives you a different, and very useful, way to look at inventory—something you probably do instinctively already. When you think of "how much" inventory you have, don't you think in terms of how long it will last until you have to replenish it? That's all "days inventory" is . . . a measure of how long your inventory will last. But now you can translate that instinct into decision-making information. You can make a judgment about the smallest number of days inventory you need on hand, and calculate how much cash you'll release by reducing your current level.

CALCULATING "DAYS OF INVENTORY"

$$\frac{\text{Dollar amount of Inventory}}{\text{Monthly Cost of Inventory}} \times 30 = \text{Days of inventory}$$

HOW MUCH CASH IS RELEASED BY REDUCING INVENTORY ONE DAY?

$$\frac{\text{Dollar amount of Inventory}}{\text{Days of Inventory}} = \text{Dollars cash per day of inventory}$$

There are some other ways you can reduce inventories and wring cash out of them, for instance:

- **Make process improvements that eliminate "idle" inventories,** such as work-in-process inventories.
- **Build-to-order when possible.** That brings in revenues before you have to produce and deliver the product, and it also lets you minimize inventory and storage space—excellent for cash management.
- **Fill your "downstream pipeline" if you have one.** Let your distributors carry a larger share of inventories if that's possible.
- **Outsource.** Have vendors do some of the manufacturing and/or sub-assembling, and maintain the inventories. This saves both inventory costs and storage space costs. Ditto for upstream suppliers/manufacturers—get them to carry the inventories.

MAKING THE MOST OF YOUR EQUIPMENT AND FACILITIES

Everyone knows it's wasteful to have idle machinery and empty facilities. No secret there. So this one is obvious—get rid of unneeded equipment and facilities. Sell them and convert them to cash, and the sooner the better.

Less obvious are obsolete or unproductive equipment and facilities. The machines look busy—they're operating all the time. The facilities are full of working people, equipment, and materials. On the surface it all looks busy and productive. But is it really? Do you have the most productive, cost-effective technology? Is your equipment being scheduled optimally? Do your people operate your equipment in the most productive manner? Could you outsource some of the work to larger, more productive operations, thus eliminating the need for equipment and facilities and at the same time driving your costs downward?

Finally, you don't have to *own* your equipment and facilities to use them. Anyone who has ever rented office space or equipment knows that. But did you know that, in some cases, you can sell your facilities or equipment to someone else and lease it back from them? Why would you do that? The sale can release a large amount of cash that you can use for growth in return for a stream of monthly payments. It's called a "sale and leaseback" arrangement. To find out if it's feasible for you, contact a commercial finance or equipment finance company (banks don't usually do this kind of deal) and see if it makes sense in your situation.

You don't want to do this kind of financing unless the cash you gain at the beginning of the deal enables you to generate revenues that more than offset the subsequent stream of lease payments. You also lose some flexibility. When you own your own equipment or facilities, you can do what you want with them. When someone else owns them, you often can't.

STRETCH YOUR ACCOUNTS PAYABLE— BUT DO IT CAREFULLY

Your accounts payable are somebody else's accounts receivable. When you stretch your payables, you are delaying their receivables—they may not be too happy about that. If you take this payables-stretching game too far, you can damage your reputation and impair your relationships with important vendors. Don't abuse your vendors. You need them, just as they need you. Think of them as partners, and if you need to stretch your payables, do it with their knowledge and their agreement. And be prepared to grant them some concessions now and then when they need your support.

Payables are the mirror image of receivables. To maximize your cash, you want to speed up collection of your receivables, but you want to slow the payment of your payables. You start by quantifying the speed with which you pay payables in the same way you measured the speed with which you collect your receivables—by calculating "days of payables." It's done the same way. You take the dollar amount of your accounts payable from your most recent balance sheet, divide that by the amount of monthly payments to vendors (from your income statement or financial records), and multiply by the number of days in the month. That tells you, on average, how many days it takes you to pay your payables.

When you calculate how much cash you free up for each day you extend your payables (divide the amount of your accounts payable by the days of payables) you have the basis for understanding the cash impact of stretching your payables. You'll have an objective way to look at the trade-off between the cash you'll free up versus the impact on your vendors.

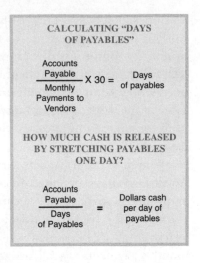

There are other ways to stretch your payables, for instance, paying in installments, or reaching agreements in which you agree to use one vendor exclusively in exchange for pricing concessions and/or the ability to make payments over an extended period of time.

As the saying goes, "Everything is negotiable." Talk with your vendors. Don't do anything unilaterally—make agreements that serve them as well as you. Look for the win-win. But don't be afraid to ask for payment concessions—they want your business, too.

INCREASING DEBT—
THE SECOND PLACE YOU LOOK FOR CASH

If you need cash, and it's not in your bank accounts, the instinct for most of us is to draw down our lines of credit, or if they're "maxed out" to get our credit lines increased. Resist that impulse, at least until you have taken advantage of all the internal opportunities to generate cash.

Debt, as you know, leverages your business, which can be a good thing, but it also increases your costs and makes your business look more risky to outsiders. Internal cash management techniques, such as those covered in this process, are, for the most part, "free." They take knowledge, time, and attention, but they add little or nothing to your expenses, and are often a way to *cut* expenses.

So don't go further into debt until you have taken advantage of the internal opportunities to generate cash flow.

ACCELERATING REVENUES—
INCREASING THE "VELOCITY" OF INCOME

The best way to increase cash flow—growing revenues—is a huge subject, and is covered thoroughly in the Marketing, Lead Generation, and Lead Conversion processes. But *growing* revenues isn't the only way they increase cash flow. You can also speed them up. Remember, the "velocity" of money through your business is the other half of your cash power formula.

Even if you can't increase the *amount* of your sales revenues, there are a number of things you can do to move them into and through your business faster, for instance:

- **Payment in advance.** The ultimate in cash management is to get your cash *before* you need it. Many businesses are able to charge their customers in advance for all or a part of the sales price. If you can do it with no ill effect on your customers, you should.
- **Cash payment.** Get cash on delivery whenever you can. You might have to offer incentives (price discounts or other inducements), but they can be worth it.
- **Shorten your payment terms.** This was already mentioned in the accounts receivable section above, but it's worth repeating.
- **Accept and encourage the use of credit cards,** when possible, instead of granting credit terms. For many credit-oriented customers, the form of credit makes little difference to them, but a credit card sale for you is nearly the same as a cash sale, whereas a sale on credit terms means delayed income.
- **Direct deposits and "auto draft."** For repeat customers, and customers who "subscribe" to your products and services (monthly payments), you can arrange to have their bank accounts automatically debited. You don't have to wait for the check, deposit it, and wait for the check to clear—you get the money instantly, on the day it's due.
- **Electronic payments and banking by computer.** You get instant information, and you can speed up the movement of money from your customers to your business.

But in all of this, take pains to make sure your customers are treated well. Do nothing that gives them the impression that you're "nickel and diming" them. If you're "grabbing for the money," they'll know it and it'll put them off. They'll understand smart business practice and respect you for it—as long as they get the service and products they want. So always keep your impact on the customer in mind as you search for better ways to manage your cash.

CUTTING EXPENSES . . . AND SOME NOT SO OBVIOUS WAYS TO BOOST CASH FLOW

Cutting expenses is one of the most obvious ways to increase cash flow. Every dollar you cut out of expenses is a dollar added to your cash flow. The whole idea of systemization is to find the most effective way to get a result *at the lowest cost.* It's a never-ending quest to always reduce costs while always improving quality and effectiveness. In short, it's the quest for ever-improving productivity.

But you know that. It's a large part of all the E-Myth Mastery work you've been doing. There's nothing to add here that hasn't already been covered extensively. Except . . .

There are *non*-cash expenses that can have cash flow effects. Sometimes it's merely a matter of making a financial decision and, with no other change, you can boost your cash flow.

Remember, there are a number of expense items on your income statement that don't involve cash. Depreciation, for instance. Or the amortization of research and development costs. And there can be others. The item appears on your income statement as an expense. If you could make the item smaller, it increases your net profit; if larger, it decreases your net profit. But, oddly, if you make such a noncash expense smaller, it *decreases* your cash flow; larger, it *increases* your cash flow.

Why? Taxes.

You pay taxes on your business's profits. So anything that reduces your profits also reduces your taxes. So if you could increase all your noncash expenses, that would reduce your profits, and also reduce your taxes. Noncash expenses have no effect on your cash flow, so increasing them doesn't impair your cash. It cuts your profits, but not your cash. But taxes *are* a cash expense to your business. So by increasing your noncash expenses, you reduce your actual tax payments, thus conserving cash for your business.

Many of these noncash expenses are simply a matter of making a management decision about how quickly to "expense" them. For instance, depreciation. If you decide to depreciate your equipment, vehicles, or facilities over a short period of time, your depreciation expense will be higher, but for a shorter period of time. So, for that period of time, your profits will be a bit down, but there will be a cash flow benefit.

There's a similar effect in cost of goods sold. When you buy the materials you use to make your products and provide services, you spend cash in the normal way. No advantage there. But accounting rules let you charge these costs through your income statement in a variety of ways, most commonly LIFO and FIFO, or "last in, first out" and "first in, first out." Meaning, for accounting purposes, you assume that (in LIFO) the last item put in inventory is the first one taken out and sold. It's as if when you add to your inventory, you throw the latest item on top of a pile. Then when you sell an item, you take it off the top of the pile. That's LIFO. You may never get to the bottom of the pile. FIFO is the opposite. You add to the top of the pile and you sell from the bottom of the pile. It doesn't matter what you actually do, this is how accountants deal with inventory costing.

So what does this LIFO/FIFO stuff mean for cash flow? Well, LIFO assumes the most recent item added to inventory is the one that's sold. The costs that went into producing it are the most recent costs (normally, given the fact that costs generally rise over time, that means the most recently produced item will be the higher-cost item). And that means your income statement reflects the higher cost of a good sold, which in turn means slightly lower profit, which means slightly lower taxes, which, finally, means a cash benefit for your business.

In general, then, for most businesses, the LIFO method of costing inventory usage increases cash flow but decreases profits. FIFO does the opposite. It's pretty complex, and unless you have large inventory turnover and/or rapidly rising product/service costs, it may not even have a significant impact on your cash.

Be careful. Tax regulations and accounting rules allow you only limited flexibility in the way you can account for noncash expenses and the tax authorities know more "tricks of the trade" than you do. So before you do anything, you *must* talk with your accountant.

Speaking of accountants, a clever, experienced, and ethical accountant can be your best ally. They know all the ways you can take legal and honest advantage of accounting rules and tax regulations. Tell them your objective is maximizing your cash flow, and ask what accounting decisions you could make that would increase your cash. There may be a surprising number of cash opportunities for you.

PURCHASING—LEVERAGING YOUR BUYING POWER

Large companies all have purchasing specialists—people whose job it is to buy equipment, materials, and supplies for their companies. They're expert at researching the highest-quality purchases and negotiating favorable prices and terms.

Small businesses can't afford purchasing specialists. But that doesn't mean small businesses can't enjoy the advantages of smart purchasing. It's a matter of attention and intention.

And the first rule of purchasing is "everything is negotiable."

Too many small business owners underestimate their own value as customers for their suppliers. They're so used to thinking of themselves as "the little guys" that they lose track of the fact that they're also customers, and as such they have enormous stature and leverage with their suppliers.

If you're worth your salt as a business owner, you love your customers. You need them. You court them. You bend over backward to please them. That's the way your suppliers see *you*. And that gives you tremendous leverage. Not to take advantage of them, but to have a fair exchange of value with them—your money and patronage for their products and services.

Start with that attitude, plus the knowledge that you can negotiate just about anything, and you'll be surprised at the ways you can boost your cash while maintaining, and even improving, your relationships with your suppliers. So everything is negotiable. What else can you do with your suppliers to improve your cash flow? Try these ideas:

- **Volume discounts.** Everybody knows that large-volume purchases will often justify substantial price discounts. So make sure you're asking for volume discounts (you'd be surprised how many businesses don't get volume discounts simply because they haven't asked for them).

  But don't forget the dimension of time. If your individual purchases don't justify volume discounts, but you make frequent purchases over time, that still amounts, cumulatively, to the equivalent of large-volume purchases, and you should benefit from them. Your supplier does.

  For example, if you buy 200 widgets every two weeks, but your widget supplier only offers his 5 percent discount for purchases of 1,000 or more, politely, but firmly, point out that you're making high-volume purchases, but over a slightly extended period of time. Ninety percent of suppliers will be happy to give you the discount. The other 10 percent should make you think about changing suppliers.

- **Just-in-time purchasing.** This is the other side of just-in-time inventory management. Purchasing raw materials, supplies, and services so they're timed to be available just when you need them rather than stockpiled ahead of time, can, in addition to dramatically reducing expensive inventories, also spread cash payments over a longer period of time, thus slowing the outflow of cash. As with any form of just-in-time management, it requires careful planning and forethought, as well as close monitoring and excellent relationships with reliable suppliers.

- **Long-term relationships.** Loyalty has value. You value loyal suppliers (who are also reliable and fair), and so do they value your long-term commitment to the business relationship. In addition to mutual trust and support, loyalty also justifies giving each other the best possible "deal." So if your normal practice is to shop around every purchase for the very best price, and you find yourself having no long-term supplier relationships, talk to the suppliers who seem to give you the best service and consistently good prices. See if they're interested in developing a long-term relationship with you and if they're willing to make some price and/or payment term concessions in return for the security of such a relationship.

  Be careful here, too. (There seems to be a "downside" as well as an "upside" to everything, doesn't there?) If you narrow your suppliers to a very few, you become vulnerable to the ups and downs of their businesses—it's the "all your eggs in one basket" effect. For every supplier with whom you commit to an exclusive relationship, make sure there are others to whom you can turn if your supplier should experience difficulty. You want to be loyal to your good suppliers, and help them in tough times just as you'd like to be helped through your own tough times. But at some point you may have to make the tough decision to change suppliers for the sake of your business and your customers.

- **Adding "upstream" value.** Sometimes your suppliers can do something that has value to you but that costs them little or nothing. For instance, a public relations company designs, writes, and produces annual reports for its clients. It outsources the printing. The printer, with space to spare in its low-rent location, stores the printed annual reports until they are needed by the PR company's clients. The storage costs the printer nothing, but is of considerable value to the PR company. The PR company has upstreamed the business function of storage to its supplier, saving storage and transportation costs that would be incurred if the PR firm had to take possession and store the items.

  There are all kinds of upstream opportunities. Can your supplier add an additional quality inspection step that you would otherwise have to do? Can they do paperwork so you don't have to do it? Can they ship directly to your customers so you don't have to receive, store, pack, and ship yourself? Can they do some of your assembly? Can they label merchandise for you? Can they do the loading or unloading?

If you look at suppliers as partners, understand something about their operations, and see the chain of events leading to your satisfied customers as one long process that includes you and your suppliers, then opportunities for "upstreaming" will become obvious. And don't forget "downstreaming" opportunities if you are a supplier.

▪ **Adding "downstream" value.** If *you* are a supplier, even if yours is a retail or service business, don't forget about downstreaming functions to your distributors, or even your customers. Once upon a time, if you made a deposit or withdrawal at your bank, the teller did the paperwork at the teller window. Then banks "downstreamed" the work of filling out deposit and withdrawal slips to their customers so tellers could be more productive. Then came ATM machines—the entire visit to the bank has been downstreamed. You don't have to talk to a teller. You don't even have to go inside the bank. And, of course, the ultimate in downstreaming for banks: home banking by computer. You don't have to go to the bank at all!

MAXIMIZING PEOPLE POWER
CONTRIBUTES TO YOUR CASH POWER

How many new employees do you need? When do you hire them? What are their required skill and experience levels? Your staffing is dictated by your organizational strategy, your systems development plan, your business plan, and your budget, all of which have their foundations in your Strategic Objective.

As a general rule, you hire permanent employees for predictable work, and you use temporary employees, overtime hours, and part-timers for nonrecurring work, peaks and surges, seasonal upswings and short-term increases in workload. The idea is to "staff up" to cover the ongoing base level of work your business experiences, but not the short-term variations.

It costs too much to acquire and train new permanent employees to hire them for a short period, let them go when the workload decreases and do it all over again every time there is a seasonal or short-term variation in your business. And the emotional and economic consequences of the hire, lay off, hire, lay off cycle are too punishing for the people involved. It's bad business and it's inhumane.

But all that is a matter of knowing your business and having the necessary plans, budgets, and organizational strategy in place. It has more to do with management of costs and profits than cash management. You'll get the cash benefits if you manage staffing costs.

Where people make a difference in your cash power is in their productivity. And you see it not in the *amount* of cash available to you, but in its *velocity* through your business. It's easy to see that an accounts receivable clerk who doesn't move receipts into your bank accounts as quickly as possible is slowing down your cash flow and thus diminishing your cash power. Less obvious, but every bit as important, is the assembly line worker who slows the line, thus slowing the movement of materials through the assembly process—materials are actually cash frozen in inventory, so slowing the line is the same as slowing cash flow. It's an aspect of your business that isn't always obvious—the speed of your business very much impacts the speed of your cash flow.

Which brings us to the subject of your business systems.

BUSINESS SYSTEMS—THEY EITHER CONSUME OR GENERATE CASH, OR BOTH

If the heart of your business is its systems (it is), and cash is the lifeblood of your business (that's true, too), then your business systems are the heart and soul of cash management. As a matter of fact, there is no such thing as a "cash management system." Your business *is* your cash management system. In other words, money and its effective use is part and parcel of every system in your business. It's not a separate, isolated system. It's integral to everything you do.

Think about the way you evaluate systems. And recall that a key indicator of every system is money. Specifically, total system costs as well as per unit costs, as well as any other key monetary impact of the system, and that includes cash flow.

Every time you look at a business system, also pay attention to its cash effects. Think about not only how to increase the revenue and cash inflow or to decrease the costs and cash outflow, but also pay attention to the speed with which cash flows through the system. Does cash (in the form of money, or in the form of materials, equipment, people, and facilities) move quickly through the system? Or does it stagnate in the form of oversized inventories, overdue receivables, underutilized workers, obsolete technology, or unproductive processes?

CASH IS A MIRROR FOR YOUR BUSINESS AND A "REPORT CARD" FOR YOU

When you get down to basics, cash is nothing more or less than a reflection of the way you run your company. If cash moves briskly and productively through your business, generating a handsome profit, you can be confident your business is working well. If your balance sheet is bloated with unnecessary assets and too much debt, and your income statement is leaking cash and is unable to produce a decent profit because of unproductive systems, then you've got your work cut out for you.

CHAPTER FOUR

The Discipline of the Management Leader

■

"Taste more often what nourishes your clear light,
And you'll have less use for the smoky oven.
You'll bury that baking equipment in the ground!"

From "The Animal Soul" in
The Soul Is Here for Its Own Joy *by Robert Bly*

There is a tendency in all of us to believe that certain benchmarks in our lives hold great significance. And, certainly, there are plenty of benchmarks in all of our lives. Each one seems the most significant prior to achieving it, and next to meaningless once we've achieved it. As soon as we've achieved it, it's "Next." Think of the benchmarks in your life. There was the first day of school, graduating from elementary school, your first date, your first kiss, your high school graduation, perhaps you went off to college, graduated from college, got married, had your first child, started your own business, among many more.

We look forward to all of these benchmarks with either fear or excitement. In either case, though, we believe that these highly anticipated events will have a significant impact on our lives. But do they? As we look forward to them, they certainly do. But in the context of our lives, the entirety of our lives, and as we sit here looking at them, can you appreciate the undue importance that we put on them? That the ones we feared, we needn't have feared, or at least so much? That the ones we were so excited about, were much less exciting than we thought, or hoped? That how we tend to assess our experiences drives the nature of our anticipation. If we tend to be disappointed by those big moments, we will expect to be disappointed in the future. And if we find thrill in them, we expect to be thrilled. Our lives are shaped this way.

And, unfortunately, our businesses are too. The absence of management leadership means that businesses become defined by the expectations of their people rather than the other way around. These businesses, from day one, are heading down a path to oblivion and don't even know it.

Let's look at how this works.

"You know that today we're going to talk about the fourth discipline, the discipline of the management leader," I said to Sarah. "The management leader is essential to the creation of a World Class Company because her job is to actively shape the management consciousness of your company in a way that moves the organizational mind-set beyond the ordinary, to World Class.

"Left to its own devices, the consciousness of an organization will be no different than the consciousness of the people who comprise it. If people in a company are living with, for example, unrealized expectations in their lives, a sense of reality that never matches the anticipation, a history of relationships with people who let them down, in other words, disappointing benchmarks, the organization will never transcend that consciousness without another force, a more powerful force, that establishes a 'highest caliber in the world' mind-set, a number one, winner, extraordinary mind-set of the World Class Company. And if we really, really look at it, with complete honesty, this mind-set does not happen naturally in most companies.

"That's why the management mind-set of your enterprise is so important, Sarah. Because it can either feed the unconscious norm of our ordinary thinking and expectations in a way that repeats the past experiences of the people who work there, or the management mind-set can tussle with the ordinary, wrestle with it, in a way that sets a new standard for experience, for results, and for benchmarks.

"And the condition of remaining stuck in the ordinary is what All About Pies has been suffering from, Sarah. It's the reason you sought me out again. Intuitively, you've understood this, though you've expressed it in different ways."

I stopped talking to give Sarah the room to take in what I was saying.

She looked at me intensely, obviously fascinated with the picture of reality I had just offered her. But, as I frequently experienced, there was something going on in Sarah that she wasn't expressing. So I asked her, "What is it, Sarah? You seem to have a question, and my gut tells me it has something to do with the implications of this for working *on* your enterprise."

"You're right, Michael. I do have a question, but I'm not certain how to ask it. It feels like it's still forming in my mind, but let me take a stab at it and see what comes out.

"If what you're saying is true, that our futures tend to mirror our past experiences—different people, different places, different circumstances, but a similar quality of experience—then how is it really possible to do things differently in our company, so that future results don't have any relationship to the good/bad, success/failure, right/wrong cycle of our lives? The magnitude of what you're saying seems to be impossible to deal with, not only given my people's experiences, but my own. My life has not been world class, not even close. How in the world do you propose that we change the trajectory of our lives?"

"I love your question, Sarah, because you're forcing me to question my assumptions and look at this dilemma earnestly with you. Which means that the reluctant coach has got to become less reluctant!"

Sarah laughed and, of course, I laughed with her, seeing as I did that, on the one hand, my contrarian position was creating an enormous challenge for myself and, on the other hand, creating nothing that didn't already exist whether I addressed it or not. In other words, the way that our past experience plays itself out in all of our lives is either related to how one manages an enterprise with integrity or not. And if we were committed to creating a World Class Company, we can do no less than engage with that question, as impossible as it seems right now.

The question for me wasn't really whether or not it was worthwhile, but whether or not I was up to the task!

Sarah immediately reacted to my suggestion, "But of course you are, Michael!"

I said, "I don't know why you're so certain, Sarah. But, let's try."

I restated Sarah's question, "If our future most often reflects our past and the company we have today is a product of our past, which is anything but world class, then how do we break free of our past and create a different future than the one our current reality would dictate?

"Put another way, how do we become what we're not?"

"This is the big question the management leader must ask. And answer. Bear with me here, Sarah, I'm feeling for an answer I know is there but haven't yet touched the center of it.

"Imagine that you are inspired to build a company that becomes world class in everything it does. And imagine that you actually pull it off. You create a McDonald's. You open up 1,000 stores. The system is flawless, or as close to flawless as any company can be. It works like a Swiss watch. Your future has been predicated on a series of successful choices you've made and institutionalized in your company at the operating level of your now World Class Company. You are a successful entrepreneur. Of course, there are challenges. Wendy's, Subway, Burger King. A continuous and relentless parade of exploding competition. The world of your 1,000 stores has created a completely altered world. Your system remains impeccable, except for the fact that it becomes harder to be number one. The people in the stores are being challenged, not only by the competition, but by the emotional turmoil inside themselves. Their perceptions of your company, their jobs, and their future are now being shaped less by the hope your company engendered when it first made its promise to them and kept it, than by the reality of their past experiences. Some of those past experiences are really good, some of them are really bad, and most of them fall into the moderate middle of the yes-no range, as most people's lives do. Something, in short, has changed. It is not the efficacy of the operating system that is driving results but the reality of the mind-set in which it operates.

"At the same time, your success has come from your commitment to holding the course, to your however-you've-discovered-it discipline, to the turnkey genius of how you do what you do, to how you pull off being 'the most successful small business in the world,' like McDonald's did. To how you differentiated and still differentiate yourself from the competition. And every single one of your managers has learned, has internalized, has enforced that genius, that discipline, that turnkey 'this-is-how-we-do-it-here' and knows, absolutely knows, from their experience, that without that discipline, without that operating commitment to how-we-do-it-here, without the system that is the genius of McDonald's, they would be as ordinary as everyone else. And if they were to become like everyone else, they would no longer be world class. And the fear of that, the absolute terror of it, of falling from grace, of losing what you and they have so zealously invented, so heroically defended and guarded and protected, would be to lose your invaluable uniqueness. And then what?

"So here we are on the horns of an E-Myth dilemma. If the 'system is the solution.' If your job is to have an operating system in your company that works like a Swiss watch. If your commitment is sacrosanct to building a brand, a franchise, that has roots, stability, predictability, has legs and stands on them boldly simply because that's what your customer and your people have grown to expect. Then how in the world do you, once again, this far into the game, after already having moved a mountain of resistance in people, become what you're not? The tendency, if the real McDonald's today is any indication, is to ask a completely different and, what I believe it will prove to be, if it hasn't already, a destructive question: *How do we keep what we have?!*

"And therein lies the conundrum.

"The conundrum about becoming what we're not, and keeping what we have.

"The conundrum about creating a future that looks nothing like the past but also retains the best of the past.

"There is a solution to this puzzle.

"And the solution lies in how we view the relationship between true creativity and stunning orchestration. It's so easy to believe that creativity and orchestration don't live in the same space, that they are antithetical or inimical to each other. That the moment we strip an operating system or process down to its essential architecture and ask everyone to produce a result in the same way, we are exiting the world of creativity. But what if we could hold creativity and orchestration as one, unified principle?

"Think about it this way, Sarah.

"Imagine the world of your McDonald's, the World Class Company you have assiduously, with enormous dedication, built over time. Imagine that the work you do is continually improving upon your already-proven-to-be-successful operating system, work we call at E-Myth: Innovation, Quantification, and Orchestration. However you got there, however you learned to do that, this is your reality. Your World Class Company is a franchise with its own separate and distinctly unique sensory package. It is a brand. You have customers who are buying from you relentlessly and competitors who are competing with you relentlessly. You have a presence. And that presence is concrete, you can point to it, it is as real as anything in this world is. The enormous value of your system educates your people, manages your people, grows your people. And you are continuously improving it. This is the company we'll call OldCo.

"OldCo is the company you've got today.

"Look at it.

"There are only two things you can do with OldCo, improve it or shut it down.

"But let's remain optimistic. OldCo is there to be improved. Until it makes no sense to improve it anymore. And certainly there comes a time in the life of every company when it no longer makes any sense to improve it, when the world has changed so much that it no longer has any relevance, any reason for being, any ability to successfully attract, serve, and keep customers. There is an inevitable end of every company. The question is not *whether* it will come or not, *but how you anticipate it.* Which brings us to NewCo, the second iteration of your life as an entrepreneur and as the management leader of your enterprise.

"To make the transition from OldCo to NewCo, a company must be able to operate on parallel tracks for some time until you are able to take the best from both and become the One World of your entrepreneurial attention. They become integrated as one.

"McDonald's, an example of the OldCo model, is 'the most successful small business in the world.' Procter and Gamble, built on the NewCo model, is the most successful *product marketing* company in the world.

"Together, OldCo and NewCo comprise the One World of the World Class Company.

"Building a World Class Company and building it to last requires both sensibilities, both the McDonald's model of brand recognition and continual improvement, and the Procter and Gamble model of relentlessly growing successful new brands in the markets they choose to dominate, to be alive and well in the enterprise.

"*How* one does that is the focus of the management leader.

"And *when* one does that he solves the puzzle of past, present, and future in the only way possible."

"The senior vice president of one large client company shared his new mantra with me sometime after we had a 'How do we become what we're not?' conversation. He had taken on 'NewCo Forever!', with an enthusiasm that is rare in my experience for a vice president in a large company.

"In his battle cry, 'NewCo Forever!' he understood the answer to the question exactly.

"He understood that the only true way to transform their large company was to approach it differently than most large companies tend to do. OldCo, in this case an insurance company, would not be able to successfully make the transition to a financial services company by trying to get the large network of commercial insurance agents to become something different, in this case, financial planners, from what they've been. This requires a parallel operation where the company is organized into OldCo and NewCo initiatives, OldCo and NewCo leadership, OldCo and NewCo management, and OldCo and NewCo marketing and finance, to develop those separate but equally important disciplines among its management team, among the people who report to them, and, most specifically, within the leadership mind-set that will distinguish an enterprise as world class from all those who aren't and never will be.

"Over time, the company will operate harmoniously as one thing, the preeminent financial services company in the world. And that will happen by thinking of their company as both a product marketing company, exactly as Procter and Gamble would, and as a network of the most successful small businesses in the world, as McDonald's would.

"Think of the NewCo opportunities as new franchise prototypes, developed to seize a very specific customer's allegiance. Think of those new franchise prototypes as Procter and Gamble would, as products to be developed and to be successfully marketed, as brands, each of which has a life of its own, bearing its own name, its own identity, under the umbrella of Procter and Gamble.

"Think of the financial planner, in this case, not as a transformed insurance agent, but as a new company opportunity, just like Procter and Gamble would. Think about this product opportunity narrowly, in a way that makes the financial planner, the person, only one part of a financial product, a financial product that is built exactly like Pampers was built, to serve a very specific consumer, to satisfy that very specific customer, in a very specifically differentiated way, to do something that needs to be done and that isn't done by any of the competing products out there for that very specific customer. Imagine a financial product built like that, in which the role of the financial planner is built into the product he sells and delivers, and that product, the totality of it, is organized into a practice, and then a business, and then, if the market is large enough to warrant it, an enterprise. A Procter and Gamble/McDonald's mindset and expertise would enable it to seed new, emerging franchise prototypes, focused on the satisfaction of specific consumer needs and to package them, organize them, test them, roll them out, and quantify the success of them. And shut them down if they're not. And when they are, expand them from a practice to a business to an enterprise.

"And, at the same time, start another one, and another one, and another one.

"If McDonald's were to approach its company this way—the McDonald's that was profitable every single quarter for 47 years until it suffered its first loss in 2002!—it would not only become known for its stores bearing the McDonald's Golden Arches, it would become known for its mastery in building an ever-expanding network of World Class Companies, the McDonald's stores plus all of the new products, the new companies, the new networks of stores, it had successfully built, grown, and managed.

"The management leader must be more than just the one who holds on for dear life. She must hold these two truths to be self-evident."

Sarah had been so patient, giving me the room to deliver a monologue about world class management that I was obviously passionate about. As I watched her while I was talking, she was pensive at moments and bursting with frustration at others. I knew that she had to be wondering how all of this applied to her little business, but I had been through enough of these moments with her that I trusted we'd get to her, ah-hah! eventually, when everything would make sense.

"Michael," Sarah said, "I'm not sure how to take all of that in. I think I understand what you mean about how people and businesses get stuck in the past, but it terrified me in moments when I thought you were suggesting that I should continue to improve All About Pies while starting another business. When I can't do this one right!"

"No, Sarah, that's not quite it. But I can understand how you might come to that conclusion from what I said. Let's see if I can clarify what the implications of this OldCo and NewCo paradigm are for you. Just like every small business owner in the world, you are too consumed with hanging on to what you've got. You need to think in a fresh way about what you're there to do. You need to think about NewCo, not OldCo, as you're preparing yourself for the role of management leader. You need to think in terms of *fundamental* change that will take All About Pies to a totally new place rather than *marginal* change that will keep you running in place. That will require some courage, to break free from the past and move into the unknown. That will require a willingness to lead your people into the unknown rather than succumb to the tendency to stay stuck in familiar ways of thinking and doing business that don't really work. That don't create juice or passion or aliveness. That don't produce world class results. No, Sarah, the last thing you need is another business. You need a new business model and that might end up looking like a very different business than All About Pies currently looks like. Make sense?"

"Relief," Sarah sighed. "Sometimes I think you say things in a far more complicated way than you need to, Michael, just to provoke me."

"What's wrong with that, Sarah, if it provokes you to reach more deeply into your experience to go beyond, if I can be blunt, the superficial kinds of things we all tell ourselves to discover what your real truth is?"

Sarah looked at me and smiled. We smiled at each other. No words were necessary.

"Let's flesh this point out a little more and go back to the insurance company I talked about earlier. It's a mature company, with an expanded network of insurance agents, which, for the longest time, were organized to do one thing, sell commercial insurance. When they stuck to that, they were very, very good. They knew what business they were in. Then somebody got the idea that with all the commercial customers they had, why not sell life insurance as well? And so they spent a fortune trying to get their commercial insurance agents to sell life insurance to their customers. Some did, but most didn't. When that didn't work, they tried something else. Well, they reasoned, if we can't get our commercial insurance agents to sell life insurance to our customers, then let's create dedicated life insurance salespeople who our commercial insurance salespeople can introduce to their existing clients and split the commissions. And that was a disaster. The commercial insurance salespeople and the life insurance salespeople felt they were competing for each other's customers so they didn't refer them. In other words, all it did was make them feel out of control.

"You think *I* complicate things, Sarah. What this company did then was to start introducing all sorts of new financial products and services. They decided to become a financial services company like CitiGroup. They initiated training of their commercial insurance agents and their life insurance agents to sell a larger array of financial products. And, of course, you can imagine what happened. It failed, miserably. Oh, they poured huge sums of money and management and experts into the project to make it work. But it never worked because it never could work. The genius of their original success, one company, doing one thing, very, very well, turned into one company doing many things, very, very badly. And all this happened because they were asking the wrong question: How can we sell more financial products to our very large customer base? The question they should have been asking was: Staying true to our vision, but not wanting to be dragged down by the past, what really exciting, new product can we develop for all of the other customers out there in the world?

"Instead of focusing on their OldCo customer, they should have turned their attention to the endless number of NewCo customers for whom they could develop unique, exciting new offers. Had they then tested them and discovered which ones were viable, they could have built new brands, new networks of agents, new businesses, each with their own customers, each intensely and singularly focused, each without a past to drag them down. Just like Procter and Gamble does.

"The management leader needs to be willing to break free of the past so that her passion has a vehicle to express itself and her company has a chance to thrive. Every assumption, every bias, every tradition, every question needs to be put into question. To create a World Class Company, Sarah, you must be able to retain the best of the past, on the one hand; on the other, there can be no sacred cows. The razor's edge between the two is where the management leader walks.

"I think I've said enough for this morning, Sarah. I'd like to give you your first assignment."

THE FIRST ASSIGNMENT

"Your first assignment, Sarah, is to ask these questions: What is it about All About Pies that, if given the opportunity to create a clean slate, you'd still want to retain? Are there any sacred cows in your answer, aspects of the current All About Pies that you're unwilling to give up, whether they support the creation of a World Class Company or not? And, having considered the first two questions, is All About Pies an OldCo or is it NewCo? Are you simply improving an old company, or are you creating a new company?"

Sarah immediately reacted to the question I was putting in front of her.

"Michael, of course All About Pies is OldCo; it already exists! Isn't that what you have been saying for the last hour or so?"

"Actually, no, Sarah, that's not what I've been saying, though I get why you would think so. What I've been saying is that you, as the management leader, need to ask two opposing questions, simultaneously: How do we become what we're not? And: How do we keep what we have? Can you feel the tension between those two questions, Sarah? The tension between those two questions creates a paradigm of opposites, which, when you as the management leader embrace them as one, will create enormous energy to move the company forward. And the question I'm asking you to ask in this assignment will help you to embrace All About Pies in a completely different way than you're used to.

"Is All About Pies OldCo, or is it NewCo? Well, the answer to that question is, *it is both!* The question is, *how* is it both? What parts of All About Pies form OldCo; what parts form NewCo? The assignment is designed to uncover those parts, making sure to identify any sacred cows that would keep you unfortunately tied to the past. And as you begin to make the OldCo list and the NewCo list, as you begin to look at All About Pies as the management leader, you will begin to see it differently. You will begin to see what you should be focusing your attention on, and how, and what simply needs to be addressed efficiently but without very much passion. In short, this question will enable you to begin to discriminate about the focus of your management passion. Some things are very, very important to the future of All About Pies. Those we'll call the NewCo attributes. Some things are only important to the present All About Pies. Those we'll call the OldCo attributes. By doing this assignment, you will begin to see where your attention is best focused."

"Okay," Sarah said, "I'm seeing it now. The management leader is responsible for what his people focus their attention on and how. And if he's discriminating between OldCo attributes and NewCo attributes, his people will always be focusing their attention on the most important things and will be living on that edge between the future and the best of the past. People can't help but be their most creative in an environment like that. And when you add orchestration to the mix, you're building something you told me about a long time ago that I've never forgotten: the perfect balance between *structure,* all the predetermined elements of a process, like scripts and benchmarks and décor and dress code, and *substance,* the spirit and energy that people bring to the process. I can see now how the perfect balance between structure and substance can only be achieved when it's resting on a foundation created by the perfect balance between the past and the future."

"I couldn't have put it any better, Sarah."

THE SECOND ASSIGNMENT

"Now that we've established that a management leader is someone who is focused on the past and the future, and you have begun to look at All About Pies in those terms, I'd like you to consider, most closely, the nature of the two roles that a management leader must play in this context, what I'll call the Good Householder and the Chief Executive Officer.

"The Good Householder is focused on maintaining the health, order, and tranquility of OldCo. The Chief Executive Officer is focused on the creation, development, validation, and growth of NewCo. One management leader, two roles.

"In your second assignment, Sarah, I'd simply like you to make a list of responsibilities of each role at All About Pies. What does each need to do to fulfill her objective? Pick the five most important responsibilities of each so that you can begin to see what the Good Householder needs to focus on so that OldCo can remain healthy, and what does the Chief Executive Officer need to focus on so that NewCo can flourish. Okay?"

Sarah smiled. "Well, that was pretty simple. I think I get it. Thanks Michael."

"Thank you, Sarah. Then let's go on to the third assignment, the organization of effort."

THE THIRD ASSIGNMENT

"Everything we've been talking about so far has been about how to organize your thinking to balance the two essential worlds that must coexist within an enterprise for it to become a World Class Company. The two worlds of NewCo and OldCo. The two management roles of the Good Householder and the Chief Executive Officer.

"The third assignment is to create a hierarchy for the organization of effort, a list, in order of importance, of the five tasks that must be done by the person fulfilling each role, every day, day in and day out, at All About Pies. Tasks that managers do.

"The purpose of this assignment is to give you an opportunity to further break down the management function in your company into specific tasks, or work that needs to get done every day. So that you can more fully understand the nature of a World Class Company in terms of a management paradigm, management responsibilities, and the actual tasks that your management team needs to perform to achieve their objectives.

"Let me give you a possible scenario to get you started in the right direction. Then I'd like you to come up with your own. So every day, your manager has a ritual. Number One is to review the operating performance of the day before and compare it with the projected performance. She wants to assess the key indicators, see how well you did, or not, see who performed best, who didn't, and formulate her strategy for the day's focus of attention. Number Two, she holds her Kick-Off Meeting with all employees who are on in the morning shift, to review with them yesterday's performance, to discuss what worked, congratulate the high performers and to discuss what didn't work and what can be improved. Every member of the staff is given an assignment for the day, over and above their normal work. Number Three, she does a routine White Glove Inspection of every area of the store, with each accountable staff member present to address what needs to be improved. And so forth. Sarah, does that help?"

"You've made this so simple, Michael. Thanks," Sarah said.

"I think you're getting through to me, Sarah," I replied.

"Maybe I'm just returning the enormous gift you've given me," Sarah said with an ease that I had not often heard in her voice. "What's next?"

"Your homework on management leadership," I answered.

"I'm ready," Sarah said with conviction.

SELECTED E-MYTH MASTERY PROGRAM PROCESSES ON MANAGEMENT LEADERSHIP

Creating a High-Performance Environment: Developing a Culture That Embraces Change

■

An old adage suggests that the more things change, the more they stay the same, but that's wishful thinking. The truth of it is that the more things change, the more things change some more. Sometimes you get to plan the change and actually invite it, but more often than not, it arrives unannounced

Creating a High-Performance Environment

DEVELOPING A CULTURE THAT EMBRACES CHANGE

Overview

The hallmark of a high-performance work environment is its ability to see change as a resource, and as an opportunity to test assumptions and systems and add to the collective knowledge. High-performance cultures perpetuate and regenerate themselves with every challenge.

Key Points

Change is the one constant for every business in today's global economy, and your success will depend as much on your ability to embrace change and use it as a resource as it will on the production of your product.

Those companies that build high-performance work environments by dedicating themselves to their purpose, creating a structure that's uniquely suited to their objectives, and giving their people the tools to get the results that are expected will create a "game worth playing" for everyone they touch. They'll draw customers, motivate vendors, interest investors, and reassure lenders with their energy and vitality.

To create a high-performance work environment, you have to focus on **vision, structure,** and **tools**. You have to clarify and integrate your company's vision into its daily life, you have to create a structure that's designed specifically for the results you want, and you have to give your people the tools they need to perform their jobs at the peak of their abilities.

Benchmarks for Creating a High-Performance Environment

- Integrate the Vision
- Build the Structure
- Train and Provide the Tools
- Quantify and Evaluate

and you have to scramble to respond. When the economy is global and technical innovation is constant, when markets fragment and re-form unpredictably, when governments deregulate and the workforce diversifies, even no-growth businesses find themselves taking affirmative steps just to maintain their positions. Change is the one constant for every business these days—from pushcart to multinational. So here's another old adage: Expect the unexpected. Because your business success will depend as much on your ability to manage and respond to change—and even to anticipate it—as it will on the production of your product. This means you have to look at change as a resource instead of an obstacle, and prepare your people to recognize the opportunities change brings and capture its advantages. And that means creating an environment where everyone is poised to take the "right action" at any given time—a high-performance environment.

THE ELEMENTS OF HIGH PERFORMANCE

A high-performance organization is not that much different from a high-performance car. The principle is the same. You take the best materials available and organize them into systems that are designed to use energy, whatever the source, in the most efficient and elegant ways available. These are not run-of-the-mill machines. They're unique and often one-of-a-kind designs created to do specific things very, very well. They're also high maintenance in that they can't be left to run down on their own. They need constant tuning. But they're worth the trouble because they accomplish their purpose better than anything else on the road, and make maximum use of any opportunity for performance. Not everyone needs a high-performance car, and you could argue that the same is true for high-performance organizations, but do you want to be the business that settled for an economy model when your competitors opted for the high end?

You don't, and there's really no need because building a high-performance environment in your business isn't a matter of money. It can be done on a shoestring, and often is. What makes a business a high-performance organization is its dedication to its purpose, its ability to consciously create a structure uniquely designed for that purpose, and its commitment to giving its people the tools they need to get the results expected. **Vision, structure,** and **tools,** in a nutshell.

But the real hallmark of a high-performance organization is its ability to see change as a resource—as an opportunity to test assumptions and systems, add to the collective knowledge, and grow the business. Change creates opportunities to see things in ways you don't ordinarily see them, and to do things in ways you don't ordinarily try. If you can use change to your advantage, it can fuel your company's growth in ways that money and technology can't, because it moves everyone out of their comfort zones, frees them to take a fresh look at the business, and drives invention and innovation.

A high-performance organization actually relishes change the way the driver of a high-performance car relishes a hill because it's an opportunity to let out the throttle and see what the machine can really do. And nothing beats the excitement of running on all cylinders. It's what the car—or the organization—was built to do, and it's in those moments of challenge that a high-performance culture perpetuates and regenerates itself.

Constructing an organization that relishes change and can "take the hill" requires thought and planning and, more than anything else, it takes the willingness to stay with it until you get it right. But it doesn't necessarily take money. It might be easier if it did because building a high-performance environment takes time, and in a growing business time can be worth more than money. But your efforts will be more than worth it because high-performance environments create a game worth playing for everyone involved. And not just employees. High-performance organizations draw customers, motivate vendors, interest investors, and reassure lenders. Their energy and vitality inspire confidence in everyone they touch.

To get you started, think about what your business would look like if it were a high-performance environment. Use the *Creating Your High-Performance Environment* worksheet to capture and clarify your ideas. Download

BUILDING A HIGH-PERFORMANCE ENVIRONMENT

Once you identify the elements of high performance, you can begin to construct the environment that will bring it to your own organization. No two businesses will do it in the same way. The object is to encourage a culture and create a structure that's best suited to accomplishing your Strategic Objective and Strategic Purpose. Here are the fundamental steps that will help you:

1. **Integrate the vision.** There are a number of ways to build your vision for your business into the culture of your organization. Some are obvious and explicit, and some are not. The most effective strategy is to examine all the possibilities for broadcasting and reinforcing the vision and its values, and systematically include them in all your activities.
2. **Build the structure.** You'll be tempted to look at your company's structure as a matter of organization charts and reporting relationships. It is, but think of structure also as those things in your organization like

rules, rewards, values, and even unconscious assumptions that influence behavior and direct
the flow of human energy. The structure of your
business is made up of all those factors and others like them that shape how and why your people do their jobs the way they do them.

Benchmarks for Creating a High-Performance Environment

Integrate the Vision

Build the Structure

Train & Provide the Tools

Quantify & Evaluate

3. **Train and provide the tools.** Peak performance
isn't genetic. Even your brightest and most
highly motivated employees need to learn how
to do it your way, and then they'll need the
wherewithal to use their training for maximum
effect. A master woodcarver, for example, needs
a very sharp, well-balanced, and specially designed knife to produce exceptional results. The
master without the knife is just potential.

4. **Quantify and evaluate.** High-performance operations of any kind
need regular attention to keep them calibrated and aligned. High-
performance people systems aren't any different. You just have to be
creative in choosing your key indicators, and then monitor your organization's performance on a regular basis.

IT ALL STARTS WITH YOU

Integrating the company's vision into the daily life of the organization is everyone's job, but it starts with the leader. The leader is in charge of articulating the
vision and reinforcing and protecting it every step of the way.

There are a number of ways to integrate your vision into the daily life of
your company, and one of the most effective ways is through business development meetings and other regularly scheduled meetings with employees.
There's no substitute for the face-to-face contact and communication between
you and your people, and this is the opportunity to paint a vivid mental picture of your dream so you can focus everyone's hopes and intentions on the future they want to create. Just remember that you can't "sell" your dream to your
people, and you shouldn't try. You don't want compliance, you want enroll-
ment. You want your people to enrich your vision with their own objectives to
create a common goal and a common spirit.

Face-to-face communication is particularly appropriate if you've just begun to articulate your vision or if it has significantly changed. You'll need the
power of your own presence to create a new consensus by communicating
your hopes for the future and the depth and sincerity of your commitment. So

spend as much time with your people as you can. Acknowledge the newness of the process and make room for a shared creation. In addition to the business development meeting, many business owners create informal opportunities for personal exchanges: Friday afternoon "beer busts," which may or may not feature beer, but create an opportunity for unstructured conversation or feedback, or monthly or bimonthly coffee hours or breakfasts with an open agenda to encourage conversation.

One of the most famous devices for creating opportunities for conversation and an exchange of ideas was a practice developed by Bill Hewlett and Dave Packard, founders of the legendary electronics manufacturing firm in California. Hewlett and Packard both would wander around through their company, engaging in conversations about work in progress or any other topics that arose. They found these opportunities to be so useful that they formalized them in a company management principle called MBWA, "management by walking around." Hewlett-Packard's published vision for how they wanted to work together was modeled and reinforced by this practice, and institutionalized as an expectation for management behavior at every level.

Modeling the vision in that way is also a powerful tool for integrating it into the daily life of your company. Once you identify the values that are inherent in your vision, you can look for concrete ways to communicate them in action. A savvy manager can make a real statement by publicly engaging in hallway or shop floor conversations about maintaining quality, meeting production obligations, or honoring customer expectations. Don't underestimate the impact on other employees when they overhear hallway instructions to "Remember, if it's not right, don't ship it!" or "He's our customer, do what it takes to satisfy him!" This is vision in action. Every employee who witnesses these exchanges comes away with a feeling of the real truth of more formal pronouncements.

Although printed materials, videotapes, and other tangible devices may not be as persuasive as face-to-face communication, they have their place in reinforcing your vision for the organization, especially if they're used as part of orientation or training materials. Where appropriate, materials from your Strategic Objective, Strategic Purpose, or other visionary writings should become part of your regularly used business documents. For example, purchase orders could feature a statement describing your impact intentions toward your vendors, invoices could display your intended impact on customers, and your employee handbook should definitely feature your intentions for the impact you want your company to have on your people. These are ways to make the written word work for you in an active and focused way. While a general statement of your company's vision and values is an important document, you can make the vision come alive—even in print—if it's integrated into your daily business procedures and tools.

Use the *Vision Integration* worksheet to take inventory of the ways your vision is currently integrated into your company's daily life, and to think of new ways to include it.

Download

While published visions and values have their place, and your personal communication and behavior modeling are even more effective, as the leader, your attitude toward your employees and their role in your company and your vision will create the foundation and tone for everything you create in your culture and your structure.

So think about this: There can't be leaders without followers, so it stands to reason that you and your people can't exist without each other. But there's always the temptation to see employees as passive participants who bring a blank slate to the game. In fact, visionary management thinking sees much more mutuality in the relationship and holds that followers are what make leaders possible. Leaders lead by consent, as any lame-duck president will ruefully admit, so just having the position doesn't guarantee you'll be able to accomplish a thing. As a leader, you'll get the best results by getting buy-in from your people, so it's buy-in you must get. If your people think you can lead, they'll align themselves with your vision and enrich it, and then let you clear the path ahead. Think of your employees as *co-creators* and you'll begin to get the picture.

Meanwhile, all those co-creators are also going to be your innovators. At least you hope they will. Your business development work depends on it. So you have to look at each employee not only as the source of ongoing innovation, but as the next possible source of the innovation that will transform your business! So they're not just co-creators, they may be heroes, too! And that's all the more reason to be sure that your organization is designed to provide them everything they need to operate at the peak of their abilities.

REMOVING THE OBSTACLES TO HIGH PERFORMANCE

Your organization chart may look like the structure of your company, but it's only part of the story. If you think of structure as everything in your business that directs, controls, and influences the flow of energy and activity, you get a much larger picture. Reporting relationships and established accountabilities certainly direct the activities and behaviors of your people, but there are other factors that have equal influence on what they produce and how they behave.

For example, the formal and informal structure of rewards and incentives has as much impact on how employees make choices and direct their energies as their job descriptions or formal position contracts. A company that's dedicated to a "don't sell . . . satisfy" lead conversation objective but only pays salespeople for sales closed has created an unacknowledged structure. Employees will understand the message and direct their energy and activities toward achievement of the reward and not necessarily the stated objective. The *real* result desired is implicit in the result that's rewarded, and people understand that.

One of the most powerful unacknowledged "structures" in an organization is its attitude toward risk. Management literature in recent years has extolled the virtues of creating business environments that promote risk taking by their employees, but the truth of the matter is that most companies still reward emulation and compliance. High-performance environments can't afford to do that because taking "right action" in response to change often means dealing with the unknown effectively, and that can mean risk. Your employees need to know how to assess the risks in the decisions they make. That means that they have to know everything they can about their jobs and the systems they operate, and particularly about the systems that feed into theirs, and that theirs, in turn, feed. The more your people have a systemic view of your business, the more they'll be able to calculate the consequences of their actions.

Once your people have a handle on assessing consequences, they'll be able to evaluate possible loss. Loss is the bottom line in most risk. For instance, your employees may use "worst-case scenarios" as a way of quantifying possible loss. Risk can also be quantified in the same way you quantify intangible indicators. In this case, "risky—riskier—riskiest" or a similar model can be used to get some sense of the relative uncertainties of various solutions. The point is to create a way to assess risk in the decision-making process. An *explicit* way that becomes part of your company culture. If you create actual tools—systems— to deal with assessing risk, you automatically make risk taking an acceptable practice in your organization. To secure its place in your company culture, you then have to reward it. And not just the successes. Imagine a company award for the best idea that didn't work and taught everyone the most!

Here are the general factors that create the "structure" of your organization:

- **Your vision:** The stated purpose of your organization will have a strong effect on the choices your employees make every day. This is a powerful tool for achieving results as long as the vision is at one with other controlling structures and documents like position contracts, standards, operations manuals, policy manuals, employee handbooks, and your rewards and incentive programs.

- **Your hierarchy:** This is the most obvious structure in your organization, and one of the major influences on the flow of energy and activity through your company. Because it is, it bears some study to determine if the structure you've chosen is designed for the terrain of your business or industry. For example, one of the major shifts in manufacturing organizations recently is the adoption of self-managed teams in place of traditional hierarchies. While it would be gratifying to see this as a trend toward more democratization in the workplace, the truth of the matter is that it's a structure better suited to remaining competitive in industries where markets are constantly shifting and quick customer responsiveness may mean survival. By moving the authority to make production decisions ever closer to where the work is actually being done, you decrease the time it takes to resolve problems and respond to change.

  This kind of structure may not make sense for your business, but here's the point. Your hierarchy, your system of reporting relationships, has to be built around what makes sense for your business, not what's traditional in your industry. The structure you create for reporting relationships has to reflect the needs of your business, not shape it.

- **"The Way We Do It Here":** This is a large part of what we call "culture" in organizations—the standards, rules, and accepted practices that shape behavior. Some of this "culture" is explicit and is addressed in vision statements and policy. Some of it is ritualized and becomes part of the organization's story and myth. But part of the culture may remain implicit and largely "unseen," in some cases running a parallel and contradictory message. A classic example of this "parallel" culture is demonstrated when companies who profess to value and honor their people, and meticulously catalog their human resources beliefs, lay off scores of workers with no notice. The truth of how they do it there is revealed in practice—and makes a very vivid lesson about what's true to their remaining employees. There's a real opportunity in a situation like that to become aware of the parallel culture and try to bring it into alignment with stated values and objectives. A high-performance organization would use that scenario as an opportunity to look at their assumptions and find a better way to integrate their vision into their practices.

- **Your beliefs about what's true:** Nothing could be more fundamental in shaping the flow of energy and activity in any organization. These are the unconscious assumptions that function as unseen, unheard, and unfelt foundations for everything you think is true. Most of the time these assumptions remain completely unquestioned, and they tend to be self-fulfilling, as well. If you unconsciously believe that people can't manage themselves or your organization, if that's really what you think even though your personal ideology would reject that notion, it will shape the choices of alternatives you see and color all your actions. You'll end up getting what you were unconsciously looking for. This is true for everyone, not just the leader. Beliefs create a structure for activity that may be more profound than any other. In a high-performance environment, the culture must emphasize a continual questioning of assumptions, especially as a part of any decision-making exercise.

TRAINING AND TOOLS—THE "RIGHT STUFF"

In a high-performance environment, everyone needs to know more than enough. More than the basics of their accountabilities, more than the systems they are operating, and more than the general purpose and direction of the company. In a high-performance environment, everyone is primed to take the "right action" because they know everything. They know what the big picture looks like, they know how their jobs fit into it and support the organization's goals, they know how to look for indications that "right action" might be necessary, and they know how to take it and make it work.

Where do you find employees like that? You already have them. They're in your company right now. All you have to do is train them and give them the tools they need to get the results you want.

If you look at it very simply, training and tools are about how to do it and how to get it done. There's a difference between them, but most business owners think they're the same thing. So lots of training goes on, but the tools are rarely passed out and most employees have to make do. It's a waste of training dollars and it won't lead to high performance.

Training is primarily about teaching job skills: how to use a cash register, how to write purchase orders, how to run the sales system, and the like. Job skills also include using the methods and devices your organization has adopted to accomplish its tasks. Documenting systems, creating an action plan, using systems evaluation and innovation techniques, methods for assessing risk and creating planned change are examples. Training should be targeted to transfer specific job-related knowledge and skills, not the least of which is how to operate the systems each employee is accountable for. Think of training as "how to do it"—a series of sequential actions that deliver a well-defined result.

KNOWING WHAT TO DO IS ONLY HALF THE JOB

Most companies do some kind of training, and a few of them do quite a lot, but very few provide the real tools their people need to "get it done." Most employees figure it out, and the more explicit the information they have about the environment, the faster that will happen. But training doesn't guarantee it. "Getting it done"—getting the expected result—can often take skills and information that never get taught.

What are some of the "tools" your people need to get their jobs done once they know *how* to do them?

The first thing they need is **information.** It's funny, but one of the most closely held resources in many companies is the one that should be given away to employees most freely, and that's information. In some organizations it's treated like money. You only get what comes with your job, and if you need more, you have to search for it. Sometimes you even have to fight for it! In some organizations, it's probably even more precious than money. Why is that? There's a good chance that it's because information is power. If you know what's happening, your ability to act is greatly enhanced.

Without information, you sometimes can't act at all. So in most organizations, information is rationed. It's on a "need to know" basis only, and the assumptions about "who needs to know what" rarely get questioned and usually run along the lines of the hierarchy. So information becomes a "control," and access to it becomes part of the organization's "structure"—one of those factors that shape activity and behavior. The result is that the people who are the daily practitioners of "getting it done" rarely know everything they need to know to recognize and interpret early signs of change or trouble.

Some companies have recognized that information is the most important tool in a high-performance environment and have instituted something called "open book management." They've trained their employees to understand financial information and then opened the books to them. Every employee has the opportunity to see the real financial implications of everything the company does, including the effect on the whole business of their own department and position. It's much easier to take "right action" if you have the whole picture.

But financial information isn't the only kind of information that can become "open book." When Steve Jobs, founder of Apple Computer, established his second company, NeXT, he posted a list of everyone's salaries on the wall outside his office. Can you imagine the energy that freed up from speculation, uncertainty, bitterness, and fear? Can you imagine having a compensation system so well thought out and fair that it would bear public scrutiny and invite serious discussions about performance? If you really think about it, there's not much information, except that protected by confidentiality laws, that can't be made available to your people. The more they know, the less they fear and the more quickly and wholeheartedly they can take "right action."

Your people need **organizational skills,** too. These are tools that help them navigate "getting it done" with other people within the framework of your company culture. In recent years, many companies have begun to teach conflict resolution and teamwork skills to their employees. The days when we could assume that everyone was on the same page with interpersonal skills are over. If there's a best way for people to interact and solve problems in your organization, you need to make it explicit. And then you need to teach people how to do it so they have the tools to get the results you want.

Training in organizational skills doesn't necessarily require expensive professional consultants. It can be homegrown. Even ongoing small group discussions that are targeted toward defining the best ways to get the work done together and take on real issues that have arisen will be helpful. What's new about this is not the notion that these skills help get the job done, but that they can be taught. Interpersonal and organizational skills are tools everyone needs to get the job done, once they know how to do it.

Along the same lines, your people and their work can also benefit from the tools of **self-knowledge** and **self-management.** And those may be the best "tools" of all if they bring your people clarity about their motivations, desires, and personal obstacles. It can be hard to teach generally aggressive and blunt employees teamwork skills if they don't have a picture of their current impact. And more retiring employees may need to first *understand* their reluctance to act before they can assert themselves on behalf of their accountabilities.

There are a number of books and training "games" that can lead people to an understanding of the impact of their personalities on others without intruding on their privacy or selling a point of view. Three well-known tools are the Enneagram, Managing Interpersonal Relationships, and Myers-Briggs personality typing (and you'll find more at your local bookstore or library). The best of these tools feature nonthreatening, fun ways to approach self-discovery and development, and can provide a way for your people to see that the development of their personal skills is just as valuable and necessary to their success at work as their job knowledge.

The *Training and Tools* worksheet process will help you inventory the training and tools you are currently providing to your people and think about what you might offer next. So take some time to think about what kinds of training you've already created, and what you might add to round out the picture.

Download

FINE-TUNING YOUR ENVIRONMENT

Like all the other systems in your business, the systems you create to build and maintain a high-performance work environment must be quantified and tracked. Like many other operations in your business, your people systems may not always be directly measurable. But they *can* be quantified.

You're familiar with quantification from your reading and other work in the E-Myth Mastery Program. You have a feel now for what you'd like to measure, and how to quantify the intangibles. So ask yourself this question: "What would tell me that we *do* have a high-performance environment in our company?" Here's a list of possible measurable and intangible key indicators for your working environment:

MEASURABLE INDICATORS	INTANGIBLE INDICATORS
Number of business development meetings held	Overall employee satisfaction
Number of training hours per employee	Employee satisfaction with company goals
Percentage of performance goals met	Employee satisfaction with job training
Percentage of performance goals exceeded	Employee satisfaction with their own performance
Number of performance awards given	Managers'/owner's satisfaction with company goals
Number of awards for risk taking given	Managers'/owner's satisfaction with employee performance
	Managers'/owner's assessment of company's ability to use change to grow

Much of the data for your measurable indicators will come right out of your personnel records and you might consider creating monthly reports to capture trends in their earliest stages. Information for your intangible indicators should come both from your own impressions and from direct feedback from your people. Employee questionnaires and some form of a 360-degree performance appraisal system are just two ways you can get the information you need. The important point is to keep these issues high on your radar screen. It's much easier to reverse unproductive trends before they become frozen into your culture.

IT'S THE JOURNEY, NOT JUST THE DESTINATION

You do best with change of any kind if you're both flexible and absolutely sure of your purpose. That may seem contradictory, but flexibility without the guiding center of your vision will bring haphazard results. You always have to know where you're going even though the landscape may modify your route and your destination. High-performance organizations make that contradiction a strength. Their well-articulated visions express their hopes and expectations for the future, and create the energy to reach their goals. And their cultures promote the collaboration and group learning that allow them to alter the path if it doesn't prove to be the best route.

And most of all, high-performance environments create *a game worth playing.* They engage people fully and create an environment where they can use all of their skills and abilities to reach higher levels of personal and professional competence with each new challenge. So while it's fun to win, the truth about great games is that most people just want to keep playing. Building a high-performance organization is the best thing you can do to keep everyone in *your* game.

Operations Manuals: Building the Authoritative Guidebook of "How We Do It Here"

▪

Your video recorder won't record. Your computer stops computing. Your self-cleaning oven won't clean. Things that worked perfectly well yesterday, suddenly don't.

But before you pick up the phone to call for help, you think, "If I can just find the owner's manual, I might be able to fix it myself!" And more often than not, you can.

Before you put the manual back in a drawer, it might occur to you that you could have saved a lot of time and trouble if you'd read that owner's manual a long time ago, *before* anything went wrong.

Unfortunately, most of us don't. Our initial success with the "on-off" switch convinces us that things operate in a rather obvious and routine way. This can be a dangerous assumption. And the same holds true in business. All too often, employees believe they know the best way to do the work of their positions, and what they don't know they can make up as they go along.

Wouldn't it be great if every job came with its very own owner's manual so when something didn't work your people could figure out how to fix it? Even better, wouldn't it be great if all your people read the manual *first* and learned to "operate" their positions effectively—from day one?

Operations manuals *are* the "owner's manuals" for every employee's position. Done well, they'll tell your people how to operate their jobs for *maximum* results. As the authoritative guidebook of how things should be done in your

Operations Manuals

BUILDING THE AUTHORITATIVE GUIDEBOOK OF "HOW WE DO IT HERE"

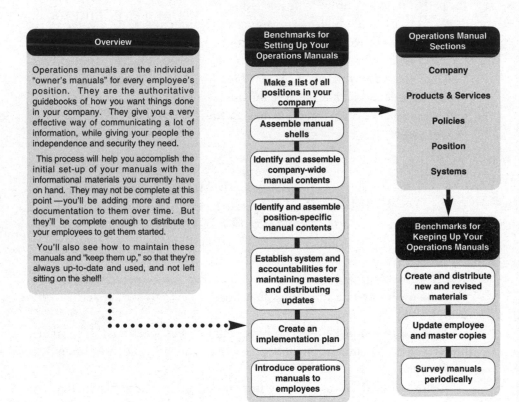

Overview

Operations manuals are the individual "owner's manuals" for every employee's position. They are the authoritative guidebooks of how you want things done in your company. They give you a very effective way of communicating a lot of information, while giving your people the independence and security they need.

This process will help you accomplish the initial set-up of your manuals with the informational materials you currently have on hand. They may not be complete at this point —you'll be adding more and more documentation to them over time. But they'll be complete enough to distribute to your employees to get them started.

You'll also see how to maintain these manuals and "keep them up," so that they're always up-to-date and used, and not left sitting on the shelf!

Benchmarks for Setting Up Your Operations Manuals

- Make a list of all positions in your company
- Assemble manual shells
- Identify and assemble company-wide manual contents
- Identify and assemble position-specific manual contents
- Establish system and accountabilities for maintaining masters and distributing updates
- Create an implementation plan
- Introduce operations manuals to employees

Operations Manual Sections

- Company
- Products & Services
- Policies
- Position
- Systems

Benchmarks for Keeping Up Your Operations Manuals

- Create and distribute new and revised materials
- Update employee and master copies
- Survey manuals periodically

company, they give you a simple yet effective mechanism for communicating a lot of information, and they give your people a sense of independence and "being in the know."

WHAT DOES AN OPERATIONS MANUAL LOOK LIKE?

Your operations manuals are made up of three distinct pieces:

1. The "shell," which is the physical container that will house the contents of the manual
2. Company-wide contents
3. Position-specific contents

The **shell** starts with a large, three-ring binder.

On the cover and spine, put the title of the manual, "operations manual for (Position Title)." Ultimately, you'll have a whole series of binders: operations manual for President, XYZ Widgets; operations manual for Vice President, Widget Service and Repair; operations manual for Manager, Customer Service; operation's manual for Widget Inspector; and so on.

Next you'll want some tabbed dividers to organize your manual into sections. We recommend these five sections:

1. Company
2. Products and Services
3. Policies
4. Position
5. Systems

You'll see what actually goes into these sections a little later in this process.

These three pieces—the binder, the title, and the tabbed dividers—comprise the shell of each operations manual.

Now let's look at what goes inside the shell. The contents of the Company, Products and Services, and Policies sections of your operations manuals will apply to everyone in the company. Everyone needs this information to understand the company as a whole, what you offer to your customers or clients, and the general policies under which you operate. These are the **company-wide contents** of your manuals.

The **position-specific contents** apply to an individual position. What a sales manager needs to know for her job is different from what the service technician needs to know, which is different from what the bookkeeper needs to know. You get the idea. This information will go into the Position and Systems sections of your operations manuals.

Unlike most owner's manuals you've seen, your operations manuals should be written in clear, concise language that makes sense, and they should tell your people how things really work: how your business operates, how their positions fit into the big picture, what they must do to achieve the results you expect from them, the standards by which they'll be evaluated, and what rules they must follow.

Think about some of the owner's manuals you've used in the past. What features and information helped you and what got in the way? If you had to learn your job all over again, what would you want to know before you start and what information would you want to find quickly as time went on?

As you build your business, you're documenting a lot of this information in the form of your organization chart, position contracts, written policies, and systems. Your operations manuals are where these documents, and others, are organized and stored so they're easy to access and use.

SETTING UP YOUR OPERATIONS MANUALS FOR THE FIRST TIME

Depending on how many positions and how many employees you have in your company right now, setting up your manuals will take some time and energy. But you don't have to do it alone. Managers, support staff, and other interested employees can help you gather materials, put the manuals together, and give you some good suggestions along the way. Here are the essential steps for creating your company's operations manuals:

1. **Make a list of all the positions in your company** and indicate how many people are currently in each position. This may seem too simple to even mention, but it's the best starting place. Use your organization chart to generate the list. Doing this will give you the big picture of what it will take to put your manuals together and show you exactly how many shells and how many copies of the contents you'll need.

2. **Assemble the shells for every manual you'll need.** At a minimum, you'll need one for every current employee. In addition, you could create manuals for:

   ▪ Upcoming and future hires
   ▪ Managers
   ▪ A company master

Remember that the shell consists of the binder, the title, and the section dividers. Three-ring binders and tabs work well, but use any type of "container" that will work in your setting. Just be sure that information can be located quickly and replaced easily when the time comes.

3. **Identify and assemble existing company-wide information.** Think about what materials you already have for the Company, Products and Services, and Policies sections of your manuals. 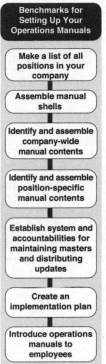 Use the *Listing of Currently Available Company-Wide Documents* to organize Download your thinking. Here's a brief description of these sections:

Company: This section gives you the opportunity to tell your people about your company and the "game worth playing"—why it exists, how it came to be, what it looks like now, and your vision for the future—in other words, what the "game" is all about and a view of how they fit into the bigger picture. It should also give employees a sense of the stability and growth of the company and help them feel that they're a part of something meaningful and bigger than themselves. Specific documents to include in this section are your:

- Strategic Objective
- Company Story
- Organization Chart
- Company History

Products and Services: Every employee, even those that don't work directly with your products and services, needs to know about them to participate fully in their jobs. Pride of affiliation is important to many people, and this section gives you the chance to show employees how your company contributes to the world by offering products and services that have value. Specific documents to include in this section are your

- Descriptions of your products and services
- Positioning statement and unique selling proposition

- Company brochures and product catalogs
- Basic information about your competition (but not detailed or defamatory) and how your company compares with them
- Documents that describe the logic behind your products and services

Policies: This section spells out the "rules for your game" that apply to everyone in your company. If your company has an employee handbook, it should already contain many of the policies that you need. You can insert the handbook right into this section of your operations manuals (or it can stand alone if it's too large to be inserted).

If you don't have an employee handbook, you may have individual policy documents that deal with such issues as: working hours, absenteeism, vacations, health and safety, compensation and benefits, equal opportunity, general rules of conduct, how to submit complaints and suggestions, how people should work together, etc.

Specific documents to include in this section are your

- Employee handbook contents
- Benefits information
- Dress code
- Facilities code
- Individual policy documents
- Documents that describe the logic behind company policies

4. **Identify and assemble existing position-specific information.** Think about what materials you already have for the Position and Systems sections of your manuals. The *Listing of Currently Available Position-Specific Documents* will help you to do this. Your managers can do much of the work to identify and collect these existing materials. Here's a brief description of these sections.

Download

Position: This section should give employees an overview of the results and accountabilities of their position. Specific documents to include in this section are:

- The position contract
- Generic, blank copies of any employment contracts and/or compensation agreements
- Documents that describe the logic behind the position

The employee's own copies of the actual employment contract and compensation agreement, containing specific figures and stipulations, are best kept in a more confidential place.

Systems: This part of the operations manual is like a "tool kit" where your employees can find all the instructions they need for doing the work of their positions. Include all the processes and procedures that you've developed over time for that particular position so that your employee can "run" his job by "running" its systems. Specific documents to include in this section are:

- System action plans
- Documents that describe the logic behind the systems

Even if some or all of these documents aren't in final form or don't conform to the business development standards you want to promote, if they're an acceptable representation of how you do business now, feel free to include them in this first version of your operations manuals. They will at least give your employees an understanding of the "body of knowledge" that exists now. And as part of your implementation plan, you can explain how the contents will be revised and updated over time.

A note about "logic": As we've described the kinds of documents that can go into each of the sections of your operations manuals, you see references to "documents that describe the logic behind. . . ." Logic is any information that gives background of context helpful to the understanding of the other information being presented.

Instead of telling your people only *what* you require of them, tell them *why*, too. This provides the rationale that gives a more complete picture and will lead to better performance and better decision making on the part of your employees. Explain the principles *behind* the work and you'll help them develop good judgment and play the game *your* way.

Materials from the E-Myth Mastery Program may be helpful because sharing information about the principles you're using to build your business will give your people a better "feel" for the business and why you're asking them to operate their positions in a specific way.

Of course, logic materials can come from other sources as well. The point is, don't be reluctant to add documentation that provides value to employees and helps them do their work with confidence and intention.

5. **Establish the system and accountabilities for maintaining masters and distributing updates.** Before you distribute their new operations manuals to everyone, decide how you will handle master sets and the distribution of new documents for inclusion. The key principle to keep in mind here is *consistency.* Everyone's manual should have the identical set of company-wide contents. Every person in a given position should have the same set of position-specific contents. And when new employees are hired, they need to be given a new operations manual that is consistent with the others. (Note: an ex-employee's copy may include inconsistencies, so exercise caution when passing on older copies to new employees.)

For company-wide contents:

- Who will maintain the master set?
- Who will be accountable for approving changes?
- Who will be accountable for distributing changes?

For position-specific contents:

- Who will maintain the master set of position-specific materials for each position?
- Who will be accountable for approving changes?
- Who will be accountable for distributing changes?

For all manuals:

- Who will be accountable for actually updating each manual when changes occur?
- Who will be accountable for assembling new manuals when needed?

For company-wide materials, usually only the president or a very senior person should be able to approve changes or additions. One person, usually in a company administration or personnel function, should be accountable for distributing updates and maintaining the master set.

For position-specific materials, these accountabilities could be the same as for company-wide materials. More typically, they are delegated to a departmental level. For example, department managers could be allowed to determine changes to the position-specific contents for their reporting employees and managers or a department administrative person could distribute updates and maintain the master set.

You'll also need to determine who will be accountable for actually placing new materials into everyone's operations manuals. Most often, this will fall to the employees themselves. But, as with everything else, be explicit about your expectation. Define it clearly. Don't just expect that people will know what to do.

And finally, who will create new manuals when a new employee is hired or when an existing manual is lost or damaged? One effective way to handle this is for a centralized person to put together the shell and insert the company-wide contents, then pass it off to the manager to insert the position-specific contents and deliver the completed manual to the employee.

Benchmarks for Keeping Up Your Operations Manuals

Create and distribute new and revised materials

Update employee and master copies

Survey manuals periodically

6. **Create an implementation plan.** Now that you've got your initial set of manuals made and have decided how they will be updated over time, create a written plan for how you'll introduce operations manuals into your company. Introducing them to managers with some simple training and opportunities for discussion will help pave the way. Then you may choose to introduce them to everyone else company-wide, by departments, or individually.

7. **Introduce operations manuals to your employees.** With the foundation in place and your materials ready, it's time to introduce the operations manuals according to your plan and hand each person their very own manual. While you'll have to explain the "mechanics" of the operations manuals, what each section means, and how to use the manual, remember to emphasize the benefits to every employee of having their own collection of all the documentation they need to answer their questions and produce the best possible results. Remember that your employees have a natural wish to please; having their own operations manuals helps them get the results you want without guessing.

KEEPING YOUR MANUALS UP-TO-DATE

Congratulations! With the introduction and distribution of your new operations manuals, you've completed another milestone in the development of your business. But you're not done yet. And, if you're doing things right, you never will be. Here's how to keep your manuals up-to-date, so that they remain a resource that's accurate and useful, and not just another binder gathering dust on a shelf.

1. **Create and distribute new and revised materials, as needed.** Over time, you will be revising some of the documents in your operations manuals, creating new ones, like new systems and policies, and you may even be eliminating some documents. As you do, simply distribute them with a cover memorandum describing the new piece and explaining exactly where to place it in their manuals and whether to remove any existing document(s).

   When you create new, company-wide policies, it helps to distribute them in a way that's instantly noticeable. Using a special format, wording, or color highlights the importance and urgency of the new rule, which can then be immediately read, implemented, and included in everyone's operations manual.

2. **Update all operations manuals, employee copies, and master copies.** Also update any copies already built for future use. Be certain to organize electronic operations manuals as well. Electronic files can be stored using the same structure outlined in this process. Depending on how you've chosen to do your updating, managers should follow up with their employees to be sure they are using new documents. The managers of the people accountable for maintaining the master sets should follow up with them as well.

3. **Survey your company's operations manuals periodically.** If operations manuals are not kept up-to-date, they become almost useless. Have your managers survey the manuals of their reporting employees periodically—twice a year is a good guideline—and you should do a survey of manuals at least annually.

TAKE THAT MANUAL OFF THE SHELF!

No manual can be self-enforcing. No matter how intelligent and clearly written, there's every chance it'll become an elegant dust catcher unless its value is continually reinforced by you and your managers. You can do that by making sure operations manuals are the official, reliable, authoritative source of information about your company, its products, and the "rules of your game."

Your operations manuals have to become fully integrated into your business. You and your managers have to use them, refer your employees to them, review their copies to be sure they're keeping them current, and make sure that up-to-date information is distributed regularly. Don't let them get lost. The minute you do, everyone will lose confidence in them.

Your operations manuals have to be "living" guides of "how we do it here"—a vital testament to your ongoing commitment to build a business that works for everyone. Remember, the business is a reflection of you, so show your conviction about this.

WHY INVEST YOUR TIME IN CREATING OPERATIONS MANUALS?

Operations manuals *sound* like a good idea; they're certainly an organized approach to conducting business and a great "system," but will people use them and will they really have any value for your business? Are they worth the time and effort it will take for you to build and implement them? Besides they're never done.

Look at it this way. Your business may run reasonably well without operations manuals. You probably know of some businesses that do.

But aren't you aiming for something more? Aren't you building a business that works—*really* works—without your having to run the whole show all the time?

Leaving anything to chance is just what you *don't* want to do. Leaving it to chance means that your employees will create their own rules, define their own jobs, and make up "how we do it here" out of their own experience—not yours. If you want it to be *your* game, you need to take the time to tell people how to play it.

Once you've created your operations manuals, you'll find they have many benefits in addition to their value as your employees' ongoing information source.

They'll help you recruit. Operations manuals will be a powerful communication vehicle about what we do here, where we're heading, and what the position entails. When you interview and hire new people, you'll have an impressive overview of everything applicants need to know.

They'll help you train. Your operations manuals will be filled with action plans, checklists, policies, and organizational information—everything your present employees or your new recruits need to know about your company and their accountabilities. Teaching employees how to do their jobs and get the best results will no longer be people dependent, or suffer from the distortions and inaccuracies that happen when training is done solely by word of mouth. Build your training agenda around the operations manual and vice versa.

They'll be your "business on a shelf." If you ever want to sell your business, your franchise prototype will be already documented in your operations manuals. Since they contain all the system solutions that run your business, you can point to your shelf of manuals and tell a potential buyer, "Here's how my business runs. It's all tested and documented. And it will work for you because it's worked for me!" What does any business person want to buy? A business that works!

CHAPTER FIVE

The Discipline of the Client Fulfillment Leader

■

**"And yet, no customer ever perceives himself
buying what the producer or supplier delivers.
Their expectations and values are always different."**

From Innovation and Entrepreneurship *by Peter F. Drucker*

At the heart of the World Class Company is its ability to satisfy the unconscious and perceived needs of its customer better than any other company can, not just by doing what any business is supposed to do—fix cars, vacuum carpets, stand behind the quality of its products, etc.—but by doing what it is not even reasonable to expect you to do. And to do that time after time.

That is the client fulfillment leader's purpose: to design, build, implement, and improve the company's Client Fulfillment Operating System, Client Fulfillment Training System, and Client Fulfillment Management System to keep the promise the company's marketing leader has determined your company needs to make to your market in order to successfully differentiate your company in the mind of your consumer from all other companies who are trying to do the same thing. So that your consumer sees your company as preferentially unique.

Quite a mouthful, perhaps, but also quite a responsibility.

For it is the ability of these three systems to work harmoniously together that will determine your company's ability to do for your customer what it is not even reasonable to expect you to do, time after time, while, at the same time, continually improving upon your performance.

It is how well these three systems work together to keep the promise you have made to your customer that turns him into a client.

Which brings us to the distinction between a customer and a client.

A customer is someone who buys from you once. A client is a customer who returns to your company time after time. A Client Fulfillment System is the method you use in the operation of your business to convert a customer into a client, and to, hopefully, retain him as one forever.

Your Client Fulfillment System includes every interaction you have with a person from the moment they become a customer. It is the number of customers who are converted into clients, how long you retain those clients, how much they buy from you for as long as they are clients, and how many of their friends and family members they refer to you that tells you how well you're doing as the client fulfillment leader of your enterprise.

Your first measure of success—how many of your customers are converted into clients—is your company's Customer Conversion Quotient.

Your second measure of success—how long your clients stay with you and how much they buy—is your company's Client Retention Quotient, the lifetime value of your client.

Your third measure of success—how many referrals your clients make—is your company's Client Multiplier Quotient.

The sum of these three measures of success, or Client Fulfillment Key Indicators, is your company's Client Fulfillment Quotient, the single most important indicator of the effectiveness of your client fulfillment system.

It tells you how meaningful a relationship your client has with you.

The client fulfillment leader looks at the world through the eyes of one who is committed to lasting relationships. *Without a commitment to lasting relationships, relationships that lead to other relationships with their friends and family, client fulfillment is an empty word.* Without a commitment to lasting relationships, no company can call itself, or be called, a World Class Client Fulfillment Company.

Without a commitment to providing your client with continual, verifiable value, beyond his expectations, beyond what your contract calls for, beyond what is reasonable for him to expect, beyond what you even promised him, a client fulfillment leader has failed to rise to the level of world class.

Let me say it again: The integrity of your Client Fulfillment System is measured by its ability to sustain genuinely valued and lasting relationships with your clients.

· · ·

Sarah and I initiated our next meeting in response to a question she asked me.

"Michael, I can understand how a client of yours could be impacted by what you've been saying. You're working with your client to improve their business. There are measures you can apply to how well you perform. Did the sales, profits, or cash flow increase? Did your client spend less time while producing more results? In my case, however, given the kind of business I'm in, it's really hard for me to think about what you're suggesting. Obviously, I want my customer to come back to my shop and buy again and again. But, given the nature of my primary business, a retail pie store, I'm hard-pressed to think about client fulfillment in the same way as you do in your business, a consulting firm. So, could you help me look at this the way I would if I were the client fulfillment leader."

"Great, Sarah. I can do that. Let's take your client fulfillment system apart for the moment and look at it from the customer-who-you-want-to-become-a-client's perspective.

"First of all," I said, "she comes in the door. Your client fulfillment system starts right there. What does she see, or hear, or smell when she comes in the door? What are her first impressions?"

Sarah was quick to answer. "She smells the fragrance of freshly-baked pie. She hears people talking at the tables, perhaps the cash register, or pie tins being stacked together, or the dishes being cleared. Oh," Sarah said, almost as an afterthought, "and she hears music. The Muzak I have piped into the store."

"Great," I said. "But, you left something out. What does she *see* when she walks in?"

Sarah laughed at the obvious omission. "Of course. She sees the store: the oak floors, the glass pie display cases, people; she sees people, customers, people who work in the store; she sees light, she sees . . . oh, you know, Michael. You've been in my store," Sarah said almost impatiently.

"I know, Sarah, but it's important that *you* know. That you see the store exactly as your customer would walking in the door. You, as the client fulfillment leader, need to take in the entire experience as your customer would, completely. Not that the customer takes it in consciously, necessarily. Very few customers take much in consciously. Our senses don't work that way. You might say there's a gestalt of sensory experience, a total experience which is all-at-once. As the marketing leader you thought about this, how to package the entire experience as a franchise, as a brand, as a unique once-only totality which is All About Pies in the mind of your customer-who-you-wish-to-become-a-client. What we're doing here is going deeper into it. Into the orchestrated experience that you, as the client fulfillment leader, can depend upon, just as you wish your client to be able to depend upon it. 'Ah,' you want your client to say, 'it's All About Pies. I remember this!'

"Now, remember what I talked about earlier, Sarah, that you need to know what the conversion of customers to clients is. You need to know what the retention and buying practices of your clients are. And you need to know how many referrals you're getting from your customers. Well, obviously, something has got to happen in this first moment, and from this moment on, if you are going to be able to quantify how well you're doing. So how would you accomplish that?"

Sarah started to answer, but I held up my hand. "Don't answer, Sarah. Because this is your first assignment. There are dozens of ways you could answer this question, all of them sound ways to achieve the objective. But, first, what's the objective we're trying to achieve here?"

"To start to quantify how many customers come in?" Sarah asked.

"Yes," I answered. "But even more. This is the first step in that client's relationship with you. Well, actually, it's not. The first step was when they first heard of you, however that happened. Either as a result of a direct mail campaign, or from someone they know, or they passed by your store a number of times and thought to themselves that one day they would come in. But, however that happened, and we'll talk more about that later, because it's obviously important to the entire relationship you're going to have with each other, this is the first step, when they come in the store, that will give you the opportunity to accomplish all of your objectives. You want to capture this moment, the name, the date, the time they came in, why they came in, what they came in for, what they actually bought, and so forth and so on. Listen, Sarah, very, very, *very* few, an infinitesimal percentage, of all retail companies capture this moment the way they could, and the way they should, and the way they absolutely need to do if they are going to build a world class client fulfillment system. And the first, most essential, component of the system is to be able to quantify the effectiveness of it. And now, when your customer walks in for the very first time, the first time you'll have with that customer, you need to record it as the beginning of your history together. And that's your first assignment."

THE FIRST ASSIGNMENT

"So the first benchmark in your client fulfillment system is the moment your prospective client walks in the door as a new customer. You need to capture this moment. How would you do it? This is what I want you to do, Sarah. I want you to make an exhaustive list of the different ways you could capture the information you want and need from your new customer, the person who just walked in your door, for whatever reason she was called to do that, so that you can begin to quantify how well your client fulfillment system works. Think about this assignment as critical to your success. You absolutely, positively need to get this one down. The first objective of this assignment, among many, is to determine what your Customer Conversion Quotient is.

"There are three rules, or standards, for achieving this objective:

1. You cannot ask your customer to do something which will make her uncomfortable, or which will feel unreasonable. In other words, it has to make sense.
2. You cannot do something that will make the transaction you are going to conduct difficult; in short, it's got to be the easiest thing to do in the world.
3. You can only do something that will positively add to your customer's appreciation of your business.

"Do you have any questions about this, Sarah?" I asked.

"Well, not a question exactly, but I would like an example of how somebody else did this. Could you give me one?" Sarah requested.

"Yes, I could. But, I'd really rather you just sit with it first and see what comes on your own. I don't want to limit your search and your creative response. Imagine that you're not looking for answers, even though they are obviously important; you're looking for questions. The questions, and your passion for discovering what they are, are the most rewarding part of this process, Sarah. And as you have already seen, even though at times it's frustrating, within the discovery of the right questions to ask, something amazing that you would never have anticipated shows up, and when it does your mind is transformed along with your business.

"Which brings us to the second assignment."

THE SECOND ASSIGNMENT

"Okay, Sarah, we now know that the first benchmark in your client fulfillment system is the moment your customer walks in the door and is greeted by all of the sensory data, in the form of her experience, that you have created in anticipation of that moment. It sounds like this: 'My customer walks in the door for the very first time. What do I want her to experience?' Do you get it, Sarah? The experience your customer has, walking in your door for the very first time, is an experience that you as the client fulfillment leader are charged with creating through your leadership of the process. It is a key component of your client fulfillment system. The second benchmark, then, is what happens next to your new customer. She walks in the door and she walks up to the counter, or what? What does she do then? What do you want her to do then? What would be the most natural thing for her to do then? Or another way of asking the question is, what do you want to happen here, Sarah? What would be perfect, both from the standpoint of your new customer and yourself, on behalf of your company. Clear your mind of whatever comes up immediately, Sarah. Think about this creatively for a time. Think about it.

Let me give you an absurd example of what I mean. You know those shooting galleries, where a figure pops up to be shot at? Imagine that the pop-up figure is life-size, and that the minute your new customer walks in the door a pop-up figure popped up right next to her. Bam! Do you see it, Sarah? Isn't that ridiculous? Obviously, you wouldn't do that, would you? Of course not, it would scare her to death! But, what *would* you do? What *would* you want to 'pop up' in front of your customer? What would you imagine could happen as benchmark two in your client fulfillment system that would move your new customer to the next step in a way that would completely captivate her? That's what I want you to do in the second assignment. I want you to make a list of possible next steps. They range from the obvious, your new customer walks to the counter, to the ridiculous, a robot hands her a sample of pie. Think about this, Sarah.

Does your new customer want to be invisible? Does she want a lot of attention? Would she simply like to conduct her business, get her pie, and leave without any fanfare? Would she love it if an entire 52-person orchestra appeared and played her favorite song? Do you see what I mean, Sarah? There's room to explore options and opportunities you have never pursued or even imagined. You're differentiating your company from all others. Think about the frustrations people have when they walk into a store for the very first time. Think about the negative experiences they have. Pursue this question, this second assignment, as though your company's life depended upon what you come up with. Write down anything and everything that comes to mind, no matter how ridiculous. Making the list, after all, is only the first step. The next step will be to think through all of the items on your list to begin to discriminate between the ones you'll pursue and the ones you won't. Do you have any questions about this, Sarah? Anything I'm willing to answer, that is."

"Actually, no, Michael. I get the point. But what's the next assignment? What's the third step in this process?"

"Glad you asked, Sarah," I said. "Because I'm hoping the third assignment will bring all this together for you in a powerful way."

THE THIRD ASSIGNMENT

"So, what we've done together to this point is to determine what the content of your Customer Conversion Quotient will be. In other words, the first few benchmarks in your client fulfillment system that will touch your new customer in such a compelling way that she will want to come back to experience your store again. What's next, of course, is to determine what the first step for your now new client will be. In other words, let's assume your new customer has now become your new client because she has completed her first business transaction with you. You have determined what you will do to make that transaction truly meaningful, captivating, exceptional in every sense of the word, so that your new customer, now your new client, will remember it favorably. What you have set out to do, Sarah, in this once-in-a-lifetime opportunity in relationship to this particular person, your new customer, now new client, is to create an association in her, an action point in her memory that, whenever she thinks of 'pies,' or 'sweets,' or 'bakery,' or 'party,' or 'gift,' or 'friend,' whatever the words are that are connected with that association for your new customer, now new client, she thinks about All About Pies. This is the hoped-for association with your company that will cause her to come back to you and buy something else. You need to know what that next decision is, when and how it is made, what the result of it is, and begin to build a rich, harvestable store of information about this new client now demonstrating her attraction to All About Pies, and the real measure of it. What is it you want to know? That's your third assignment, Sarah. What do you want to know about your client? And your fourth assignment is, now that you know it, what do you do about it? What steps do you take to reward her, and to benefit from her attraction to All About Pies? How much is just enough, how much is too much? And what is the medium through which all of this activity takes place? Does it happen when she walks in again? Does it happen after she leaves? Do you have an active web-based program? A membership program? An e-mail-reminder program? A gift program? A surprise-in-the-mail program? What are the benchmarks of your continuing interaction and engagement with your client to look like? Forever. Not just one step at a time, but completely, over time.

"In short, your client fulfillment system is something you will create as a complete entity, from the beginning of your relationship with your client to the end of your relationship with your client, thinking through and addressing everything you can possibly imagine doing for the life of your client, to thank her, to reward her, to acknowledge her, to invite her, to help her, to respond to her, to engage with her, to surprise her, to please her, to help her, to serve her, like no company has ever done it before.

"Your client fulfillment system, Sarah, could be thought of as an after-market program. But that's not really what it is. It is taking into consideration every component of your client fulfillment system, the visual, emotional, functional and financial aspects of it, that can be manipulated to behave in a way of your choosing, to stimulate your client in ways she has never been stimulated before, to give her options she has possibly never thought about before, all in the form of your products and potentially rich store of services. What would those products and services be, given the business you are in, and what business are you in after all? Just your name will tell you, Sarah: All About Pies. Meaning, anything and everything to do with the subject of pies. The world of pies. Pie stuff that no one has ever heard of before. That's your world, and now it's your client's world, Sarah. And no one knows more about the world of pies than All About Pies does.

"And that raises another question we haven't looked at yet, Sarah. What is a pie? Until now, all you have thought about are fruit and cream pies, because that's what prompted you to create your store. But what about all the other kinds of pies? Meat pies, seafood pies, and veggie pies. Pies for breakfast, for lunch, for dinner and for snacks. Every kind of pie known to woman. Why, there must be a veritable treasure trove of history surrounding the pies. Do you know what it is, Sarah? And if you don't, who does, and how do you immerse yourself in it to become the true maven of pies, the true creator of All About Pies, to the degree you can?

"Do you get my point, Sarah? The client fulfillment leader needs to consider everything. Not just about how to make the customer happy. It's more complicated than that. Because you can't make a customer happy unless you make the person who is waiting on that customer happy. And you can't make the person who is waiting on the customer happy unless you know who that person is, what they want, what's missing in their life. And you can't know any of that unless you ask them. And even when you ask them, if you don't ask the right questions, you won't get the truth back. In fact, the person who is working for you will rarely tell you the whole truth, not because they don't want to tell you the total truth (oh, they might want to tell you the truth, but that's even more reason for what I'm trying to say here to you), but because they don't know what the whole truth is. And neither does your customer, now a client, know what the truth is. Nor could they tell you what they would love you to do for them, except in relationship to a frustration you have created for them. If the pie didn't taste good. Or if an employee of yours was rude. Or if you made a promise and failed to keep it. Or if your store was supposed to be open on Monday at 9:00 A.M., but you didn't open it until 9:10 the day they happened to come by. And so forth.

"My point is, Sarah, that your process for creating your client fulfillment system must include all of these components—the ones related to marketing, human resources, customer service, organizational development, pricing, operations, sales, direct mail, or IT, the list goes on—as One Thing. Your client fulfillment system is part of One Thing. One Total Thing from the very first moment you conceive it. It's what is referred to by some as your business model. It's what's referred to by others as your business plan. It's what's referred to by even others as your business strategy. But whatever it's called, it's always and forever about client fulfillment. And that's where we are right now in the process. It is a huge discipline, client fulfillment, at the core of your company, and it will call for all of the attention and creativity you can give it. What you are called to do here as the client fulfillment leader is to think through your lifetime relationship with your client, every aspect of it, and to mine your imagination for the most original, responsive, thoughtful impressions you can make about that client, that will, over the time she has shared her life with you, cause her to think about you endearingly, yes, lovingly, and respectfully, as one might a very close friend. Hard to do? Absolutely. But it can certainly be done. And when it's done, it stands out remarkably from all the rest that has never done it. This is what marks the attention of the client fulfillment leader. She thinks about these things. She takes them in, deeply. She cares about these things in a way that could be almost embarrassing for most of us. She envisions doing the impossible for every single client, always. And then coming up with something else that was unthinkable. Unthinkably original. Just like the robot serving samples in a place you would never expect to see one. That's how remarkable this client fulfillment thing could be that we're discussing here now, Sarah. Delightfully shocking and stunningly effective. And that, dear heart, is your job!

"So, let's go on to look at the work of the client fulfillment leader to see how many different ways you can practice this thing of ours. Okay?"

"You leave me speechless, Michael." Sarah smiled. "Have you even noticed, Michael, that no matter what the discipline we're working on, you always make it sound like it's the most important one to me?"

"That's because it is, Sarah. Each of the disciplines is the most important one, simply because we're talking about it. They are all One Thing. Remember that. Everything you do touches everything you do. It is all One Thing. This entire conversation is all about One Thing. You can't do anything without touching everything. And that's why I say this with such conviction, Sarah. That to engage fully with each discipline as though your life were at stake would be the very best way to do what it is we're doing together. Only because our lives are at stake, and not, each and every moment. Right now. Right this very moment, Sarah. Stop. Remember that? Remember yourself. Remember that? Come back to this moment. Now. And then you'll feel the passion flowing in you. And as you feel the passion flowing in you, Sarah, you will feel the reality of this moment, not as a series of steps into the future, but as this moment and this moment alone. And then this moment will come alive.

"So let's do that, right now, Sarah. Let's Stop and see what happens. And then I'll give you your homework on the work of the client fulfillment leader."

I stopped. Sarah did too. The silence was pregnant with both discomfort and remarkable possibilities.

SELECTED E-MYTH MASTERY PROGRAM PROCESSES ON CLIENT FULFILLMENT LEADERSHIP

Your Client Fulfillment Baseline: Determining "Where Are We Now?" in Client Fulfillment

■

While all of the Seven Centers of Management Attention (leadership, marketing, money, management, lead generation, lead conversion, and client fulfillment) are important and deserve your attention, client fulfillment is what your *customers* care most about. It's the one that gives them what they want from you—the one they're paying their money for. It's the ultimate proof that you did what you promised to do.

For your customers, nothing about your business is as important as client fulfillment. It's what will put you ahead of your competition and allow you and your business to thrive.

So client fulfillment deserves special attention because it's the only sure way into the hearts and minds of your customers. Customers don't really care if your financial systems are in place, if your leadership is inspired, if your lead generation is attracting just the right people, or what style of management your key people practice. What they do care about is whether you manage to consistently provide them with a quality product that meets their needs, whether you're able to get that product into their hands quickly, reliably, and at

Your Client Fulfillment Baseline

Overview

Evaluating your client fulfillment process is key to understanding and addressing what your customers care most about.

Client fulfillment, in addition to the actual design of your product or service, consists of three main processes:

- Production
- Delivery
- Customer service

The baseline for your production, delivery, and customer service processes is the quantified status of the process as it exists now.

Your baseline is your starting point for planning and for measuring improvement.

Evaluation of your processes and establishing their baselines are both described in terms of the key indicators that describe their inputs, their outputs, and their costs.

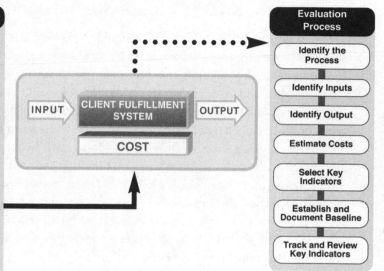

INPUT → CLIENT FULFILLMENT SYSTEM → OUTPUT

COST

Evaluation Process

- Identify the Process
- Identify Inputs
- Identify Output
- Estimate Costs
- Select Key Indicators
- Establish and Document Baseline
- Track and Review Key Indicators

an attractive price, and whether your customer service processes are helpful and efficient. That's what *they* care most about, and if you want to keep them as customers, that's what *you* need to care about!

YOUR BASELINE TELLS YOU WHERE YOU ARE AND LETS YOU MEASURE PROGRESS

The key question, then, is how do you establish the very best possible client fulfillment process for your business, or more accurately, for your customers? You're going to do this by looking at the three major processes that make up client fulfillment (production, delivery, and customer service) and evaluating the input, output, and costs for each of those processes, which will enable you to clearly and specifically document your current performance level—your baseline.

Why do you need a baseline? If you don't know where you are now, it's rather difficult to figure out where you're going! You care very much where you're going, and a baseline—by telling you exactly where you are right now—will provide the point of reference from which you can set goals and measure your progress. By documenting your current baseline and tracking changes over time, you're going to have a clear sense of how effective your improvements to those processes have been.

That's what this business development process, your Client Fulfillment Baseline, is all about—evaluating the major components of your client fulfillment process and establishing the baseline from which you'll set goals and measure your progress.

WHAT, EXACTLY, IS CLIENT FULFILLMENT?

First things first. What *is* the client fulfillment process?

Client fulfillment consists of the product itself plus three major processes—production, delivery, and customer service—the combined result of which is to put your product or service into the hands of satisfied customers.

Production. Production is what it takes to make your product or service a reality. It starts where product design leaves off. In other words, once you've identified the product or service you want to offer for sale and have specified its particular attributes—what will make your product different and better than anyone else's—production is how you actually create, make, or acquire that product or service so you can sell it.

What does production look like in *your* business? If you have more than one dissimilar product or service, you probably have more than one production process. The kinds of things you do in production and the number of

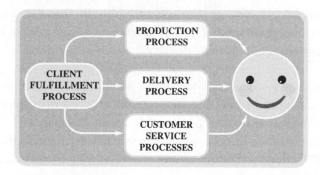

steps there are from beginning to end vary widely from one type of business to the next. But every business has at least one production process.

Identify those systems that are part of your production process. Where does the production process begin and where does it end? It begins at the point where your product is no longer an idea, but begins to take some tangible form. And it ends when you have a complete product or service ready for sale or delivery to your customer.

- If you're in the retail grocery business, your production process might include identification of vendors, purchasing, and receiving.
- The production process for a company manufacturing kits for children's toys might incorporate testing, purchasing, assembly, quality control, and packaging.
- For a carpet cleaning business, production might involve recruiting, providing necessary training, purchasing or leasing equipment, buying cleaning supplies, and of course the actual cleaning process itself.

Delivery. This is getting your product or service from your business to your customers. It begins where your production process leaves off. Delivery always has the element of transportation. During your production process, you took raw materials and added value to those materials with the end result being your actual product or service. Delivery transfers the value of that product or service to your customer.

Inbound. For an inbound business, your customers become an active partner in the "delivery" of your product or service. Even though they come to your location, you still accomplish delivery to them. For inbound businesses (e.g., grocery store, amusement park, restaurant, department store, gas station, airline, barber shop, dentist), the focus is less on the physical transfer of a product or service, and more on the experience of the transfer itself.

Outbound. With outbound delivery, the physical transfer of value to the customer is more prominent, but the experience should still not be ignored. There are two types of outbound delivery:

- In-business production. You create a product or service at your location and transport it to your customers (pizza delivery, mail order businesses, manufacturers of all kinds, newspapers, magazines, door-to-door sales business). The toy kit manufacturer might deliver his product by way of mail, shipping (air, rail, or sea).
- On-site production. You go to the customer's location to create your product or provide your service (carpet cleaners, in-home nursing care, janitorial service, electricians, contractors, management consultants, etc.).

Many companies use several forms of delivery. For instance a furniture store will usually allow you to take your purchase with you like an inbound business, but may also provide outbound delivery services with their own trucks and crew or through third parties such as Federal Express or local trucking companies.

Customer service is what you can and do provide over and above the minimum requirements the customer expects as honest value for his money. Customer service is what causes your customers to perceive your product or service in a better light. The customer is not paying for these "extras," and they are not "necessary" in order to acquire or use your product or service. A good rule of thumb is that if it's not an inherent element of your product or service, it's probably customer service.

It can be difficult to define what falls into this category because there are so many possibilities. Opportunities for customer service can happen whenever any part of your business interacts with a current or potential customer. Customer service might include any of the following types of service: attitude, assistance, information and advice, training, maintenance, and credit/financial arrangements.

- The grocer might offer recipe cards to spotlight seasonal produce, trim meat to customers' individual specifications, carry groceries to customers' vehicles, or feature a nutritionist offering menu suggestions for selected food items.
- The toy manufacturer might provide a toll-free number to help with assembly problems, in-house demonstrations of the full

capabilities of the finished toys, or an insert that suggests games and activities for those children ultimately receiving the toys.

▪ The carpet cleaner might provide handouts on dealing with stains, offer suggestions for protecting carpets in the future, or perhaps offer a free "carpet life analysis."

ESTABLISHING THE BASELINE FOR YOUR PRODUCTION, DELIVERY, AND CUSTOMER SERVICE PROCESSES

Let's have a step-by-step look at how you establish your baseline.

1. **Identify the process.** You'll begin identifying the elements of your three main client fulfillment processes (production, delivery, and customer service) by listing the beginning point, the ending point, and, perhaps, some of the key components within each process. The individual systems that collectively make your product or service a reality are your production process. In the same manner, identify your delivery process—the systems that are needed to put your product or service into your customer's hands. Finally, identify your customer service process, which consists of the systems you have in place to add additional value to your product or service above what's promised. There are three *Process Identification* worksheets to help you keep track. Remember, for baseline Download purposes, you won't be looking at the individual systems within the production, delivery, and customer service processes, but at the way each process operates as a whole.

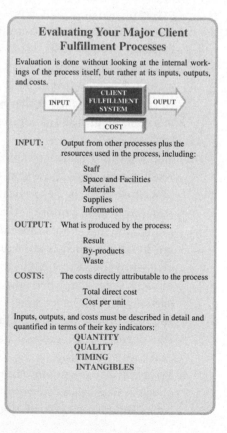

Evaluating Your Major Client Fulfillment Processes

Evaluation is done without looking at the internal workings of the process itself, but rather at its inputs, outputs, and costs.

INPUT → CLIENT FULFILLMENT SYSTEM → OUPUT

COST

INPUT: Output from other processes plus the resources used in the process, including:

Staff
Space and Facilities
Materials
Supplies
Information

OUTPUT: What is produced by the process:

Result
By-products
Waste

COSTS: The costs directly attributable to the process

Total direct cost
Cost per unit

Inputs, outputs, and costs must be described in detail and quantified in terms of their key indicators:
QUANTITY
QUALITY
TIMING
INTANGIBLES

2. **Describe the process inputs.** Identify the main resources needed for this process to function, and describe them in terms of their key system indicators. If it's labor intensive, how many man-hours are required? If it's a function of facilities, how much space, tools or equipment are needed to ensure that the process can do its job? If the process relies on raw materials, what sort of supplies need to be available and in what quantities? If the process is data driven, what sort of information is needed? Use the *Process Baseline* worksheet to track your work in this step and the next two.

3. **Describe the process outputs.** Identify the result, by-products, and waste products produced by the process in terms of its key indicators. Output is the final result of the process you're evaluating. Think about why this process was put into place and what importance it has in the overall client fulfillment process. Be sure to identify any by-products (wanted or unwanted) that result from this process.

4. **Estimate process costs.** What costs can be directly tracked to this specific process? Remember not to include general or overhead costs in your calculations. Do your best to collect cost information that is compatible with your accounting system. Get the precise accounting information if you can, estimate if you can't.

5. **Select key indicators.** Your job here is to identify a small number of revealing indicators, those that will give you the ability to monitor the process objectively. Key indicators may include such measures as total cost, cost per unit of output, numbers/amounts of key resources (like headcount, man-hours, amounts of supplies or raw materials) and output measures (such as units produced or delivered, customers served, etc.)—any indicators that let you take the pulse of the important parts of the process and, when taken as a whole, allow you to monitor it. As part of your criteria for selecting key indicators, consider the impact on your customers, the impact on your business, and the overall effectiveness of the process. Use the *Key Indicators* worksheet to record and track your choices.

6. **Establish and document your baseline.** Using the key indicators you selected, establish where your level of performance is at this particular time. Be sure to record not only the final result (dollars, time,

input/output ratios, units delivered/consumed, etc.) but also your rationale and any assumptions you made in your calculations. This baseline will be the key to understanding your current performance level and to evaluating the effectiveness of changes or improvements you put into place. You'll have the objective data to see and quantify improvements and you'll know precisely where to get the "best bang for your buck!"

7. **Track key indicators and review periodically.** Assign a responsible individual the accountability for tracking your future progress against these baselines. Make it a part of your periodic review of key strategic indicators to track your client fulfillment processes quarterly, or in some regular time frame that is consistent with your business.

EXAMPLE: SWEETTOOTH, INC.

Let's see the evaluation process in action by looking at how it worked for the client fulfillment processes of SweetTooth, Inc., makers of hand-dipped chocolates. The owner, Betty Rappel, began by working through each step of the system evaluation process. We've simplified SweetTooth's actual process to make the example clearer.

1. **Identify the process.** To begin, Betty took an "overview" look at her three main client fulfillment processes (production, delivery, and customer service) by filling out a Process Identification worksheet for each of them. (All of her worksheets are shown at the end of this process. As you read them, you'll be able to see how her reasoning progressed as she worked through each step.)

   Betty wanted to make sure that she was seeing each of the three processes in a clearly defined way, and that she was "assigning" her various, individual subsystems to their "right" client fulfillment process. She wasn't going to look at each one of those subsystems in detail yet, but she wanted all her production activities included in production, all delivery activities in delivery, and ditto for customer service.

   She had a few systems that were difficult to pinpoint and that required some thought in order to classify into one process or another. For instance, she provides a "Certificate of Purity" with each box of chocolates. Is the certificate part of her production process or is it a customer service? Because it's packed inside each box, she decided it's part of production.

   Now that Betty has clearly identified the parameters of the three processes, she's ready to pick any one of them, complete the rest of the benchmarks for that one, and then do the same for the other two processes. (We'll discuss them collectively.)

2. **Describe the process inputs.** With her systems identified, Betty next listed the major resources needed for each of these processes to function. She focused on the "big ticket" items, those that had the greatest overall impact on the process she was examining (the largest quantities, the most expensive elements, those that contributed most to the taste, the machinery that contributed most to the process, staffing, etc.). She worked through each phase of her production, delivery, and customer service processes to identify needed inputs using key indicator data to objectively describe them. She recorded her findings on the *Process Baseline* worksheet.

Download

3. **Describe the process outputs.** Betty examined each process to identify its primary end result (expected outcome), any by-products (wanted or unwanted) that were produced, and any waste that was a function of each process. She also recorded these on the *Process Baseline* worksheet.

4. **Estimate process costs.** Betty found that in some areas (production for example) it was relatively easy to determine her costs. She had requisitions and invoices that told her exactly how much she had spent on materials, equipment, and floor space; and she knew the salaries of those employees who were employed in the production area. In other areas (customer service), the nonspecific nature of the process made it very difficult to pin down exact costs. In those cases, she used what data was available and came up with estimates for the costs she felt were reasonably representative of the actual amounts involved.

5. **Select key indicators.** At this point, Betty had quite a list of inputs, outputs, and costs associated with each client fulfillment process. And with it came a sense of accomplishment and clarity beyond what she had expected at the outset.

But she was not done yet. Next, Betty examined the information she'd collected, carefully looking at the costs and other items of significance. "Which pieces of information will be the most useful in telling me whether or not my process is doing what it's supposed to?" Looking at the data from this perspective, Betty found the items, or indicators, that would allow her to assess the ongoing effectiveness of her client fulfillment processes. These same indicators will point her in the most fruitful directions for making improvements where they will have the most substantial impact.

Example: SweetTooth, Inc.
PRODUCTION PROCESS BASELINE WORKSHEETS

Process Identification Worksheet

YOUR PRODUCTION PROCESS

My production process, the way I make the idea of my product or service a reality, is: (*write one or two sentences*) receive orders, purchase ingredients, mix chocolate, dip fruits and shape individual pieces, wrap them in individual foil wrappers, and assemble in 1-lb assortments, along with special orders.

The production process begins with: identification of vendors and purchase of ingredients and packaging materials.

and ends with: fully assembled assortment boxes ready for shipment and delivery.

and the key steps in between are: Receiving materials, storage of materials, mixing chocolate recipes, dipping and shaping fruits and nuts, hand wrapping each piece, assembling various assortment boxes, quality inspection and testing, maintenance and cleaning, preparing cartons for shipment.

Process Baseline Worksheet

INPUTS:	PRODUCTION PROCESS:	OUTPUT:
Fresh raw materials (perishables, wrappers, boxes), staff, equipment, floor space, recipes	Purchasing, storage, mixing, dipping, shaping, quality inspection, assembly and packing	1-lb boxed assortments
	COST: Total monthly production costs = $75,600. Unit cost = $1.75 per 1-lb box.	

		QUANTITY	QUALITY	TIMING	INTANGIBLES
INPUT (1-lb box)	Candy ingredients ($19,958 per month)		84% = Grade A 11% = Grade B 5% = Grade C		Fresh ingredients' cost variable by season
	Supplies		Standard #43(a) wraps = Grade 2 wax paper		
Staff	Production payroll = $27,775/m			Need average of 4 days to train new employee in procedures	Dipping, shaping & wrapping employees are gaining weight!
Equipment	Maintenance average = $208/m				
Floor space	436 sq. ft devoted to production				
Recipes	7 unique mixture recipes		THE BEST!		
OUTPUT	1-lb Assortment (apx. 24 individual pieces)		Quality rejection rate at 4.9% (88 boxes/mo)		
	Production rate = 1800 cartons per month		Returned merchandise @ 43 cartons/mo (2.4% return rate)		

Key Indicators Worksheet

Process PRODUCTION   **Date** April 200X

KEY INDICATORS	Baseline	Previous Period	Current Period
Production volume: cartons per day	180 per day		
Cost of perishable ingredients: price per carton	$11.08		
Total ingredient cost per month	$19,958		
Inventory availability for ingredients: days of inventory on hand at standard production rate	2.73 days avg.		
Accuracy of assembly (number of boxes rejected per day by quality inspection for inaccurate/faulty mix)	88 boxes/mo 4.9%		

Example: SweetTooth, Inc.
DELIVERY PROCESS BASELINE WORKSHEETS

Process Identification Worksheet

YOUR DELIVERY PROCESS

My delivery process, the way my product or service passes from me to my customers, is: (*write one or two sentences*) by several methods. I have an on-site sales outlet. I also ship to specialty and department stores throughout a wide area. I am just beginning a catalog sales operation that will require mailing and commercial carrier.

The delivery process begins with: Receipt of fully packaged cartons from production, including completed packing slips and inspection charts. For in-house sales, the delivery process begins with direct requests for pieces from the in-house sales coordinator.

and ends with: receipt by our customers (or distributors) of our assortments.

and the key steps in between are: prioritizing shipments, preparing shipping labels, deciding on mode of transportation, arranging pickup. For in-house sales: transporting items from production floor to sales outlet and restocking as needed throughout day.

Process Baseline Worksheet

INPUTS: for outbound orders: Packing/shipping materials, trucks, mail/shipping costs, staff. For in-house orders: staff, restocking costs.

DELIVERY PROCESS: Two major delivery systems: those for outbound orders & those for in-house sales. Catalog sales delivery system still in planning stages

OUTPUT: On-time, accurate delivery of product to customers & distributors with no damaged goods en route. For in-house sales: accurate on-time transportation from production area to sales room.

COST: $0.50 per 1-lb box
Total monthly delivery cost
(per 6/30/9X budget) = $21,760

	QUANTITY	QUALITY	TIMING	INTANGIBLES
INPUT (1-lb box) OUTBOUND SHIPMENT				
Packing/ labeling	24 boxes per carton	Std. Lined #73	Stock on hand to allow for such shipments	Box more functional than attractive!
Shipping staff		5 employees		
Carrier Selection		Expense vs. accuracy considerations in selection of shipper		
Company trucks	2 currently in service Upkeep cost $218/mo			
Mail UPS	2000 boxes/mo 3500 boxes/mo		4 mail runs a day 3 UPS pickups per day	
IN-HOUSE SALES OUTLET	Average 18 boxes & 75 assorted individual pieces per day		Random throughout day, higher volume during holiday seasons	
OUTPUT	1800 cartons per month	30 boxes per month damage (1.7%)	Average 3 days delivery to distributors	

Key Indicators Worksheet

Process DELIVERY

Date April 200X

KEY INDICATORS	Baseline	Previous Period	Current Period
Speed of delivery to distributors	Avg. 3 days for 74% of distributors		
Spoilage during delivery cycle (chocolate melting, fresh ingredients over-ripe)	30 boxes/mo 1.7%		
Average cost of delivery (per carton)	$12.00		
via UPS	$11.18		
via mail	$10.86		
via company truck	$13.96		
Percent of total deliveries lost during shipment	3.4% (61 boxes)		
Percent of UPS deliveries lost during shipment	3.9%		
Percent of U.S. mail deliveries lost during shipment	7.6%		
Percent of deliveries lost on company truck	0%		

Example: SweetTooth, Inc.
CUSTOMER SERVICE PROCESS BASELINE WORKSHEETS

Process Identification Worksheet

YOUR CUSTOMER SERVICE PROCESS

The customer services I provide to my customers include: unique holiday and special-occasion wrapping and ingredients, hand-printed messages for gift, made-to-order assortments, options on seasonal fruits exotic nuts

I identify new customer service opportunities by: including customer surveys in selected assortment boxes, having a suggestion box to encourage ideas from my employees.

My employees practice good customer service by: (1) freely offering their opinions for making me aware of comments they receive from suppliers and clients (good or bad!); (2) responding to complaints within 24 hours of receipt; (3) money-back guarantee if customer is dissatisfied for any reason.

Process Baseline Worksheet

INPUTS: Custom ingredients and wrappings, staff time for custom services and adjustments	CUSTOMER SERVICE PROCESS:	OUTPUT: Potentially happier & MORE customers
	COST: In-place custom and adjustments services = $540 per month plus "soft" costs	

	QUANTITY	QUALITY	TIMING	INTANGIBLES
INPUT (1-lb box)				
Customer surveys	Included in 1 out of 5 boxes		Slow return on responses. Difficult to determine origin	Cannot respond to anonymous comments. Many suggestions contradictory
Employee suggestions	Average 15 suggestions per month	Some excellent ideas have emerged from this system		Employees feel more involved in the company & in their jobs!
OUTPUT				
Shipment tracking service	Average 24 inquiries per month		Immediate (real time) information	Very favorable feedback — happier customers.
Custom boxes, wrappers	Adds $.43 to cost of producing	Excellent, but may not be worth additional expense		

Key Indicators Worksheet

Process CUSTOMER SERVICE   **Date** April 200X

KEY INDICATORS	Baseline	Previous Period	Current Period
Number of custom-wrapped assortments per month	87 (4.8% of total)		
Cost of custom wrapping per box	$.43 per box		
Customer complaints received per month	9		
Average time to resolve customer complaints	2.7 days		

At the end of her assessment, Betty selected those *key* indicators for each of the three client fulfillment processes. These would serve as her guideposts to success.

6. **Establish and document a baseline for key indicators.** Betty pinpointed the current levels of performance for the key indicators she had selected and recorded those baselines on the *Key Indicators* worksheet. Download

7. **Track key indicators and review periodically.** Betty was surprised that she had been able to document so many specifics about her client fulfillment processes, and she acknowledged that it was vital to the future of her business to use those baselines as a foundation for future improvements. She assigned her production manager the task of periodically tracking the production process against its baseline; her delivery supervisor was charged with keeping track of progress for the delivery baseline. Betty decided to personally track her customer service baseline. All three managers understood that their job was to not only sustain current levels in high performing areas, but also to measure progress in areas where improvements were indicated.

CUSTOMERS: LOVE 'EM OR THEY'LL LEAVE YOU!

Client fulfillment is not an easy task. Customers can be fickle and they're not always going to tell you when and why they're unhappy. It's up to you to do the groundwork to determine how well you're meeting and hopefully exceeding their expectations. You can't afford the luxury of not providing exactly what your customers want, need, or expect. To quote noted magician Henning Nelms: "Any relationship between what you want to present to the paying public and what they want to see is purely coincidental." Your business is no magic act. Evaluating your client fulfillment process tells you if what your customers want and what you consistently deliver are one and the same!

Systems Innovation:
Analyzing and Improving Your Business Systems

■

Pick a system. Observe it. Evaluate it. Fix it. Watch it work. That's the essence of the systems innovation process. There's a lot more to it than that, of course, and some systems are enormously complex and detailed, but the process holds for any system in any business. Once you learn the basic process, you can "fix" any system, make any system better, invent a new system. And you don't need a

Systems Innovation

ANALYZING AND IMPROVING YOUR BUSINESS SYSTEMS

The Systems Innovation Process

- Select a System for Innovation
- Observe the System On-Site
- Diagram the System
- Determine System Baseline
- Analyze Work Flow
- Apply the Innovation Checklist
- Diagram the Innovated System
- Estimate Performance & Compare with Baseline
- Install & Test the Innovated System

Definitions

Systems innovation is the creation or improvement of business systems.

Every system can be improved. It's the basic assumption behind systems innovation.

A system consists of a series of work steps, or "benchmarks," that work together within the system to produce a result. A system may connect with other "external" systems that provide it with inputs or depend on its output.

Key Points

When innovating a system, go see it. Get a firsthand "feel" for it. Talk to the people who operate it. Learn how it works in great detail.

Diagram the system using the box-and-arrow technique. Show the system's benchmarks (contained within its "black box") and showing connections with other systems in your business (outside the "black box").

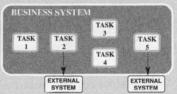

Describe the key indicators of the systems performance using the input-output-costs technique and describing the key indicators in terms of quantity, quality, timing, and intangibles.

Analyze all four types of work flow — task flow (the benchmarks of the system), materiel flows, management information flow, and the physical layout and traffic flows of the system.

Use the innovation checklist to help discover and create new ways to operate the system. Diagram the innovated system with its new benchmarks, and estimate its new input-output-cost performance. If the "innovated" system doesn't exceed the performance of the "old" system, go back to the innovation checklist and try again. If your estimate is an improvement over the "old" system, decide if the improvement is sufficient to justify changing to the innovated system. Keep cycling through the innovation checklist until you have developed an innovated system that is worth implementing in your business. Then install and operate the innovated system.

Ph.D. in engineering to do it. You only need your common sense and a process that walks you through what has to be done.

According to the E-Myth point of view, business development is a process of "innovation, quantification, and orchestration" and you do it through business systems. Systems innovation, then, is the leading edge of the business development process. A couple of quotes from *The E-Myth Revisited* illustrate the idea of innovation:

> Innovation is often thought of as creativity. But as Harvard Professor Theodore Levitt points out, the difference between creativity and innovation is the difference between thinking about getting things done in the world and getting things done.

The E-Myth goes on to say:

> It is the skill developed within your business and your people of constantly asking, "What is the best way to do this?" knowing, even as the question is asked, that we will never discover the best way, but by asking we will assuredly discover a way that's better than the one we know now.

The whole idea of systems innovation is to find the better way. And here's how you do it.

FINDING THE BETTER WAY

Every system can be improved. Do you believe it? You should. It's the working assumption at the core of all your systems innovations. Even if you have a system that's light-years ahead of anything you've ever seen and beats the pants off anything your competitors have, you can take it on faith it can still be improved. The only real question is one of priorities. Which of your systems will you work on now and which ones will have to wait a bit?

It comes down to the question of need—your customers' needs and the needs of your business.

You know about your customers' needs. That was the idea behind the psychographic profile you created earlier (see Part Two, Chapter Two). It's also the idea behind product strategy and design work. The products you produce, your delivery process, your customer services, your sales processes, and your advertising all have to serve your customers' needs.

But your systems also have to serve your business. And that comes down to economics and quality of life for you and your people. The economics require minimizing costs, maximizing profits, and ultimately increasing the value of your business. Quality of life issues revolve around creating business systems that are productive and satisfying for your people.

THE SYSTEMS INNOVATION PROCESS

Here's an overview of the process (some of the steps are discussed in more detail following the outline):

The Systems Innovation Process

- Select a System for Innovation
- Observe the System On-Site
- Diagram the System
- Determine System Baseline
- Analyze Work Flow
- Apply the Innovation Checklist
- Diagram the Innovated System
- Estimate Performance & Compare with Baseline
- Install & Test the Innovated System

1. **Select a system for innovation.** Which system? Select a system your intuition tells you needs attention.

   Actually, the real answer to the question "Which system should you innovate?" is *every* system. You'll take the most important systems and those that need attention most urgently first, but eventually, every system in your business should be put through the systems innovation process.

2. **Observe the system on-site.** See it. Watch it in action. Talk to the people who operate it. Get their experience, their "feel" for the system. Read the system documentation. Get to *know* the system.

3. **Diagram the system.** Use the box-and-arrow format on the right to make a simple diagram of the benchmarks of the system. Give each benchmark a brief name and number them in sequence. Make your diagram spacious, not cramped. You're going to use it for a number of purposes and you'll need the space.

4. **Determine the system baseline by looking at its input/output/cost.** Input includes the resources required to operate the system (staff, facilities, equipment, supplies, and information). Output is the result produced by the system plus any by-products and waste the system generates. Costs are the costs directly attributable to the system over an accounting period (month) and the

per-unit costs when the system produces units of output. Quantify and describe input and output in terms of its key indicators (quantity, quality, timing, and intangibles). Having gathered this information, you now have the baseline against which you will measure future performance.

5. **Analyze the system's work flow.** Work flow is the progression of activities, materials, and information into, within, and out of a system. Work flow has four components—task flow, materiel flow, information flow, and layout. Task flow consists of the steps you showed in your box-and-arrow diagram. Materiel and information flows may or may not be significant for any one system, and they may or may not coincide with the task flows—it depends on your specific business. Layout is the physical arrangement of work stations, workspace, and the traffic patterns in the working area.

    Work flow includes connections with other systems in your business and even connections with outsiders like suppliers, regulators, creditors, and others. The system you're working on occupies a place in the overall business and is interrelated with other systems. You'll need to look at those interrelationships to understand their balance and their interdependencies, and the effect the system has on the larger scheme of things at your business.

    Later in this process you'll find a list of specific guidelines for analyzing each of the four work flow components.

6. **Apply the Innovation Checklist.** Use the *Business Systems Innovation* checklist to explore opportunities for improvement. The checklist includes a series of specific techniques for improving the work flow of any system. Some may be appropriate, some may not. If you're inventing a completely new system, the checklist is an Download excellent way to avoid mistakes in system design.

7. **Diagram the innovated system.** Decide what improvements to try, or the best configuration for a new system, and diagram it. Again, the box-and-arrow diagramming technique works well. Take advantage of people who populate the "old" system to develop suggestions and give their experienced opinions on various ideas for innovating the system.

8. **Estimate the performance of the innovated system and compare with the current system baseline.** Quantify and describe the key indicators of your newly conceived system. If you want to try to generate an even more effective version, cycle back through steps 6 and 7. If the system is acceptable, go on to step 9.

9. **Install and test the innovated system.** This will require planning, training, probably some preliminary on-site experimentation, and maybe even a period of continued testing and observation (like the "beta test" period used in developing new computer software). When the system has settled into its normal pattern of operation, you'll want to determine the "norms" of its operation (the normal range of input, output, and costs, again expressed in terms of key indicators), and document and use ongoing monitoring as part of your "orchestration" process.

YOU HAVE TO SEE IT TO UNDERSTAND IT— GO AND LOOK

You may already know your business systems so well you could describe them in detail from memory—but don't do that. Most memories aren't that trustworthy, especially when it comes to the details of business systems. But even if you have a superb memory, go look at the system. Get a direct "feel" for it. Talk to the people who operate it. Find out what corners get cut, and why. Find out what ideas they have, and why. Find out what they've tried that worked or didn't work, and why. Get a sense of how people, materials, and equipment move in and about the system. See how the system relies on other systems for input and feeds its output to other systems, and talk about it with people operating the other systems.

In other words, don't make it a study, make it an *experience*. If you make it a study, you're limiting yourself to logic. Logic is powerful and essential, but your brain also works in nonlogical ways. If you experience the system firsthand, you're feeding the intuitive and instinctive parts of your brain. You're picking up clues and observations you might not even be aware of, but that will serve you well as you move into the truly innovative steps of the process.

BOXES AND ARROWS—SIMPLE YET SOPHISTICATED

If you're trained in systems analysis or if you want to use any of the many excellent software programs to diagram your systems, by all means use them. But they're not necessary, and they can sometimes get in your way because they can give you a false sense of precision and they don't capture the "feel" of the system.

The box-and-arrow diagram gets the job done very well and it's the simplest way to do it. Besides, unlike most other techniques, you can add your own notations and sketch in useful observations and ideas if you like. Like all the tools and techniques presented in the E-Myth Mastery Program, you adapt it to your business, make it your own, use it your way.

There are a few rules you should follow:

- Make your diagrams roomy, with plenty of space to add notes.
- Boxes represent work activities, tasks. They're also called "benchmarks."
- Each box should be labeled with a word or two to identify the task. Numbering helps.
- An arrow shows the sequence of tasks, how tasks are linked.
- The entire system is enclosed within a larger box (representing the "black box" idea).
- External systems are shown by boxes outside the "black box" and are connected with arrows showing where they provide input to or receive output from the system's tasks.
- Invent any other rules that work for you. Add any notations to your diagram that help you.

Here's what a system diagram might look like:

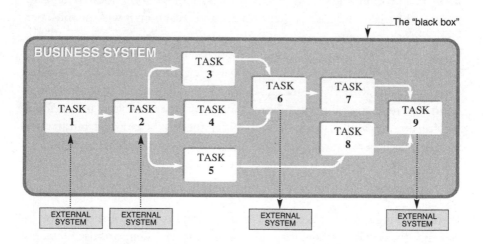

WORK FLOW ANALYSIS—
LOOKING INSIDE THE BLACK BOX

Work flow requires you to look closely at the inside of the black box, at its inner workings. You do that by identifying all the benchmarks, the steps, that make up the system you want to examine, diagramming them in the box-and-arrow format, and closely defining the system's dynamics—what is called its "work flow." Work flow is the pattern of tasks, materiel movement, information flows, and physical layout that form the system.

Understanding is what you're after. The idea is to understand completely and in detail how the system works. You'll be tempted to jump to solutions and new approaches as they occur to you and your people, but resist. Force yourself to *completely* understand the system before taking on the task of innovation. Otherwise, you'll leap to premature conclusions and incomplete solutions based on partial information. It doesn't take that much longer to do a complete analysis, and the end result will be systems that are significantly more effective.

YOU CAN'T UNDERSTAND ANY SYSTEM UNLESS YOU UNDERSTAND ITS WORK FLOW, AND THAT MEANS DETAILS, DETAILS, DETAILS

The trouble with business systems is that you can't understand them, and you certainly can't create or improve them, unless you immerse yourself in the details—in understanding them and insisting on getting them right. You can't systemize your business looking at it through a telescope. It takes a microscope. You can *evaluate* a system from the big picture point of view, and you do that, as you've seen, by looking at its external manifestations, its inputs, outputs, and costs. But you can't even begin to innovate your systems without looking into the innards of your business systems and absorbing both their logic and their "feel" at the most detailed possible level. You have to dig into the "black box" and there's no way around it.

But that's actually good news. Details are your friends. The details will set you free. When you've dug into the details of your systems and gotten them running like a Swiss watch (or today's high-tech equivalent), then you step back to the big picture viewpoint and monitor your systems through their key indicators. You innovate at the detail level; you monitor at the big picture level. Get the details right and you don't have to deal with them anymore, except when something goes wrong or when the time comes for another round of innovation.

Industrial engineers with advanced degrees spend their entire careers immersed in work flow. They use tools like PERT charts (Program Evaluation and Review Technique) and linear programming and use words like "critical path" and "time and motion study." And, no, you won't be doing any of those things. You don't need to.

You'll be taking the practical, nontheoretical, no-nonsense approach. You'll look at the work flows of your systems and answer two questions: "What gets done by the system?" and "How does it get done?" Your tools will be your own eyes, some low-tech box-and-arrow diagrams, a floor plan, and the experience and common sense of you and your people.

THE FOUR FACES OF WORK FLOW

The heart of any system is its work flow. Get the work flow right and you've got a system that works right. Work flow can be complex, but if you approach it the right way, it's straightforward. First off, you need to know the four kinds of work flow:

1. **Task flow**—the work activities of the system, what you show in your initial box-and-arrow diagram.
2. **Materiel flow** (yes, it's spelled correctly)—the equipment, apparatus, and supplies used in the system, including information when information is part of the work and is integral to the result.
3. **Management information flow**—accounting data, operating instructions, key indicators, management information . . . information *about* the system.
4. **Layout and traffic flow**—the physical location of workstations and the traffic in and around them.

THE FOUR COMPONENTS OF WORK FLOW

TASK FLOW

MATERIEL FLOW — LAYOUT & TRAFFIC

MGMT INFO

You may need as many as four diagrams, one for each type of work flow. Three of them are copies of the basic box-and-arrow diagram you've already drawn showing task flow. You just make copies and on one you trace materiel flows, on another you trace management information flows. You might only need one or two diagrams, depending on the size and complexity of the system. Sometimes you can draw all three on one diagram. You want to make your diagrams large and roomy so you can write notes and ideas directly on them. The fourth diagram is a map of the system—a floor plan or other sketch of the physical layout and patterns of movement of people and equipment.

These diagrams don't have to be masterpieces of engineering or artistry. They merely have to capture the details of the system clearly enough for you to understand. They're your working papers, and you're the only one they have to satisfy . . . you and anyone you ask to work with you on it. The trick is to get the right information onto your diagrams. What information? Here are some guidelines:

Task Flow

- The tasks—the benchmarks, or steps—of the system
- Sequence—the order in which the tasks are performed
- Dependencies—which tasks have to be done before or after other tasks
- Balance—matching outputs and inputs; output from one task is input for another

Materiel Flow

- Types and amounts of supplies, raw materials, components, information, equipment
- Point of origin/entry in the system
- Interim stops within the system
    - Productive stops (when the materiel is put to productive use)
    - Idle stops (when the materiel is between operations or in temporary storage)
- Point of exit from the system or consumption within the system

Management Information Flow

- Types of information, and form (paper? electronic? how transported?)
- Point of origin or point of capture
- Interim stops within the system
    - Productive stops (when the information is put to use)
    - Idle stops (when the information is not in use or not moving to a destination)
- Point of exit from the system

Layout and Traffic Flows

- Configuration and nature of the physical space
- Location and arrangement of workstations (task locations)
- Utilities—type, access, and capacity
- Traffic patterns—movement in, around, and between workstations and other systems
    - People
    - Machines
    - Materials

That's a lot to think about, but unless you go to that level of detail, you can't be sure your systems are operating to their potential.

But take heart! Even though there's a lot to consider, innovation is fun. It's creative. And it's rewarding. Approach your innovation process and the guidelines presented in the *Business Systems Innovation* checklist with enthusiasm. If you do, you'll get extraordinary results.

Download

DON'T RUSH IT!

Don't jump to premature conclusions and innovations! Discipline yourself to thoroughly understand the system . . . the *complete* system. As you begin to look at the details of the system, you're likely to see immediate opportunities for improvement, but don't rush the process. Don't make "fixes" as they occur to you. Go through every step of the work flow analysis. Get the whole picture. *Then,* and not before then, move on to the innovation work. That way you'll avoid false starts, impulsive tinkering that you'll have to reverse later on, partially effective solutions to problems, and low-yield innovations.

Remember that effective, robust systems are at the very heart of the successful businesses. And systems innovation is the only way to keep those systems effective and robust, and your business healthy and thriving, year after year. You now have the power to create and implement positive change in your business. Use it often, wisely, and well.

CHAPTER SIX

The Discipline of the Lead Conversion Leader

■

**"... serendipity is when you're looking for something
and you find something else that's even better.
Penicillin. Columbus, too, I guess. Synchronicity is
when two independent variables happen at the same
time, in a pseudo-meaningful way. Serendipity is
scientific, synchronicity isn't."**

From Tropic of Night *by Michael Gruber*

I'd like to start by defining some terms.

In the E-Myth vocabulary, a "lead" is any revenue opportunity—any response, inquiry, expression of interest or complaint, any contact with your company—made by a prospective customer, a new customer, a new client, or a maturing client, whether initiated by your company or by the contact.

A prospective customer is someone who has never bought from you.

Though we already covered this in the previous chapter, a new customer is someone who has made his first purchase from you, and a new client is a new customer who has come back and bought something a second time from you.

A maturing client is someone who has come back a number of times to buy from you.

Lead conversion, therefore, is the process through which your company "converts" a revenue opportunity into revenue. Which means that every contact made by a prospective customer, a new customer, a new client, or a maturing client, with your company, is either a revenue opportunity or a revenue enhancing opportunity, which boils down to one thing, more revenue.

Which says that every contact made with your company is a revenue opportunity.

The lead conversion leader is committed to that premise, whole hog plus the postage.

The fifth, sixth, and seventh disciplines—client fulfillment, lead conversion, and lead generation—comprise the Core Operating System of a World Class Company.

The core operating system of lead generation, lead conversion, and client fulfillment is the way in which you make a promise to a prospective customer, convert that prospective customer's expression of interest into revenue, and therefore into a new customer, and fulfill that new customer's expectations, based upon the promise you made to him, as well as the ones that he came to you with, over and over and over again, as your customer becomes a client and your client matures, better and more completely, than he could have possibly imagined, thereby increasing the lifetime value of that client to your company, and the lifetime value of your company to your client.

Therefore, the lead conversion leader, the client fulfillment leader, and the lead generation leader are each focused on one part of a seamless, intricately complex, effective and efficient system of interactions with your prospective customer, new customer, new client or maturing client when your core operating system is working at its best.

The core operating system in a World Class Company is One System, with three components, not three systems. As I've said again and again, the entirety of it must be seen as One Thing, as though from above. It is the seeing of the One Thing your company is that *is* Your Vision. The One Thing your company is is the manifestation of your vision as a systematic whole. The purpose of your company is to manifest your vision as absolutely, positively, physically, concretely, visually, emotionally, functionally, financially—*articulately*—as it possibly can.

The disciplines enable you to do that. They are the means through which you articulate your vision.

The lead conversion discipline enables you to convert every possible opportunity your company will ever have into revenue, to the degree that is possible, which in turn will grow your company, which in turn will expand your company's reach, which will in turn touch more people, which will in turn create more awareness, acceptance and preference for your brand, which will in turn achieve your objective, which is to become the preeminent company in your chosen market, in your chosen industry, in your chosen world, the ultimate realization of your vision.

Which is to say, without a disciplined focus on lead conversion, your company cannot achieve the objective of becoming world class.

Let's take a look at each category of consumer to better understand the lead conversion possibilities inherent in each.

The prospective customer. Your prospective customer calls on the phone, comes in the door, visits your website, writes you a letter, responds to a cold call, a direct mail solicitation, a coupon, an advertisement, a catalog, a referral from a friend or acquaintance. This prospective customer has never done business with you before. Now what?

Sarah looked at me and said, with a smile, "Is that a question?"

"Yes," I said. "How would you approach that question, Sarah?"

"Well, first of all," Sarah began, more seriously, "I would have to organize the list of possible ways that customer came to my company. Did she just happen to walk by and feel drawn to walk in? By the name of the store, or the pies in the window, or the look of the store? Or was it that they intended to drive to the store because they had always wanted to, but never did? Or was it that they received one of my 'A tiny, free, delicious pie' invitations, a letter I send out to a new list of prospective customers every week in a lovely bond envelope, stamped first-class, with the red wax seal on the envelope flap to distinguish it from any other mail they might receive, as something very special." She smiled at me, "I just made that up! Or was it that they came in with a friend who's already been in before. Until I know what category they fit into, I can't begin to think about the conversion process because, in each case, it would be different.

"On the other hand," Sarah continued, warming up to the subject, "how would I know which category they fit into without asking them, and how could I possibly ask every prospective customer who comes to me through whatever means they come to me, why they came to my store, where they heard of my store, what prompted them to do it, and, if that's not too difficult a question, how could I possibly capture all of that information, especially through an employee who is already too busy, and where would we store all that information, before it gets entered into the computer, and who would enter it? The complexity of the problem seems to outweigh the size of the opportunity, by far."

"Great question and great start, Sarah," I said. "It's so important that you see the lead conversion opportunity presented by each and every prospective customer, despite the size of the challenge of different prospective customers with different motivations and different agendas. So, let's pursue the question you just asked so that you could, with each and every prospective customer, accomplish the purpose of your lead conversion system, to produce three distinct results: (1) revenue; (2) information, and (3) a better system for producing 1 and 2.

"So, first you need to categorize your prospective customers in a way that makes sense. Second, you need to brainstorm about different ways to respond to each of those categories, to produce revenue, information and a better system. The product of that brainstorming should be a methodology for organizing your process for pursuing the three results of your lead conversion system for each category of prospective customer. Can you begin to see the concentration, discrimination, organization, innovation, and communication possibilities in this, Sarah?

"Imagine that you've been assembling the management system you need to lead the process of lead conversion in your company. You're creating a hierarchy of opportunities, first, by identifying the categories of prospective customers; second, by determining how you would determine which category they fit into when you interact with them; third, by capturing all the information you have decided you need to know enough about your prospective customer to convert her into a new customer, to improve the effectiveness of your lead generation system, your lead conversion system, your product development system, and so forth, so you can continually improve the performance of your company. Without this information, you're guessing. With this information, you're making intelligent guesses, which can then be validated, as true, or not, through further experience. In other words, Sarah, knowing how to successfully convert a prospective customer into a new customer is the foundation for the continual improvement of your business. That's why it's so critical to organize the field of data so that you can study it, conscientiously, as a lead conversion leader would.

"In short, Sarah, every maturing client has a history. As the lead conversion leader of your company, your job is to know, and to make sure your people know, what that history is. That history starts the instant a prospective customer comes into contact with you. In that instant, that contact needs to be distinctive, reassuring, welcoming, promising and productive. How would you do that for each category of contact? What words would your lead conversion people say so that the prospective customer is moved to purchase something, discovers more than she thought she would, leaves feeling she received more than she expected, and begins, with your company, a long and healthy relationship?"

THE FIRST ASSIGNMENT

"So this is your first assignment, Sarah. To list 10 specific actions you could take that would accomplish this objective. How would you touch, move, respond to, delight your prospective customer in the process of completing the transaction that converts her into a new customer? And how would you capture that information?"

The new customer. So now that you have a new customer, how do you convert her into a client?

"Not so fast," Sarah said, "I haven't figured out yet how to turn a prospective customer into a new customer. Aren't we going to talk about that?"

"Yes, Sarah, we will. After you've completed the assignment. I think if we touch on the logic in each of these consumer categories, it will help you see the whole of your lead conversion process as part of the whole of your core operating system. That's what's important right now. Developing a world class perspective on lead conversion. Okay?"

Sarah nodded in agreement and I went on. "I want to talk about the revenue generating opportunities that may not be obvious to you. These are the ones that you can only see by stepping back and observing from the outside what's going on on the inside. Not just on the inside of your company, but on the inside of your new customer.

"I'm asking you to step back and look at her on the inside so that you never make the mistake of dehumanizing her. Your new customer is not just a lead, a source of new revenue, a pie buyer, she's also an elderly woman who's just lost her husband, or a young girl who's just found her first lover, a middle-aged woman who hasn't been in a relationship for years. They are all looking to your pies for nourishment. Who is this person who just walked in your door for the second time? How do you find out? You don't have the time, and even if you did, she probably wouldn't share herself, her story, with you. Why should she? You're a perfect stranger. And while you could get to know her by inviting her out for coffee, that's not practical or desirable. So the question is, how do you accomplish the same thing at a feeling level, through other people working for you, as your company grows to include thousands of new customers, each of whom has her own story? Who is this person who is standing in front of me, right now? Your people need to live with this question constantly, it needs to become the deep, coursing refrain underneath all of your hiring and training and inspiration and interest. And even though you may never know really, just asking the question in front of a new customer, something becomes more alive, more awake, more stirring inside your employees, and in the interaction with your new customer as a result. And if you're lucky, no, if your leadership drills this question—Who is this person who is standing in front of me?—deep into your employees' souls, it will bring them to the even more important question, Who am I? And there they'll be, your employees, face-to-face with the awareness of how little they really know about the customer standing in front of them and how little they know about themselves!

"Which brings us back to the essence of the work we're doing together, Sarah, and the work you will be doing continually on your own, to awaken the passion within your company, within your people, the passion that is already there, lying dormant, by asking living questions over and over again. The vitality, the juice of our lives, lives in the questions."

THE SECOND ASSIGNMENT

"Which brings us back to the new customer, and your second assignment, Sarah. Just like in the first assignment, I'd like you to make a list of 10 different methods you could use to convert a new customer into a new client and be sure to cover how you would capture that information. Remember, Sarah, the objective is to bring your new customer back to buy again. And to do that, something remarkable has to happen that causes your new customer to *feel* like a new client. She needs to *feel* the relationship she's having with your company as opposed to feeling like another business transaction. The *feeling* of relationship, the *feeling* of being seen is everything. When it comes to lead conversion, the feeling is everything."

The new client. The new client is a new customer who has returned once more to your store, or by phone, to place an order or to pick up an order or to buy something she wants, even if she's not sure what it is.

"Think about her for a moment, Sarah. Can you see someone like that in your mind?"

Sarah responded immediately. "Yes, of course I can. Interestingly, I see faces and bodies, clothes and mannerisms, but I can't see names. Wow, I never thought about that before, Michael. I can't see names! In the thick of doing business in the store, taking orders, getting them ready, writing them up, I realize I never talk to the customer by her name. I'm also realizing that I don't, Michael, because I don't think of it as important."

"Isn't that remarkable when you think about it Sarah? That you've never thought of your customer's name as being important? So, what if I never used your name? How would that affect our relationship?"

"But that's different, Michael. This is a relationship we're having. You know so much about me. You're my coach, my guide. I've shared so many personal things with you. It would be unnatural for you not to use my name."

"But, you see, Sarah," I answered, "that's what's so remarkable about this process. You're beginning to think about your customer, in this case, your new client, differently than you ever have. Let's look at this name thing more closely.

"At Safeway, like many grocery chains, they use 'loyalty cards' to develop maturing clients by giving them discounts on certain items when they return to shop. You know how it works. You swipe your card into the system at the counter and your discount appears. And, if you forget your card, all you have to do is give the clerk your phone number and the system finds you and credits you automatically with the discount. But what the system also does is provide the clerk with your name, so that when the transaction is completed, the clerk, whether we have ever seen each other or not before, says, "Thank you, Mr. Gerber." And when she does, I feel seen. Think about that, Sarah. I love it when she says, 'Thank you, Mr. Gerber.' Even though I know she doesn't know me from Adam. How easy am I?

"Here's another example I love. When I check into my exercise club— 24-Hour Fitness—I swipe my membership card into a similar system, and each time I do, the person at the counter hands me back my card and says—and this happens every single time—'Have a good exercise, Michael.' Have a good exercise, Michael. Can you believe it? Every time that happens, Sarah, I feel seen! They know me, even though they don't. Just like me, your client wants to feel seen, and using her name is one of the simplest ways to satisfy her need."

THE THIRD ASSIGNMENT

"So, here's your third assignment, Sarah. Come up with a list of 10 things you can do to convert a new client into a maturing client as well as how to capture that information. And remember, if it doesn't *feel* good, it's not. Okay?"

"You're relentless, *Michael*," Sarah said with a grin on her face. "And, *Michael*, thank you."

And I felt it like I do every time.

The maturing client. Conventional wisdom will tell you that getting a customer is harder than keeping one. I don't think so. I think that keeping a customer, turning that customer into a client who never goes away, who always buys from you because they love you, because you've become a necessary and important part of their life, is a hard job. Because we take so much of what we have for granted. We're all pursuing the thing we don't have, hoping it will give us what we don't have. Our maturing clients, the ones who have been the most loyal, often bear the brunt of our forgetfulness, our lack of attention, our lack of true interest, our lack of passion. If we were more attentive, how many more maturing clients would we have?

Sarah knew what I was saying was true. "You know the people I see in my shop over and over again? I do take them for granted, even though I love seeing them, the ones who come in repeatedly over months, and some over years. They give me a sense of stability, a feeling that something about my business is dependable. What's interesting is that I never think about the ones who don't come back any more. In other words, they did come in, from time to time, they were 'steadies,' and then they were no longer here. But I rarely notice. I rarely say to myself, 'Whatever happened to What's-Her-Name?' Because, I suppose, I'm so busy. But maybe it isn't even that. Maybe it's because I haven't really focused my attention on them, that I don't really have a relationship with them. I have just taken their coming and going for granted. Even though it makes me feel good that they come back, I've never really wondered about why they do, when they do, what they buy, what their 'history,' to use your term, is with me. I don't really know them, as you say, and what's worse, if I weren't in the store, they wouldn't be seen by anyone who works for me. I wonder what it feels like to them?" Sarah asked, as though to herself. "I wonder what it feels like to be on their side of the counter, when they come back, when they make another purchase, when we make them feel invisible."

"Yes, Sarah, they feel invisible. Which is such a common experience for us all that most of the time we don't notice how invisible we feel. Until someone makes us feel visible. Then we notice. That's the responsibility of the lead conversion leader. To be aware of the hunger that lives in all of us—in every prospective customer, new customer, new client, and, most of all, in every maturing client, that it is always there, whether they know it or not—to feel seen."

THE FOURTH ASSIGNMENT

"I can only imagine you're anticipating the fourth assignment, Sarah, which is to make a list of 10 ways you intend to remind your maturing client that you never forget her, never diminish her value, never take her for granted, so that she feels it, so that she says, if only to herself, 'All About Pies didn't have to do *that!*' What would *'that'* be, Sarah? Write it down. Okay?"

"Thank you, *Michael,*" Sarah said grinning.

"My pleasure, as always, Sarah. Our next task is the work of the lead conversion leader. I'm going to give you your homework and see what else we can do to shatter your pictures of reality," I said grinning back at her.

SELECTED E-MYTH MASTERY PROGRAM PROCESSES ON LEAD CONVERSION LEADERSHIP

Your Lead Conversion Process: Giving Your Customers the Opportunity to Say "Yes"

■

"I'm interested! I'll take it! I love it!"

If you're in business, this is your "dream" sale! This is how you always hope it will be! No "selling," just a responsive, confident customer, the right product, and an inevitable sale.

But more often than not, "selling" isn't this easy. It's hard, and it feels like work. Trying to convince someone to do something they may or may not want to do *is* work. And that's what "selling" usually feels like—convincing, cajoling, and struggling against resistance—and it's not always successful.

So how do you get from "selling" to a "dream" sale? And where do you find those responsive, confident customers who recognize the value of your products or service and don't need to be "sold"?

The first thing you do is stop "selling." Selling is about the *seller*. It focuses on *you* and what *you* need. If you're thinking about what you need to do next to make the sale, you won't be focusing on your customer.

So think about your customers. They'll value your business and its products through their own perceptions. What do *they* need? After all, you're in this together. *You* need their patronage to grow your business, and *they* need products and relationships that will gratify them. When you forget about the "sale" and look for the ways you can satisfy your customers' needs, the sale—when it comes—will be the inevitable result of giving your customers what they need to make the purchase decision. You won't have to "sell" them.

IF IT'S NOT SELLING, WHAT IS IT?

When you make a sale you don't always create a customer. Selling has a short horizon and focuses on a single transaction. But a customer isn't a one-time thing. At least not the customer *you* want. Depending on your business, your contact with your customers may be fleeting or sustained, daily or infrequent, but when they have a need for *your* product or service, you want them to come to *you*. You want a relationship. And that's what your customers want, too.

Products or services *and* relationship, because the help they need to make the right purchase decisions for themselves will come from you. At least, they hope it will. It's your job to make them believers. To convert their interest and hope into the conviction that you can give them what they need.

And what they need is support for the decision they've already made. By the time your potential customers—your leads—get to you, they've already made their way through the early steps in the purchase decision chain (see *Customer Perceptions and Behavior,* pp. 151–155). They *want* your product, and now they're looking for the logical confirmation and emotional support that will make them comfortable with their purchase decision.

So we call the selling process "lead conversion," because it recognizes your prospects' willingness to become your customers if you can give them what they need. Not if you can "sell" them.

If you want those responsive, confident customers—the ones in your "dream" sale—you'll have to create them yourself. And here's the good news— you can! You just have to remember that *their* needs, and not the mechanics of sales technique, must drive your lead conversion process.

CUSTOMERS ARE MADE, NOT BORN

You'll create a customer every time you use a needs-based selling system that delivers the emotional impact and credibility your prospects need to be comfortable with their purchase decisions. That means they have to experience the sincerity of your intentions and the believability of your information. And it can't be faked. The only way you'll convince your potential customers that their interests come first is if they do! And your selling process will tell them everything they need to know. If they're pressured, pushed, or manipulated, they'll know. If your selling process serves you and not them, they'll know.

So, as crazy as it sounds, you have to become indifferent to the sale. Focus instead, on the process. Do the best job you can of accommodating your prospects' decision-making needs (presumably you've already seen to their product needs), then let the chips fall where they may. If you've done your job well, you'll have communicated your intention to create a long-term relationship dedicated to satisfying your customers' needs, and you'll convert a very high percentage of your leads to customers—people who'll return to you time and time again when they need what you sell. They'll return because they know they'll get what they need, and that you've made it your business to put their needs ahead of your own.

Your Lead Conversion Process

GIVING YOUR CUSTOMERS THE OPPORTUNITY TO SAY "YES"

Overview

Your lead conversion process should be designed to create customers and not "sales." The sale should be the inevitable result of having the right product for the right customer in a selling process that recognizes customer purchase decision needs as the driving force.

When considering your product, prospective customers will have purchase decision needs represented by the Seven Selling Functions — information, understanding, needs clarification, advice, assistance, reassurance, and transaction processing. The specific needs of individual customers will depend on their perception of the *impact* the purchase will have on them and the *confidence* they feel in making the decision to buy. Your job is to satisfy those needs so they can find the rational and logical support for the emotional decision to buy that brought them to you.

There is a universal lead conversion process through which to meet your customers purchase decision needs that fits any business or product and can be customized for your target market. Each step of the process builds on the last to give your customers the support they need for their purchase decisions.

Key Points

There are two essential elements of your lead conversion infrastructure that will affect how you structure your selling process: **people** and **paths**. These are the ways you staff your sales process and the channels you choose to sell your product.

Think about who best sells your product. The five most customary sales force configurations are:

1. Automated
2. Order-taking
3. Conventional
4. Consultative
5. Inside or external staff

A general rule of thumb in choosing a selling mode is that the more selling functions your customer requires for the purchase decision, the more important the relationship-building qualities in your sales method.

How does your selling message best get to your customer? Familiar sales channels include:

1. Telephone
2. Mail
3. Direct response print media
4. Face-to-face selling
5. Stores or other on-site outlets
6. The Internet

Take a fresh look at your lead conversion staffing and channels. There may be alternative ways to accomplish your goals even though they're not traditional in your industry.

The Universal Lead Conversion Process

Engage with Your Prospective Customer

Repeat the Emotional Message

Determine the Customer's Needs

Provide a Solution

Offer the Product

THE UNIVERSAL FIVE-STEP LEAD CONVERSION PROCESS

Now that you've given up "selling," how *do* you design a lead conversion process that accommodates your prospects' decision-making needs? Where do you start?

No matter what your product or business, the heart of your selling process will always be the encounter with your customer. It's where the rubber hits the road and your marketing and product strategies produce real-time results. So your lead conversion process can't leave anything to chance. You've promised your customers satisfaction, and now you need an orchestrated approach to meeting their needs. You need a system!

There are five steps in your lead conversion process, and each one builds on the last to give your customers the support they need for their purchase decisions. They'll work for any business and any product, and they provide the structure for customizing your selling process for *your* target market. Here are the five benchmarks:

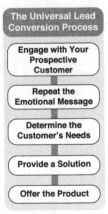

The Universal Lead Conversion Process

Engage with Your Prospective Customer

Repeat the Emotional Message

Determine the Customer's Needs

Provide a Solution

Offer the Product

1. **Engage with your prospective customer.** This is the step that gets the ball rolling and sets the tone for your future relationship. What kind of relationship do you want it to be? What about your customers? What do *they* want it to be? Here's where you declare your intentions!

2. **Repeat the emotional message of your "promise."** Your customers came to you with a provisional decision to buy your product because it promised to meet their emotional needs. What were they and what did you promise? How can you remind them that they've come to the right place?

3. **Determine the customer's needs.** The more you know about exactly what a given customer wants and needs, the better you'll be able to meet those needs. What does the customer really want? Why do they think they want it? Will your product meet the customer's perceptions, and if it does, what support do they need to take action on the decision to buy that brought them to you?

   Your salespeople must have a basic set of questions that will elicit customers' needs, and point them toward which of your products to offer a particular customer and how to offer them.

4. **Provide a solution.** Here's where you can offer your customers unique, customized responses to their purchase decision needs. If they need confirmation of their product perceptions, you can supply it. If they need more information, advice or reassurance, you can provide that too. Think about the best teacher you ever had—the one who was more interested in *you* than in merely explaining the subject matter—and try to be more of a teacher than a salesperson. Here's where you meet your customers' needs by "educating" them about your product.

5. **Offer the product.** Either your customers will accept the "solution" or they won't. If they do, you need a purchase transaction to process the details. If they don't, you've built the foundation for a long-term relationship with your attention to their needs. The door to a future relationship is wide open!

With the five-step universal lead conversion process as your starting point, you can build a selling system that is specifically tailored for your business and your market. You'll see how in a moment. Then, you can apply *your* process with *your* customers in a way that satisfies each customer's specific and individual needs. (You'll see an example of that later on in this process.) So you start with a generic process that applies to everyone, but you end up serving the unique needs of each individual customer. It's the best of both worlds: the efficiencies of an orchestrated process and the customer focus of a completely customized process. And here's how you do it!

DESIGNING YOUR LEAD CONVERSION PROCESS

How do you adapt the universal lead conversion process to your own business? You start with an understanding of the significance of each step to your customer so you can apply the five steps in a way that satisfies each customer's specific and individual needs. Let's take the five steps one by one to see how they play out in your customer's experience.

1. **Engage with your prospective customer.** This step is easy to dismiss as a mere formality, but it's where your customers begin to build their expectations of getting what they want—or not. To engage with them means *to show or create interest.* More than a simple greeting and a few pleasantries, it's an opportunity to demonstrate your commitment to giving them what they want out of your relationship.

   If you're a self-serve cafeteria and your customer base is focused on quick, cheap food, this step may be respectful but brief. Even that, in its way, establishes your responsiveness to what your customer wants out of the relationship. If you're selling an expensive automobile, you may want to take a more leisurely and exploratory approach to the initial engagement in order to give your customer room to get comfortable with you and their own concerns about the purchase.

More than anything else, keep the focus on your customer. Make your own interest in them and their concerns clear, whether that means giving them physical space to browse, asking if they have time to talk with you before you start talking, or relieving them of responsibility for any interaction at all, as in the case of the cafeteria. You're setting the tone for the rest of the relationship in this step, and creating your customers' interest in pursuing it. What you need to be saying with words and actions is that their needs and comfort will be the overriding consideration every step of the way.

2. **Repeat the emotional message of your promise.** Your customer responded to something in the broadcast of your promise through your lead generation process. Repeat the promise! That might be as simple as restating your unique selling proposition (USP) as you begin to respond to the customer's questions, or it might involve a more elaborate description of the product's features and benefits that produce the effect your customer was drawn to. This step easily links to the first step in the lead conversion process, because it's intended to reassure customers that they're in the right place to get what they want—something that's bound to create interest!

Your sensory package is also a powerful tool for reinforcing the emotional message of your promise. Make sure it's in keeping with the promise of gratification you made in your lead generation. If you're selling baby clothes to a target market that values hearth and home, and your advertising kindles childhood memories and nurturing impulses, decorating your store with severe postmodern leather furniture and harsh light is not going to keep your promise! This is an excellent opportunity to test and fine-tune the decisions you made about your company's image and sensory package.

3. **Determine the customer's needs.** What do your customers want and why do they think your product can give it to them? What is their perception of your product? And what do they need to be comfortable with the provisional emotional decision to buy that they made as the result of your lead generation process?

The easiest and most straightforward way to determine the specific needs of individual customers is by asking them a series of questions, designed to elicit the exact information you want. So, as you consider the two main categories of needs discussed below—your customers' needs and perceptions with respect to your product or service itself, and what they need to actually make the decision to buy—write down your ideas for questions you can ask to discover these underlying needs on the *Determining Customers' Needs* worksheet.

Also, think about options for asking your customers these questions and for how salespeople will "track" or remember the answers. While some of this may seem to be "dictated" by the very nature of your lead conversion process, keep an open mind.

Oral and written approaches, or a combination of the two, are the most standard for both asking the questions and for the customers' responses. Questionnaires, surveys, and checklists are examples of ways to ask and answer questions in writing, and work well when you need to refer back to what customers have said.

Newer technologies can also be used to both your and your customers' advantage. Audio recording, videotape, personal computers, and the Internet are other methods for learning more about individual customer needs and documenting them. An interesting example can be seen in the proliferation (and success) of video dating services. The videotape is actually a recorded needs analysis! The "counselor" asks the "date seeker" a series of predetermined questions, the responses are captured on tape, and the counselor (or other date seekers) then finds the best "matches"!

Let's look in a little more detail at the two main areas of customer needs: their product perceptions and their purchase decision needs.

Your Customers' Product Perceptions:

All your marketing and product strategy work has been directed at communicating and delivering the promise you believe your customers want to hear, and your research and strategy have been aimed at your "target market." But in your lead conversion process, the individual is paramount. Two customers for the same product may have very different individual perceptions of it. So you need to understand how your customers perceive your product and your business, and especially, which attributes are most important to them and will be decisive in their purchase decision. When you know that, you can contribute to the decision in the way that best serves the customer.

For example, if you own a Mercedes-Benz dealership and you've researched your target market, you've aimed your marketing at a group of affluent, quality-oriented buyers who value prestige and performance. Your first customer, a self-made man who has won his success through talent and hard work, sees the Mercedes as both a reward for his accomplishment and the fitting automobile for his new status in the world. He is convinced on all levels to buy the car, and he certainly has the means to do it. But something's in the way.

It turns out that this man had great regard for his father—a hardworking, devoted family man who never made much money and was hardheaded and practical with whatever he had. And his dad always drove a Ford. It would never have occurred to him to drive anything other than the most practical, reliable, inexpensive car on the road. That was his dad's measure of value. Your customer can't help thinking that he should be doing the same thing! That if the Ford was good enough for his father, it should be good enough for him! He wants the Mercedes, he values its quality and performance, he can afford it . . . but he can't find the comfort he needs because of these underlying perceptions and associations related to automobiles.

Your second customer presents a whole different picture. While your marketing and lead generation approach may have emphasized the Mercedes' luxury, status, and prestige, this customer could care less! For him, the Mercedes is a *machine*—the best you can buy, or so he's told. And that's all he cares about. He wants to drive the best-engineered car on the road. And if you're busy sharing your perception of your product as the height of prestige and beauty, you're not helping him. He doesn't care! And he's starting to think this isn't for him. He's starting to think your product is all about appearance and status, and that makes him uncomfortable. Maybe this *isn't* the car for him.

So how can your salespeople approach people whom they know nothing about, as individuals, and discover what they need to know? What could our Mercedes-Benz dealership owner ask in his lead conversion process to uncover the differing needs and perceptions of prospects looking at a Mercedes? How about:

- Tell me a little bit about the cars you had in your family while you were growing up, and other cars you've owned. How does that affect what you're looking for today?
- What are you driving now? How do you feel about it? What do you like most about your current vehicle and what do you like least?

- What combination of qualities would your "ideal" automobile have?
- What have you heard or what do you think about the Mercedes that doesn't appeal to you? Why is that?

You could ask these same questions to every prospect, and get replies that would lead you exactly in the right direction for finding the best product offering you have for them and positioning it in an appealing way. What's your version of these questions? Use the *Determining Customers' Needs* worksheet.

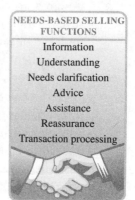

Download

Once you know how your customer perceives your product, you need to determine what support he or she needs for the purchase decision. How do you do that? How do you design a lead conversion process that accommodates your prospect's decision-making needs? And what are they?

Your Customers' Decision Needs:

The seven "selling functions" identify customer needs and translate them into the core of a needs-based selling process. These are the things your lead conversion process must offer. Your customers may not need *all* the selling functions to develop comfort with their purchase decisions, but they'll need some. How many of the selling functions, and which ones, will depend on two factors: your customers' perception of the purchase *impact* of your product, and their *confidence* in making the decision to buy that product.

> **NEEDS-BASED SELLING FUNCTIONS**
> Information
> Understanding
> Needs clarification
> Advice
> Assistance
> Reassurance
> Transaction processing

Confidence and impact determine which of the seven selling functions you need to build into your lead conversion process. What does your process have to do to make sure your customers have the confidence to make the purchase? If they don't have it, they'll never reach the level of comfort they need to make the purchase decision.

Confidence is a funny thing. Some of your customers will have it from the start, some will need you to help them build it (through the seven selling functions), and some—quite a few, actually—never generate their own confidence. They "borrow" it from you or someone else they respect and trust.

Here's where your knowledge of your customers and their perceptions of your product are indispensable. For example, there's an obvious difference between a candy bar and a new car, but a computer and a home theater, though matched in cost, may present very different purchase decision challenges to the same customer. Both products are costly and have a significant financial impact, but each may require a different level of personal confidence for the purchase decision.

The home theater, as elaborate as it is, may still be just a television set to your customer. The technology is familiar and the product is relatively simple to use. But the computer is another story. The technology is relatively new and can be intimidating, especially for a first-time buyer. Even customers who generally feel very confident about making high impact decisions may have difficulty in bringing that confidence to a purchase decision about an unfamiliar product. So, the same customer could need a different combination of selling functions for each product.

Your lead conversion process needs to take this into account. Don't assume that high cost, alone, will dictate all seven selling functions, or that an ordinarily high-confidence customer will bring that confidence to every purchase decision. Use your knowledge of your customers to design a process that's customized to their needs, because even the seven selling functions can mean different things to different customers. For example, "reassurance" doesn't mean the same thing to an adult patient in a doctor's office as it does to a teenage customer in a clothing store.

And what you don't know, ask! (In a tactful way, of course.) Two teenagers in a clothing store may feel very differently about their level of confidence in selecting what they should wear and how much reassurance they need to complete the purchase. You need to know what *your* customer perceives "reassurance" to be.

When you know how your customers see the impact of the purchase of your product, and how confident they feel in making that purchase decision, you'll know which selling functions need to be included in your lead conversion process. Use the *Purchase Decision Needs* worksheet to list the specific decision needs your prospective customer is likely to have, and what you can do in your selling process to meet them. You'll now have a more complete idea of the logical and rational support your customers need for their purchase Download decisions and what you can do to supply it.

For example, if your customers perceive the purchase of your product to have a high impact on their lives, and only feel moderate confidence in making this particular purchase decision, your selling process will have to include a lot of information, understanding, and advice. Your customers will need facts, an interpretation of those facts in light of their needs, and guidance about their choices.

But remember, in the lead conversion process you're still dealing with an individual customer. So as you consider each of the seven selling functions, use the worksheet list questions that will help you understand the individuals' decision needs. Be prepared to concentrate on the decision needs your target market is *likely* to have, but build in the flexibility to discover and respond to all the decision needs an individual customer actually *does* have.

4. **Provide a solution.** This is the step in your lead conversion process that looks the most like traditional "sales." Ordinarily, this is the place where you "convince" the customer to buy your product. But if you remember "don't sell . . . satisfy," this is not where *you* convince the customer. This is where your customers convince themselves! This is where they discover, with your help, whether your offering solves all or most of the needs they have. And this is where they get everything they need to be comfortable with their purchase decisions.

Your main goal in the solution presentation is to educate your customers about how your product or service will satisfy their exact needs. You know that they already believe it will on the emotional level and that they have high hopes! Now you want them to enjoy the same assurance on the rational or logical level. So this is your opportunity to share all your knowledge about the value of your product with your customers.

But beware of pushing too much information on them. Be prepared with *all* the information, but only give as much as the customer has an appetite for. Be responsive, respectful, and on the customers' track, not *your* track. Too much information can overwhelm them and detract from their growing confidence.

If you think back to the best teacher you ever had, you'll find the tone you want to take: excitement about the material and its benefits for your life, a pleasure in sharing information with you, and an offering of the information without strings. Your best teacher never tried to "sell" you. It was always information and insight freely given.

Think back to the two customers looking at the Mercedes-Benz. How could the solution presentation be tailored to meet both their needs?

The first customer wants the Mercedes prestige, but doesn't want to abandon the qualities of good value, practicality, and reliability that were important to his father, who drove Fords. Does he know that if he buys the Mercedes he'll probably never have to buy another car as long as he lives—unless he wants to? This customer perceives *some* of the attributes of your product, but not the whole story. He needs the part that's missing to be completely comfortable with his purchase decision.

The second customer won't have any problem with his purchase decision if you'll just get out of the way and not "push" the part of the message about luxury, status, and prestige. He knows exactly what he wants, the best driving machine available, and only needs a narrow band of precise information to be sure he's making the right purchase. He doesn't need to have his perceptions broadened. He just needs confirmation of his expectations.

So aim your solution presentation at meeting your customers' needs. Anticipate and encourage questions, and give them every opportunity to develop the level of comfort they need to make the purchase decision.

5. **Offer the product.** This is the final step in the lead conversion process. Your customers should now have their questions answered and all the logical support they need for buying the product you offer. This is the point where you'll be most tempted to push for a positive response. But remember, if you focus on this "sale" rather than on creating a relationship of mutual trust with this customer, you may be giving up all the sales to this prospect in the future.

So make your offer from your customers' point of view. Does the product meet their needs? Does it deliver what it promises? Are all their selling needs met? If the answers are "yes," you've got a sale. If the customer is still not there, keep the door open. If you've done it right, he or she will be back.

DON'T FORGET THE OVERALL EFFECT

Now that you've seen the detail of the five universal benchmarks of a lead conversion process, don't forget that none of the parts will work unless the overall effect meets the purchase decision needs of your customers. This includes all the things you do to offer your product to your customer. Things like your sensory package, the quality of the interaction between your salespeople and the customer, the way product information is communicated through selling aids—even the words you choose to greet prospects or describe your product.

All of these things must be aimed at meeting your customers' purchase decision needs, and should be linked to the particular selling functions that are most important to your prospects.

For example, new patients in a doctor's office are like potential customers in any business. Because of the nature of the services they are looking to "buy," they have a high need for reassurance, advice, and understanding. A flippant, lighthearted, and comic presentation of the doctor's services would not meet the usual customer's needs. The doctor and his or her staff need to choose a décor, a manner, and even words of greeting and communication that will have the emotional impact and credibility that will make patients feel they're in the right place. Subdued colors, authoritative information, and warm and friendly attention from staff all serve to present the doctor's services in a way that meets the potential customer's needs. And while your family doctor may no longer wear the white coat as part of his or her presentation—choosing the more accessible and friendly presentation that street clothes create—many specialists and hospital-based doctors still wear this traditional "uniform" because of the professionalism and authority it conveys. When you need specialized advice, the white coat—as the badge of the medical professional—helps to reinforce your faith in the education and knowledge of the expert.

But the flippant, lighthearted, and comic presentation, and bright colors and loud noise might be just right in a video games store! Those customers probably want a sense of fun, irreverence, and adventure, and engaging them on that level will meet the needs they hope to satisfy with their purchase decision.

So when you think about showcasing your product and your business in your lead conversion process, think about the overall effect you want to communicate to your potential customer.

THE INFRASTRUCTURE OF LEAD CONVERSION— PEOPLE AND PATHS

There are two essential elements of lead conversion that directly affect how you move through the universal five steps: the way you staff your sales process and the channels you choose to sell your product. These are strategic considerations, but they directly affect how you'll achieve the purpose of each of the steps in your selling process.

People: Who best sells your product to your target market? The five most customary sales force configurations are automated, order-taking, conventional, consultative, and in-house or external. Each one tends to be appropriate for particular products or services, but don't let conventions get in your way. If you think there's a better solution to your potential customers' sales needs than the traditional approach, it may be the thing that differentiates you from your competition. Just be sure to look at your choice through the eyes of your customers and keep the following guidelines in mind:

Automated selling requires no human contact. Vending machines and computerized order-taking systems are prime examples of this mode that is particularly well suited to low-impact, low-confidence purchases where even the purchase transaction can be accomplished by a machine. An automated system is geared for sheer convenience, and can be unforgiving of customer errors or questions. Its best use is the simplest of sales transactions, where relationship building is irrelevant to repeat sales.

Order-taking is a sales method characterized by telephone operators, cashiers, waiters, and newsstand attendants. More people-friendly than an automated process, it does allow for an exchange of information and sometimes limited advice and reassurance, but it won't create as many opportunities for relationship building as conventional or consultative sales approaches. It is best suited for sales processes where customer confidence is relatively high given the impact of the purchase, and where technical product information is simple and obvious.

Conventional selling techniques are the kind usually found in retail stores, and they generally involve a one-on-one process between a salesperson and the customer. This is the sales approach that offers the most versatility in developing a sales process that addresses multiple decision needs. It also has the most potential to create relationships, because the salesperson can customize the system to the needs of the particular customer.

Consultative sales personnel are generally "experts" like financial planners, stockbrokers, insurance agents, lawyers, and other independent professionals, as well as those selling highly complex products like computers or real estate. Consultative selling is most appropriate when the purchase decision has a high impact and requires specialized knowledge.

Inside staff or external agents are two choices for a sales force. Sometimes it's more cost effective to use independent agents to sell your product, especially if your sales territory is large but doesn't warrant a full-time, in-house sales force.

Your product and the purchase decision needs of your potential customers will shape your selling mode, but here's a general rule of thumb: the more selling functions your customer requires for the purchase decision, the more important the relationship-building qualities in your sales method.

If your choice of selling method includes the use of people, you need to think about what kind. For example, if you sell computers, you'll be looking for salespeople with the patience to learn about the technical features of the product, and the ability to communicate the attributes of each model to the customer. They may not initially need a lot of knowledge, but they'll have to be willing to learn and have the ability to communicate complex information clearly. A salesperson for a clothing store might not need to be able to grasp detailed, technical information, but may need the ability to give advice and communicate reassurance credibly.

What knowledge, abilities, and personality traits would the ideal salesperson for your product and customer have?

Paths: How does your selling message best get to your customer? It depends on your product and how your customer feels about its purchase, but some products lend themselves more easily to some communication channels rather than others. Traditional sales channels include the telephone (telemarketing), the mail (catalog sales and direct mail), direct response print media (magazines, newspapers), face-to-face selling at your location or your customer's, and selling at stores or other on-site outlets. Here again, don't let customary practices limit your view. There are new selling channels, like the Internet, developing all the time. Until relatively recently, most selling was thought of as a one-to-one, in-person activity, but changes in lifestyle and technology have created new selling channels for many products. Catalog shopping, especially for high-end products, has been one of the biggest changes in retailing since the advent of the department store. Customers, increasingly strapped for time and less willing to venture out at night to shop, find catalogs and their television equivalent—home shopping networks— attractive and convenient replacements for in-store shopping. The home shopping networks even use automated order-taking, something the high-touch retail selling world would have considered unthinkable just a few years ago!

So take a fresh look at your lead conversion path. Could a new sales channel be more effective than your current choice? Or could it be an addition? Have you overlooked possibilities for expansion because they're not traditional in your business?

INNOVATING YOUR LEAD CONVERSATION PROCESS

You now have all the pieces you need to innovate your lead conversion process: an understanding of your customers' purchase decision needs and what you could do to satisfy them, a set of structured benchmarks for selling to your customers, and some considerations about the people and paths you might use to offer your product to your customer. And here's how you do it.

Just as you used the process *Systems Innovation* (see pp. 294–304) to innovate your production, delivery, and customer service processes, you're going to use this tool to get your lead conversion process in order. You simply follow the now familiar benchmarks until you reach the innovation step. But this time, in addition to the *Business Systems Innovation* checklist, you also have the universal five-step lead conversion process, plus what you've learned about lead conversion infrastructure to guide your innovations. You're doing nothing different, you simply have more information to work with. Once you've completed the innovation process, use the *Lead Conversion Process* worksheet to draw a box-and-arrow diagram of your new system and identify which of the universal five steps of lead conversion each benchmark represents.

Download

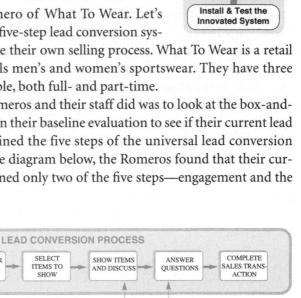

The Systems Innovation Process

Select a System for Innovation

Observe the System On-Site

Diagram the System

Determine System Baseline

Analyze Work Flow

Apply the Innovation Checklist

Diagram the Innovated System

Estimate Performance & Compare with Baseline

Install & Test the Innovated System

EXAMPLE—WHAT TO WEAR REVISITED

Meet Joan and Tony Romero of What To Wear. Let's look at how they used the five-step lead conversion system to clarify and innovate their own selling process. What To Wear is a retail clothing business that sells men's and women's sportswear. They have three stores and employ 22 people, both full- and part-time.

The first thing the Romeros and their staff did was to look at the box-and-arrow diagram they drew in their baseline evaluation to see if their current lead conversion process contained the five steps of the universal lead conversion process. As you'll see in the diagram below, the Romeros found that their current selling process contained only two of the five steps—engagement and the solution presentation.

LEAD CONVERSION PROCESS

| OBSERVE CUSTOMER | ASK IF CUSTOMER NEEDS HELP | SELECT ITEMS TO SHOW | SHOW ITEMS AND DISCUSS | ANSWER QUESTIONS | COMPLETE SALES TRANS-ACTION |

Step 1
ENGAGE WITH CUSTOMER

Step 5
OFFER THE PRODUCT

Here's how the Romeros set out to revamp the lead conversion process at What To Wear:

STEP ONE—ENGAGE YOUR PROSPECTIVE CUSTOMER

Joan and Tony Romero have been in business for almost 20 years. Although most of their time is involved with management tasks, Joan still sells on the floor several afternoons and Saturdays each month. She has always been an effective salesperson, and although she has had excellent help on and off over the years, her salespeople have never been consistent. Joan thinks the ability to sell is a "gift"—you either have it or you don't—and this makes recruiting a hit-or-miss operation. It's hard to tell if someone has the "gift" or not in an interview. A bubbly, outgoing personality doesn't always indicate the ability to sell.

But Joan and Tony are determined to systemize their lead conversion process. They've identified some patterns of behavior that seem common to the best salespeople they've had and, using the five steps of the universal lead conversion system as the benchmarks, they're going to construct a process for all their salespeople to follow.

Referring back to their lead conversion baseline, Tony and Joan see that their engagement with the prospective customer doesn't really start until a salesperson happens to notice that someone's in the store. It's hit or miss, in a way, because if the salespeople are busy, a customer could wander around without being greeted or acknowledged for a fair amount of time. Joan has noticed that some people just walk out, and she's afraid that she not only lost a potential sale, but gained a reputation for poor service! She's also noticed that her salespeople don't really engage with the customer until the customer begins to ask serious questions about their clothing. They may greet them pleasantly, but they don't *engage*—they don't show or create interest. There's plenty of room for improvement here.

Joan and Tony called an employee meeting and asked for everyone's input for improving their selling process. First, they shared the work they had done on the box-and-arrow diagram they created for their present system, and then worked with their employees to identify which of their own steps fit into the steps of the universal lead conversion process. Once they did that, they began to focus on the first step—engaging with the customer. They figured that if they could envision the perfect engagement step, they could identify its components and work on including them in everyone's actions. Then they could set standards to measure their own performance and any improvements they could make. It seemed like a strange thing to do for "selling," but the Romeros' staff was intrigued by the idea. Creating the "perfect sale" was a great game and gave them an opportunity not only to be creative, but to voice their pet peeves about the whole process.

Everyone at What To Wear agreed that the greatest weakness in their sell-ing activities was their approach to the customer at the front end. They didn't always know when a new customer entered the store and, if they were busy with another customer, it might be 10 or 15 minutes before they could break away and say hello. This was far too long to let a customer wander through the store without any acknowledgment.

The staff decided that every customer had to be greeted and engaged as soon as they entered the store. One of the salespeople suggested that they in-stall a device that gave off a soft tone when someone came through the door. That would alert them that they had a guest. They also decided that whatever they were doing short of actually processing a sales transaction, they would ex-cuse themselves and greet the new customer just as if they were a newly arrived visitor to their home. The greeting would include giving the customer their name, a question about whether they'd been in the store before, and the assur-ance that they would return to the customer in just a few minutes. They didn't know if this would be better—would the customer being served be offended if the salesperson took a moment to greet a just-entering customer?—but they decided to test it for a month. What To Wear's new standard for engaging the prospective customer was created!

STEP TWO—REPEAT THE EMOTIONAL MESSAGE

What To Wear's USP is "Good taste for every occasion!" It's a promise of ap-propriateness and variety. A customer can expect to find sportswear for casual, work, and evening wear, all in the same location. The Romeros and their staff discussed what this means to their customers, and how they could reinforce the promise they were making and distinguish themselves from other retailers.

As they continued to think about what they could do to communicate the emotional part of their message to customers coming into their stores, they listed the following things:

- State What To Wear's unique selling proposition (USP).
- State their positioning statement, or a version of it.
- Emphasize the quality and selection of the clothing.
- Emphasize their attention to individualized service.
- Explain how the store is organized.
- Offer a children's activity center as a customer service.
- Pave the way for finding out more about the customer's particular needs.

They felt that this was a sound and realistic list of what salespeople could consistently do to establish or reestablish an emotional connection with customers. And the staff became excited about the potential for being able to communicate this important aspect of what What To Wear has to offer, and their role in creating customers, as compared to their traditional view of themselves as "sales clerks" who do little more than show merchandise and transact sales.

STEP THREE—DETERMINE THE CUSTOMER'S NEEDS

When the Romeros and their staff took the time to think about how they were accomplishing this step in the lead conversion benchmarks, they realized that they had been giving it short shrift. They decided to take some time to discuss the purchase impact of their product and the confidence level of their customers in order to fine-tune their lead conversion process.

When they looked at their selling process with the customer, they realized that they usually only asked a few questions ("What are you looking for? What kind of dress, suit, gown, etc.? What's your size?"), rather than creating an opportunity to learn a lot about the customer and what he or she really needed. So they decided to take some time to discuss the purchase decision from their customers' point of view. What did *their* customers need?

The Romeros and their staff decided that the financial impact of their customers' clothing purchases was moderate, but that their customers were very concerned with how they looked. Their purchases could have a high impact on their customer's self-image. Their experience also told them most of their customers needed to develop some confidence about their purchases, and that some of that confidence would come from the reassurance and advice of the staff.

So they designed a series of questions that would give them basic information about what the customer was looking for. Then, they created some additional questions that would tell them how the customer felt about making the purchase, the occasion they were buying the clothing for, and how they felt about shopping. This would allow them to assess how much information, advice, assistance, or reassurance each individual customer needed. Everyone now felt they had a systematic and foolproof method for learning what customers wanted and considered important, and for giving them the help they really wanted.

STEP FOUR—PRESENT THE SOLUTION

With the customer's needs well in mind now, the Romeros and their staff felt that they could really showcase their skills in helping people find flattering, appropriate clothing. This part of the lead conversion process included their identifying specific articles of clothing that would meet the needs of the occasion. Then, because each salesperson had taken the time to determine the customer's needs, they could also speak to his or her concerns and uncertainties, explaining why a particular garment would be a good choice, or comparing the features of several possible choices, so that the customer could weigh the relative advantages more easily. The Romeros always felt they had what customers wanted, but they were depending on "star" salespeople to communicate that to customers. By sharing everyone's best ideas and customer assistance practices, and then including the ones they liked best in a selling process they would all use, the owners and staff of What To Wear felt that *anyone* could use their new sales system and be an excellent salesperson.

STEP FIVE—OFFER THE PRODUCT

Many of Joan and Tony's salespeople falter at this step because they're not sure how to "close" a sale. They wait for the customer to indicate interest or they press too hard. It's a step that's full of uncertainty because they're not sure exactly what to do. Some of the Romeros' staff—the "stars"—don't seem troubled at this point and are very successful, but for most of What To Wear's sales force, this is the weakest point of the process.

Joan and Tony felt that clarifying their expectations for this point in the selling process might help their staff create a different approach. They explained that their business had been built on service to the customer, and that their niche as a specialty shop meant that building a loyal customer base with repeating business was the key to their success. They spent a lot of time repositioning the selling process with their salespeople, placing the emphasis on satisfying customer needs rather than forcing a sale. They explained that their measure of success was returning customers and not the daily sales total, and that the sales would come if they focused on the customer—what products they wanted to find in the stores and what kind of help they needed with their purchase decisions.

This was a new slant for most of the Romeros' staff. Until now, most of them thought selling was about convincing and most of them didn't like it. They loved working with customers and they were proud of their merchandise, but they hated that final confrontation of the "close." Somehow, in that last step, they felt they had to give up all the relationship building they did naturally and try to get the customer to buy.

The Romeros and their staff decided on a format for offering the product that emphasized the value of the purchase to the customer, in light of the customer's expressed needs. They didn't try to "sell." They trusted their customers to make the decision for themselves once they had all their needs met, and they agreed that the customer should never feel uncomfortable about not buying. What To Wear's doors would always be open to their customers no matter what the outcome of their visit.

The Romeros captured their ideas for formatting the five steps of the lead conversion process, and their best practices in serving customers, through a revised box-and-arrow diagram. They now had a system with a series of benchmarks for their selling process.

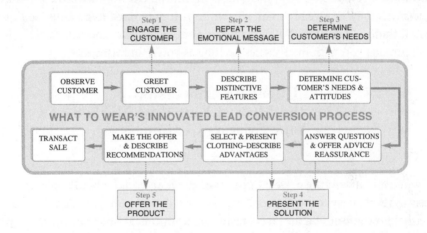

What next? How will the Romeros and the What To Wear staff translate their new lead conversion system into real and effective interactions with customers?

In the next business development process, you'll learn to create presentation scripts you can customize for your business and your target market that will guide your salespeople and your customers step by step through this interaction. Although any selling encounter can be unpredictable, scripts create a structure for insuring that each customer gets consistent information and service.

You'll also need to quantify the results your new system is getting to see how well it's working to give your business what it needs. There are two ways to do this. First, by creating ten indicators of lead conversion so you can monitor your progress, and second, by creating a tracking report that will show you the effectiveness of the individual benchmarks in your newly innovated lead conversion process. This will allow you to pinpoint *exactly* where the process is working best and where to focus attention to get even better results.

IT'S NOT A SALE, IT'S A RELATIONSHIP

Everything you've learned in this business development process has been geared toward building a relationship of mutual support with your prospective customers. By taking your focus off the "sale" and concentrating on your customers' needs, you'll send a powerful message of concern for customer satisfaction that will earn you continued patronage.

But what about the "sale"? Don't you need that, too? You do. That's why you're in business. But your sales won't come from "selling." They'll come from the assistance you give your customers in finding comfort with the purchase decisions they've already made. So while you may have to give up "selling," you'll trade a "sale" for a relationship of mutual support and satisfaction that will provide you with many "sales" as long as you're in business.

Client Re-Conversion: Making the Most of Your Best Market— Your Existing Customers

■

If you could invent the perfect target market, what would it be? People who are easy to reach. Easy to "sell." People you know will buy from you. People who already know about you and have favorable opinions about your business and your products.

You don't have to invent this perfect target market. You already have it. It's your existing customers.

Do you think of them as a target market? You should. And if you know how to do it, they're your best, most productive, most loyal market.

A good starting point is to understand the basic customer dynamics and put that understanding to use for your benefit and theirs.

CUSTOMER DYNAMICS: "IF YOU AIN'T KEEPIN' 'EM, YOU'RE LOSIN' 'EM"

Your "customer base" consists of all customers who buy from you. They range from your frequent buyers, who love you and your products and are the light of your business life, all the way to dormant customers, who have bought from

Client Re-Conversion

Definitions

Your customers are a market segment unto themselves, possibly several market segments. They're your best market.

Your "customer base" consists of all customers who buy from you. They range from frequent buyers to dormant customers, who don't buy frequently and haven't bought recently. Lost customers were once customers, but aren't anymore. They left for one of three reasons — they moved or became otherwise unavailable; they were disappointed; or they were attracted by your competition. Dormant customers are likely to buy from you when they buy again, but lost customers are gone and require extraordinary efforts to recover, and often can't be recovered in any case. It's more cost-effective to retain customers than to try to regain lost customers.

Client re-conversion is (a) the recognition that customers are a high-priority target market, and (b) the ongoing generation of repeat sales from them.

Client Re-Conversion

Key Points

Client re-conversion has three main benefits for your business:

· Repeat business

· Referral business

· Enhanced reputation and market image

For effective customer communications and re-conversion activities, you need the best, most complete customer database you can afford.

· The "minimum" customer database is, essentially , an address book.

· A "good" customer database also includes customer history (purchases, amounts, dates, and customer contacts).

· The "best" customer database also includes detailed demographic and psychographic information.

The secret to successful client re-conversion isn't selling; it's adding genuine value to the customer relationship, and acting in your customer's best interests rather than being self-serving and acting only in your own best interests. Ultimately, the customer's best interests *are* your best interests.

Customer communications fall into three categories:

▪ Administrative — Integral to doing business with a company. Important.

▪ Service — Something "for my benefit." A service for me. Also important.

▪ Sales — They're "selling" me something. For the benefit of the company. Unimportant. Often ignored. Often annoying.

Do your best to keep your customer communications in the first two categories. You can include some sales messages, but make them more like service announcements than advertisements.

Targeting Your Customer Base

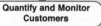

Designate Customers as a Target Market

Gather Information about Them

Create Value-Added Programs

Establish Communications

Quantify and Monitor Customers

you at some point in time, but don't buy frequently and haven't bought recently. Until you contact them, you can't tell dormant customers from lost customers, but it's an important distinction because lost customers are gone and require extraordinary efforts to recover, while dormant customers are likely to buy from you when they buy again.

If you want to keep your customers, you have to pay attention to them. Keep them aware of the value they receive from you. Continually court them. Make sure your promise is the right one for them. And continually exceed that promise.

The diagram below, labeled "Customer Dynamics," shows the ways your customer base grows and shrinks. It shrinks by losing customers because of disappointment or because of effective competitors or simply because they're no longer accessible to you (e.g., moved away, deceased). It grows by adding new customers through your lead generation and lead conversion, and through word of mouth and referrals. Re-conversion doesn't increase your customer base, but by retaining customers, it slows your attrition rate. Re-conversion, however, can dramatically increase your sales revenues by increasing the frequency and average sale amount of existing customers.

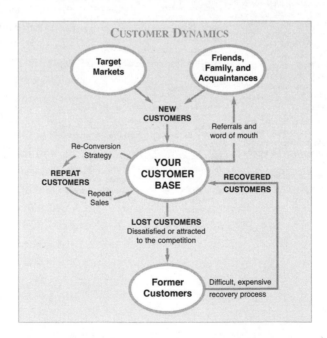

In this process, you're going to concentrate on developing repeat business from your customers—larger and more frequent purchases—and increasing customer loyalty. That's "client re-conversion."

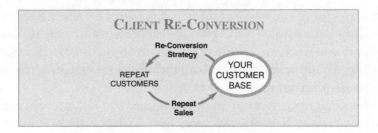

THE UPSIDE AND DOWNSIDE OF
CUSTOMER RELATIONSHIPS

There's an old saying in business: "Your best customer is the one you already have." It's true, but only if you keep them happy. If you fail to meet their expectations, they'll leave. And if the competition offers them something better, they'll leave. They might give you the benefit of the doubt for a while, but if you don't deliver the value they want, they're gone. And like a disappointed lover, when they leave, they leave with bitterness. They'll talk about their disappointment to anyone who'll listen. And that's a lose-lose scenario. You lose and they lose.

But you already know the downside of your customer relationships. That's why you created the powerful customer experience. That's why you put your quality management systems in place. That's why you designed your products and services to meet their every conscious and unconscious need. That's why you study your customers under the strongest possible microscope and do everything you can to bring them value and satisfaction.

Aside from the happy fact that customers buy from you, what's their upside opportunity? Three things: repeat business, referrals, and reputation.

Repeat business is obvious—if their experience is satisfactory and if they're not lured away by your competition, your customers will buy from you whenever the need for your products or services arises. But it's not automatic. You have to keep them aware of you and it has to be a favorable awareness. And for some products and services, the sense of need has to be stimulated. Dentists and automobile repair shops know this well. Their customers often forget about them until something goes wrong. Then they "need" something and make a purchase. But the smart dentists and auto repair shops communicate with their customers, offer preventative care programs, and provide great value while increasing their own profitability. A win-win strategy for all concerned.

Referrals are new customers who come to you because your existing customers told them to. They are the friends, family, and acquaintances of your customers. Your customers have told them of their positive experience of your business and your products, and they want the same for themselves. So they walk in your door already "sold." The flip side of referrals happens, of course, when your customers have a negative experience of your business and tell their friends, family, and acquaintances about their disappointment. Referrals offer you a special opportunity.

Reputation is the word of mouth—good or bad—that your customers spread about you to the people they come in contact with. In the end, your reputation in your markets comes from your customers. Your advertising and public relations can improve your reputation somewhat, but the bottom line of your reputation, of your image in your market, is what your customers say it is.

All of these—repeat business, referrals, and reputation—can be improved in major ways by looking at your customers as a very special, high-opportunity market segment, and creating a marketing strategy tailored for them.

Here's how you do it.

TARGET MARKETING TO YOUR CUSTOMER BASE

Like everything else in the E-Myth Mastery Program, you first shift your point of view, then take it one step at a time. In this case the shift of viewpoint brings your customer base into sharp focus as a target market—your most important target market, deserving all the attention your highest-priority target markets get. Then it's a matter of learning more about them, creating the programs that will serve their needs—and yours—communicating with them, and quantifying and monitoring them so you can do ever better in the future. Five steps define the process.

1. **Designate customers as a target market.** If you don't already view your customers as a special target market, you need to shift your point of view. Describe the Central Demographic Model and Central Psychographic Model. If your business has a customer base made up of different segments, you may want to establish more than one customer segment. For instance, a well-known discount stockbrokerage firm found that its customers were of two distinct types—"traders" who watch the markets closely and buy and sell their stocks frequently, and "buy-and-hold" investors who don't watch the stock markets very closely and hold their investments for long

Targeting Your Customer Base

Designate Customers as a Target Market

Gather Information about Them

Create Value-Added Programs

Establish Communications

Quantify & Monitor Customers

periods of time. Each customer segment required very different communications and services. Targeting the "heavy users" (frequent purchasers or big spenders, for instance) is a common practice for many businesses.

2. **Gather information about them.** Don't assume you know your customers. You certainly know a lot about them, but don't assume you know everything. And don't assume you know about their customer experience. Find out. Be sure. That's the key to increasing your revenues from them and to increasing their sense of value from you. Find out what works and do more of it. Find out what doesn't work and do less of it.

There are two avenues for gathering customer information—market research and internal information gathering. A market research study follows the same process you'd use to learn about any other target market segment. Use the *Customer Information Collection Plan* to determine how you'll gather the customer information you'll need.

Download

Internal information gathering is inexpensive, quick, accurate, and easy if you dovetail it into your existing business systems. It's as simple as asking your customer to fill out a customer information card or warranty card, or asking a few short questions during telephone conversations, or including short questionnaires with bills, statements, or order confirmations. There's no limit to the possible ways you can gather customer information.

But keep two cautions in mind: respect confidentiality and don't be intrusive. Most people will tell you about themselves if they know it's for their own benefit. So assure them that the information you gather will be confidential and will be used for your own purposes (product design, service improvement, etc.) and won't be given to anyone else without their permission. Don't burden them with excessive information gathering (too frequent, too time consuming, too personal) and don't intrude on their lives with telephone calls at dinner time, excessive "junk" mail, and the like.

Merely gathering customer information isn't enough. You have to organize it, store it, use it to understand your customers and communicate with them.

You need a customer database.

The simplest form of customer database is an address book—names, addresses, and telephone numbers. That's the absolute minimum, and it's pretty crude, but it's a start. Better is a database with all the contact information of an address book, and also including customer history (purchases, amounts, dates, and customer contacts). And best of all is a complete customer database with all contact information, customer history, and detailed demographic and psychographic information. You should have the best, most complete customer database you can afford.

3. **Create value-added programs.** If you want your customers to do more for you, first you have to do more for them. It's up to you to provide the motivation in the form of something they value. Value added can take any form that represents value to your customers—the possibilities are virtually unlimited. You can offer information, products, services, and even psychological satisfactions (special memberships, recognition, birthday cards)—anything that will be valued by your customers and which enhances their experience of your business and products.

> **TYPES OF VALUE-ADDED RE-CONVERSION PROGRAMS**
>
> **Price concessions and "freebies":** Frequent flier programs; eat here and get the 10th meal free; discounts; coupons; rebates; etc.
>
> **Extras:**
>
> ■ Information (statement stuffers, newsletters, bulletins and announcements, "inside" information that gives the customer some advantage)
>
> ■ Services (free pickup and delivery, free periodic maintenance, house calls)
>
> ■ Merchandise (desirable items apart from your product or service such as calculators, radios, umbrellas, caps, T-shirts)
>
> ■ Experiences (vacations, meet a celebrity, special events)
>
> **Recognition and status:** "Exclusive" membership for good customers; special treatment in the store, restaurant, etc.; public recognition for reaching a milestone; or special categories of service such as "platinum" credit cards, "red carpet" rooms at airports, etc.

Probably the most well-known customer re-conversion is the frequent flier program offered by the airlines— fly with the same airline, and after you accumulate enough mileage, you get a free flight. It's so effective that virtually every airline has had to adopt a similar re-conversion program or risk a significant outflow of customers.

Remember, though, that the best motivation for customer loyalty is value. If you provide the best value, repeat business is assured.

4. **Establish customer communications.** Communication is probably the single most important aspect of customer re-conversion. Re-conversion communications are much like lead generation communications, and you determine the channels and messages in much the same way. Use communication channels that fit into the customer's normal behavior patterns, and use messages that your psychographic information tells you will resonate with their needs and attitudes. The *Customer Communication* worksheet will help you Download determine this.

You have enormous advantages when communicating with your

customers, especially if you have a good customer information database. In the first place, you know your customers far better than you know your target markets in general (you do, don't you?). In the second place, you already have ready-made channels to reach them.

When you make a sale to a customer, there's an interaction—person to person, by telephone, over the Internet, by mail—there's always some connection. That's one of the best possible communication channels, and you should use it for re-conversion as well as for the original sales transaction. You can gather information (ask them questions and record the results, hand them a short information card to fill out, offer them a "membership" in your "club"—there's no limit to the possibilities). You can give them coupons, special offers "for customers only," announcements for future events like sales or new product introductions, or anything else that will motivate them to come back to you. For many businesses, there are monthly bills, statements, newsletters— some form of ongoing frequent communication that is a normal part of your business. You should add re-conversion messages to those existing channels.

There are two cautions:

Maintain your credibility. Customers, while they know and understand that you want to sell them something, don't want to be badgered. If you make it clear that your re-conversion efforts are in the best interests of your customers—truly in their best interests, not merely words—that you're offering something of value to them, not just more sales for you, then you'll maintain your credibility. Better, you'll demonstrate your genuine respect for your customers. To illustrate, think about all those letters you've seen that begin with "Dear valued customer." The words are correct—a business does value its customers— but the tone is impersonal, condescending, manipulative, and, frankly, phony. And customers hate that. Be genuine. Keep your customers' best interests in mind, and you can't go wrong.

Be nonintrusive. Telemarketing calls at dinner time, junk mail, and anything that sounds or reads like "hype," are intrusive and irritating to customers. Incidentally, don't be confused between "hype" and high energy or boldness. "Hype" (short for "hyperbole") means deliberate exaggeration to the point of misrepresentation. It has overtones of manipulation and doesn't respect the intelligence of your audience. High energy, boldness, and impact are a different matter.

Be sure your communication channels dovetail with the normal behavior of your customers and the business they conduct with you, and that their tone, appearance, and content are appropriate. "Appropriate" means respectful, helpful, for their benefit.

5. **Quantify and monitor customers.** If your business is bigger than a hot dog stand, you need customer tracking systems and a customer database. In fact, we can all learn a good lesson from hot dog vendors. They know their customers, do them favors, pay attention to them. Their businesses are small enough that their customer tracking systems and customer databases are all in their heads. Yours isn't that small and you can't keep all the information you need in your head. So you need formal systems and a way to store, organize, and analyze your customer information.

You've been through strategic, business, and systems indicators, systems evaluation and innovation, and marketing quantification, so there's no need to restate it all here. Just keep in mind that your customers are your most valuable target market, and construct your quantification and tracking systems with that level Download of priority in mind. You can sketch out your plan in the *Re-Conversion Program Outline.*

GATHERING CUSTOMER INFORMATION— MAKE IT PAINLESS FOR THEM AND EFFICIENT FOR YOU

Gathering customer information should be easy. All you have to do is identify the points of access in your business process and create an "instrument" to collect the information you want. And make sure it's done in a way that respects your customers and doesn't annoy them.

The points of access are those points in your lead generation, lead conversion, or client fulfillment processes at which you have some interaction with customers. As long as you're interacting with them anyway, with a little foresight, you can gather the information you need to understand them better.

For instance, if you do lead generation by direct mail, it's easy to add a few brief questions to your response card or to the telephone script used by your telemarketing people. Or in your lead conversion process, it's easy to design a short information card the sales person completes for each customer. Or include some customer information questions on your product warranty card. Or have your customer service people gather a few facts during the calls they receive from customers. Or add a brief questionnaire to your bills and account statements. Or ask customers to answer a one-minute series of questions while they're on line at your website. Or mail them questionnaires offering them a chance at a prize for returning the completed questionnaire. Or . . . well, use your imagination.

A key point to remember is that many customers will think some information is just "none of your business." There are facts that customers believe are too personal, or that expose them to risks that they don't want to take. Some customers don't like to tell anyone their age or income, for instance, and those are two very important demographic indicators. And many don't want to tell you their Social Security numbers, or their credit card numbers. You can see that some kinds of information are more sensitive than others.

So, how do you get sensitive information? There are three proven techniques—show them that they'll benefit, protect their privacy, and depersonalize the information for them.

- Show them the benefit. Tell them, in writing if you need to, that the information they provide will be used to improve your products and services.
- Protect their privacy. Assure them you won't sell their information to mailing list houses or any other parties who might use it in a way the customer might not like. Promise confidentiality. And don't just promise it; make sure you protect their information. Do what you tell them you're doing. And don't do what you tell them you won't do.
- Depersonalize the information. If income is a sensitive subject, for instance, ask them the income question in a way that depersonalizes it. You might ask them to check the box indicating their annual household income in the following list:
  - ❏ Zero to $24,999
  - ❏ $25,000 to $49,999
  - ❏ $50,000 to $99,999
  - ❏ $100,000 or over

That way, you have useful information, but your client hasn't revealed anything he or she considers too personal.

And, of course, some customers just won't give you information they consider sensitive no matter how respectful you are and no matter how well you protect their privacy. Sometimes you simply can't get every bit of information you want.

THE THREE CATEGORIES
OF CUSTOMER COMMUNICATION AND
WHY THEY'RE IMPORTANT TO YOU

In a 1992 study conducted for a major U.S. corporation, there was an interesting finding about customer communications. It gives important guidance and some useful insights about how to make your re-conversion communications as effective as they can be. The findings are paraphrased to protect the confidentiality of the sponsor of the study.

When asked about the communications they get from companies they do business with, customers respond with descriptions such as "junk mail," "important mail," product solicitations and offers, bills, statements, newsletters, marketing "stuff," surveys, and advertising. As they talk about these various kinds of communications, it becomes clear that they perceive three categories, which can be described as:

Administrative Communications are integral to doing business with a company—bills, account statements, administrative forms (e.g., change of address), changes of contractual agreements, announcements of procedural changes, and other items of an administrative nature. Administrative communications are always thought of as important, always taken seriously, and often saved in some sort of file.

Service Communications are perceived to be for the customer's benefit. Product information and announcements (if not obviously sales-oriented and full of "hype"), newsletters (again, if not thinly disguised sales materials), worksheets, product response cards, questionnaires that call for information that will clearly help the company provide better products and services (once again, if not disguised sales materials), announcements of changes that affect customers, and the like. Service communications are also thought of as important, although not as important as administrative communications. They're taken seriously and sometimes saved for later reference.

Sales Communications consist of attempts to sell the customer something. The most infamous example is so-called "junk mail." Even high-quality, desirable communications fall into this "junk" category if their primary purpose is to sell something.

Sales communications have a credibility problem and customers view them with skepticism. They are assumed by customers to be self-serving, slanted in favor of the company, and primarily for the benefit of the company, not the customer. Interestingly, product catalogs seem to be perceived more as service than sales communications, even though their purpose is clearly selling.

The lesson of this research is clear. If your communications with your customers have the impact of "sales" communications, they will be perceived as being in the interests of your business, and will be seen as less important, maybe even undesirable. If your communications have the impact of "service" or "administrative" communications, even if they have some appropriately presented selling information, they will be perceived as being in the customer's best interests, and will have far greater effectiveness.

CUSTOMERS ARE LIKE EVERYBODY ELSE, BUT MORE SO

Here's a bit of marketing philosophy that you might already know, but it's worth repeating. It has to do with respect.

Everybody everywhere wants to be treated with a certain basic amount of respect. It's human nature. We're all that way.

Somehow, today, too many "professional" marketers have lost sight of that basic fact of being human. So we see advertising that offends us with its pandering, its extreme claims and exaggerations, its misleading information, and its half-truths, all in the name of getting customers in the door. We see companies who do as little as they can for their customers to make their sales numbers. We see uncaring service . . . or no service at all.

There's a special feeling to being a customer, but it's fragile. It's not a big factor in the customer's life; in fact, the customer probably doesn't think much about it and may not consciously recognize it. But it's there. There's a link. There's an expectation of trust, however faint. There's an expectation for service, value, quality. There's a desire for that basic respect that we all deserve merely for being here on the face of the planet.

So if you treat them like the "professional" marketers do, your customers will be a bit reluctant about you, and their connection with you will be weak. They'll leave you in a nanosecond for someone who treats them better, more respectfully.

And respect means more than just politeness and saying the right things. In the long run—and aren't you in business for the long run?—actions speak louder than words. Real respect for your customers shows in the quality of your products—you make your products better than you have to because it's right, because it respects your customers. Your customer services add value because that honors your customers. Your delivery process delights your customers. It's the right thing to do, not just what you have to do to move product. It's what transforms customers into clients.

And, in the end, the way you treat your customers says a lot about the respect you have for yourself.

CHAPTER SEVEN

The Discipline of the Lead Generation Leader

■

"When a skillful martial artist uses his sword, he should
be able to cut a fly off his friend's nose without cutting
his nose. To have the fear of cutting his nose is not true
practice. When you do something, have a strong
determination to do it! Whoosh! (Sound of sword
cutting air.) Without any idea of skillful or not,
dangerous or not, you just do it. When you do something
with this kind of conviction, that is true practice.
That is true enlightenment."

From not always so *by Shunryu Suzuki*

And finally, the discipline that everyone is hungry for. The discipline that
prompts and promotes the continual flow of abundance to your doors, the
flow of prospective customers who, in turn, become new customers who become new clients who, ultimately, become the prized well of devoted, mature
clients who you know, you just know, are the answer to your prayers, will make
your life easier, will become what you had hoped for, dreamed about, at the
very beginning of your business, the elixir of abundance, the sweet nectar of a
financially fulfilled life, the bliss of Forever and Always Enough.

"If I could only get them to come in my door."

"If I could only get their attention."

"If I could only . . ." I probably have heard that expression 10,000 times or
more from the mouths of small business owners, followed always, inexorably,
with the one word that punctures their hopes and their confidence in anything
I could possibly say to them. And the word is "But." "*But* I don't have the
money." "*But* I don't know what to do." "*But* the competition is killing me." Or
"*But* I've tried everything, and nothing works."

"If only . . ." and "But . . ." pretty much sums up an all too common but profound sense of resignation when it comes to lead generation, a reflection of a part of many small business owners that has succumbed to a no-way-out, end-of-the-road approach to life. The place that consumes all the air and leaves nothing for passion or vitality . . . or hope.

So now what?

Sarah and I had been working nonstop for many months. We were coming to the end of one road, and the beginning of many others. New roads, new obstacles, new places to go, new attractions, new distractions, all of them, however, leading to a very different place than the road that the reluctant entrepreneur travels. Sarah's reluctance hadn't left her. She was simply seeing it clearly, engaging with it rather than being consumed by it, observing herself in the throes of turmoil that allowed her to see that it wasn't really turmoil at all. But simply what her mind did given its choice to do what it does, given the freedom to run anywhere it pleased, like a goat in an unfenced pasture. All of the work we'd been doing had come to this place, to the discipline of the lead generation leader, as naturally as a river seeking its own level. It's as though Sarah and I had been preparing All About Pies for a **Grand Opening**! which Sarah had conceived first, in the drawing room of her mind, then in her heart, then back in her mind again, then on the blank pieces of paper proliferating on her desk, and after all that, fearing the worst, hoping for the best, she opened the doors and throngs of people were waiting to come in! All those people! Isn't this what a business is supposed to be like? Isn't this what every small business lives for, the people? For months and months, Sarah and I had been doing nothing other than the work of getting ready for this last of the seven essential disciplines where it all comes to roost.

Lead generation is the process through which the promise that lives at the heart of the enterprise is made, repeatedly, nonstop, to those for whom the promise was created, your most probable consumer.

The discipline is rooted in the nonstop nature of the job of the lead generation leader.

Lead generation is a nonstop endeavor. When lead generation stops, so does the company. Even if it doesn't happen right away, stop generating leads and I can assure you your company will die. A company that stops generating leads is borrowing from the past, just like a fruit tree that is no longer cared for. As hardy as that tree might be, there will come a time when it will stop bearing fruit.

When it comes to lead generation, you've got to, if you're serious about building a World Class Company, take all the stops out. There's a time to get ready and once you are, once you know exactly what you're going to do, what your promise is, what your client fulfillment system is, what your lead conversion system is, what your core operating system is, then you have to start the engine. To start the lead generation engine in earnest, and to make certain that you have the determination to *keep it running full-time.* It is the function of a World Class Company to continually attract people to it. And to never stop.

THE FIRST ASSIGNMENT

"Which brings us to your first assignment about lead generation, Sarah. Most people, the people who live by 'If only . . . ' and 'But . . . , ' would tell you that lead generation is difficult. It really isn't. Someone said recently that, in our government's failure to prevent 9/11, we suffered from a 'lack of imagination.' I don't think that's quite true, Sarah. I think what's really true is that most people, whether they own a small business or administer in the government, suffer from a lack of—what else?—passion. Passion sparks imagination. There is no imagination without the fuel that passion creates. Passion for the result. Passion for the role we play. Passion for pursuing what it is we are accountable for, committed to, wish for, relentlessly. So what I'd like you to do here, Sarah, is to create a list of every single idea you can muster about methods for attracting people to your door. I'd like you to sit down for that purpose and that purpose only, 15 minutes every day, for seven days, writing down whatever comes to your mind, including the words you might use, the promotions you might have, the media through which you would accomplish your objective. In other words, brainstorm with yourself about the medium of lead generation, the content of the offer, and process you'll follow. Write everything, even what you consider foolish or superficial. The most important thing to remember as you do this assignment is not to think about *doing* any of the things you write down. Don't get caught up thinking about *how* to do them, the possible obstacles, the money you don't have, etc. You know what I mean, the endless number of complications that we can always imagine that put the breaks on our passion. Any questions, Sarah?"

Sarah looked relieved. "Actually, no, Michael. I feel so freed by not having to think about how I would get these things done. Generating ideas comes easily to me. That's the most fun. It's the doing that stresses me out. Like you said, where's the money going to come from? What kind of ad should I write? And what about the graphics and printing and mailing, all the mechanics of getting stuff done that takes up so much time? Brainstorming is easy. It's *doing* what I brainstorm about that isn't."

"I know, Sarah. The more entrepreneurial passion and energy you allow yourself to express, the more the wants and needs of the entrepreneur in you will replace the wants and needs of the technician in you. True entrepreneurs want to spend their time generating ideas. They don't want to do the work. Which is why an entrepreneur can build a World Class Company that a technician has no interest in. A World Class Company doesn't depend on the owner to produce results. A World Class Company is systems-dependent. A true entrepreneur learns very quickly how to replace himself in the tactical functions he doesn't want to do by creating systems that his people are trained to use. Your role as the lead generation leader has more to do with unleashing your passion to discover the opportunities that exist in your imagination than it has to do with *doing* anything. The opportunities to generate leads are always endless, Sarah. And therein lies the joy. They're endless if and when you pursue them without any sense of limitation, without any sense of how difficult it will be to get any of them done. Your job is to lead, not to do. You simply have to trust that as you lead, as you pursue the endless opportunities, you will discover an entirely new life. This assignment is the first step. It will liberate you, Sarah, if you let it. So will your second assignment."

THE SECOND ASSIGNMENT

"Now that you've liberated your imagination through your passion in service of the generation of leads for your company, your next assignment, Sarah, is to do the same thing with your employees. Small business owners always seem to have a similar complaint which sounds something like: 'Why do I have to come up with all the ideas? Why aren't my people more creative?' Does that sound familiar, Sarah?"

Sarah nodded her head, yes. "Always, and forever, Michael," she said. "It drives me crazy. But isn't it true that if you're going to hire relatively inexperienced people to use the system you've created, it's unreasonable to also expect them to be creative?"

"Very good question, Sarah.

"Think about it this way, Sarah. Your people are no different than you. They get lost in their passion; they are living more in the future than in the present. They're spending far too much time wondering what's going to happen to them, where are they going to be in a year, in two years, what are they going to be doing? They are consumed by the question every one of us is consumed by, 'What's going to happen to me?' That question consumes our energy, and is rarely addressed directly by people who own their own business. Their promises to their people are usually pretty empty. Make the commitment, most owners say to their people, make a commitment to growing inside our company, and one day, as we grow, you'll be rewarded. But that day rarely comes. The day-to-day experience of most people working in a small business is that the needs are always greater, far greater, than the resources to satisfy them. That's your people's experience, Sarah. And your people, like people everywhere, are in need of something more than what they've got, and, frankly, more than what you've got. They need stimulation. They need inspiration. They need their own aliveness. And the way you can do that is to help them to find their own creativity, like my friend did building her first house from scratch, as you did as a little girl writing in your journal, as you've done again over these months we've been together. Tell me, Sarah, have you ever told the story of The Little Girl Who Wanted to Write a Book to your people?"

Sarah's face lit up.

"Never," she said. "I would have never thought of doing that!"

"I know, Sarah. Very few small business owners ever share intimate stories, true stories, stories that moved them, changed their lives with their people. Too personal. But that's what everyone is interested in. They are hungry for intimacy. Hungry for something real in their lives. Something other than the empty patter of, if you stay, and if you work very, very hard, you have a future in our company. Sarah, they don't want a future in your company. They want a future in their lives. And that's the only conversation that will transform your relationship with them. An earnest conversation that engages them where they live.

"Do you see why this is so important?"

"I just never thought about it before, Michael, about what my people *really* need. But, as always—when I finally understand what you're saying, that is"— Sarah said poking fun at me—"you make complete sense."

"I'm glad, Sarah," I said, "Let me share a short story about a big company I consulted for.

"I spent some time working with a very large franchise company which came to me to talk about how E-Myth could help their struggling stores. I spent some time in their stores, talking to their people. I was astonished by how surprised their people were that I was interested in them, not in their jobs. They were reluctant at first. They didn't trust me. An old white guy in a dark navy suit, white starched shirt and tie, you get my point. I wasn't like them. They knew I didn't live in their world; they knew I had no idea what their world was like, what it felt like to them to go home after work. I needed to know where they lived, what they did, what they were interested in. And gradually, as they began to trust me, they began to open up. At first they were hostile. Their negative energy rushed out like a flood. But as they saw I wasn't reacting to them, that I still remained interested, and, most of all, as I began to share with them some of my life, my story, where I grew up, what my hits and misses were, they began to slow down, to really talk.

"Sarah, no one in that company had ever talked to them. Truly talked to them. No one was really interested. They simply wanted to get the job done. They saw their people as a means to an end. People cannot discover their own creativity when they feel seen as a means to an end, when no one is interested in them as a creative being. When I went back to the corporate offices, the guys in the home office dismissed my advice: If you want your stores to grow, if you want your customers to turn into real clients, follow your people home. Follow them home and see what it's like to live in their shoes. And that's exactly what you need to do in order to generate more customers, and turn them into clients. Follow them home, see where they live. Experience their experience. That's where the creativity is, where it will come alive, where your opportunity resides.

"Did I answer your question, Sarah?"

"I'd say so, Michael," Sarah said.

"Can we go on to your second assignment?" I asked Sarah, who nodded yes.

"Then your second assignment is to have your employees do exactly the same exercise as your first assignment. Write down all the lead generation ideas they can come up with, regardless of how workable they think they are, for 15 minutes every morning, for seven straight days. Invite them to share their creativity with you. Some will, some won't. Some will have remarkable fun, some will look at it as a test. Some will take to it like a duck to water, some will be sullen, resentful, and awkward with it. But in the end, you will begin to see how easy it is to create new ideas to generate new leads. Which brings us to the third assignment, Sarah."

THE THIRD ASSIGNMENT

"Once you and your people have plumbed the depths of your imagination to create every single lead generation idea you can come up with, I'd like you to get together and share them with each other.

"For this I would take one day, planned especially for the purpose of looking into the possibilities. And begin the process of discovering with each other where the real creative opportunities are, organizing them into Medium, Content, and Process. Medium means the kind of lead generation activity: Direct Mail, Internet, etc. Content refers to the offer you're making, the words you use, the design of the finished product, a letter, a brochure, etc. Process is the method by which you implement the activity, Step One, Step Two, Step Three, Step Four. This organization achieves several purposes simultaneously, Sarah. First, it creates a Culture of Organization within your company. This culture supports the idea that for anything to be done well it needs organization. It speaks to the hunger in most people for a world that makes sense. A world that is governed by logic. A world in which things can be created as opposed to simply reacted to.

"The second purpose is to give your people a sense of their own creativity. They will discover that even though they know nothing about lead generation, they have a capacity to generate rich ideas, ideas that can produce revenue, not only for the company, but should they choose, for themselves as individuals. This awareness produces a Culture of Creativity in an emerging World Class Company.

"The third purpose for your daylong meeting with your people is to begin to raise their expectations of ordinary life to a completely new level, to reveal to them the Culture of Responsibility, for the life they have been given.

"The Culture of Organization, the Culture of Creativity, the Culture of Responsibility is a matrix of potentiality, the seeds for which can be planted during one simple day in which everyone comes together to discuss the opportunities that abound to create an enormous number of leads to grow our company!"

"Michael, I have been sitting here listening to you rhapsodize about creativity and people," Sarah said. "And I'm feeling pretty self-centered at the moment. I realize how consumed I've been by what I want, my own desires, my own life, my own business. Not only do I take my long-term customers for granted. I also take my people for granted. I forgot they were human! I see that I just haven't been *interested* in them. It's embarrassing to say this, but I've simply looked at them as tools to make my business work. And when they didn't work, I got infuriated with them. Of course they couldn't be creative."

"I see you see it, Sarah. Think about it. You'll know what to do.

"For now, let's go on to the work the leader of lead generation needs to do so we can finally put the last piece of this puzzle of ours in place. Okay? Are you ready for the last homework assignment?"

"I'm so ready," Sarah said with conviction, conviction that was hard-won.

Lead Generation Channels:
Reaching Your Target Markets

■

In the mid-1960s, Canadian educator Marshall McLuhan coined a phrase that was to become one of the defining expressions of the 20th century: "The medium is the message."

The truth in these words is that the *way* one chooses to convey a message—the vehicle, the medium, the channel of communication—is as important and has as much impact on how the message is received, as the actual content of the message itself.

For many years, *The New York Times Magazine* has carried the advertisements of Steuben Glass. These ads are simple, artistic photos of this company's beautiful crystal figures, and carry a minimum of text. Although, technically, these ads could run in any magazine, newspaper, or even on television, you won't see them there. The reputation and "élan" of *The New York Times Magazine* as the selected lead generation channel has become as much a part of the association in our minds as the words and images we see on the page.

You don't have to be Steuben Glass—or advertise in *The New York Times*—to have this kind of impact on your potential customers. You just have to know which lead generation channels speak as eloquently and persuasively to your target market as *The New York Times* does to Steuben's.

In this business development process, you'll review some of the many channels that are available to generate interest in your business, evaluate which channels will give you the best results for the least amount of money, and create a lead generation implementation plan so that the channels you use help you achieve your lead generation goals in the most extraordinary way possible.

BUT WHAT, EXACTLY, IS A CHANNEL?

"Channel" has a number of meanings, but here it's used in the sense of a "means of communication" or a "path of communication." A lead generation channel, then, is any method, medium, or vehicle you use to communicate your lead generation message. It's *how* you broadcast your promise to your target markets.

Lead Generation Channels

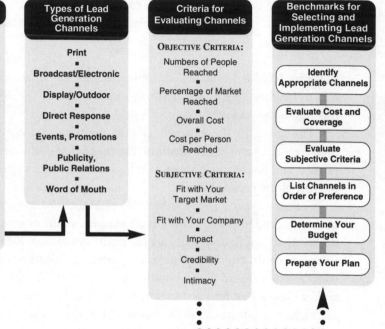

Overview

Lead generation channels are the methods, media, or vehicles you use to communicate the messages of your business to prospective customers. Channels are the "how" and messages are the "what." Together, they attract attention and create impressions that cause customers to respond. The right channels, combined with the right messages, will give you the response you want—interest in your offer and an ongoing relationship with your company.

Types of Lead Generation Channels

Print
▪
Broadcast/Electronic
▪
Display/Outdoor
▪
Direct Response
▪
Events, Promotions
▪
Publicity, Public Relations
▪
Word of Mouth

Criteria for Evaluating Channels

OBJECTIVE CRITERIA:

Numbers of People Reached
▪
Percentage of Market Reached
▪
Overall Cost
▪
Cost per Person Reached

SUBJECTIVE CRITERIA:

Fit with Your Target Market
▪
Fit with Your Company
▪
Impact
▪
Credibility
▪
Intimacy

Benchmarks for Selecting and Implementing Lead Generation Channels

Identify Appropriate Channels

Evaluate Cost and Coverage

Evaluate Subjective Criteria

List Channels in Order of Preference

Determine Your Budget

Prepare Your Plan

There are many types of channels available to you, and new variations are being created all the time. Some of the most common channels are: print advertising, like magazines and newspapers; broadcast advertising, like radio and television; direct mail; billboards; and word-of-mouth referrals from satisfied customers.

CHOOSE YOUR CHANNELS; DON'T LET THEM CHOOSE YOU

When selecting which channels to use for lead generation, most small businesses make the mistake of using one of these approaches:

- **"Everybody else does it this way."** In this approach, you choose the most common channel or the one that your competitors and others in your industry use. "If they're doing it, it must be the best way."
- **"It was handed to me on a silver platter."** In this approach, you choose the method that requires the least effort on your part. "The advertising guy called me and it sounded good, so I signed up."
- **"Shot in the dark."** In this approach, you try one method for a while and if it doesn't seem to be working, you try something else. "For the money I can afford to spend, they're all about the same, anyway."
- **"I've always done it this way."** In this approach, you just keep advertising the way you always have, even though you have no idea if the channels you're using are giving you the results you want. "I know my name's getting out there and, besides, I can't afford the time, effort, or money to generate leads any differently." This is also known as the "throwing good money after bad" approach.

THE IMPORTANCE OF SELECTING THE RIGHT LEAD GENERATION CHANNELS

With so many choices, how can you pick the best lead generation channels for your business? And does it really make a difference? Why not just place an ad in the local newspaper and be done with it?

The channels you select are important. The right choices will expand the value of every dollar you spend. Unless you have money to burn, your lead generation dollars need to be as well targeted as your message. Three key elements to consider in choosing your channels are reach, attraction, and cost.

Reach

You can't attract new customers if they don't know you exist. You must reach out to them with a compelling message, and your lead generation channels are the carriers of that message. When considering the various channels, remember that your customers won't go out of their way to get your message, and they shouldn't have to. So you want to work with channels that reach your customers as a regular part of their lives.

The Marketing Funnel

TARGET MARKET POPULATION

MARKET COVERAGE

LEAD
GENERATION

SALES

Look at the marketing funnel. "Market coverage" can be defined as the extent to which your marketing activities reach your targeted customers; and the lead generation channels you use are the main vehicles for reaching them. In other words, your ability to reach your target customers, which is a prerequisite for creating customers for your business, is vitally dependent on the lead generation channels you use. And if you don't reach sufficient numbers of your target market, lead generation and sales will suffer.

Attraction

Once the channel and its message have reached a target customer, you hope that that customer will pay attention to the message and be attracted by it—in fact, attracted enough so that he will take action.

But, guess what! Before customers can be attracted by your message, they must first be attracted by the messenger—the channel carrying the message. Put another way, if you've selected a channel that your customers are either not interested in or, worse yet, one that repels them, they'll never even get to the message, no matter how compelling that message may be.

Have you ever thrown out a piece of direct mail without even opening it up to see what was being offered? Or hung up on a telemarketing phone call before the caller was able to say more than "Hello . . ." These examples (and you can probably think of many more) prove that the channel you select *is* an important part of the attraction equation.

Of course, many businesses use direct mail and telemarketing quite successfully. Which only proves the point that you must really know your target customer. What attracts one person does not necessarily attract another. And what repels one person does not necessarily repel someone else.

How do you determine which channels will attract your target customers? Consider these criteria:

- **Credibility**—Is this medium believable? Do your customers trust it?
- **Appropriateness**—Does this medium have the right kind of impact? Is this the way your customers want to be approached and communicated with? Is it consistent with their picture of themselves?
- **Associations**—What other thoughts does this medium bring to mind? Are they pleasant or unpleasant?

If you can successfully choose the lead generation channels that will attract customers, they'll be more likely to be receptive to your message and drawn irresistibly into the "magnetic field" of your business.

Cost

You are running a business, after all. So, unless you're extremely profitable or have unlimited money to spend, cost will be a factor in selecting the lead generation channels you'll use.

First, you'll look to the financial condition of your business, your budget, and your revenue goals to see how much money you'll need to get the results you want. Then you'll evaluate the efficiency and effectiveness of the various channels available to you. The most efficient channels will give you the most "exposures" in your target market for the least cost. The most effective channels will give you the most qualified leads for the least cost.

What's an "exposure"? Let's say your target market is doctors. A hundred doctors drive to work every day between 8:00 and 8:30 A.M. and listen to a particular radio station. A block away from their medical center is a large billboard. If you play a radio ad at 8:15 every morning, you will have 100 exposures every day—100 doctors hearing the ad once at 8:15. If you advertise on the billboard, you will have 200 exposures every day—100 doctors seeing the billboard twice a day; in the morning on their way to work and in the evening on their way home. Reach times frequency equals exposures.

What if your radio ad and your billboard both cost the same amount of money per month? If the radio ad brought in more inquiries from doctors than the billboard, it would be more effective, even though the billboard was more efficient with twice as many exposures for the same price.

Effectiveness in your channels is ultimately more important than their efficiency. But if you haven't yet determined the effectiveness of the channels you want to use, trying the most efficient ones, consistent with the reach and attraction criteria discussed above, may be your best strategy.

BENCHMARKS FOR SELECTING AND IMPLEMENTING YOUR LEAD GENERATION CHANNELS

With so many possible channels, so many variations in how your customers think and behave, so many other demands for your money, and so many other factors to consider, you definitely need a system for selecting and implementing the best possible lead generation channels for your business. Here are the six benchmarks that will guide you successfully through that process, and more easily than you might imagine.

1. **Identify a range of appropriate channels that fit your target market.** Review the lead generation channels described in this process and make a list of any others you know. Then, create a specific picture in your mind of your target customers—how they live their day-to-day lives and what types of channels might reach them at home, at work, and at play.

   With a clear picture of your target customers in mind, go through your list of available channels one by one and identify those that best "fit" your target market. Which ones are part of their daily routine; vehicles they see, hear, or experience in the normal course of their lives? And which channels, in and of themselves, create positive associations and negative associations within the minds of your customers? You probably won't want to consider using a lead generation channel that your customers instinctively reject, no matter how prevalent or inexpensive it may be.

   The result of this benchmark will be a "customized" list for your business of those lead generation channels that best fit the customers you most want to attract. You can use the *Lead Generation Channels* checklist to develop it. (As a general guideline, this list of channels that best "fit" your target market should have a minimum of 5 and no more than 12 channels.)

Benchmarks for Selecting and Implementing Lead Generation Channels

- Identify Appropriate Channels
- Evaluate Cost & Coverage
- Evaluate Subjective Criteria
- List Channels in Order of Preference
- Determine Your Budget
- Prepare Your Plan

Download

2. **Evaluate each channel in terms of cost and coverage.** This step will require some research or, at the very least, some educated guesswork. Using the *Lead Generation Channels Cost and Coverage Evaluation* worksheet, write down the names of the channels you're going to evaluate. Then, write how much it costs for one "placement" in the channel, for example, the cost of one radio ad, one magazine ad, one direct mailing, etc.

   Download

   Keep the variables as consistent as possible. You don't want to compare the cost of a quarter-page magazine ad with a full-page newspaper ad, or a one minute radio ad with a 30-second television ad. Because of all the variations among the many different types of channels, one easy technique is to cost everything at its smallest available cost, and then do any necessary "equalizing" later. For example, one local newspaper may take no ads smaller than an eighth of a page, whereas another newspaper may accept smaller placements.

   At this stage, consider only those costs you'd pay to an outside party to place your message in the channel. Don't add in your internal costs, such as preparing advertising copy or writing press releases, because these are highly variable and under your control. If you're considering unpaid, "nonadvertising" channels, like word-of-mouth referrals, press releases, or trade articles, document them on the worksheet, even though the costs will be "zero." You'll still need to compare their reach and coverage with the higher-cost alternatives.

3. **Evaluate each channel in terms of relevant subjective criteria.** Although cost and coverage are important factors in your channel selection process, there are a number of other criteria you need to consider. The main ones are:

   - **The channel's fit with your company's image and strategic objective.**

     The channels you use should be consistent with the image you want to portray to the outside world, most particularly to your target market, and with the strategic goals and objectives you have for your business. Once your business is associated with a particular medium, it may be hard to shift the association in people's minds. Think strategically and with a long-term view; use your "double vision." Be wary of choosing those channels that are most expedient in the moment, if they don't serve your company's future vision.

- **Your company's ability to use the channel effectively.**
Does your company have the internal resources, skills, and talents to make the best use, or even adequate use, of the channel you're considering? Do you have the writing talent to create an effective press release? Do you have the artistic and copy writing skills to develop four-color magazine ads? Do you have the financial resources to produce a television ad? Do you have the marketing, administrative, and logistical resources to plan and carry out a community event?

  Be realistic and objective in assessing your company's abilities. Better to choose a more modest channel and execute it well than to be overly aggressive and end up with a sloppy, unprofessional result.

- **Other subjective qualities of the channel,** like its impact on your customers, its credibility, and the level of intimacy or connection it promotes.

  Impact is the conscious or unconscious feeling that your customers associate with a given channel and the way that feeling influences their behavior. For example, the lead generation channel of telemarketing is a "fit" with the vast majority of target markets— almost everyone has access to a telephone. But repeated instances of receiving telemarketing calls at inconvenient times, during dinner or late at night, and the cold or pushy attitude of some of the callers, have caused many people to feel angry and resentful at the channel of telemarketing itself. The behavior many customers adopt based on this feeling is to automatically reject any offer made via telemarketing.

  To determine the impact of the channels on your list, put yourself in the shoes of your target customers and ask yourself how they would describe or react to each of those channels. Do your customers think billboards are exciting and fun, or intrusive and tasteless? Do they think the Internet is contemporary and cutting edge, or complicated and scary?

  Credibility is the level of believability, trust, and confidence that your customers have in the channel. And different people have different views on the credibility of the various lead generation channels. Some people believe anything that's printed in a newspaper, but little of what they see on TV. In general, unpaid channels tend to be more credible in people's minds than paid advertising.

  Intimacy is the extent to which the channel fosters a close, personal connection between the customer and the message being delivered. How well does the channel draw the person into your "magnetic field" and, thereby, into a relationship with your company? Does it touch them? Does it move them? Does it reach them inside, where they live? Intimacy is established through strong emotional associations, personal identification, and engagement through as many senses as possible. Attending an event sponsored by your company would be more intimate than seeing your company's product on a billboard. This is also why an advertisement featuring a celebrity gets better results than the exact same ad featuring an unknown actor or model—people perceive that they "know" or are familiar with the celebrity and, therefore, are more likely to express an interest in the product.

Your goal is to identify channels that have strong, positive impact and high degrees of credibility and intimacy. Use the *Lead Generation Channels Subjective Criteria Evaluation* work- Download sheet to document your comments regarding these criteria with respect to each of the channels you're considering.

4. **List channels in order of preference based on your evaluations.** So far, you've developed a list of the most appropriate lead generation channels for your specific target market and evaluated each of those channels based on the objective criteria of cost and coverage, and various subjective criteria. Each of those evaluations reveals facts, figures, and impressions that will inform your channel selection process. Now you must go through your lists and evaluations and create your final list in order from "best to worst" or "most appropriate to least appropriate" lead generation channels for your business. If you find any of the channels from your original list are, in fact, not appropriate or a good fit, take them off the list entirely. Record your final list of channel selections on the *Lead Generation Channels Selection* Download *List* worksheet.

5. **Determine your budget.** This benchmark requires you to leave the world of lead generation channels behind, momentarily, and shift your attention to the world of money. How much money do you have available to spend on your lead generation activities during the year? Your budget should give you the answer to this question. If you think your budget does not accurately reflect the amount you can or want to spend, put some serious thought into determining what would be the right amount. How much of this money do you want to spend on your

primary target market and how much on other markets? Moving on to the next step and being able to get your lead generation "house" in order depends on your having a realistic budget number to work with. The *Lead Generation Budget Planning* worksheet will guide you through the process of allocating your budgeted money for the market you're working on now among the channels Download you want to use.

6. **Prepare your lead generation channels implementation plan.** This step will propel all of your lead generation planning and development into actual implementation and results. It will give you and your staff a firm footing for your weekly and monthly lead generation activities. And as one of the key products of your lead generation system, it will provide a basis for innovating, quantifying, and orchestrating this critical area of your business.

Your plan should be a one-year plan, starting sometime within the next two to three months. (If one year into the future seems too difficult to think about right now, try it anyway. You can revise your plan later on, if needed.) Your plan should show the market being targeted, how you want to position your business to that market, which specific channels you'll use, when you'll use them, how much you'll spend, who is accountable for the activity, and what result you are expecting. A complete description of the contents and format of this plan will be discussed later in this business development process.

THE VAST ARRAY OF LEAD GENERATION CHANNELS

The marketplace is populated with a huge variety of channels that companies can use to reach the hearts and minds of prospective customers. Some of these channels, like signs, placards, and word of mouth, have been in existence since businesses began; others, like the Internet, are as new as the latest technology.

There are two main categories of lead generation channels: paid channels and unpaid channels. Paid channels are commonly referred to as advertising, which is clearly paid for and sponsored by the company with a vested interest in doing so. Unpaid channels are typically thought of as publicity or, in a broader sense, public relations.

Many small businesses depend on word of mouth to help generate leads. Spontaneous word of mouth, especially coming from someone who is well known and respected, can be very effective. Because of this, some word of mouth has crossed over into the "paid" arena via compensated referral programs. Of course, when it becomes known that someone is being paid to promote a certain company or its products, the credibility factor drops.

Because of the different types of channels and the many variations on each type, sticking to hard-and-fast categorizations is difficult and, fortunately, of little benefit. As companies create new ways to use lead generation channels, changes appear in the market rapidly. And that's the good news. Because, while there are many types of lead generation channels that exist, what you choose to do is limited only by your own imagination. So don't be afraid to pick and choose, combine different ideas, or create something completely unique.

WHICH CHANNELS ARE "RIGHT" FOR YOUR BUSINESS?

So many different lead generation channels to choose from! How can you possibly decide which ones to use? Actually, it's not as difficult as you might think.

Earlier in this process you read about the three general criteria of reach, attraction, and cost and how they apply to your lead generation channels. Now we'll reexamine those in terms of the specific criteria you can describe and evaluate to make the best decisions about which channels are best for you.

Review the criteria for evaluating lead generation channels in this section, then apply them to each of the channels you're considering. The Profile of Key Lead Generation Channels chart on page 366 will give some additional guidance.

Objective Criteria

Reach: Reach is the number of people (or households or businesses) exposed to a particular channel at least once during a specified time period. For example, a newspaper might have a circulation, or reach, of 100,000 people a day; a spontaneous word-of-mouth referral from a satisfied customer to a friend would have a reach of one.

Market Coverage: Market coverage is the percentage of the target market you reach. Reach divided by the total number in the target market population gives you the percentage of market coverage.

Cost: Cost is the dollar amount required for the channel provider to carry your message. This could be the cost for one 30-second radio ad, the printing and postage costs for 1,000 pieces of direct mail, and so forth. You will also want to calculate the cost per person reached by the channel.

Frequency and Exposures: These are not technically criteria for evaluating channels, because they are as dependent on your own discretion (and on your

Lead Generation Channels Listing

PRINT ADVERTISING	**EVENTS & PROMOTIONS**
Newspapers	Business Conventions, Trade Shows
Magazines	Fairs, Exhibits
Newsletters (external)	Contests
Trade/Organizational Directories	Premiums/Novelties (calendars,
Telephone Directories	note pads, key chains, magnets,
Catalogs, Brochures, Flyers	etc.)

BROADCAST/ ELECTRONIC ADVERTISING	**PUBLICITY, PUBLIC RELATIONS**
Television	Press Releases
Radio	Feature Articles
Facsimile	Product Announcements
Internet	Newsletters (internal)

DISPLAY/ OUTDOOR ADVERTISING	Speeches
	Seminars
Signage	Annual Reports
Billboards	Community/Charitable Events
Placards	Charitable Donations
Posters	Sponsorships, Endorsements
Bumper Stickers	Alliances with other businesses
Vehicle Signage	**WORD OF MOUTH**
Vehicle Advertising	Spontaneous Word of Mouth

DIRECT RESPONSE	Referral Programs
Direct Mail	Testimonials
Telemarketing	

budget) as they are on the channel you use. But they're worth mentioning because they are related to the channels and their reach, and will play a part in your channel selections. Frequency is the number of times within a specified time period that an average person is exposed to the message, such as running your ad in the sports section and the business section of the newspaper with 100,000 circulation. In this case, 100,000 people would see your message twice, resulting in 200,000 exposures. As was mentioned earlier, reach times frequency equals exposures. Exposures is an important concept to consider because it often takes multiple exposures to a message before a potential customer is moved to take action.

Subjective Criteria

Fit with your target market: At the beginning of this process, you made a "broad brush" evaluation of which channels best fit your target customers. Now you'll want to consider in more specific terms, and document on the worksheet, how each channel is suited to the lifestyle of the people you most want to attract. Do they read the newspaper every day from cover to cover, watch TV occasionally, and never listen to the radio? Do they open and read every piece of mail they get, or routinely toss out direct mail? Are they "networkers" who join organizations and refer to their directories regularly?

Fit with your company: There are two ways to look at the fit between a particular channel and your company. One is its "strategic" fit—its appropriateness to your strategic objective and the image you want to project. The other is more of a "practical" fit—the capability of your company to use this channel effectively.

Impact: Impact is the force or influence exerted on a person by the channel, usually due to a feeling or an association it has raised. When evaluating the impact of a channel on your target customer, think about the feeling that channel produces and how your customer responds to it. Different people respond differently to the same feeling. A sensory laden "infomercial" may produce feelings of anxiety or personal involvement which one person responds to by taking action (inquiring about the product), while another responds by rejecting it.

Don't consider the impact of the message at this stage; think only about the impact the channel, itself, has. It may take a little effort on your part to separate the channel and the message as you try to determine impact on your customers, but do your best.

Credibility: Credibility is the level of believability, trust, and confidence your customers have in the channel. To most people's minds, certain channels are more credible than others. What's in the minds of your customers? Do they believe the messages that are conveyed by this channel or are they unsure?

Intimacy: Intimacy is the extent to which the channel fosters a close, personal connection between the customer and the message being delivered. Is the channel really speaking to me? Is it drawing me in, or keeping me at a distance? Is it compelling me to respond?

The worksheets already referenced will help you record your thoughts and observations about these criteria. Modify them, if you like, to suit your particular needs. Remember that the result you're after is a clearer, more refined picture of exactly which lead generation channels are "right" for your business—or, more to the point, which ones are the best matches for your target customers.

IT WON'T WORK WITHOUT A PLAN

Creating your lead generation implementation plan is the culmination of your work in this business development process. It will give you the tool for delegat-

Profile of Key Lead Generation Channels

CHANNEL	DESCRIPTION	ADVANTAGES	DISADVANTAGES
NEWSPAPERS		Very accessible; timely; variety of options for size and "sophistication" of ad; excellent coverage of targeted locations; high credibility; repeat exposures from one placement; reasonable cost	Lack of distinctiveness; high level of skimming and skipping; short "shelf life;" relatively poor production quality
MAGAZINES		High prestige and credibility; many options for targeting specific geographic and demographic markets; repeat exposures from one placement; high-quality production; "pass along" readership	High cost; long lead time for placement
TRADE, ORGANIZATIONAL DIRECTORIES/ EXTERNAL NEWSLETTERS	Booklets published by a particular group for distribution to its members, clients, or other specific constituencies, containing name/address/telephone listings and/or advertising	High level of targeting to specific markets; repeat exposures; prestige through association with the sponsoring group; relatively low cost	Inconsistent quality; lack of distinctiveness among listings; text and graphic constraints; may need to meet criteria or requirements for inclusion
TELEPHONE DIRECTORIES		Very accessible; excellent coverage of targeted locations; repeat exposures; long "shelf life"; relatively low cost	Relatively low quality production; long intervals between changes/updates; high clutter
TELEVISION		Multi-sensory; high attention; high impact; high level of coverage of most markets; ability to target demographics	High production cost; high placement cost; fleeting exposure; multiple placements generally required to generate response
RADIO		High level of coverage; ability to target geographic and demographic markets; reasonable cost	Fleeting exposure; moderate level of production effort required to produce effective ad
INTERNET	A collection of international computer networks linked together to form one large network, which provides easy access to information from businesses, universities, governments, and other organizations	Active engagement by customers; convenient; repeat exposures; message and presentation can be changed frequently	High level of effort and expertise to initiate and maintain; lack of access in many markets
DISPLAY/OUTDOOR	A variety of signs generally found in outdoor locations including: signs in windows or on buildings at business locations; small placards and posters hung in various locations; large billboards, usually in heavily trafficked locations along roadways; vehicle displays, such as bumper stickers, signs painted on or attached to your own company vehicles, and your company's advertising displayed on busses, taxis, subways, etc.	High visibility; high repeat exposure; high attention; relatively low cost	Little ability to target demographics
DIRECT MAIL	Marketing/lead generation messages sent individually, via mail, usually to large numbers of potential customers	Ability to select specific, targeted customers; ability to personalize the message; length and depth of message	"Junk mail" image
TELEMARKETING	Marketing/lead generation messages communicated individually, via telephone, to large numbers of potential customers	Ability to select specific, targeted customers; ability to personalize the message; length and depth of message; ability to interact with customer; high level of engagement; ability to get customer's commitment to "next step"	"Nuisance" image
BUSINESS CONVENTIONS/ TRADE SHOWS	Events sponsored by industry, commercial organizations to bring buyers, sellers and other constituents together for a variety of activities, including meetings, information dissemination, demonstrations, networking	Ability to target very specific markets; high attention and engagement; many options for disseminating your message; ability to interact with customer and personalize message; multi-sensory; ability to get customer's commitment to "next step"	High level of effort required; for small businesses, can disrupt normal course of business
PRESS RELEASES/PRODUCT ANNOUNCEMENTS	Information written or prepared by your company and released to various lead generation channels for the purpose of securing non-paid space in those channels to promote your company, product, brand, etc.	High credibility; accessible; timely; excellent coverage of targeted locations; "no" cost	No certainty that items will be placed; lack of control over what ultimately appears

ing your ongoing lead generation work to others in your company with the confidence that they know what to do, when to do it, how much money they can spend, and what result they're after—and that they have the underlying logic to support them in their day-to-day decision making. If yours is a small business and you're the one implementing the plan with little or no support from others, it will act as your personal lead generation "agenda," giving you relief from having to think up your lead generation activities from week to week, and freeing you to focus on the results of what you're doing, rather than on the mechanics of it.

The recommended format for your lead generation implementation plan has three parts:

1. A statement of overall positioning strategy
2. Your monthly lead generation plans
3. Your monthly controlling calendar

Lead Generation Implementation Plan— Part 1: Statement of Overall Positioning Strategy

Your lead generation implementation plan needs to begin with a statement of the overall positioning strategy you've designed for the particular target market you're planning for. The preliminary work for this should be already done. You have already clearly defined your central demographic and psychographic models and your positioning strategy, and created your unique selling proposition and positioning statement for this market in Part Two, Chapter Two. In addition, you should also include a general description of the channels you've selected for this population and your expectations for the lead generation results you're striving for.

This process provides the underlying logic and foundation for the specifics which follow in the rest of the lead generation plan. It also is a necessary link between the two steps of creating the channels plan and then creating the actual messages that will be carried by each of the channels. Here's an example of what this portion of your implementation plan might look like:

LEAD GENERATION IMPLEMENTATION PLAN FOR
WESTERN DISTRIBUTORS, INC.
TARGET MARKET: APPLIANCE RETAILERS (SMALL)

Our primary target market is owners of small retail appliance stores in rural and sub-urban areas of our territory. This segment makes up 78 percent of the appliance businesses (the other 22 percent being large retailers and department stores) and 61 percent of the dollar volume of sales.

The central demographic model of this market segment is male, 45 to 60 years old, business owners with little or no college education, married with three children, and an average total household income of $52,000 per year.

The positioning strategy for this market is:

General classification:	Brand preference
Relative standing:	Preemptive persuasion
Gratification mode:	Interpersonal
Purchase preference:	Value

Western Distributors' positioning with clients is a combination positioning. We are closely identified with the sole manufacturer we represent, which is one of the best-known names in the appliance industry. It is not the "top of the line" manufacturer, but is known more as the "workhorse" appliance for the average household. Although retailers are not compelled to carry our line, it is a great fit with their own preference for value. Our products are the best for the price. We also want to create our own positioning which distinguishes us from other distributors our clients have dealt with. Appliance retailers are often frustrated by distributors' lack of personal attention and lack of ongoing contact with the retailer. We want to play heavily to the interpersonal characteristic of our clients by stressing that our staff will provide friendly, personal service and that it will be easy for the client to maintain contact at whatever level works best for them.

UNIQUE SELLING PROPOSITION: The right products, the right price, the right people.

POSITIONING STATEMENT: As the exclusive representative in your area, we're the trusted experts at providing you with the full range of household appliances that meet all of your valued customers' needs, at a price that fits their lifestyles. We're always here for you to make sure you're able to provide these quality products to your community. Your customers will come back to you, year after year.

Channels and messages should focus heavily on interpersonal elements. Our primary lead generation channels for this market will be: trade show exhibits, trade journal advertising, phone contacts, direct mail reminder cards, follow-up visits to retail locations, and premiums handed out at trade shows and delivered to retail locations.

Our lead generation goals for the plan year will be to increase our market coverage from 60 percent to 90 percent (there is no reason why every small appliance store in the territory shouldn't be exposed to our message) and to increase our sales appointments from three per month per sales representative to one per week in the first four months and up to two per week in the remaining eight months. Our territory is a sufficient size to support this.

Lead Generation Implementation Plan— Part 2: Monthly Lead Generation Plans

This section should have 12 pages, one for each month of the year you're planning. The name of your target market and the month and year should be prominently displayed. It often helps to set up each of the 12 pages with this basic information, and to develop your monthly comments for all 12 months before beginning the detailed planning. This gives you a broad overview from which to construct your plans. Here is a sample plan for one month of Western Distributors' lead generation activities.

LEAD GENERATION PLAN
FOR: APPLIANCE RETAILERS
JUNE 1998

Channel	Comments	Cost	Accountability	Timing
TRADE SHOW	Continue preparations for July trade show	$3,700	Vice President, Marketing	N/A
TRADE JOURNAL	1/2 page ad in Appliance Monthly (Regional Edition)	$ 475	Marketing Assoc.	1 per month automatically placed
PHONE CONTACTS	Introduce company & invite retailer to booth at trade show	0	Marketing Assoc.	10 calls per day, 1st 2 weeks of June
REMINDER CARDS	Follow-up to phone call & others not reached Total 200 cards	$ 150	Marketing Assoc.	Mail by June 22
FOLLOW-UP VISITS	Prepare list for target visits	$ 300	Sales Rep.	5 visits per week
PREMIUMS	Check inventory	0	Marketing Assoc.	6/1
		Total $920		

Comments: Busy month for retailers due to graduations and Father's Day. Lay groundwork for the July trade show with phone calls, reminder cards and delivery of premiums.

Lead Generation Implementation Plan— Part 3: Monthly Controlling Calendars

Completing your implementation plan is a controlling calendar, which takes each monthly plan you've generated and translates it into discrete and specific benchmarks that will accomplish the results you want. Use the *Controlling Calendar Template* to create your own. Remember that the activity on your monthly plan may actually take weeks or even months to plan and execute, and some additional time to follow up. So, while your individual monthly plans give an overall picture of lead generation activities for the month, your controlling calendar provides the necessary plan and detail for how those activities will be accomplished.

Download

BEWARE OF "FALSE PRECISION"

The facts and figures you'll be documenting as you evaluate these channels may tempt you to believe that formulas and worksheets will lead you to a clear conclusion about the "correct" lead generation channels for you. You may even see circulation numbers and demographic data and market research "proving" that one channel is better for you than the others. But beware— don't fall into the trap of believing that data and statistics alone will give you all the answers.

Choosing your lead generation channels is as much an art as a science. Numbers and research aren't as exact or as clear as they seem. Understanding real people isn't a precise exercise, and numbers and research—no matter how precise they seem—are not precise.

Numbers and research are useful in a general way. They can highlight general trends and point you in directions that you probably had not seen before. So, by all means, use them. But use your common sense and experience, too. Ultimately, you'll learn more about your markets from your own tracking and observations. Identifying the right key indicators, tracking them over time, and seeing your lead generation results improve will tell you if you're using the right channels for your customers.

CHANGING CHANNELS . . .

Communicating with your customers is fundamental to the success of your business. Unfortunately, it's anything but obvious, which means of communication will "do the job." Which channels will convey your message in exactly the way you want it conveyed? Which will have the exact impact you want

CONTROLLING CALENDAR

June 1998

ITEM	1	2	3	4	5	8	9	10	11	12	15	16	17	18	19	22	23	24	25	26	29	30
Trade Show													Staff mtg		Prepare Check list	← Assemble Materials →						
Trade Journal										Rec. journal				Review ad								
Phone Contacts	Prepare script	Call 10	Call 10	Call 10	Call 10	Call 10	Call 10	Call 10	Call 10	Call 10	follow up		follow up									
Reminder Cards		Design mtg	Draft copy	Draft art	Review	Final draft		To printer		Review proof	Prepare labels	Receive from printer		Mail								
Follow-up Visits			Prepare list	Review list	Visit 5			Visit 3		Visit 2				Visit 5				Visit 3	Visit 2			Visit 5
Premiums	Check inventory															Collect items for trade show						

them to have? Which will create exactly the right impressions in the minds of your customers?

Your dedication to the work of lead generation is important. As you select the best lead generation channels for your business and your customers and design a plan for using them—and beyond that, as you immerse yourself in the process of doing this work, which you will do over and over again—you will receive tangible and far-reaching results in your business. Results you can measure; results you can feel.

What results? Not only will your business be exposed to larger numbers of qualified leads than ever before, but those leads—those people—will feel more strongly connected and attracted to you than ever before. They'll be queuing up outside your door, calling you, or doing whatever they need to—ready, willing, and able to become lifelong customers. Because you've cared enough to reach them in a way that addresses them as individuals; that speaks to them, touches them, and recognizes their needs and preferences. This is one more piece of your business kaleidoscope that can distinguish you from all the other businesses out there who are vying for your customers.

Application of Lead Generation Principles: Reaching Your Target Markets with Impact

■

We're all flooded daily with information and sensory stimulation. It's surprising that any of us can remember anything! So for an advertiser to be successful at: (a) getting your attention, (b) stimulating your interest, and (c) motivating you to buy the product, everything about the message has to be in sync—not just one isolated element in an otherwise uninspiring ad.

Think of an advertisement or radio or television commercial that really stands out in your mind. What was the product or service? How did the ad affect you? Did you laugh? Cry? Did it make you want the product? Did you take the next step?

If you did, then the advertiser knew her stuff. She knew her ad needed to move her audience through the three phases of lead generation:

- The "instant of connection"
- Reinforcement of the connection
- Transition to lead conversion

In this process you're going to learn the 10-step process for using the elements of lead generation communication to create a message—a magnetic

Application of Lead Generation Principles

Overview

Effective lead generation pieces use the 11 core elements to move the audience through three phases. This booklet explains the 10-step process for creating effective lead generation pieces.

A lead generation "piece" is an advertisement, commercial, or other communication used in lead generation. The six most commonly used channels for lead generation pieces are:

- Print publications (magazines, newspapers, newsletters, directories, etc.)

- Mail (letters, postcards, promotional pieces, etc.)

- Radio (commercials, announcements, special programming, etc.)

- Television (commercials, infomercials, announcements, etc.)

- The Internet (web sites, advertising on the world wide web, etc.)

- Display advertising (billboards, signs, bumper stickers, vehicle signage, etc.)

While the process can seem complex and detailed, at its core it's simply this: Know your target market, get their attention, and tell them what you can do for them.

THE THREE PHASES OF LEAD GENERATION

1. The "Instant of Connection"
2. Reinforcement of the Connection
3. Transition to Lead Conversion

THE ELEVEN ELEMENTS OF AN EFFECTIVE LEAD GENERATION PIECE

1. Context
2. Headline
3. Imagery
4. Sensory elements
5. Brand identity
6. Layout
7. Essential information
8. Format
9. Logic
10. Qualifiers
11. Action steps

Creating Effective Lead Generation Pieces

- Specify Desired Results
- Determine Context Constraints & Opportunities
- Create the "Instant of Connection"
- Define the "Logic" of the Piece
- Determine Essential Information & Establish Format
- Establish Qualifiers
- Include Brand Identification
- Present the Action Steps
- Integrate the Elements
- Produce the Piece

message—that will make your target market fall in love with your product and want to buy it.

THE 10-STEP PROCESS

There's a 10-step process for creating pieces that move prospective customers through the phases of lead generation and accomplish the desired results. The 10-step process applies to all forms of lead generation, all messages, and all channels. The *Ten-Step Process for Creating Effective Lead Generation Pieces* worksheet helps you walk through the process one step at a time to create your own lead generation pieces or help you manage outside experts to do it for you.

Download

Don't expect outside experts like advertising agencies, graphic artists, or copywriters to know this 10-step process. They won't. But the good ones will understand the principles even if they don't know the 10 steps. The others won't understand it and may even resist it. But make sure, even if your outside service providers don't understand the process, that they cover all the points of the process, (you can use the worksheet as a checklist).

The 10-step process is described below.

1. **Specify the desired results.** There are three kinds of results you want your lead generation pieces to achieve with your target market audience:

   ▪ Create favorable impressions about your business and your products and services.
   ▪ Move prospective customers as far along the purchase decision chain as is reasonable.
   ▪ Motivate them to take the action steps you provide in the piece.

   So your first step is to specify exactly what results are achievable for you, given the channel you have selected—exactly what impressions you intend to produce, how far along the purchase decision chain the piece should move

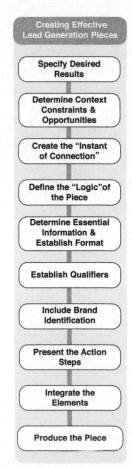

Creating Effective
Lead Generation Pieces

Specify Desired
Results

Determine Context
Constraints &
Opportunities

Create the "Instant
of Connection"

Define the "Logic" of
the Piece

Determine Essential
Information &
Establish Format

Establish Qualifiers

Include Brand
Identification

Present the Action
Steps

Integrate the
Elements

Produce the Piece

prospective customers, and specifically what action you want them to take.

2. **Determine context constraints and opportunities.** The channel you select (magazine, radio, television, etc.) and the specific "vehicle" within that channel (*Playboy* magazine, *Field and Stream, Modern Bride, National Geographic,* etc.) play a major role in shaping your lead generation pieces. Each channel has its constraints and offers its own special opportunities for lead generation.

   You have to look closely at each vehicle and determine its market coverage (how many of your target customers does it "reach"); the likely state of mind of the audience when reading, hearing, or viewing the vehicle; the appropriateness of the vehicle for your products and services; and the surrounding informational and advertising material. Toward the end of this process there is a table, Context Analysis: Channel Constraints and Opportunities, to help you. As you do your context analysis, you may have to adjust some of the results you want to achieve and revise step 1 above.

3. **Create the "instant of connection."** Connection is established with the headline, the primary image presented in the piece, and the sensory elements of the piece. Establishing connection with the target audience, especially doing it within the very brief time you have before you lose them, is truly an art, not a science. There are no hard-and-fast rules. The examples later in this process show some ways to think about how to do it.

   There's an easy way to increase your skill at creating headlines, images, and sensory elements so you can make the most of your opportunity to "connect" with your target market. It won't make you an expert, but it will improve whatever level of skill you already possess.

   What you do is . . . pay attention. When you watch television, listen to the radio, read a magazine or newspaper, or read your mail, pay attention to what you're seeing. Notice the headlines, the images, and the sensory elements in all the advertising that comes your way throughout the day. You might even take some notes. The key is to notice which headlines and images capture your attention and draw you in. The simple act of paying attention will build your skill.

   But it's not quite that simple. You are not your target market, and you're probably nothing like them. So you have to put yourself in the shoes of your target market as best you can. Think like them. See all that advertising the way they see it, not the way you see it. That alone will make you more skillful at creating the "instant of connection" in your lead generation pieces.

Better yet, research your market. Find out what actually does capture their attention, what actually works. Your research can take the form of either market research surveys or your direct experience with your own lead generation. As your knowledge of what works grows, your ability to instantly connect will improve, and your lead generation pieces will yield better and better results.

4. **Define the "logic" of the piece.** If your "instant of connection" is successful, your prospective customer is emotionally inclined to take the next step toward buying your product. But remember from your work in *Customer Perceptions and Behavior* (pp. 136–156), that decisions are made both rationally and emotionally—by the conscious and unconscious minds. The conscious mind provides the rational justification for the emotional decision already, if tentatively, made. So your lead generation piece has to have the necessary rational justification, even if it's only implied.

If that's not clear, think of it this way: If the customer were to ask you, "Why should I do what you're asking me to do?" how would you answer? That's what your lead generation piece has to say to the prospective customer, either explicitly in words or implicitly through images and associations.

Logic is communicated by believable statements—claims and assertions about your business and your products. The statements can be either explicit or implied, but they must be credible. You can establish credibility for your claims in one or a combination of five ways:

- **Self-evident.** The best claim is one that is self-evident to the potential customer—something that is understood to be true with no further support needed. In advertising, there aren't many claims that are self-evident to customers, so other support is usually necessary.
- **Reasoning.** Fact A plus fact B leads to conclusion C. Or, if A then B.
- **Preexisting knowledge, beliefs, or attitudes.** The impressions and assertions made by your lead generation piece have to be consistent with what the prospective customer already knows, believes, thinks, or likes . . . or your piece must reverse contrary views

(much harder than using existing beliefs and attitudes for support).

- **Evidence** in the form of believable data from credible sources or in the form of convincing anecdotes the prospective customer can relate to.
- **Testimony** from experts or credible celebrities.

5. **Determine essential information and establish the format.** When you have the logic for your piece, you have to determine the points of information—the content points—that you'll use to convey the logic and also the format you'll use to make it easy to read (or hear or see) and understand.

Then you write it. It's best to use professional copywriters and script writers—they understand the subtleties of communication and have the necessary writing skills. If you have to do it yourself, *always* have a professional proofreader or editor review it. It's an inexpensive step and can prevent major errors and embarrassments.

The key questions you should consider are "How much do you write?" and "What's the best format?"

How much information you provide depends on three things—the particular communication vehicle you're using (radio commercial, advertisement in a magazine, billboard, mailed brochure, etc.), your product, and the preferences of your target market.

- **The communication vehicle.** The more time and/or space the vehicle provides, the more information you can provide. A television infomercial gives you a half hour, even a full hour, of information and allows you to communicate extremely complex ideas and information, if that's what's needed to accomplish the result you want to accomplish. On the other hand, a billboard alongside a busy highway, while large, gives you only a few seconds of a driver's attention, and limits your content to a very few, simple messages and impressions.
- **Your product.** If yours is a simple product, already well-known to your markets, you need very little information and very little of the customer's attention to communicate it. If yours is a complex product, not well-known in your markets, you'll need more extensive communication and significant time and attention for the customer to absorb it. For complex products and services, it's best to

limit the results you want from your lead generation to simple impressions and easy responses to your pieces. Or you'll need to select vehicles that accommodate more images and information.

- **Your target market.** If the target market's purchase decision process is complex and needs lots of support and interaction with your business, then lead generation is probably only the very front end of the process, and your lead generation pieces can only take you a little ways along the purchase decision chain. If the purchase decision is simple and quick, the opposite is true. Also, some markets are more receptive to visual communication, some want information to read, some want interaction, some don't. Always consider the behavior of your target market.

Format, like so much in lead generation, is an art, not a science. In general, long blocks of undifferentiated text or narrative get ignored, no matter how valuable the information they contain. So, if you have a great deal of information, make extensive use of eye-catching subheadlines, boldface type, underlining colors, shapes, images interspersed with the text—anything that helps the major points stand out and attract the eye of the reader. For audible communications, sound effects, pacing, dialogue (rather than narrative), and volume shifts (shouting to whispering, for instance) add interest and draw the listener's attention to important points.

Don't overdo these attention-drawing devices. An advertisement full of subheadings, boldface type, bullet points, and eye-catching type fonts defeats its own purpose. It all adds up to clutter and confusion, and readers will reject it. Use attention-getting devices sparingly and only to draw attention to key points.

There are no hard-and-fast rules for formatting. The only reliable guidance is to know your target audience, and focus on the key points—key points from the customer's point of view, not yours. If you must present a lot of information, make it easy to skim.

6. **Establish qualifiers.** Your lead generation pieces can't screen out unqualified potential customers—anyone can respond who wants to respond, qualified or not. But you can design your pieces so unqualified leads screen themselves out and qualified leads "screen" themselves in. And you can do it in ways that avoid negative impressions of exclusion or arrogance on your part. Think explicit and implicit, and inclusive and exclusive.

Implicit qualification is built into your lead generation piece automatically if you design it to appeal primarily to qualified leads. If you know who your target market is, including a thorough psychographic profile, then implicit qualification should be automatic. Your message and all the other elements of the piece will be designed for qualified leads and will appeal mainly to them and not unqualified leads.

Explicit qualification occurs when you specifically identify the kinds of people who need your product or service and will be attracted by your business. A headline such as "If you fly more than 50,000 miles a year, you should fly Aeromax Airlines" is an explicit qualifier. (If Aeromax also wants to attract infrequent fliers, however, this headline would tend to screen them out.)

Every advertisement you'll ever see for Rolls-Royce automobiles will feature images relevant to wealthy people who enjoy the finer things in life. That's an implicit qualification, designed to appeal to economically upscale people.

An inclusive qualifier indicates what kind of people *should* respond to the piece. An exclusionary qualifier indicates those who *should not* respond. As a general rule exclusionary qualifiers aren't a good idea, especially explicit ones, because they tend to be demeaning or insulting. Can you imagine Rolls-Royce using a line in its advertising such as "If you make less than a half a million a year, don't bother"?

7. **Include brand identification.** Brand identification is as important as it is easy. Always, always, always include the product or service name and your business's name in every piece. In print or other visible vehicles, also include your logo and appropriate brand identification images if you have them. In audible pieces, also include any sound "images" if you have those (such as theme songs, jingles, or other distinctive sounds that are associated with your brand).

You can mention or show brand identifiers anywhere in each piece, but you should also position them as follows:

- **Print and display pieces.** Show product and company names and logo at the lower right corner. The eye travels from upper left to lower right, so, generally, the last thing a reader sees, and the last impression made, is that of the logo, product name, and company name.
- **Broadcast pieces.** Show names and logo, and announce names and audible brand indicators at the end of each piece. Again, the last

impression, if the rest of the piece has done its work, identifies the product and is a key element of reinforcement.

8. **Present the action steps.** This step is simple but critical. The idea is to make it easy for a customer to buy from you or to take the next step into your lead conversion system. You need to be clear about the results you intend the piece to achieve, then make it a "no-brainer" for the customer to act.

There are two parts to each action step. First you have to tell the prospective customer what you want him or her to do; then you have to provide the mechanism for doing it. If you want them to telephone you, then ask them to call, and make it easy with an easy-to-remember, toll-free telephone number. If you want them to mail you a response, include an easy-to-complete, postage-paid, preaddressed response card.

And, of course, make it as risk-free as you possibly can—no obligation to buy, money-back guarantee, and similar assurances. Risk, from the customer's point of view, means financial risk and the risk that your product or service might not be satisfactory, but it also includes the "risk" of annoyance, hard sell, and any other kind of personal discomfort that might occur when they contact you.

So tell them what you want them to do. Make it easy for them to do it. Make it as risk-free as possible.

9. **Integrate the elements.** At this point in the process, you have all the elements of an effective lead generation piece. But there's one more step before production—integration. It's the layout step. Everything must fit together as a unified, balanced whole—it's not a bunch of parts; it's one unified thing. If it's a visual piece, make sure it's visually "balanced" and appealing to look at—or shocking if that's the effect you want. Make sure nothing stands out unless you want it to stand out. If it's an audible piece, make sure it sounds right, balanced, with the right pace, the right mix of sounds, creating the impact you intend it to create.

The point of the integration step is to arrange the elements so the audience's attention flows smoothly (or jerkily, if that's the effect you want) from one element to another and so the entire piece is a unified whole.

The best way to develop the layout and integrate the elements is "draft and sketch." For print-only pieces (for publications, display pieces, or brochures), you make sketches showing the relative positions of the various elements and draft the text portions, including the format elements. For auditory pieces, you draft the script, annotating the various sound effects, music, etc. For visual/action pieces, you draft the script, as you would for auditory pieces, and also sketch a "storyboard." A storyboard is a series of sketches, each showing a key part, or "scene" of the piece. Sketches can be extremely rough; you don't have to be an artist to get the idea and a general impression of the impact of the piece.

You may have to go through several draft-and-sketch cycles before the piece begins to approach its final, most effective configuration. Even then, you won't know until it's in almost final form. Typically, even the professionals fine-tune their pieces right up to the last minute before final production, often making adjustments during the production process itself.

Each time you complete a draft-and-sketch and have a layout and sequence that seems right, ignore for a moment the logic of the various elements. You've done your rational best developing the draft-and-sketch. Now, look at the piece as a whole, and see if it makes the impact you want it to make. This is the "gut feel" test where your intuition and sense of taste and balance take over. If it feels "off," then something probably is "off" and needs adjustment.

Remember this. You pay a lot of attention and put a lot of thought into each lead generation piece. Your target customers don't. If they notice it at all, they see it fleetingly, hear it with only "half an ear." It's the holistic impact that will capture them, so each piece has to work in a holistic way until the attention of the audience is captured. Then, and only then, will they pay attention to any of the details of the piece. The integration step may, in the end, be the most important of all.

10. **Produce the piece.** Once you've completed the previous nine benchmarks, it only remains to produce the piece, place it in the selected communication vehicle, and wait for results. And, of course, quantify the results and learn from your quantified experience how to improve each piece.

SIX COMMON LEAD GENERATION CHANNELS . . . PLUS ONE

The previous process, *Lead Generation Channels,* identified 12 kinds of channels you can use to communicate your lead generation messages, and the advantages and disadvantages of each. In this process, you're going to focus on the six most commonly used ones. You'll also look at brochures, which are not actually a "channel" (they're often used as a lead conversion piece, after a qual-ified lead is contacted), but which also follow the same 10-step process and have the same 11 elements as do lead generation pieces. These most commonly used channels are:

Publications
Mail
Radio
Television
Internet
Display Advertising
Brochures

Don't feel limited by these seven. If you're successfully using other channels, by all means, stick with them, improve them. And keep your mind open for other opportunities.

Each channel provides opportunities for lead generation communica-tions, but each also has constraints and limitations associated with it. The table on the following pages outlines some of the opportunities and constraints.

IT'S ALL ABOUT PEOPLE WHO NEED YOU

There's a lot of seeming complexity in lead generation. Three phases. Eleven el-ements. Ten steps. It seems almost mathematical. Mechanical. Clinical. It's easy to lose sight of the fact that, at its core, lead generation is really quite simple.

It's all about people with needs.

It's not mechanical. It's human.

At its most basic level, lead generation is identifying people with needs you can satisfy, and telling them so in ways they can understand quickly and easily. It's getting their attention and talking to them. Keep that in mind and the rest is detail. Important detail—people can be amazingly complex and subtle—but detail nonetheless.

Identifying people who need what you have to offer is the heart of the channel selection process you saw in the previous process, "Lead Generation Channels." Telling them what you can do for them is the heart of lead genera-tion communications.

So, while immersed in the details of context analysis, designing images, writing headlines, sketching layouts, drafting scripts, and all the other details of the process, keep in mind that you're merely communicating with people who need what you have to offer. All you have to do is get their attention and tell them what you can do for them.

Context Analysis: Channel Constraints & Opportunities

CHANNEL	CONSTRAINTS	OPPORTUNITIES
PUBLICATIONS (Examples: magazines, newspapers, newsletters, directories, etc.)	■ Print only; no sound or motion. ■ Schedule requirements or limitations. ■ Limited to the size and shape of the pages of the publication. Sometimes limited to black and white or limited colors or print quality. ■ Look for editorial content and surrounding advertising that is compatible with your business and your products and is appropriate for your target market. ■ Look for distribution/circulation that matches your target market profile, including psychographics.	■ Extremely versatile as to size, colors, images, layout, formatting, placement within the publication. ■ Good ability to reach your target market. ■ Costs easy to control. ■ Repeat exposures likely. ■ Enormous variety of publications available – you're almost certain to find several that work for your target markets. ■ Can carry large amounts of text if needed.
MAIL (Examples: post cards, letters, promotional pieces, etc.)	■ Print only; no sound or motion. ■ Mail "clutter" makes it hard to draw and hold customer's attention. ■ Copy writing and formatting are critical. ■ Hard to avoid perceptions of "junk mail." ■ Some size and weight constraints due to costs, but easy to control. ■ Can be screened out by household members or by assistants.	■ Good to excellent ability to reach your target market, depending on quality of mailing list. ■ Extremely flexible; can include a wide variety of items, sizes, colors, shapes, formats, etc. ■ Can control reach precisely to control inflow of leads. ■ No "context" problems because mail is standalone. ■ Easy to personalize.
RADIO (Examples: commercials, announcements, specials, etc.)	■ Limited ability to focus on your target market; a lot of "wasted" reach. Seemingly low cost may be high based on actual target market reached (cost per lead). ■ Sound only; no visual elements. ■ Linear; limited to sequential presentation of information. ■ Commercial clutter. ■ Look for programming content and surrounding advertising that is compatible with your business and products and appropriate for your target market. ■ Look for days and times of day that work for your target market.	■ High energy, music, drama available. ■ Extremely versatile. Can do everything from narrative only to exciting drama. ■ Extremely accessible; radio stations will often assist you with production.
TELEVISION (Examples: commercials, announcements, infomercials, etc.)	■ Very limited ability to focus on your target market; a lot of "wasted" reach. ■ High cost. May be even higher based on actual target market reached (cost per lead). ■ Commercial clutter. ■ Look for programming content and surrounding advertising that is compatible with your business and products and appropriate for your target market. ■ Look for days and times of day that work for your target market.	■ Extremely versatile. Any combination of print, audio, visual, action. ■ The most powerful channel with highest potential for impact and information. Simultaneous multisensory impact possible (image plus print plus action plus voice plus sound effects).

Context Analysis: Channel Constraints & Opportunities

CHANNEL	CONSTRAINTS	OPPORTUNITIES
THE INTERNET (Examples: websites, advertising on the Web, etc.)	▪ Reach limited to people with access to computers and knowledge of how to use them. ▪ Market coverage statistics not readily available, hence difficult to plan communications campaigns and estimate results. ▪ Mainly print and images. ▪ Computers of viewers vary, so screen size and other visual elements may not be perfectly communicated. ▪ Internet clutter. ▪ Some technical skills necessary for design and production.	▪ For the right kinds of businesses, can provide explosive growth. ▪ Highly versatile; mainly visual, but sound and action available. ▪ Extremely rapid growth. Reach getting broader daily. ▪ Can be interactive, hence can move customers a long way down the purchase chain.
DISPLAY ADVERTISING (Examples: billboards, signs, bumper stickers, vehicle signage, etc.)	▪ Print/visual only; no auditory or action. ▪ Brief attention opportunity limits amount and complexity of images and information to a very small amount. Can't move the customer very far along the purchase decision chain. ▪ Location site and placement at the location site are critical to effectiveness for stationary pieces. ▪ Make sure location and surroundings are appropriate for your target market.	▪ Generally very low cost. ▪ High incidence of repeat viewing. ▪ Simplicity – relatively easy to design and write.
BROCHURES (Examples: booklets, fliers, catalogs, etc.)	▪ Visual and text only; no sound or motion. ▪ High front-end development effort and cost, especially for larger, more complex pieces. ▪ No context problems because it's a stand-alone piece.	▪ Highly flexible; everything from fliers and handouts to multi-page booklets and catalogs. ▪ Unlimited use of pictures and other images. ▪ Unlimited use of text (although formatting can get complex when making large amounts of information readable and skimmable).

EXAMPLES

Example 1: Publications Channel— Advertisement in Trade Magazines

■

SWENSON AND SONS

Swenson and Sons has manufactured exercise and athletic equipment for three generations. Its lead generation communications have never been as successful as the owner wished, in spite of the fairly large budget devoted each year to advertising and other promotions.

Let's see what happened as Mike Swenson worked through the process for creating an advertisement, which will run in trade magazines. First he identified the results he wanted to achieve and the steps that would motivate his potential customers into action.

> Our target market is fitness equipment retailers and health clubs around the world, and occasionally individuals who want to purchase home fitness equipment directly from us. Exercise equipment is not an "impulse buy," so we don't expect our advertisement to result in an instant purchase.
>
> I want our lead generation message to accomplish several things. First, I want it to tell people how committed we are to the quality of our products, and to show the pride with which we produce them. We've been in business for more than three generations, and I want people to know that we're not a fly-by-night fitness company that sells flimsy, faddish equipment. I also want our message to encourage more retailers and health club owners to carry our brand in their stores and in their gyms. And, since we do sell directly to individuals, I also want to introduce our equipment to the public at large. We'll give them an 800–number to call for a free catalog, as well as our website address where they can view the catalog online.

Next, Mike took a closer look at the particular channel he chose to work with:

> We decided to place our ad in fitness and exercise trade magazines because of their ability to reach our target market through repeated exposure. We've analyzed the surrounding messages in the magazines that we've chosen. They consist of ads for juice drinks, power bars, other fitness equipment manufacturers, vitamins, health clubs, and exercise clothes. Our target market is fitness-oriented and seeks top-quality and innovative fit-

ness equipment that will last for a long time. And they're willing to pay extra for it.

With a clear idea of the results he wanted and the "context analysis" that told him what would be appropriate to the trade magazine channel, Mike put together the elements of an effective print advertisement. He summarized his thought process as follows:

We want people to associate the hard work they do on their bodies in the gym with the hard work we do in manufacturing our products. We choose for our headline:

YOU SWEAT. WE SWEAT.

This will be placed top center, in a large, easy-to-read style of font. To reinforce the headline, we'll have a background image of one of our employees assembling a piece of our equipment.

The logic and essential information of our message will be centered below the headline, in a smaller, contrasting font style:

YOU WANT THE BEST FITNESS EQUIPMENT THAT MONEY CAN BUY.
YOU WANT IT TO LAST.
YOU WANT GUARANTEED SERVICE WHEN YOU NEED IT.
YOU'VE GOT IT.
WE PUT AS MUCH SWEAT INTO BUILDING OUR PRODUCT AS YOU DO IN
BUILDING YOUR BODY.

Finally, we'll include the following "evidence" to support the logic of the piece:

---

500 FITNESS CLUBS AROUND THE WORLD USE OUR EQUIPMENT EXCLUSIVELY.

VOTED NUMBER ONE BY THE WORLD FITNESS EQUIPMENT
MANUFACTURERS ASSOCIATION.

"I OWN A GYM IN SAUSALITO. WE ONLY USE SWENSON AND SONS
FITNESS EQUIPMENT BECAUSE OF ITS QUALITY
AND EASE OF USE."—GYM OWNER IN SAUSALITO, CA

Mike chose not to include an explicit qualifier in his message because he advertised in magazines specifically focused on his target market—therefore, he felt that the audience was already prequalified. So he finished his lead generation message with the action step, brand identification, and logo.

CALL FOR OUR NEW 1999 CATALOG. 1-800-456-9999, OR VISIT OUR WEBSITE
AT WWW.SWENSONANDSONS.COM

SWENSON AND SONS. MAKERS OF QUALITY FITNESS EQUIPMENT SINCE 1932
[LOGO PLACED IN LOWER RIGHT CORNER]

Example 2: Mail Channel—
Direct Mail letter to Local Businesses

■

COUNT ON US!

Count On Us! is a small bookkeeping firm owned by Susan Meadows. Susan's business generates about $500,000 in annual gross revenues and she has eight employees. Her business primarily involves entering and reconciling budgetary, financial, and accounting data for local businesses. Susan's business is busy with her present clients, but she feels like she doesn't have enough new business walking through her door.

Susan produced a direct mail piece that was mailed to local small businesses in her community.

I'm really proud of my business and my employees. We do a great job! And I want my potential customers to experience that when they read my direct mail piece.

My preferred way of introducing myself is by phone or in person. Since that's too time-consuming, I decided to do a direct mail piece that will encourage them to contact me for a free, half-hour consultation. I'll enclose a postage-paid response card for their convenience in responding.

I chose direct mail because of its precise ability to reach my target market, which consists of responsible, busy, lower- to middle-class businesspeople and tradespeople. They want dependability and proven quality; also, they're cautious and sometimes mistrustful. I believe that using this channel, direct mail, is the best use of my budget and will have the greatest impact.

I've analyzed other direct mail pieces, and I want to avoid as much as possible being perceived as "junk" mail. To do that, I'm going to send an upscale, very businesslike letter, as opposed to a postcard, which reflects a lack of privacy and resembles "junk" mail—confidentiality is important in my business.

With direct mail the "instant of connection" happens twice—first with the envelope, and then with the letter. The envelope connection is subtle and implicit—no message on the envelope but it will be high quality, very professional, and understated so the connection will be based on unconscious association (classy, upscale, and businesslike, inferring "that's like me," or "that's like I want to be").

Susan knew from some recent research from her trade association that all bookkeepers are highly accurate and about the same price, so that wasn't the way to establish "preferential differentiation." She decided to focus on the three most common frustrations with accounting and bookkeeping services, which were: slow turnaround time; bookkeepers "don't understand my business"; and poor performance of special requests. Here's her direct mail letter:

> *Wouldn't it be great if your bookkeeping service was fast, knew your business better than anyone except you, and did what you wanted when you wanted it? That's our promise to you, and I'd like to talk with you about it.*
>
> *We specialize in providing bookkeeping and accounting services to individuals and small businesses of 25 employees or less, and we'd like to introduce you to our services by way of a free, 30-minute consultation.*
>
> *Please return the enclosed postage-paid card, and we'll contact you to set up an appointment. Or, if you'd prefer, call us at our toll-free number: 1-800-123-7000. We'll be happy to answer any questions you might have.*

I know that short paragraphs and bolding or underscoring key words are essential to keeping someone's attention in a direct mail piece. So I'm going to highlight words like "fast," "better," "promise," and "free."

My logo is located at the top of the letterhead, and I will place my USP at the bottom center.

COUNT ON US! OUR NAME SAYS IT ALL.

Example 3: Radio Channel—Local Radio Advertisement

■

CHAN'S DELECTABLES

May Chan owns the best gourmet deli and gift store in her community. She receives most of her business solely by word of mouth, although she occasionally does some advertising. But for the most part, she doesn't do anything at all to generate new customers.

My business just kind of grew up around me. But now that my business is growing, I'd really like to reach beyond my community. And word of mouth—which is how I've gotten customers all these years—can only go so far. I'd like my customers to perceive my business as a gourmet deli, specializing in the finest imported foods and gifts in the area. I'll encourage them to come in for lunch, or to stop on their way home to pick up something for dinner.

I know that radio commercials aren't especially effective at reaching specific target markets. But I don't need to reach my entire market. For what I wish to accomplish, the cost of doing this commercial seems reasonable enough.

I'm going to advertise during the morning weekday rush hour so that I reach people before they start thinking about what they're going to do for lunch that day. The radio station I chose plays soft rock music and is geared toward my target market of people in their 30s to 50s who eat out at lunch and can afford more than fast food. They seek variety and a better than average lunch experience.

My commercial will be dialogue between two people who are having lunch in my deli. For the background music I chose Vivaldi's "Four Seasons" because it will contrast but not conflict with the surrounding material on the radio station. The music will be playing softly in the background while they're dining. The surrounding conversation is lively, but not intrusive.

Sue: "Wow, James. Chan's is such a great place! How'd you find it?"
James: "It's been here for a long time. I come here about twice a week. They always have something new and exciting on the menu, and the ingredients they use are always fresh. I like to bring clients here because the ambiance is so nice. But you can still get in and out within an hour."
Sue: "Bringing clients is a great idea, but I can also come for a quick lunch."
James: "And they're open late, so I like to stop on my way home to pick up something for dinner."
Sue: "That's great. I'm going to tell everyone at work about Chan's."

Friendly, male announcer:

Chan's Delectables, at the corner of First and Main in Bridgeport, has been a downtown institution for more than 20 years. Come in for lunch, or stop by on your way home to pick up dinner for the family.

Example 4: Television Channel—
Advertisement on Local Television Station

■

WHAT TO WEAR, INC.

What To Wear, Inc. is a retail clothing business owned by Joan and Tony Romero. Their three stores specialize in men's and women's sportswear and they employ about 22 people. They've been in business for 20 years.

The sale of our women's clothing has been on the rise in recent months, but our men's clothing sales have slumped. Men typically dislike the shopping experience, and will only step foot into a retail clothing store if they absolutely must. Or they send their wives or girlfriends in to shop for them. Even though that often results in sales, it also results in more returned merchandise when men are unhappy with the selection. So we want to encourage more men in our target market to shop in our stores.

We chose a television commercial because of its visual appeal. Even though the cost is high, we believe it will have the greatest impact on our target market. These are men and women in their late 30s to mid 50s, married, middle- to upper-income. Their recreational activities revolve around their children's baseball or soccer games, and occasional games of golf. They don't spend a lot of money on things outside of their homes or children. And they don't make impulse purchases—they have a very clear idea of what they want and in what style and brand.

Our commercial will be shot inside one of our stores on a busy Saturday morning. The female announcer will be walking down the aisle toward the men's department, where a male customer is engaged by a "personal shopper" who is showing the customer a few articles of clothing. They're both smiling.

We're going to air the commercial during weekday evening television shows appearing on our local station between 5:30 and 9:30 P.M., and during morning news programs and televised golf tournaments on weekend days.

Our headline will be:

DOES SHOPPING FOR CLOTHES EXCITE YOU
ABOUT AS MUCH AS DOING YOUR TAXES?

At What To Wear we want your shopping experience to be better than that. To make it easier for you, one of our personal shoppers will ask you questions about your sizes and preferred styles and brands of sportswear. Then, whenever you're ready to shop for clothes, all you have to do is call us and we'll have a selection of your favorite styles for you to look at when you arrive. That's it. Easy and stress-free.

We carry a large selection of the latest men's fashions. Come see our new line of Men's Club Sportswear—perfect for casual Fridays or weekends.

What To Wear . . . Come in and experience a different way to shop for clothes.

Example 5: Internet Channel—Website on the Internet

▪

THE OUTER EDGE COMPANY

The Outer Edge Company manufactures and distributes canvas products for outdoor leisure activities such as camping, hunting, fishing, and nature sports. Its main line of products is knapsacks, tents, and weather-resistant outerwear. The Outer Edge is owned by John Grayson.

It's quite expensive to produce a three-color catalog, four times a year, and deliver it to our entire target market. We've decided to put our catalog online for our new and existing customers to browse through as well as make online purchases. If they still want a printed catalog, we'll provide that as well. Ideally, the result I'd like to achieve is for the customer to make an actual online purchase, or call our 800–number to place an order. Alternatively, we'd like customers to send us their names and addresses to be placed on our catalog mailing list.

Our target market is upscale, adventuresome types who want products that are functional, attractive, durable, and dependable. They get bored easily and are somewhat dissatisfied with their day-to-day lives. They crave adventure. They probably fantasize about climbing Mount Everest, but realistically they're satisfied climbing the pseudorock wall at their local gym. Our website will contain images of those "higher" experiences that they would like to envision themselves doing—for instance, climbers reaching the summit of Mount Everest; kayakers on a raging river; the Tour de France bicycle race.

My market is fairly upscale, and the majority of them are computer savvy and have their own computers. And, while the Internet itself is still fairly complex and difficult to control, it's also the latest and greatest in technology and my customers love that. So I think a website will appeal to them.

Layout is critical in a website, not only to capture and hold the customer's attention, but also to help move him to information of interest and to bypass information of no interest. John's thoughts about the layout were:

Our name and logo will be placed at the top of every page.

The central image on the first page will be that of a string of climbers reaching the summit of Mt. Everest. The caption next to it will be our USP, which is:

The Outer Edge Company. Performance for Adventure!

Along the bottom will be a series of icons and captions which, when clicked, will lead the customer through our website. These will be labeled:

➤ **View our catalog.** When clicked, this will take the customer to the first page of the online catalog. From this point, he will make further selections based on the type of equipment he is looking for. Each of these categories will contain images pertaining to that particular activity. Within each category will be the option to place an order or search for an item by name or number. The customer won't waste time paging through hundreds of items of no interest. With just a few mouse clicks, he'll zero in on exactly what he's looking for. He'll stay engaged because he'll only see what he wants to see.

➤ **Make a purchase.** If you already know the item number of the item you wish to purchase, click here.

➤ **Request a catalog.** If you'd like to be placed on our mailing list and receive a catalog, click here.

➤ **Customer service.** If you have questions about our products or about an order you've placed, click here.

➤ **About our company.** To learn about our company or to review current job opportunities, click here.

➤ **Questions or comments?** Click here to send us an email.

➤ **Want to talk to us?** Call 1-800-999-1234. We have representatives available to answer your questions or take your order 7 days a week, from 8 a.m.–10 p.m., Pacific Standard Time.

There will be links on each page for all of the above options so that the customer can get anywhere in the website without having to go back to page one.

■

STERLING KITCHENS AND BATHS

Sterling Kitchens and Baths is a home remodeling business owned and operated by Millie Stone and her two sons, Ethan and Stuart. They work with property owners to design and renovate kitchens and bathrooms, and act as general contractors to accomplish the remodeling of their clients' homes.

Ours is a face-to-face business—customers typically come to see us after we've talked to them on the phone. We realized that we needed some kind of "in-between" communication for our customers to take with them when they leave our store, because we usually don't make a sale in the first meeting. We want to provide our customers with information that they can review on their own time. So, although our brochure won't result in an instant sale, we think it will provide our customers with the information they need in order to move toward a purchase.

Our target market are middle- to upper-income, married homeowners with children, who have lived in their homes for more than five years. These are people who value their privacy, and may have never experienced contractors in their homes for an extended period of time. So one of the things we want to stress is how professional we are, and how their homes and their lives will be disrupted as little as possible. We also want to impress upon our customers the beauty and quality workmanship of our remodeling projects.

On the front cover of the brochure will be three overlaid photos of some of the kitchens and bathrooms we've designed. The caption below it will read:

FUNCTION MADE BEAUTIFUL

We want to make an upscale, classy impression, with lots of high-quality photos of our work, so our brochure will be full-sized (8½ x 11), four-color, heavy paper stock with a semiglossy finish.

We'll place our name at the top of the front cover, and our logo, address, and phone number will be placed bottom center.

On the inside front cover we'll have the following text:

Sterling Kitchens and Baths has been making rooms beautiful for over a decade. We use only the highest-quality materials, and our

craftspeople and contractors are recognized as the best in the industry.

We understand how awkward it can be to have strangers working in your home while remodeling. We will make that experience stress-free and enjoyable. You and your home will be treated respectfully and professionally from beginning to end.

Our work is 100% guaranteed. At Sterling Kitchens and Baths, your home remodeling project isn't finished until you say it is.

The rest of the brochure will be a multipage booklet with before-and-after photos of kitchens and baths we've designed. Next to each picture we'll have a few major points about the particular layout, such as the materials used, the space needed for installation, and an estimate of cost depending upon the materials chosen. We'll make notes in the brochure as we lead the customer around our showroom so that they will recall what they looked at after they leave.

The photos will be lush and rich, showing the beauty and quality of the demonstrated rooms.

The last two pages will be blank, and there will be plenty of white space throughout so customers can take notes.

On the inside back cover we'll place the following text in the middle, right above slots where the salesperson will insert her business card:

IF YOU HAVE ANY QUESTIONS ABOUT ANY OF OUR KITCHENS OR BATHS, PLEASE CONTACT US AT 1-800-4BEAUTY.

On the outside back cover, bottom center, we will place our name, logo, address, and phone number.

Example 7: Display/Signage Channel— Outdoor Billboard Advertisement

■

BUGGBUSTERS, INC.

BuggBusters, Inc. is a growing pest control company with an innovative, high-tech method for exterminating termites. It is owned by Mike Furgeson.

Mike discussed his reasons for choosing this particular channel for his lead generation message, and the pros and cons of doing so.

I know I can't move people very far down the purchase decision chain us-ing this particular channel, but that's fine because people don't call me unless they need me anyway! I just want people to become familiar with our name and what we do.

It was easy for me to choose a billboard because my services can be needed any time, in any place. So virtually anyone that drives by could become a customer. Fortunately for my business, termites aren't discriminating!

The downside of choosing this channel is that I have very little time for my message to grab someone's attention when they're traveling down the highway at 65 mph. I also know that people are probably not going to stop to jot down my phone number so that they can give me a call. But the repeat exposure will be great, and I think my billboard will be catchy enough that people will remember my name.

My target market is low- to middle-income homeowners who live in the suburbs. I'm going to place my billboards near the neighborhoods in which they live, as well as along major commute routes.

Mike realized that he needed to accomplish a lot in very little time and space so his message had to be short and to the point. He chose to incorporate all of the elements of his message in the following information:

> Image on the left: A big bug in a red circle.
> Caption below: Now you see 'em . . .
> Image on the right: A green circle with BuggBusters logo in it.
> Caption below: Now you don't.
> **BuggBusters**
> **1-800-BUG-BUST**

EPILOGUE

"You must do the thing you think you cannot do."

Eleanor Roosevelt

So here we are, on the mountain together. Few people ever get this far! And at this place, and at this time, having struggled mightily to get where we are, all of us, you, me and Sarah, have three choices: go back down the mountain, back where we started, and give up the climb; stay where we are and settle down, to build a little house, a fence, and raise some chickens; or continue to climb.

Only three options.

What shall it be?

I promised Sarah months ago that I would share with her how the story at my company ended. When the time was right. Well, I think this is the right time. Now that we've made it this far. And we're looking at the options from here.

I had the same three options back then. When the storm of disaster almost overtook me. When I faced financial ruin, emotional devastation of the worst kind, chaos and confusion beyond belief, angry people all around me doing their utmost to undo me, believing in their heart of hearts that I deserved it, and that my company would never withstand the unmerciful tidal wave they had unleashed.

They were wrong. While the option to file bankruptcy and start over was always tempting us, while the option to continue to limp along in the undignified state of insolvency was always lingering around, while these two options were always *there,* the only truly viable option for us was to climb, an inch at a time if necessary, until we found much higher ground. This was the only option that honored the commitment we made when I started the company in 1977: to become the premier provider of small business services world-wide.

So, in the middle of a tumultuous storm, without a tent, a backpack, or anything to tether me to the earth, with no guide I could trust, with only my warrior wife at that time and partner, Ilene, and a handful of strong-minded, willful, and dedicated climbers, we started up the mountain, ready to respond to whatever life handed us.

The decision to persist, to continue to pursue my vision, to make things right for the innocent people who were hurt by my ignorance and stupidity, created, more than anything, the miracles, and I mean miracles, that led us out of the blinding storm to the place on the mountain where we could see the most spectacular views through clear, blue skies.

Here are a few of the miracles.

I remember the day that Ilene returned to the office to tell me about her visit to Pac Bell, the telephone company to whom we owed $140,000, the largest past due balance in their history we were told. That they didn't cut off our phone service was a miracle in and of itself. Ilene had walked into their 10,000-square-foot open office in San Jose, filled with endless workstations, to hand a woman the last check, the final payment, and everyone in the office stood up and cheered! I guess they had heard our story. I guess they had never known anyone like Ilene, who made promises and kept them.

I remember the day that we were waiting to hear the outcome of a five-day arbitration in San Francisco, where one of the ex-franchisees had sued us for all sorts of horrible crimes, and we had countersued for breach of contract. Despite the fact that all of the other franchise suits had been settled out of court, despite the fact that we had made several generous offers to this particu-lar ex-franchisee to avoid litigation, he persisted in his pursuit of his $2 million claim. While we were realistically anticipating some modest, perhaps $50,000, award in his favor for technical violations of the franchise law, when the call came, when our attorney's secretary called us to read us the arbitrators' deci-sion, it was a miraculous *$620,000 award in our favor!* The vindication we had waited for for six long years had finally come. I remember that Ilene, who was eight months pregnant with our daughter Alex at the time, laughed and cried so hard that she left a puddle of pee on the carpet in my office.

And I'll never forget the morning two very stern-looking marshals came into our office to execute on a judgment and planted themselves in the finance area to wait for the postman to deliver the day's mail, and how, miraculously, our normally integrous, but definitely uncourageous, finance manager, with absolute daring and not a single thought about the consequences to himself, slid out of the office unnoticed at the exact moment that the postman was coming up the walk, to collect the mail and separate out the envelopes that looked like they had checks in them so that the mail that ended up in the marshals' hands had no money in it.

And I'll never forget that breakfast at the Westin Hotel, at the San Francisco Airport, in 1991—after six unbearable years of struggle, after feeling about as close to being forced to close our doors as I ever had, after so many meetings with potential investors who got our hopes up and sent us into crashing disappointment—with a man who told us, in this strangely genuine way, that he could "write a check for $250,000 without thinking twice." Somehow, Ilene and I just knew, in that moment, that our torture was miraculously about to end. He was, in fact, the real deal and loaned the company the money it needed to retire its remaining debts and start on a path to healing. We paid him back, too.

In between these miraculous moments, which, at the time, seemed too few and far between, but are now unforgettable, the whole thing felt like it was going to destroy us. At times, many times, we just knew we couldn't make it, but then one of us would say to the other, let's just get through today. And we would, moved by the spirit of our people or our clients or a generous creditor, by the love of our shared mission, the soulful, grounded incredible vision we shared, as we climbed and climbed, up, up, up.

The nights were the worst. Most nights Ilene and I felt like we were going to die.

The mountain was a monster.

But I'm here to tell you, we climbed it. And the company that we envisioned is more than alive and well.

It's a completely different world.

Since I wrote *The Power Point* in 1992, the company has grown three times its size and is continuing to grow. We long ago paid off all the debt. Other than lines of credit we use from time to time for operating purposes—a miracle in itself given what a pariah we were in the banking community for so many years—the company is debt free. It generates very respectable profits and there is plenty of cash in the bank, tons of it from my perspective, after all the years we lived with a negative cash position. And the culture of financial oversight and attention that we developed out of need continues to proliferate. The company works better than most and is always improving, always becoming more systematized, always reaching for that scintillating something far off in the sky, called Perfect.

And Ilene and I no longer work in the company. Just as we teach the clients who are interested, we have freed ourselves from day-to-day operations and have turned the reins over to professional management, led by a world class chief executive officer whose mandate it is to hit specific growth targets over the next four years. Ilene and I are the primary shareholders, and hold positions on the board. Ilene regularly consults with the company and lives a life she has crafted out of the freedom the company has provided for her. I am the company's chief rainmaker, writing and speaking to expanding audiences. My books have sold more than two million copies, have been published in 19 languages, and are on the most successful business books of all time lists.

E-Myth Worldwide is a stunner, a joy to behold, a true product of love, and stamina, and mystery and magic. It brings magic to the people who made it, and magic to the people for whom it was made. For countless small business owners who were looking for something they didn't have. That's been our calling. That's been our blessing. That's been the fire that wouldn't go out.

Sarah looked at me with soft eyes and took in a deep breath.

"That was a gift, Michael. I've been sitting here listening to you tell the end of your story and I'm left feeling so full, so rich and full and complete. I feel like the world has opened up to me. For the first time, I'm okay with who I am and where I am. For the first time in my life, I don't want to be anywhere other than exactly where I am. It feels, Michael, like the work I'm doing, the vision I'm becoming connected to, and my passion and this practice have all become aligned, around a new sense of purpose, a true sense of purpose. I'm in love with it. I don't know how else to put it, but I know that I will one day."

Sarah paused for a moment, and then, as if realizing something she had wanted to say, reached over and touched my hand. "Michael, this *has* been an adventure, just like you said it would be. And all the work that is left to do is nothing when I realize that it isn't the work, it isn't the end game, it isn't any of that that calls me, that feeds me; it is this extraordinary connection I now have with the magic. It's the magic, Michael. It's always been about the magic. I just didn't let myself feel it before. But listening to you. Now I know it's me. It's not you, it's not E-Myth, it's not All About Pies. The magic is me, Michael. And I've fallen in love with my magic."

"And just think," I said to Sarah, "it's always been there."

A FULL LIST OF THE REFERENCED WORKSHEETS AVAILABLE AT
www.emythmastery.com

INDEX

BOOKS BY MICHAEL E. GERBER

THE E-MYTH PHYSICIAN
Why Most Medical Practices Don't Work and What to Do About It
ISBN 0-06-093840-4 (paperback)
Gerber shares powerful insights that will lead independent physicians to successful practices and enriched lives.

THE E-MYTH CONTRACTOR
Why Most Contractors' Businesses Don't Work and What to Do About It
ISBN 0-06-093846-3 (paperback)
Gerber applies his E-Myth Revolution specifically to contractors—the largest group of clients Gerber serves.

E-MYTH MASTERY
The Seven Essential Disciplines for Building a World Class Company
ISBN 0-06-072318-1 (hardcover)
ISBN 0-06-075924-0 (audio CD)
Presenting practical exercises to help small business owners recover their vision and passion, Gerber clears a path for getting back to the basic disciplines for business success. *E-Myth Mastery* is the ultimate business development program that will help you recover your passion and turn your company into a world-class operation—a turn-key machine for the money and satisfaction that only a successful entrepreneur can enjoy. Get started today!

THE E-MYTH MANAGER
Why Most Managers Aren't Effective and What to Do About It
ISBN 0-88-730959-3 (paperback)
Drawing on lessons learned from working with more than 15,000 organizations, Gerber offers a fresh, provocative alternative to management as we know it.

THE E-MYTH REVISITED
Why Most Small Businesses Don't Work and What to Do About It
ISBN 0-694-51530-2 (audio)
ISBN 0-06-075559-8 (audio CD)